P9-DMW-375

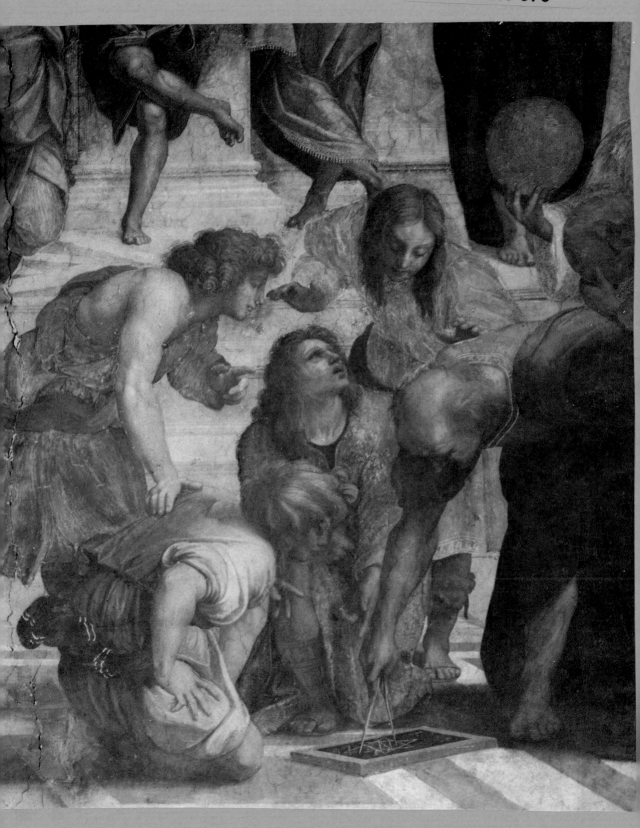

KENNETH CLARK
Civilisation

Other works by Kenneth Clark

Leonardo da Vinci

The Gothic Revival

Landscape into Art

The Nude

Looking at Pictures

Ruskin Today

Rembrandt and the Italian Renaissance

Piero della Francesca

KENNETH CLARK

Civilisation

A PERSONAL VIEW

British Broadcasting Corporation
and John Murray

Published by the
British Broadcasting Corporation,
35 Marylebone High Street,
London, W1M 4AA
SBN: 563 08544 4
and
John Murray,
50 Albemarle Street,
London, W1X 4BD
SBN: 7195 1933 0

First Published 1969
Second Impression 1969
Third Impression 1969
© Kenneth Clark 1969

Printed in England by
Jolly and Barber Limited,
Rugby, Warwickshire

Contents

Colour Illustrations

Black and White Illustrations

Acknowledgements

Illustrations 83, 92, 93 and 104 are reproduced by gracious permission of Her Majesty the Queen.

Acknowledgement is due to the following for their permission to reproduce illustrations in this book. References are to plate numbers; bold figures denote colour plates. Albertina, Vienna, 85, 103, 110; Alinari/Mansell, 2, 9, 39, 52, 53, 54, 55, 58, 59, 60, 61, 62, 63, 64, 65, 66, 67, 68, 74, 76, 78, 81, 82, 84, 86, 87, 88, 89, 91, 95, 96, 98, 101, 102, 107, 116, 117, 119, 120, 123, 124, 126, 127, 128, 129, 130, 131, 132, 134, 135, 140, 144, 147, 156, 159, 164, 171, 176, 206, 210, 214, 216, 237; Almasy, 4; Archiv für Kunst und Geschichte, 169; Art Institute, Chicago, 215; Ashmolean Museum, Oxford, 198, 234; Austrian National Library, **10**, 37; Bayerische Bibliothek, 24; Bibliothèque Nationale, Paris, **12**, 8, 25, 204, 205; Bibliothèque Royale, Brussels, 44; Birmingham City Museum and Art Gallery, 40; Joachim Blaüel, **21**, **24**; Bord Failté, 5; British Museum, **1**, **2**, 1, 6, 14, 17, 29, 46, 105, 106, 108, 109, 112, 121, 145, 146, 180; Camera Press, 238; Cathedral Library, Winchester, 30; J. Allan Cash, 114, 194; Courtauld Institute of Art, London, 3, 236; Eric de Maré, 41; Deutschen Zentral für Fremdenverkehr, Frankfurt, 160, 161; Dutch National Tourist Office, 158; Fitzwilliam Museum, Cambridge, 21 (left); Frans Halsmuseum, Haarlem, **26**, 137; Giraudon, **5**, **7**, **11**, **36**, **37**, **43**, **44**, 27, 49, 50, 148, 177, 181, 202, 203, 207, 208, 235; Walter Hege, 94; Hans Hinz, **20**, **22**; Hirmer Fotoarchiv 4; The Iveagh Bequest, Kenwood, 143; Peter Keetman, 176; F. L. Kennet, 56, 80, 115; A. F. Kersting, **30**, 15, 31, 32, 36, 38, 40, 113, 153, 155, 168, 170, 172, 173, 178, 228; Kunsthistorisches Museum, Vienna, 12; Kunstsammlung, Basle, 97, 99, 100, 111, 190; The Louvre, Paris, **6**, **9**, **33**, 163; Magdalene College, Cambridge, 48; Marburg, 20, 22; Marchioness of Cholmondeley, **34**; Mauritshuis, The Hague, 142, 149; Paul Mellon Foundation, 175; Ann Münchow, 16, 18, 19; Museum of City of New York, 231; Museum Folkwang, Essen, **39**; Museum of Modern Art, New York, **42**; Reproduced by Courtesy of the Trustees, National Gallery, London, **25**, **38**, **47**, 35, 47, 51, 70, 139, 150, 200; National Gallery of Art, Washington, 69; National Gallery of Scotland, **32**; National Maritime Museum, Greenwich, 151, 192, 220, 221; National Museum, Stockholm, **35**, 201; New York Historical Society, 185; Palazzo di Capodimonte, Naples, **23**; Phaidon Press, 31, 218, 219; Radio Times Hulton Picture Library, 223, 230; Réunion des Musées Nationaux, **8**, 77, 212; Rijksmuseum, Amsterdam, **27**, 138; Royal Academy of Arts, London, 197; Royal Hospital, Greenwich, 154; Scala, **13**, **14**, **15**, **16**, **17**, **18**, **20**, **28**; Science Museum, London, **46**, 152; Service Photographique, Versailles, **8**; Edwin Smith, 7, 23, 28, 57, 73, 75, 133, 141, 157, 183; Soane Museum, London, 174; Society of Friends, London, 224; Stadt-und Universitätsbibliothek, Frankfurt, 21 (right); Stedelijk Museum, Amsterdam, **48**; Stiftsbibliothek, St Gallen, 13; Tate Gallery, 182, 189, 195; Thames and Hudson 3, **45**; Trianon Press, 33, 34; University of Glasgow, 179; Universitetets Oldsaksamling, Oslo, 10, 11; USIS 187; Vatican, Rome 90; Victoria and Albert Museum, **19**, **26**, **43**, **45**, 71, 162, 166, 196, 199, 232, 233; Virginia State Travel Service, 188; John Webb **41**.

Foreword

This book is made up of the scripts of a series of television programmes given in the spring of 1969. Writing for television is fundamentally different from writing a book, not only in style and presentation, but in the whole approach to the subject. People who settle down to an evening's viewing expect to be entertained. If they are bored they switch off. They are entertained as much by what they see as by what they hear. Their attention must be held by a carefully contrived series of images, and often the sequence of images controls the sequence of ideas. The choice of illustration is itself determined by certain material accidents. Some places are inaccessible, some buildings defy the camera, some locations are too noisy for sound recording. All these considerations have to be in the writer's mind from the beginning, and modify or direct his line of thought. But more important still, every subject must be simplified if it is to be presented in under an hour. Only a few outstanding buildings or works of art can be used as evidence, only a few great men can be named, and what is said about them must usually be said without qualification. Generalisations are inevitable and, in order not to be boring, must be slightly risky. There is nothing new in this. It is how we talk about things sitting round the room after dinner; and television should retain the character of the spoken word, with the rhythms of ordinary speech, and even some of the off-hand imprecise language that prevents conversation from becoming pompous.

Going through these scripts and comparing them in mind with the actual programmes, I am miserably aware of how much has been lost. In almost every one of them the strongest impact depended on factors that could not be conveyed in words. To take examples from one programme only, 'The Fallacies of Hope': the sound of the *Marseillaise* and the prisoners' chorus from *Fidelio*, and the marvellous photography of Rodin's *Burghers of Calais*: all these said what I wanted to say about the whole subject with a force and vividness which could never have been achieved by the printed page. I cannot distinguish between thought and feeling, and I am convinced that a combination of words and music, colour and movement can extend human experience in a way that words alone cannot do. For this reason I believe in television as a medium, and was prepared to give up two years writing to see what could be done with it. Thanks to skilful and imaginative directors and an expert camera crew, I believe that certain moments in the film were genuinely moving and enlightening. They are lost in a book.

So why have I allowed the book to be printed? Partly weakness – I hate saying no, and in this case I should have had to say it, or write it, hundreds of times. Partly vanity – few people can resist the opportunity of airing their opinions. As the series proceeded I found myself saying out loud a number of things I should never have said otherwise. Just as the Bourgeois Gentilhomme was delighted to find that he spoke prose, so I was astonished to discover that I had a point of view. And then, perhaps, I may be allowed one less disreputable motive: gratitude. As I looked through the scripts I recognised that they were an expression of gratitude for all the life-giving experience I have enjoyed in the last fifty years. I don't know why it should be considered praiseworthy to give thanks in public, but it is recommended in almost every liturgy, so I suppose it is excusable.

Naturally I thought first of filling out my summary scripts and giving them a more literate form. I soon discovered that to amplify every allusion and support every generalisation would take a year's work and would deprive the book of a certain ease and speed, which may be counted in its favour. There was nothing for it but to accept the limitations imposed on me by the medium, changing or omitting those passages that would have been incomprehensible without the accompanying film. A line of argument determined almost entirely by visual evidence does not make for logic or completeness; and in the programmes it led to a number of omissions of which I am ashamed. Even the most rapid survey of civilisation should have said more than I have done about law and philosophy. I could not think of any way of making them visually interesting. This defect is particularly serious in my treatment of Germany. I talk a lot about Bavarian Rococo, and hardly mention Kant or Hegel. Goethe, who should have been one of the chief heroes of the series, makes only a brief appearance, and the German romantics are left out altogether. Other omissions were simply due to shortage of time. I had originally planned a programme on the classical tradition from Palladio to the end of the seventeenth century. It would have allowed me to include Corneille and Racine, Mansart and Poussin, and might have been one of the most satisfying of the whole series. But thirteen is the canonical number of television programmes, and it had to go. In consequence Baroque is over-emphasised at the expense of Classicism.

Music played a great part (some people thought too great a part) in the series; poetry was less often quoted, and I am uneasy at my treatment of Elizabethan England. To bring in Shakespeare simply as the great pessimist, the culminating figure in half a century of necessary doubt, is obviously absurd. But to pad out the end of the programme with a few commonplaces about *A Midsummer Night's Dream* or *Romeo and Juliet*, would have been worse.

Some of the most offensive omissions were dictated by my title. If I had been talking about the history of art, it would not have been possible to leave out Spain; but when one asks what Spain has done to enlarge the human mind and pull mankind a few steps up the hill, the answer is less clear. *Don Quixote*, the Great Saints, the Jesuits in South America? Otherwise she has simply remained Spain, and since I wanted each programme to be concerned with the new developments of the European mind, I could not change my ground and talk about a single country.

This leads me to say a word about the title of the series, which I have retained for the book. It was an accident. The BBC wanted a series of colour films on art, and thought that I might be able to advise them. But when David Attenborough, then responsible for BBC 2, asked me to do so, he used the word *Civilisation*, and it was this word alone that persuaded me to undertake the work. I had no clear idea what it meant, but I thought it was preferable to barbarism, and fancied that this was the moment to say so. In a very few minutes, while the lunch of persuasion went cheerfully on around me, I had thought of a way in which the subject could be treated, and from that first plan I departed very little. It was concerned only with Western Europe. Obviously, I could not include the ancient civilisations of Egypt, Syria, Greece and Rome, because to have done so would have meant another ten programmes, at least; and the same was true of China, Persia, India and the world of Islam. Heaven knows, I had taken on enough. Moreover, I have the feeling that one should not try to assess a culture without knowing its language; so much of its character is connected with its actual use of words; and unfortunately I do not know any oriental languages. Should I then have dropped the title *Civilisation*? I didn't want to, because the word had triggered me off, and remained a kind of stimulus; and I didn't suppose that anyone would be so obtuse as to think that I had forgotten about the great civilisations of the pre-Christian era and the East. However, I confess that the title has worried me. It would have been easy in the eighteenth century: *Speculations on the Nature of Civilisation as illustrated by the Changing Phases of Civilised Life in Western Europe from the Dark Ages to the Present Day*. Unfortunately, this is no longer practicable.

'I should like to thank': at this point one usually stops reading; but my debt to my directors, Michael Gill and Peter Montagnon, and my director-researcher Ann Turner, is of a different kind to that owed to librarians, photographers, secretaries and the other standard recipients of acknowledgement. The discussions that preceded the planning of each programme went far beyond choice of locations and other problems of production. They were a source of ideas, and as often happens when people are working closely together, we could not afterwards remember who had the first thought of certain lucky strikes. The technical objections raised were themselves a spur to invention. I could see the truth of those familiar words 'How often has a difficult rhyme led me to a beautiful thought'. This is only one part of my debt to the BBC. No one has ever had more generous, trusting and efficient masters and in conclusion they provided me with an editor for this volume, Mr Peter Campbell, whose quick intelligence and indefatigable energy make him a lazy author's dream.

Catherine Porteous my secretary, and the members of the unit who worked with me for almost two years helped me in many ways, and their names should be recorded in this book of the series:

Lighting Cameraman, A. A. Englander; Camera Operator, Kenneth Macmillan; Camera Assistant, Colin Deehan; Grips, Bill Paget; Lighting, Dave Griffiths, Jack Probert, Joe Cooksey, John Taylor; Sound Recordist, Basil Harris; Sound Assistant, Malcolm Webberley; Supervising Film Editor, Allan Tyrer; Film Editors, Jesse Palmer, Michael Shah Dayan, Peter Heelas, Roger Crittenden; Research Assistant, June Leech; Producer's Assistants, Carol Jones, Maggie Houston.

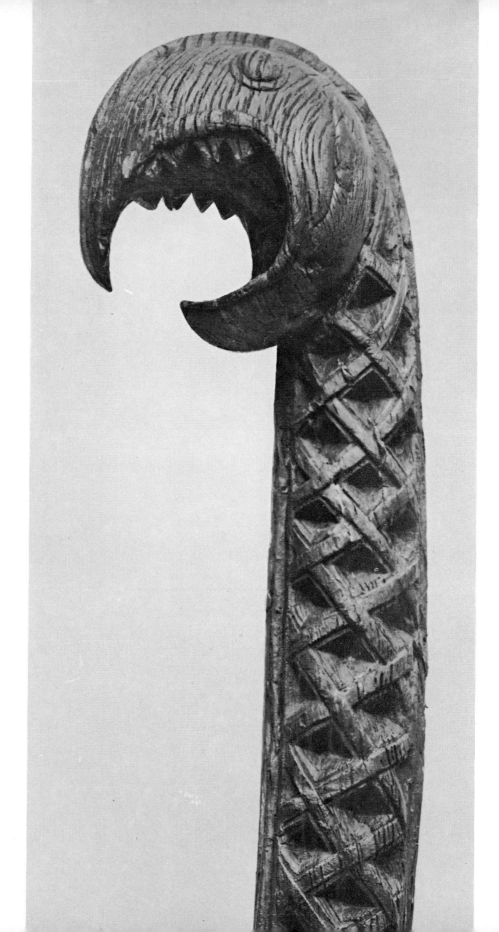

1 The Skin of our Teeth

I am standing on the Pont des Arts in Paris. On one side of the Seine is the harmonious, reasonable façade of the Institute of France, built as a college in about 1670. On the other bank is the Louvre, built continuously from the Middle Ages to the nineteenth century: classical architecture at its most splendid and assured. Just visible upstream is the Cathedral of Notre Dame – not perhaps the most lovable of cathedrals, but the most rigorously intellectual façade in the whole of Gothic art. The houses that line the banks of the river are also a humane and reasonable solution of what town architecture should be, and in front of them, under the trees, are the open bookstalls where generations of students have found intellectual nourishment and generations of amateurs have indulged in the civilised pastime of book collecting. Across this bridge, for the last one hundred and fifty years, students from the art schools of Paris have hurried to the Louvre to study the works of art that it contains, and then back to their studios to talk and dream of doing something worthy of the great tradition. And on this bridge how many pilgrims from America, from Henry James downwards, have paused and breathed in the aroma of a long-established culture, and felt themselves to be at the very centre of civilisation.

What is civilisation? I don't know. I can't define it in abstract terms – yet. But I think I can recognise it when I see it; and I am looking at it now. Ruskin said: 'Great nations write their autobiographies in three manuscripts, the book of their deeds, the book of their words and the book of their art. Not one of these books can be understood unless we read the two others, but of the three the only trustworthy one is the last.' On the whole I think this is true. Writers and politicians may come out with all sorts of edifying sentiments, but they are what is known as declarations of intent. If I had to say which was telling the truth about society, a speech by a Minister of Housing or the actual buildings put up in his time, I should believe the buildings.

But this doesn't mean that the history of civilisation is the history of art – far from it. Great works of art can be produced in barbarous societies – in fact the very narrowness of primitive society gives their ornamental art a peculiar concentration and vitality. At some time in the ninth century one could have looked down the Seine and seen the prow of a Viking ship coming up the river. Looked at today in the British Museum [1] it is a powerful work of art; but to the mother of a family trying to settle down in her little hut, it

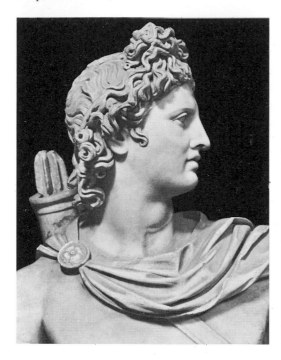 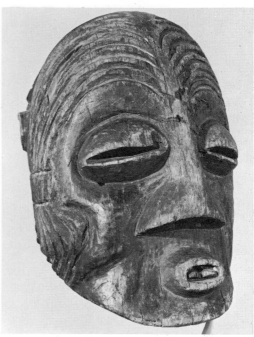

would have seemed less agreeable – as menacing to her civilisation as the periscope of a nuclear submarine.

An even more extreme example comes to my mind, an African mask that belonged to Roger Fry [3]. I remember when he bought it and hung it up, and we agreed that it had all the qualities of a great work of art. I fancy that most people, nowadays, would find it more moving than the head of the Apollo of the Belvedere [2]. Yet for four hundred years after it was discovered the Apollo was the most admired piece of sculpture in the world. It was Napoleon's greatest boast to have looted it from the Vatican. Now it is completely forgotten except by the guides of coach parties, who have become the only surviving transmitters of traditional culture.

Whatever its merits as a work of art, I don't think there is any doubt that the Apollo embodies a higher state of civilisation than the mask. They both represent spirits, messengers from another world – that is to say, from a world of our own imagining. To the Negro imagination it is a world of fear and darkness, ready to inflict horrible punishment for the smallest infringement of a taboo. To the Hellenistic imagination it is a world of light and confidence, in which the gods are like ourselves, only more beautiful, and descend to earth in order to teach men reason and the laws of harmony.

Fine words: and fine words butter no parsnips. There was plenty of superstition and cruelty in the Graeco-Roman world. But, all the same, the contrast between these images means something. It means that at certain epochs man has felt conscious of something about himself – body and spirit – which was outside the day-to-day struggle for existence and the night-to-night struggle with fear; and he has felt the need to develop these qualities of thought and feeling so that they might approach as nearly as possible to an ideal of perfection – reason, justice, physical beauty, all of them in equilibrium. He has managed to satisfy this need in various ways – through myths, through dance and song, through systems of philosophy and through the order that he has imposed on the visible world. The children of his imagination are also the expressions of an ideal.

Western Europe inherited such an ideal. It had been invented in Greece in the fifth century before Christ and was without doubt the most extraordinary creation in the whole of history, so complete, so convincing, so satisfying to the mind and the eye, that it lasted practically unchanged for over six hundred years. Of course, its art became stereotyped and conventional. The same architectural language, the same imagery, the same theatres, the same temples – at any time for five hundred years you could have found them all round the Mediterranean, in Greece, Italy, France, Asia Minor or North Africa. If you had gone into the square of any Mediterranean town in the first century you would hardly have known where you were, any more than you would in an airport today. The so-called Maison Carrée at Nîmes is a little Greek temple that might have been anywhere in the Graeco-Roman world.

Nîmes isn't very far from the Mediterranean. Graeco-Roman civilisation stretched much further than that – right up to the Rhine, right up to the borders of Scotland, although by the time it got to Carlisle it had become a bit rough, like Victorian civilisation on the North-West Frontier. It must have seemed absolutely indestructible. And of course some of it was never destroyed. The so-called Pont du Gard [4], the aqueduct not far from Nîmes, was materially beyond the destructive powers of the barbarians. And a vast mass of fragments remained – the Museum at Arles is full of them. 'These fragments have I shored against my ruin.' When the spirit of man revived, they were there to be imitated by the masons who decorated the local churches: but that was a long way off.

What happened? It took Gibbon six volumes to describe the decline and fall of the Roman Empire, so I shan't embark on that. But thinking about this almost incredible episode does tell one something about the nature of civilisation. It shows that however complex and solid it seems, it is actually quite fragile. It can be destroyed. What are its enemies? Well, first of all fear – fear of war, fear of invasion, fear of plague and famine, that make it simply not worthwhile constructing things, or planting trees or even planning next year's crops. And fear of the supernatural, which means that you daren't question anything or change anything. The late antique world was full of meaningless rituals, mystery religions, that destroyed self-confidence. And then exhaustion, the feeling of hopelessness which can overtake people even with a high degree of material prosperity. There is a poem by the modern Greek poet, Cavafy, in which he imagines the people of an antique town like Alexandria waiting every day for the barbarians to come and sack the city. Finally the barbarians move off somewhere else and the city is saved; but the people are disappointed – it would have been better than nothing. Of course, civilisation requires a modicum of material prosperity – enough to provide a little leisure. But, far more, it requires confidence – confidence in the society in which one lives, belief in its philosophy, belief in its laws, and confidence in one's own mental powers. The way in which the stones of the Pont du Gard are laid is not only a triumph of technical skill, but shows a vigorous belief in law and discipline. Vigour, energy, vitality: all the great civilisations – or civilising epochs – have had a weight of energy behind them. People sometimes think that civilisation consists in fine sensibilities and good conversation and all that. These can be among the agreeable *results* of civilisation, but they are not what make a civilisation, and a society can have these amenities and yet be dead and rigid.

So if one asks why the civilisation of Greece and Rome collapsed, the real answer is that it was exhausted. And the first invaders of the Roman Empire became exhausted too. As so often happens, they seem to have succumbed to the same weaknesses as the people they conquered. It's misleading to call them barbarians. They don't seem to have been particularly destructive – in fact, they made some quite impressive constructions, like the Mausoleum of Theodoric: a bit heavy and megalithic compared to the little Greek temple at Nîmes – the shallow dome is a single piece of stone – but at least built with an eye to the future. These early invaders have been aptly compared to the English in India in the eighteenth century – there for what they could get out of it, taking part in the administration if it paid them, contemptuous of the traditional culture, except insofar as it provided precious metals. But unlike the Anglo-Indians, they created chaos; and into that chaos came real barbarians like the Huns, who were totally illiterate and destructively hostile to what they couldn't understand. I don't suppose they bothered to destroy the great buildings that were scattered all over the Roman world. But the idea of keeping them up never entered their heads. They preferred to live in pre-fabs and let the old places fall down. Of course, life must have gone on in an apparently normal way for much longer than one would expect. It

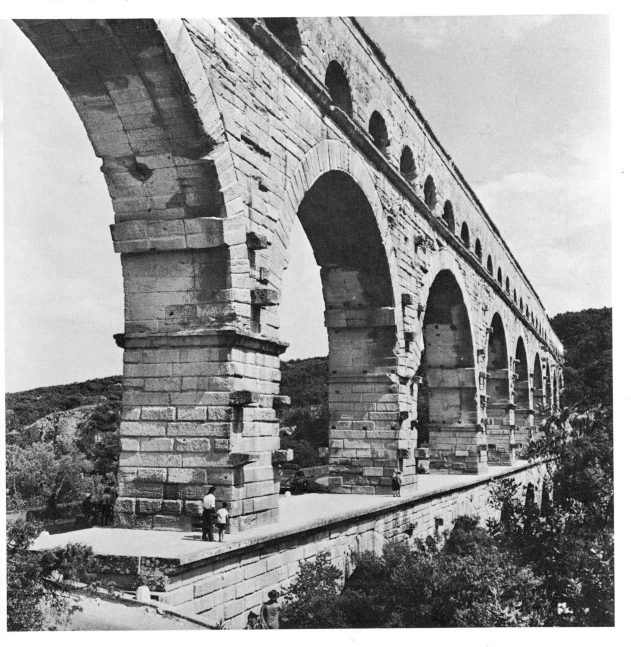

always does. Gladiators would have continued to fight each other in the amphitheatre of Arles; plays would still have been performed in the theatre of Orange. And as late as the year 383 a distinguished administrator like Ausonius could retire peacefully to his estate near Bordeaux to cultivate his vineyard (still known as Château Ausone) and write great poetry, like a Chinese gentleman of the T'ang dynasty.

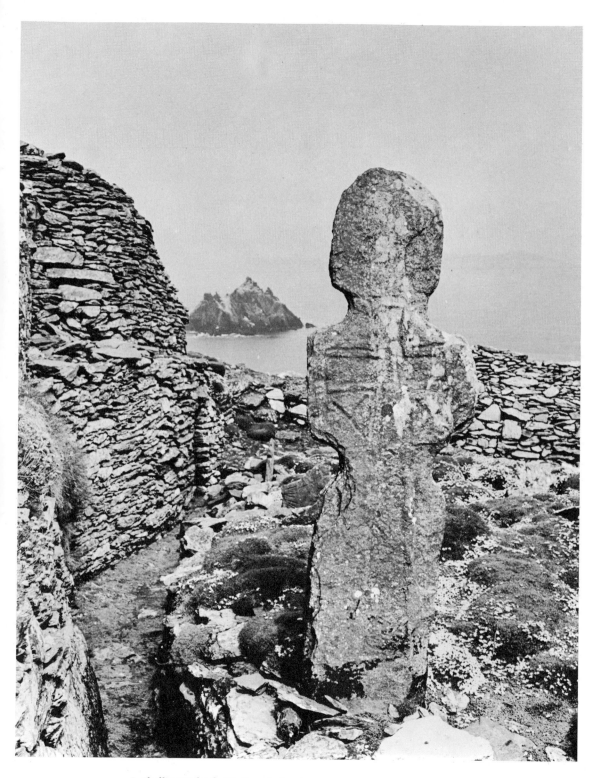

5 Skellig Michael, Western Ireland

Civilisation might have drifted downstream for a long time, but in the middle of the seventh century there appeared a new force, with faith, energy, a will to conquer and an alternative culture: Islam. The strength of Islam was its simplicity. The early Christian Church had dissipated its strength by theological controversies, carried on for three centuries with incredible violence and ingenuity. But Mahomet, the prophet of Islam, preached the simplest doctrine that has ever gained acceptance; and it gave to his followers the invincible solidarity that had once directed the Roman legions. In a miraculously short time – about fifty years – the classical world was overrun. Only its bleached bones stood out against the Mediterranean sky.

The old source of civilisation was sealed off, and if a new civilisation was to be born it would have to face the Atlantic. What a hope! People sometimes tell me that they prefer barbarism to civilisation. I doubt if they have given it a long enough trial. Like the people of Alexandria they are bored by civilisation; but all the evidence suggests that the boredom of barbarism is infinitely greater. Quite apart from discomforts and privations, there was no escape from it. Very restricted company, no books, no light after dark, no hope. On one side the sea battering away, on the other infinite stretches of bog and forest. A most melancholy existence, and the Anglo-Saxon poets had no illusions about it:

> A wise man may grasp how ghastly it shall be
> When all this world's wealth standeth waste
> Even as now, in many places over the earth,
> Walls stand wind beaten,
> Heavy with hoar frost; ruined-habitations . . .
> The maker of men has so marred this dwelling
> That human laughter is not heard about it
> And idle stand these old giant works.

Yet it was probably better to live in one of these tiny houses on the very edge of the world than in the shadow of one of the old giant works, where at any moment you might be attacked by a new wave of wanderers. Such at least was the view of the first Christians who came to the West. They came originally from the eastern Mediterranean, the first home of monasticism. Some of them settled at Marseilles and Tours; then when life became too dangerous they struggled on in search of the most inaccessible fringes of Cornwall, Ireland or the Hebrides. They came in surprisingly large numbers. In the year 550 a boat-load of fifty scholars arrived at Cork. They wandered about the country looking for places that offered a modicum of security and a small group of like-minded men. And what places they found! Looking back from the great civilisations of twelfth-century France or seventeenth-century Rome, it is hard to believe that for quite a long time – almost a hundred years – western Christianity survived by clinging on to places like Skellig Michael [5], a pinnacle of rock eighteen miles from the Irish coast, rising seven hundred feet out of the sea.

Apart from this small, enclosed society of scholars, what kept that wandering culture alive? Not books. Not building. Even allowing for the fact that most of the buildings were in wood, and so have vanished, the few surviving stone structures are pitifully humble and incompetent. It's amazing that they couldn't do better – but the wanderers seem to have lost the impulse to make durable habitations. What did they have? The answer comes out in the poems: *gold*. Whenever an Anglo-Saxon poet wants to put into words his ideal of a good society he speaks of gold.

> There once many a man
> Mood-glad, gold bright, of gleams garnished
> Flushed with wine-pride, flashing war-gear,
> Gazed on wrought gemstones, on gold, on silver,
> On wealth held and hoarded, on light-filled amber.

The wanderers had never been without craftsmen; and all their pent-up need to give some permanent shape to the flux of experience, to make something perfect in their singularly imperfect existence, was concentrated in these marvellous objects. They achieved, even in the chasing of a torque, an extraordinary intensity. But nothing shows more clearly how the new Atlantic world was cut off from the Graeco-Roman civilisation of the Mediterranean. The subject of Mediterranean art was *man*, and had been ever since early Egypt. But the wanderers, struggling through the forests, battling with the waves, conscious chiefly of the birds and animals that hung in the tangled branches, were not interested in the human body. Just before the last war two hoards of treasure were discovered in England – both in Suffolk, about sixty miles from each other. They are both now in the British Museum. The one from Mildenhall [6] is decorated almost entirely with human beings – all the old characters from antiquity, sea gods, nereids and so forth. The drawing is a bit wobbly, because this dates from the very end of the ancient world, when belief in man had grown insubstantial, and the old outlines have been filled in without much conviction. The other hoard was from the ceremonial ship at Sutton Hoo [1, facing page 12]. Two hundred years have passed – perhaps a little more – and man has almost vanished. When he appears, he is a decorative cypher or hieroglyphic; and in his place are fabulous animals and birds – and I may add that the men of the Dark Ages took a less patronising view of birds than do the makers of Christmas cards. But although the subject is what we call barbarous, the sense of material and the craftsmanship is finer and more confident and technically more advanced than it was in the Mildenhall treasure.

This love of gold and wrought gemstones, this feeling that they reflected an ideal world and had some kind of enduring magic, went on right up to the time when the dark struggles for survival were over. It is arguable that western civilisation was saved by its craftsmen. The wanderers could take their craftsmen with them. Since the smiths made princely weapons as well as ornaments, they were as necessary to a chieftain's status as were the bards whose calypsos celebrated his courage.

But the copying of books needed more settled conditions, and two or three parts of the British Isles offered, for a short time, relative security. One

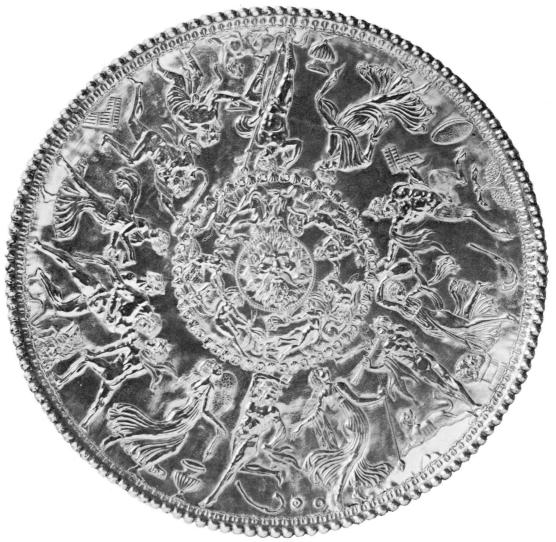

6 Neptune dish from Mildenhall treasure

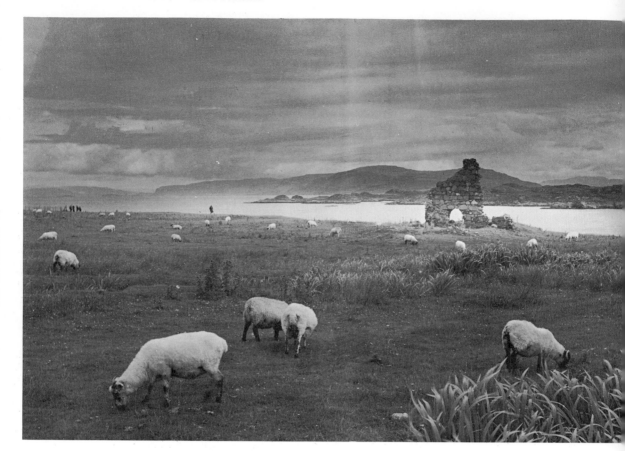

of them was Iona [7]. Secure and sacred. I never come to Iona – and I used to come here almost every year when I was young – without the feeling that 'some God is in this place'. It isn't as awe-inspiring as some other holy places – Delphi or Assisi. But Iona gives one more than anywhere else I know a sense of peace and inner freedom. What does it? The light, which floods round on every side? The lie of the land which, coming after the solemn hills of Mull, seems strangely like Greece, like Delos, even? The combination of wine-dark sea, white sand and pink granite? Or is it the memory of those holy men who for two centuries kept western civilisation alive?

Iona was founded by St Columba, who came here from Ireland in the year 543. It seems to have been a sacred spot before he came and for four centuries it was the centre of Celtic Christianity. There are said to have been three hundred and sixty large stone crosses on the island, nearly all of which were thrown into the sea during the Reformation. No one knows which of the surviving Celtic manuscripts were produced there and which in the Northumbrian island of Lindisfarne; and it doesn't really matter, because

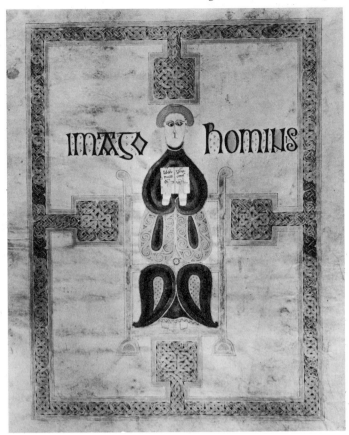

they are all in what we rightly consider an Irish style [**2**, facing p. 13]. They are beautifully written and their clear, round lettering carried the word of God all over the western world. They are also elaborately decorated, and the strange thing is how little consciousness of classical or Christian culture these decorations reveal. They are all gospel books but they are almost devoid of Christian symbols, except for the fierce, oriental-looking beasts who symbolise the four Evangelists. When a man appears he cuts a very poor figure. In one case the scribe has thought it best to write *Imago Hominis* – the image of a man [8]. But the pages of pure ornament are almost the richest and most complicated pieces of abstract decoration ever produced, more sophisticated and refined than anything in Islamic art. We look at them for ten seconds, then we pass on to something else that we can interpret or read. But imagine if one couldn't read and had nothing else to look at for weeks at a time. Then these pages would have an almost hypnotic effect. The last work of art to be produced in Iona was, perhaps, the Book of Kells [9]. But before it was finished, the Abbot of Iona was

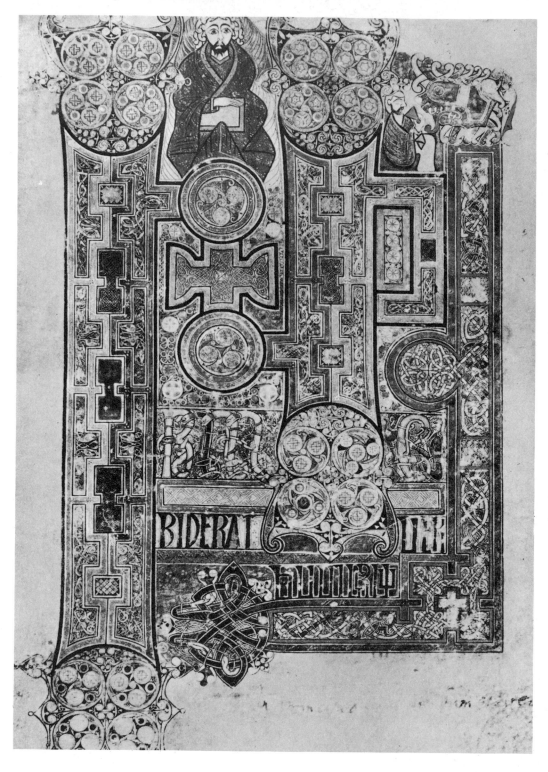

BIDERAT

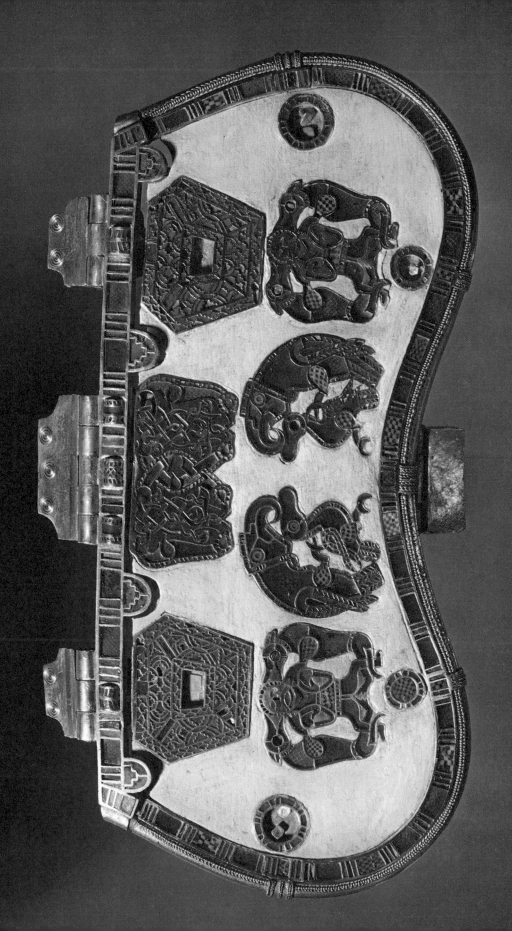

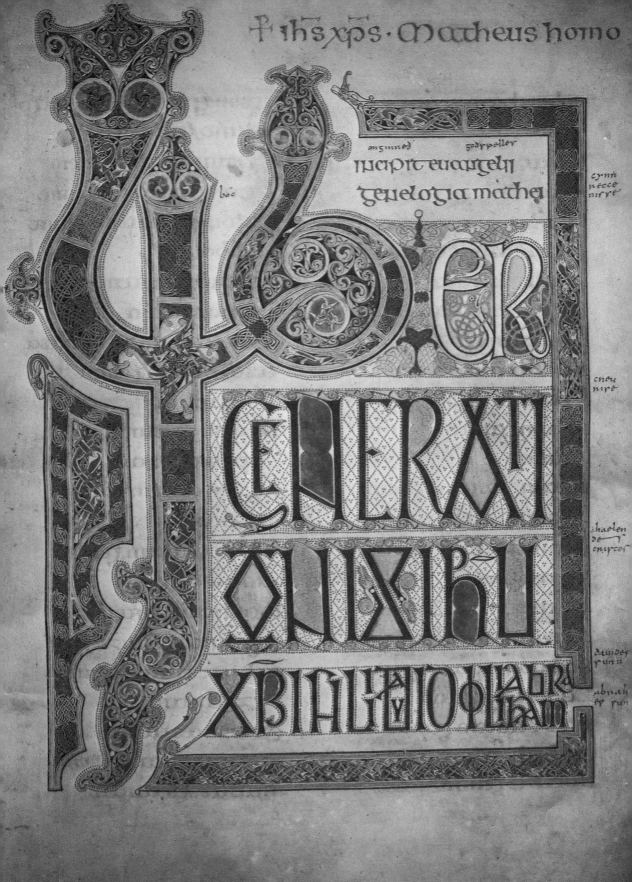

✝ ihs xps · Mattheus homo

incipit euangelii
genealogia Matthei

LIBER
GENERA
TIONIS
XPIHUIFILIDAUIDFILII
ABRAHAM

forced to flee to Ireland. The sea had become more menacing than the land. The Norsemen were on the move.

'If there were a hundred tongues in each head,' said a contemporary Irish writer, 'they could not recount or narrate or enumerate or tell what all the Irish suffered of hardships and of injuring and of oppression in every house from those valiant, wrathful, purely pagan people.' The Celts haven't

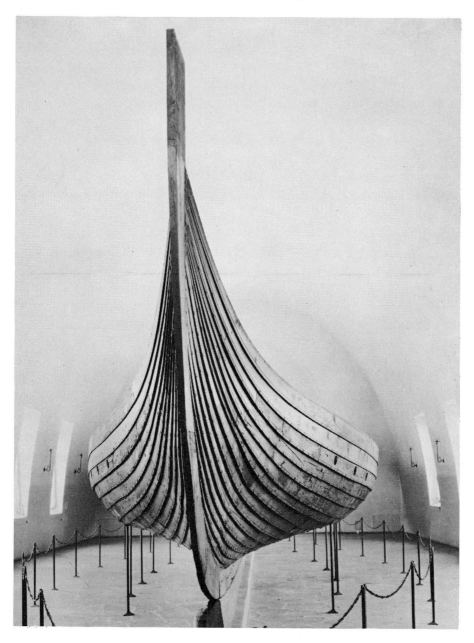

10 Gokstad Ship, Oslo

2 The beginning of the Gospel of St Matthew, from the Lindisfarne Gospels

changed much. Unlike the earlier wanderers, the Vikings had a rather splendid mythology, romanticised for us by Wagner. Their runic stones give one the feeling of magical power. They were the last people of Europe to resist Christianity. There are Viking gravestones from quite late in the Middle Ages that have symbols of Wotan on one side and Christian symbols on the other – what is called hedging your bets. A famous ivory casket in the British Museum has Weyland the Smith on the left and the Adoration of the Magi on the right. When one reads scarifying tales of them, one must remember that they were almost illiterate, and the written evidence about them was recorded by Christian monks. Of course they were brutal and rapacious. All the same, they have a place in European civilisation, because these pirates were not merely destructive, and their spirit did contribute something important to the western world. It was the spirit of Columbus. They set out from a base and with unbelievable courage and ingenuity they got as far as Persia, via the Volga and the Caspian Sea, and they put their runic writing on one of the lions at Delos, and then returned home with all their loot, including coins from Samarkand and a Chinese Buddha. The sheer technical skill of their journeys is a new achievement for the western world; and if one wants a symbol of Atlantic man that distinguishes him from Mediterranean man, a symbol to set against the Greek temple, it is the Viking ship. The Greek temple is static and solid. The ship is mobile and light. Two of the smaller Viking ships, which were used as burial chambers, have survived. One of them, the Gokstad ship [10], was intended for long voyages and in fact a replica of it crossed the Atlantic in 1894. It looks as unsinkable as a gigantic water-lily. The other, the Oseberg ship [11], seems to have been more like a ceremonial barge, and was filled with splendid works of craftsmanship. The carving on its prow has that flow of endless line that was still to underlie the great ornamental style we call Romanesque. When one considers the Icelandic sagas, which are among the great books of the world, one must admit that the Norsemen produced a culture. But was it civilisation? The monks of Lindisfarne wouldn't have said so, nor would Alfred the Great, nor the poor mother trying to settle down with her family on the banks of the Seine.

Civilisation means something more than energy and will and creative power: something the early Norsemen hadn't got, but which, even in their time, was beginning to reappear in Western Europe. How can I define it? Well, very shortly, a sense of permanence. The wanderers and the invaders were in a continual state of flux. They didn't feel the need to look forward beyond the next March or the next voyage or the next battle. And for that reason it didn't occur to them to build stone houses, or to write books.

11 Oseberg Ship, Oslo

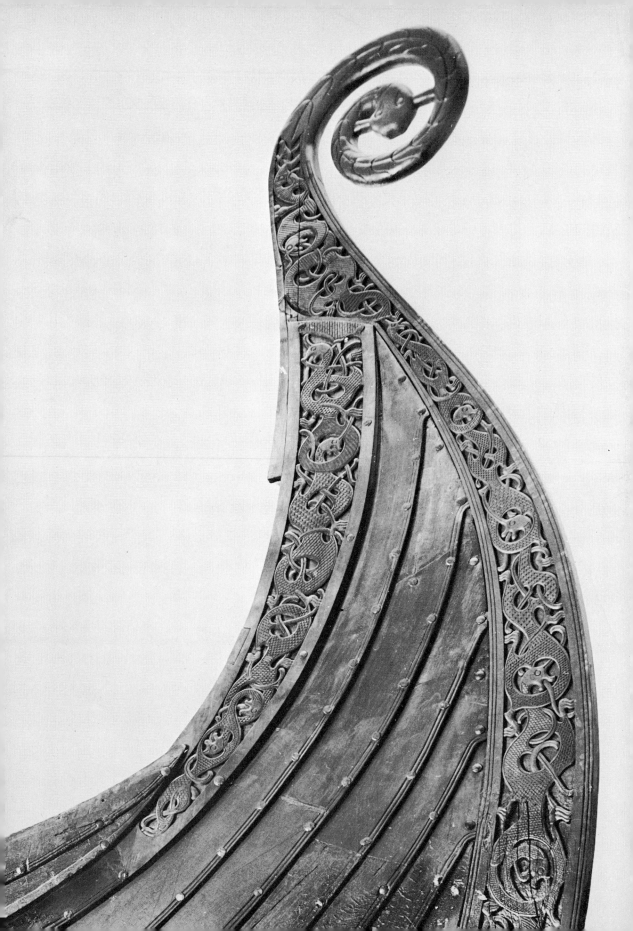

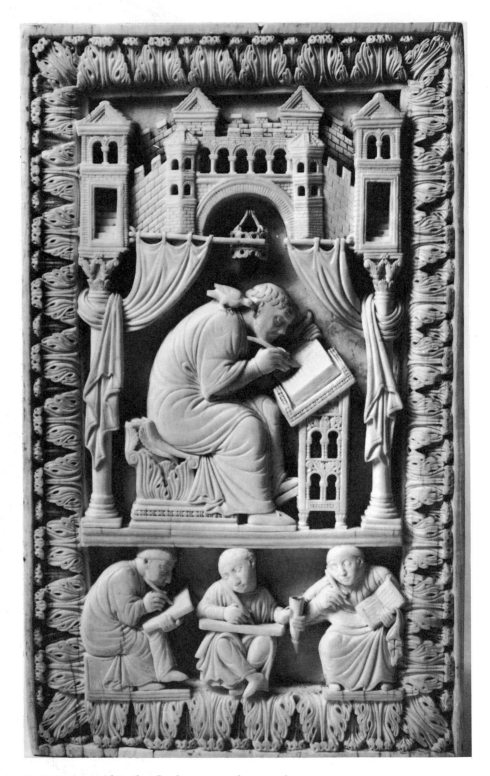

12 St Gregory and Scribes (book cover, tenth century)

Almost the only stone building that has survived from the centuries after
the Mausoleum of Theodoric is the Baptistry at Poitiers. It is pitifully
crude. The builders have tried to use some of the elements of Roman
architecture, capitals, pediments, pilasters, but have forgotten their
original intention. But at least this miserable construction is meant to last.
It isn't just a wigwam. Civilised man, or so it seems to me, must feel that he
belongs somewhere in space and time; that he consciously looks forward
and looks back. And for this purpose it is a great convenience to be able to
read and write.

For over five hundred years this achievement was rare in Western Europe.
It is a shock to realise that during all this time practically no lay person, from
kings and emperors downwards, could read or write. Charlemagne learnt to
read, but he never could write. He had wax tablets beside his bed to
practise on, but said he couldn't get the hang of it. Alfred the Great, who
was an exceptionally clever man, seems to have taught himself to read
at the age of forty, and was the author of several books, although they were
probably dictated in a kind of seminar. Great men, even ecclesiastics,
normally dictated to their secretaries, as they do today and as we see
them doing in tenth-century illuminations. Of course, most of the higher
clergy could read and write, and the pictures of the Evangelists, which
are the favourite (often the only) illustrations of early manuscripts, become,
in the tenth century, a kind of assertion of this almost divine accomplishment.
But St Gregory, who looks so intensely devoted to scholarship on a tenth-
century ivory [12], St Gregory himself is credited with having destroyed
many volumes of classical literature, even whole libraries, lest they
seduced men's minds away from the study of holy writ. And in this he
was certainly not alone. What with prejudice and destruction, it's surprising that the literature of pre-Christian antiquity was preserved at all. And in
fact it only just squeaked through. In so far as we are the heirs of Greece and
Rome, we got through by the skin of our teeth.

We survived because, although circumstances and opportunities may
vary, human intelligence seems to remain fairly constant, and for centuries
practically all men of intellect joined the Church. And some of them, like
the historian, Gregory of Tours, were remarkably intelligent and unpreju-
diced men. It is hard to say how many antique texts were available in the
Celtic monasteries. When Irish monks came to Europe in about the year
600 they found Roman manuscripts in places like Tours and Toulouse.
But the monasteries couldn't have become the guardians of civilisation
unless there had been a minimum of stability: and this, in Western Europe,
was first achieved in the Kingdom of the Franks.

It was achieved by fighting. All great civilisations, in their early stages, are based on success in war. The Romans were the best organised and most ruthless fighters in Latium. So it was with the Franks. Clovis and his successors not only conquered their enemies, but maintained themselves by cruelties and tortures remarkable even by the standards of the last thirty years. Fighting, fighting, fighting. Incidentally drawings of the ninth century show, almost for the first time, that the horsemen have stirrups [13], and people who like mechanical explanations for historical events maintain that this was the reason why the Frankish cavalry was victorious. One sometimes feels that the seventh and eighth centuries were like a prolonged 'Western', and the resemblance is made more vivid by the presence, already in the eighth century, of our old friends, the sheriff and the marshal; but it was really far more horrible, because unredeemed by any trace of sentiment or chivalry. But fighting was necessary. Without Charles Martel's victory over the Moors at Poitiers in 732, western civilisation might never have existed, and without Charlemagne's tireless campaigning we should never have had the notion of a united Europe.

Charlemagne is the first great man of action to emerge from the darkness since the collapse of the Roman world. He became a subject of myth and legend. A magnificent reliquary in Aix-la-Chapelle [3, facing p. 28], made about five hundred years after his death to hold a piece of his skull, expresses what the High Middle Ages felt about him in terms that he himself would have appreciated – gold and jewels. But the real man, about whom we know quite a lot from a contemporary biographer, wasn't so far from that myth. He was a commanding figure, over six feet tall, with piercing blue eyes – only he had a small squeaky voice and a walrus moustache instead of a beard. He was a tireless administrator. The lands he conquered – Bavaria, Saxony, Lombardy – were organised a good deal beyond the capacities of a semi-barbarous age. His empire was an artificial construction and didn't survive him. But the old idea that he saved civilisation isn't so far wrong, because it was through him that the Atlantic world re-established contact with the ancient culture of the Mediterranean world. There were great disorders after his death, but no more skin of our teeth. Civilisation had come through.

How did he do it? First of all, with the help of an outstanding teacher and librarian named Alcuin of York, he collected books and had them copied. People don't always realise that only three or four antique manuscripts of the Latin authors are still in existence: our whole knowledge of ancient literature is due to the collecting and copying that began under Charlemagne, and almost any classical text that survived until the eighth century has survived till today. In copying these manuscripts his scribes arrived at

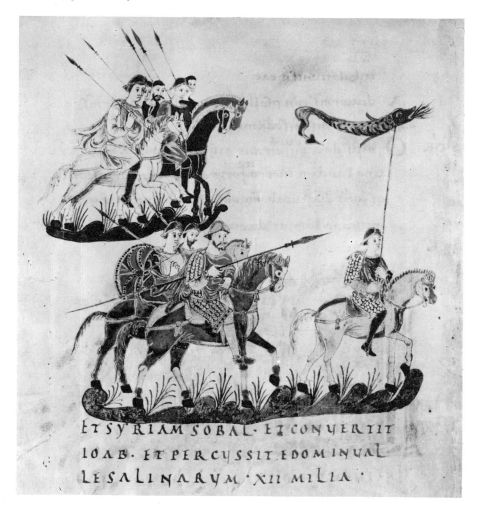

ETSYRIAM SOBAL· ET CONVERTIT
IOAB· ET PERCUSSIT EDOM INVAL
LESALINARUM ·XII MILIA·

the most beautiful lettering ever invented; also the most practical, so that when the Renaissance humanists wanted to find a clear and elegant substitute for the crabbed Gothic script they revived the Carolingian [14]. And so it has survived, in more or less the same form, until the present day. Like most able men who have had to educate themselves the hard way, Charlemagne felt strongly the value of education, and in particular he saw the importance of an educated laity. He issued a series of decrees to try to achieve it. But the words of these decrees are revealing: 'In every bishop's see instruction shall be given in the psalms, musical notation, chant, the computation of the years and seasons, and grammar.' 'The computation of the years and seasons'! What we call a liberal education was still a long way off.

Charlemagne's adoption of the imperial idea led him to look not only at antique civilisation but at its strange posthumous existence in what we call the Byzantine Empire. For four hundred years Constantinople had been the greatest city in the world, and the only one in which life had gone on more or less untouched by the wanderers. It was a civilisation all right. It produced some of the most nearly perfect buildings and works of art ever made. But it was almost sealed off from Western Europe, partly by the Greek language, partly by a religious difference, chiefly because it didn't want to involve itself in the bloody feuds of the western barbarians: it had its own eastern barbarians to deal with. A little of its art had filtered through and provided a model for the first figures that appear in eighth-century manuscripts. But on the whole Byzantium was more remote from the west than Islam which had established a basis of evolved intellectual life in southern Spain. No eastern emperor had visited Rome for three hundred years, and when Charlemagne, the great conqueror, went there in the year 800 the Pope crowned him as the head of a new Holy Roman Empire, brushing aside the fact that the nominal emperor ruled in Constantinople. Charlemagne was afterwards heard to say that this famous episode was a mistake; and perhaps he was right. It gave the Pope a claim to supremacy over the emperor which was the cause, or pretext, for war for three centuries. But historical judgements are very tricky. Maybe the tension between the spiritual and worldly powers throughout the Middle Ages was precisely what kept European civilisation alive. If either had achieved absolute power, society might have grown as static as the civilisations of Egypt and Byzantium.

On his way back from Rome Charlemagne went to Ravenna, where the Byzantine emperors had erected and decorated a series of splendid buildings that they never visited. He saw the mosaics of Justinian and Theodora in the church of San Vitale [15], and realised how magnificent an emperor could be. (I may add that he himself never wore anything but a plain blue Frankish cloak.) And when he returned to his residence at Aix-la-Chapelle (he settled there because he liked swimming in the hot springs), he determined to build a replica of San Vitale as his palace chapel. It couldn't be an exact replica. His architect, called Odo of Metz, hadn't mastered the complexity of the earlier building. But when one thinks of the crude stone buildings that preceded it, like the Baptistry at Poitiers, it is a most extraordinary feat [16]. Of course, the craftsmen, like the marble columns, have come from the east, because under Charlemagne Western Europe was once more in touch with the outside world. He even received an elephant from Haroun al Raschid, of the *Thousand and One Nights,* called Abbul Abuz: it died on a campaign in Saxony and its tusks were made into a set of chessmen, some of which still survive.

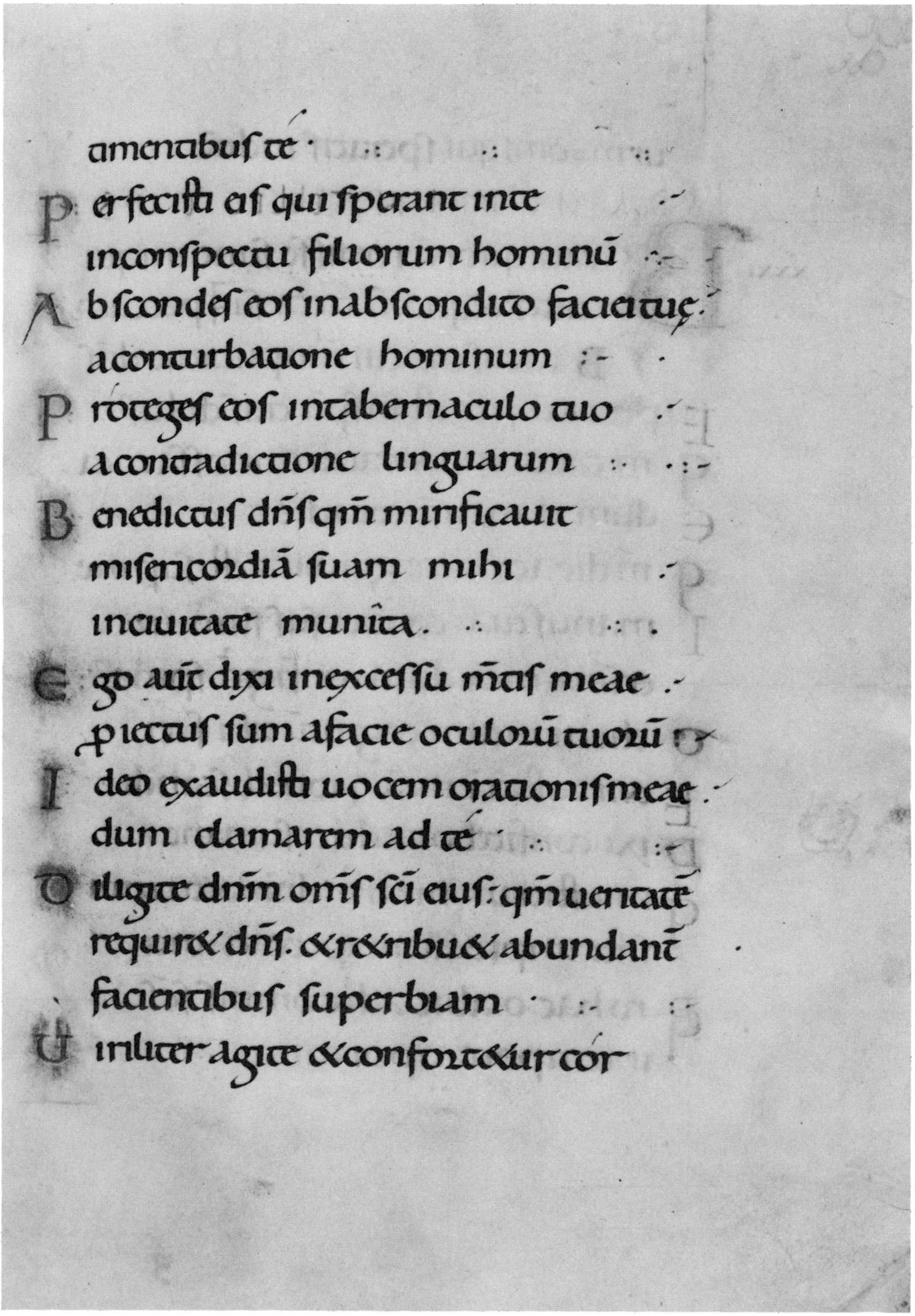

amentabus te

Perfecisti eis qui sperant inte

inconspectu filiorum hominū

Abscondes eos inabscondito faciei tue

a conturbatione hominum

Proteges eos intabernaculo tuo

a contradictione linguarum

Benedictus dns qm mirificauit

misericordiā suam mihi

inciuitate munita.

Ego aut dixi inexcessu mtis meae

proiectus sum afacie oculorū tuorū

Ideo exaudisti uocem orationis meae

dum clamarem ad te

Diligite dnm oms sci eius: qm ueritate

requiret dns. & retribuet abundant

facientibus superbiam

Uiriliter agite & conforteturcor

14 Page from Carolingian manuscript

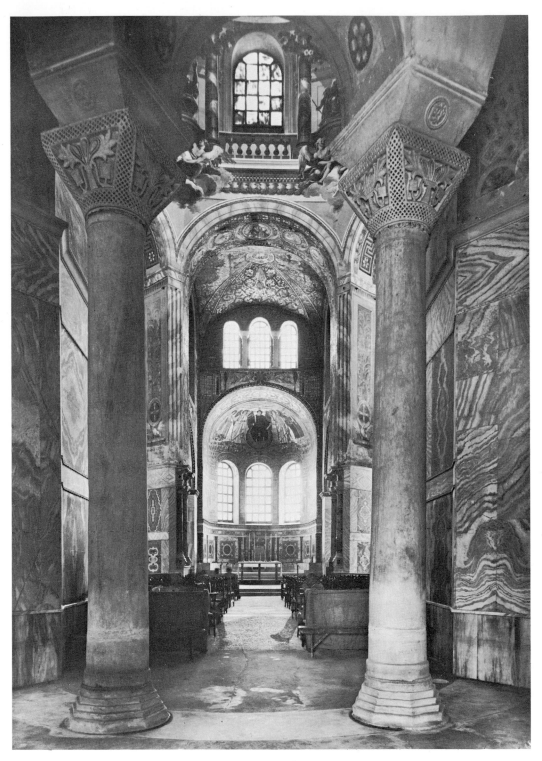

15 San Vitale, Ravenna

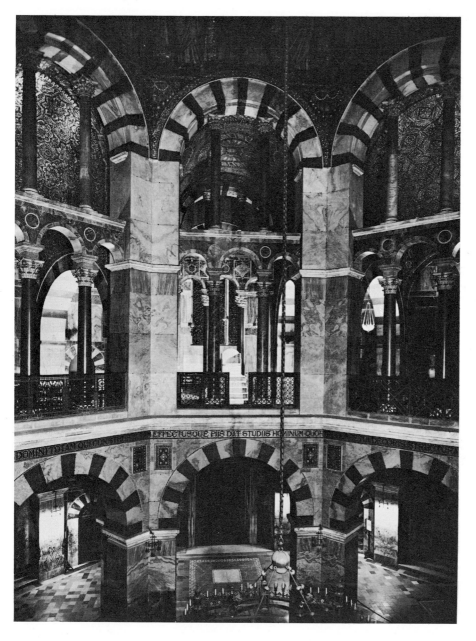

As ruler of an empire stretching from Denmark to the Adriatic, he amassed treasure from all over the known world – jewels, cameos, ivories, precious silks. But in the end it was the books that mattered – not only the texts but the illustrations and the bindings. In both of these there was a long tradition of skill, and the works of art produced under the influence of Charlemagne's revival are masterpieces. There have never been more splendid books than those illuminated for the court library, and sent as presents all over Western Europe. Many of the illustrations were based on a late antique or Byzantine model, the originals of which are lost. Like the texts of Roman literature, they are known to us only through Carolingian imitations. Most curious of all are pages which are derived from the style of antique wall-painting – those architectural fantasies that spread all over the Roman world from Spain to Damascus. In their own day these books were so precious that the practise arose of giving them the richest and most elaborate bindings conceivable. Usually they took the form of an ivory plaque surrounded by beaten gold and gems. A few of them are still in this form, but even when the gold and jewels have been stolen, the ivory plaques survive; and these small pieces of sculpture are in some ways our best indication of the intellectual life of Europe for almost two hundred years [4, facing p. 29].

From the break-up of Charlemagne's empire there emerged something like the Europe we know, France to the west, Germany to the east and Lotharingia, or, as we should say, Lorraine, a contentious strip between them. By the tenth century the German part was in the ascendant under Saxon rulers, the three Ottos who, one after another, were crowned as Emperor.

Historians usually consider the tenth century almost as dark and barbarous as the seventh. That is because they look at it from the point of view of political history and the written word. If we read what Ruskin called the book of its art, we get a very different impression, because, contrary to all expectation, the tenth century produced work as splendid and as technically skilful, even as delicate, as any other age. Not for the last time in studying civilisation one learns how hard it is to equate art and society. The amount of art is astonishing. The princely patrons like Lothar and Charles the Bald commissioned quantities of manuscripts, with jewelled book covers, and sent them as gifts to their fellow rulers or to important ecclesiastics. An age when these beautiful things could be valued as instruments of persuasion could not have been wholly barbarous. Even England, which during the lifetime of Charlemagne had been sunk in provincial darkness, recovered in the tenth century and produced works of art that have scarcely been equalled in this island. Is there a finer English drawing than the Crucifixion, which is the frontispiece of a psalter in the British Museum [17]? King Aethelstan is not a very clear or heroic figure in English history, but his collection, which is described in some detail, would have made Mr Pierpont Morgan, who was very fond of gold, go purple in the face with envy. Of course these marvellous objects usually contained relics of the saints: that was the normal

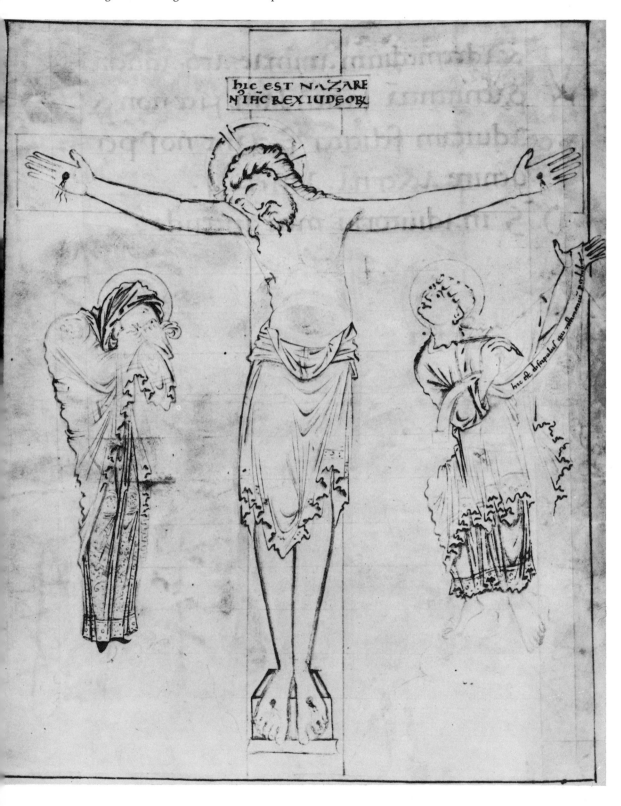

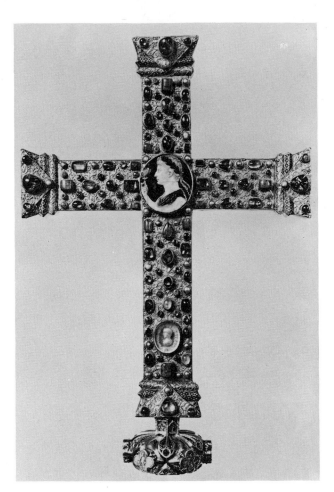

pretext for the artist to use his most precious materials and his utmost skill. The idea that material substances could be made spiritual by art alone belongs to a later phase of medieval thought. And yet this use of art to encase objects of religious value was really an indirect expression of the same state of mind. In these splendiferous objects the appetite for 'gold and wrought gem-work' is no longer the symbol of a warrior's courage and ferocity, but is used for the glory of God.

In the tenth century Christian art took on the character it was to retain throughout the Middle Ages. To me the cross of Lothar [18 and 19] in the treasury of Aix-la-Chapelle is one of the most moving objects that has come down to us from the distant past. One side is a beautiful assertion of imperial status. At the centre of the gems and gold filigree is a cameo of the Emperor Augustus, an image of worldly *imperium* at its most civilised. On the other side there is only a flat piece of silver, but on it is engraved an outline

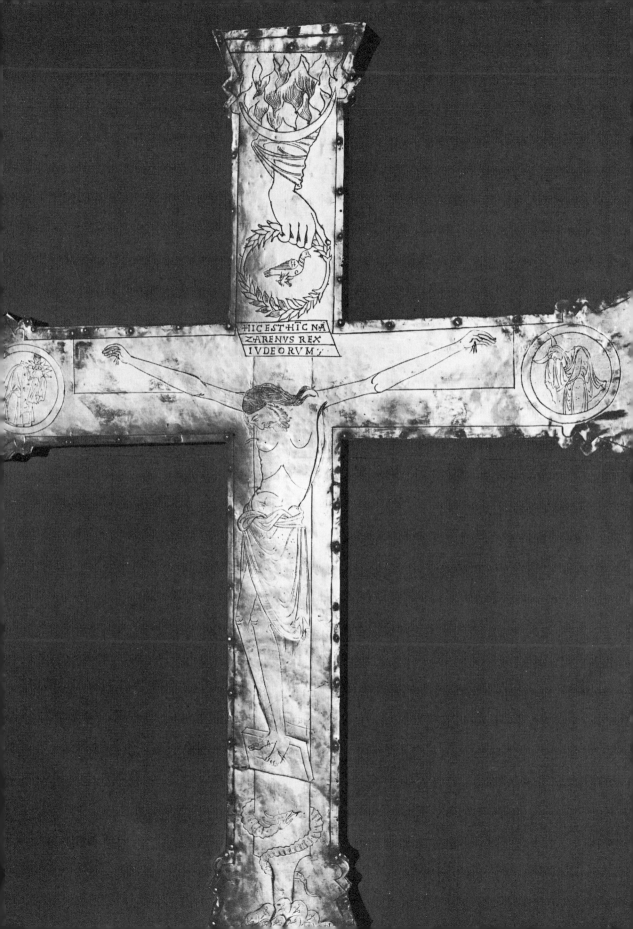

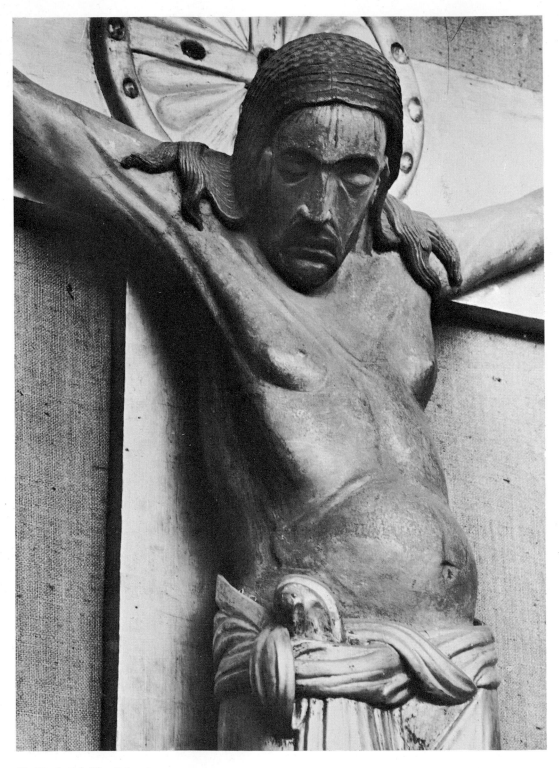

20 Gero's Crucifix, Cologne

3 Reliquary in the form of the head of the Emperor Charlemagne

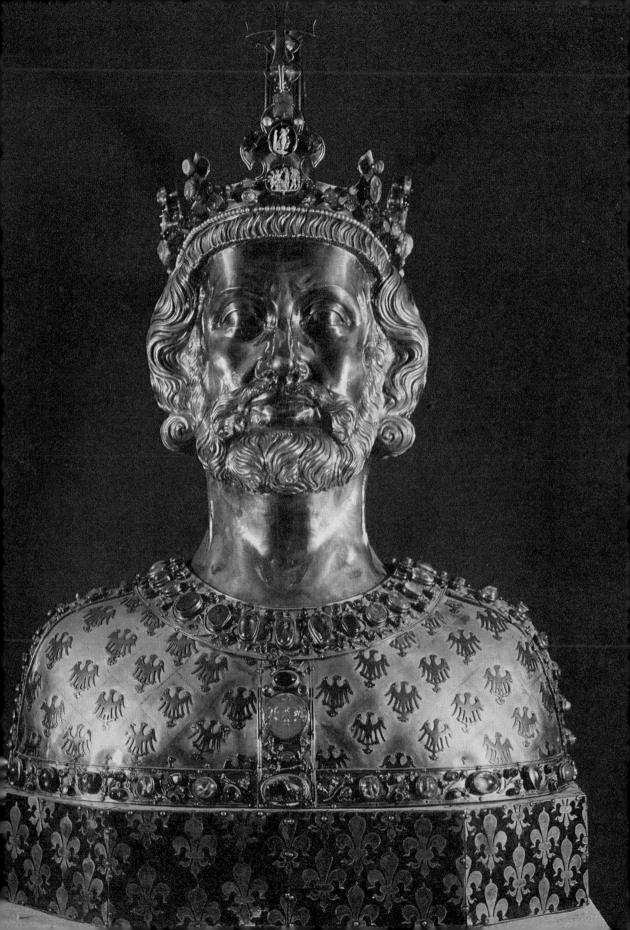

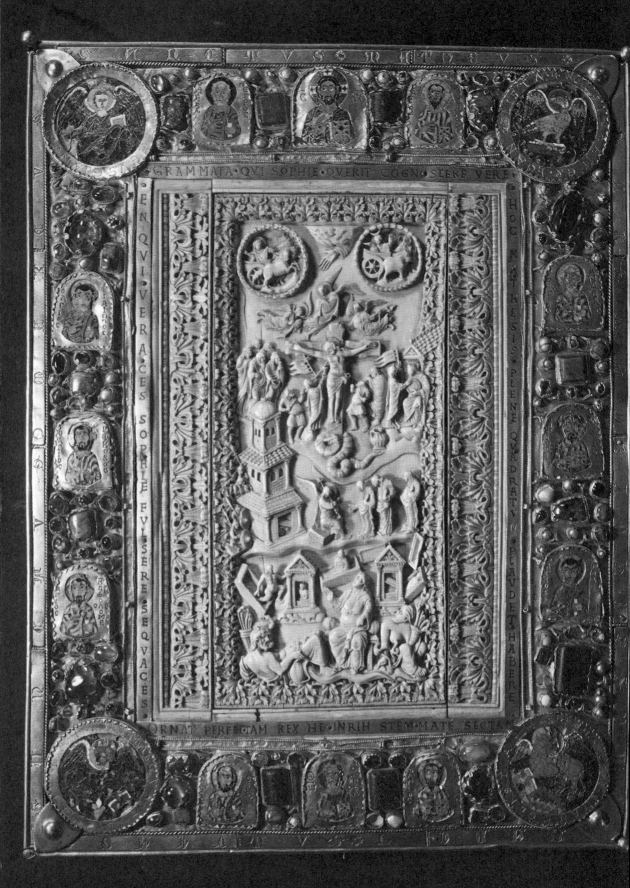

GRAMMATA·QVI·SOPHIE·QVERIT·COGN·SCERE·VERA

EN·QVI·VERACES·SOPHIE·FVLSERE·SEQVACES·

HOC·MATHESIS·PLENE·QVADRATVM·PLAVDET·HABERE·

ORNAT·PERFECTAM·REX·HE·INRIH·STEM·MATE·SECTA

drawing of the Crucifixion, a drawing of such poignant beauty as to make the front of the cross look worldly. It is the experience of a great artist simplified to its essence – what Matisse wished to do in his chapel at Vence, but more concentrated, and the work of a believer.

We have grown so used to the idea that the Crucifixion is the supreme symbol of Christianity, that it is a shock to realise how late in the history of Christian art its power was recognised. In the first art of Christianity it hardly appears; and the earliest example, on the doors of Santa Sabina in Rome, is stuck away in a corner, almost out of sight. The simple fact is that the early Church needed converts, and from this point of view the Crucifixion was not an encouraging subject. So, early Christian art is concerned with miracles, healings, and with hopeful aspects of the faith like the Ascension and the Resurrection. The Santa Sabina Crucifixion is not only obscure but unmoving. The few surviving Crucifixions of the early Church make no attempt to touch our emotions. It was the tenth century, that despised and rejected epoch of European history, that made the Crucifixion into a moving symbol of the Christian faith. In a figure like the one made for Archbishop Gero of Cologne it has become very much what it has been ever since – the upstretched arms, the sunken head, the poignant twist of the body [20].

The men of the tenth century not only recognised the meaning of Christ's sacrifice in physical terms: they were able fully to sublimate it into ritual. The evidence of book illustrations and ivories show for the first time a consciousness of the symbolic power of the Mass. In the tenth-century manuscript known as the Uta Codex one sees the oriental splendour which the Ottonian thought appropriate to Church ritual. Points of theology are made visible in great detail. This could be achieved only in a secure and triumphant Church. And look at this ivory book cover [21], with its solemn, columnar figures chanting and celebrating the Mass. Are they not, almost literally, pillars of a great new establishment?

These confident works show that at the end of the tenth century there was a new power in Europe, greater than any king or emperor: the Church. If you had asked the average man of the time to what country he belonged, he would not have understood you; he would have known only to what bishopric. And the Church was not only an organiser; it was a humaniser. Looking at Ottonian ivories, or at the marvellous bronze doors [22] made for Bishop Bernward at Hildesheim at the beginning of the eleventh century, I am reminded of the most famous lines in Virgil, that great mediator between the antique and the medieval world. They come when Aeneas has been shipwrecked in a country that he fears is inhabited by barbarians. Then as he looks around he sees some figures carved in relief, and he says:

4 Binding of *Book of Pericopes* belonging to Henry II

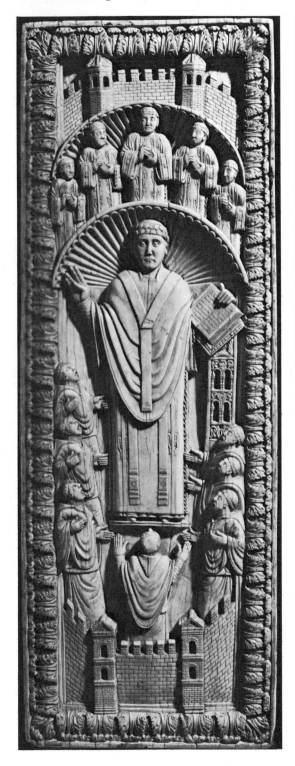
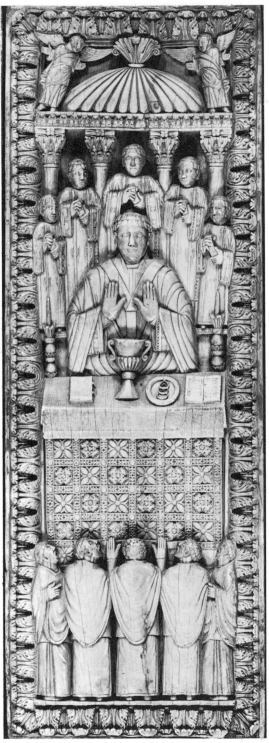

'These men know the pathos of life, and mortal things touch their hearts.'

Man is no longer *Imago Hominis*, the image of man, but a human being, with humanity's impulses and fears; also humanity's moral sense and belief in the authority of a higher power. By the year 1000, the year in which many timid people had feared that the world would come to an end, the long dominance of the barbarian wanderers was over, and Western Europe was prepared for its first great age of civilisation.

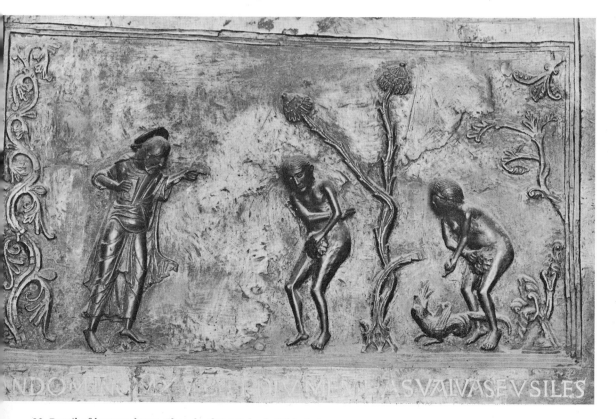

22 Detail of bronze doors, Church of St Michael, Hildesheim

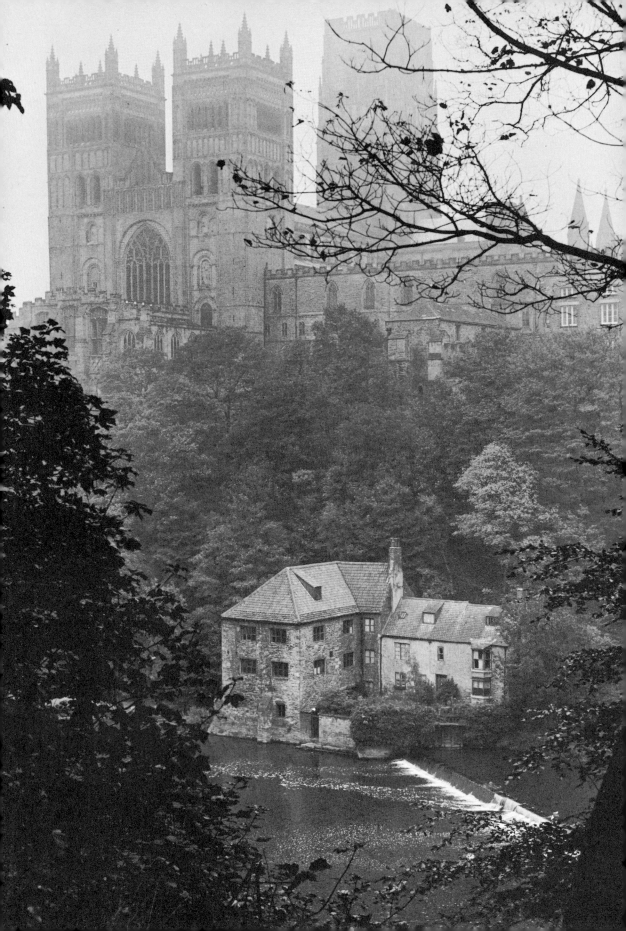

2 The Great Thaw

There have been times in the history of man when the earth seems suddenly to have grown warmer or more radio-active . . . I don't put that forward as a scientific proposition, but the fact remains that three or four times in history man has made a leap forward that would have been unthinkable under ordinary evolutionary conditions. One such time was about the year 3000 BC, when quite suddenly civilisation appeared, not only in Egypt and Mesopotamia but in the Indus valley; another was in the late sixth century BC, when there was not only the miracle of Ionia and Greece – philosophy, science, art, poetry, all reaching a point that wasn't reached again for 2000 years – but also in India a spiritual enlightment that has perhaps never been equalled. Another was round about the year 1100. It seems to have affected the whole world; but its strongest and most dramatic effect was in Western Europe – where it was most needed. It was like a Russian spring. In every branch of life – action, philosophy, organisation, technology – there was an extraordinary outpouring of energy, an intensification of existence. Popes, emperors, kings, bishops, saints, scholars, philosophers were all larger than life, and the incidents of history – Henry II at Canossa, Pope Urban announcing the First Crusade, Heloise and Abelard, the martyrdom of St Thomas à Becket – are great heroic dramas, or symbolic acts, that still stir our hearts.

The evidence of this heroic energy, this confidence, this strength of will and intellect, is still visible to us. In spite of all our mechanical aids and the inflated scale of modern materialism, Durham Cathedral remains a formidable construction [23], and the east end of Canterbury still looks very large and very complex. And these great orderly mountains of stone at first rose out of a small cluster of wooden houses; everyone with the least historical imagination has thought of that. But what people don't always realise is that it all happened quite suddenly – in a single lifetime. An even more astonishing change took place in sculpture. Tournus is one of the very few churches of any size to have survived from before the dreaded year 1000, and the architecture is rather grand in a primitive way. But its sculpture is miserably crude, without even the vitality of barbarism. Only fifty years later sculpture has the style and rhythmic assurance of the greatest epochs of art. The skill and dramatic invention that had been confined to small portable objects – goldsmith work or ivory carving – suddenly appear on a monumental scale.

24 'Ecclesia', manuscript illustration

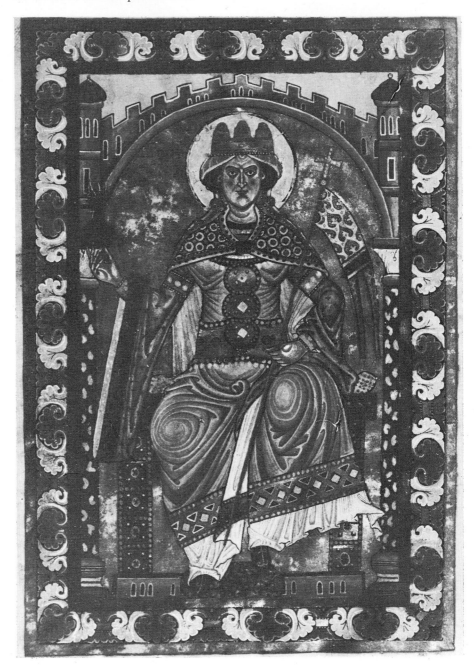

These changes imply a new social and intellectual background. They imply wealth, stability, technical skill and, above all, the confidence necessary to push through a long-term project. How had all this suddenly appeared in Western Europe? Of course there are many answers, but one is overwhelmingly more important than the others: the triumph of the Church. It could be argued that western civilisation was basically the creation of the Church. In saying that I am not thinking, for the moment, of the Church as the repository of Christian truth and spiritual experience: I am thinking of her as the twelfth century thought of her, as a power – Ecclesia – sitting like an empress [24].

The Church was powerful for all kinds of negative reasons: she didn't suffer many of the inconveniences of feudalism; there was no question of divided inheritances. For these reasons she could conserve and expand her properties. And she was powerful for positive reasons. Men of intelligence naturally and normally took holy orders, and could rise from obscurity to positions of immense influence. In spite of the number of bishops and abbots from royal or princely families, the Church was basically a democratic institution where ability – administrative, diplomatic and sheer intellectual ability – made its way. And then the Church was international. It was, to a large extent, a monastic institution following the Benedictine rule and owing no territorial allegiance. The great churchmen of the eleventh and twelfth centuries came from all over Europe. Anselm came from Aosta, via Normandy, to be Archbishop of Canterbury; Lanfranc had made the same journey, starting from Pavia. The list could be extended to almost every great teacher of the early Middle Ages. It couldn't happen in the Church, or politics, today: one can't imagine two consecutive archbishops of Canterbury being Italian. But it could happen – does happen – in the field of science; which shows that where some way of thought or human activity is really vital to us, internationalism is accepted unhesitatingly.

In so far as the intellectual and emotional lives of men and women of the twelfth century rose above mere necessity, they were inspired and directed by the Church. I suppose that they led narrow and monotonous lives, given rhythm only by the occupations of the months. Much of the year was spent in darkness, in very cramped conditions. What must have been the emotional impact of the inconceivable splendour, so much richer than anything that has come down to us today, which overwhelmed them when they entered the great monasteries or cathedrals.

This expansion of the human spirit was first made visible in the Abbey of Cluny. It was founded in the tenth century, but under Hugh of Semur – who was abbot for sixty years, from 1049 to 1109 – it became the greatest church in Europe, not only a huge complex of buildings, but a great organisation and a power – on the whole a benevolent power – in Church politics. The building was destroyed in the nineteenth century – used as a quarry like the buildings of ancient Rome. Only part of the south transept remains and a few fragments of sculpture. But we have many descriptions of its original splendour [25]. The abbey church alone was 415 feet long and 118 feet wide – the size of a large cathedral – and on feast days the walls were covered with hangings. The floors were of mosaic with figures, like a Roman pavement. Of the treasures it contained, the most astonishing was a seven-branched candlestick of gilt bronze, of which the shaft alone was eighteen feet high – a formidable piece of casting, even today. So much for those who say that the beliefs and institutions of the early Middle Ages were conditioned by technical incompetence. Of all this nothing remains, and practically nothing like it – no hangings, no figured mosaic floors, except in the cathedral of Taranto; only a few candlesticks, later and much smaller. One of them, made for the Cathedral of Gloucester, is only about eighteen inches high, but so highly wrought that one can imagine it eighteen feet [26]. It is an extreme example of Cluniac elaboration.

The first great eruption of ecclesiastical splendour was unashamedly extravagant. Apologists for the Cluniac style tell us that its decorations were subordinated to philosophic ideas, and I am bound to say that the few remaining sculptures at Cluny itself do deal with rather difficult concepts – they are a series of capitals representing the tones in music, which, ever

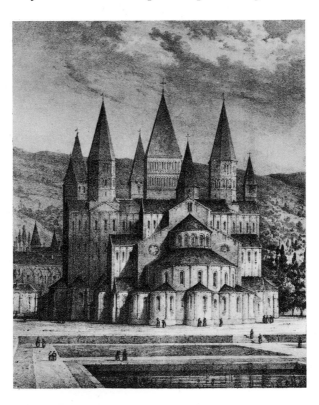

25 The abbey church of Cluny in 1879

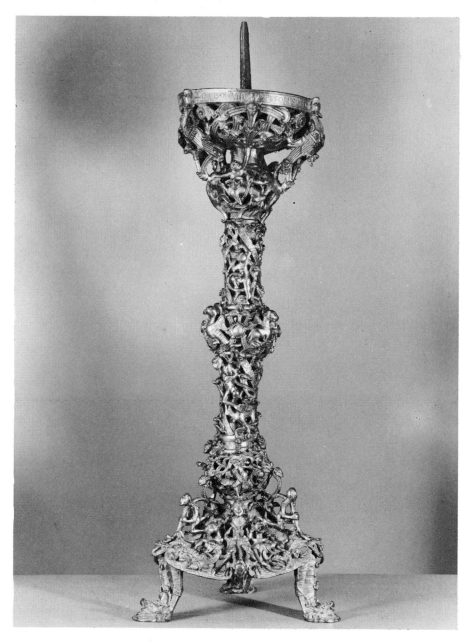

since Charlemagne, had played a leading part in medieval education. But my general impression is that the invention which boiled over into sculpture and painting in the early twelfth century was self-delighting. As with the similar outburst of the Baroque, one can think up ingenious interpretations of the subjects, but the motive force behind them was simply irrepressible, irresponsible energy. The Romanesque carvers were like a school of dolphins.

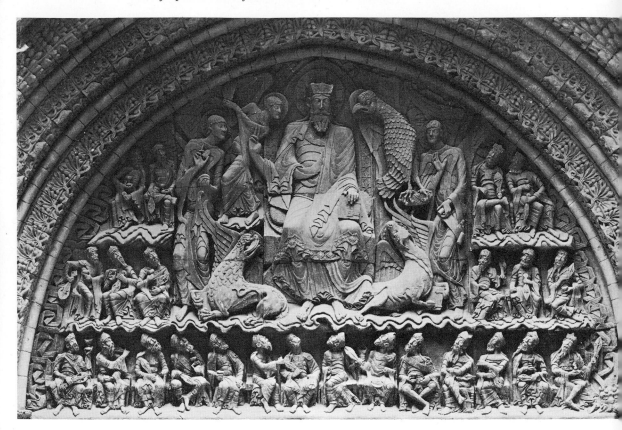

All this we know, not from the mother house of Cluny itself, but from the dependencies that spread all over Europe. There were over 1,200 of them in France alone: a fairly remote one, the Abbey of Moissac in Southern France, was important because it was on the pilgrimage route to Compostella. The carvings have much that is typical of the Cluniac style: the same sharp cutting, the same swirling drapery, the same twisting line, as if the restless impulses of the wandering craftsmen, the goldsmiths of the Viking conquerors, still had to be expressed in stone. Moissac is a peculiar case, because the chief sculptor who worked on the portal door seems to have been an eccentric of the first order, a sort of Romanesque El Greco. What could be stranger than his crazy-looking old men with their twisted limbs and fabulous mustachios [27]? Something could, and that is the central mullion of the door with its fabulous beasts. When one considers that they were once brightly coloured – Cluniac ornament seems to have been painted, as manuscripts show us, in bright primary colours – one realises that they must have looked even more fiercely Tibetan than they do today; and I can't imagine that even the medieval mind, which was adept at inter-

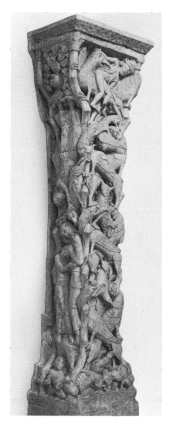
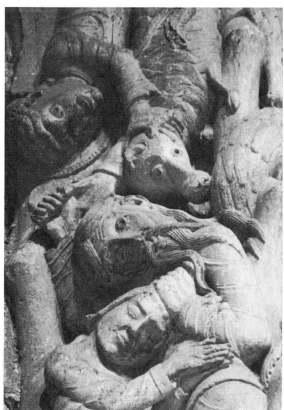

preting everything symbolically, could have found in them much religious meaning.

The Moissac master produced an even more liberated piece of self-expression in the mullion of the church of Souillac [28], which is surely one of the most bizarre and terrifying works of art ever produced in Western Europe before the present century. It *is* a work of art – no doubt about that. The gigantic birds, with their evil-looking beaks, and the cowering mortals achieve their effect on our emotions by plastic power and perfect mastery of means. It is an epitome of forest fears, a kind of totem-pole of western man at the end of his wanderings. But what has this column to do with Christian values – with compassion, charity or even hope. It isn't surprising that the most powerful churchman of his day, St Bernard of Clairvaux, should have become the bitter and relentless critic of the Cluniac style. Some of his attacks are the usual puritan objections, as when he speaks of 'the lies of poetry' – words that were to echo through the centuries and become particular favourites in the new religion of science. But St Bernard had an eye, as well as an eloquent tongue:

And in the cloisters, under the eyes of the brethren engaged in reading, what business have those ridiculous monstrosities, that misshapen shapeliness and shapely misshapenness? Those unclean monkeys, those fierce lions, those monstrous centaurs, those semi-human beings. Here you see a quadruped with the tail of a serpent, there a fish with the head of a goat. In short there appears on all sides so rich and amazing a variety of forms that it is more delightful to read the marble than the manuscripts and to spend the whole day in admiring these things, piece by piece, rather than in meditating on the Divine Law.

The last sentence shows clearly enough that Bernard felt the power of art; and in fact the buildings done under his influence, in what we call the Cistercian style, are closer to our ideals of architecture than anything else of the period. Most of them are abandoned and half-ruined, simply because it was part of St Bernard's doctrine that they should be built far from the worldly distractions of towns; so when, after the French Revolution, town monasteries were turned into local churches, the Cistercian monasteries fell into ruins. Yet in a few of them the monastic discipline has survived. It can be seen to this day, bringing the old buildings back to life, and it makes us realise how much we have lost by turning churches into museums.

This way of life is concerned with an ideal of eternity, and that is an important part of civilisation. But the great thaw of the twelfth century was not achieved by contemplation (which can exist at all times), but by action –

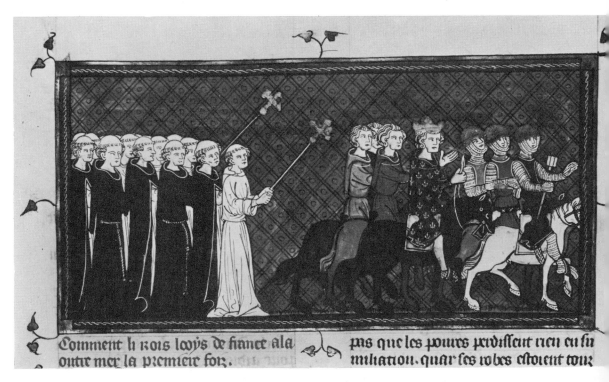

29 The King of France going on a crusade (manuscript illustration)

a vigorous, violent sense of movement, both physical and intellectual. On the physical side this took the form of pilgrimages and crusades [29]. I think they are among the features of the Middle Ages which it is hardest for us to understand. No good pretending that they were like cruises or holidays abroad. For one thing, they lasted far longer, sometimes two or three years. For another, they involved real hardship and danger. In spite of efforts to organise pilgrimages – Cluny ran a series of hostels along the chief routes – elderly abbots and middle-aged widows often died on the way to Jerusalem.

Pilgrimages were undertaken in hope of heavenly rewards: in fact they were often used by the Church as a penitence or a spiritualised form of extradition. The point of a pilgrimage was to look at relics. Here again we like to rationalise in modern terms and compare the pilgrim looking at a large fragment of the True Cross in Constantinople with the tourist cricking his neck in the Sistine Chapel. But this is quite unhistorical. The medieval pilgrim really believed that by contemplating a reliquary containing the head or even the fingers of a saint he would persuade that particular saint to intercede on his behalf with God. How can one hope to share this belief which played so great a part in medieval civilisation? Perhaps by visiting a famous place of pilgrimage – the little town of Conques, dedicated to the cult of St Foy. She was a little girl who in late Roman times refused to worship idols. She was obstinate in the face of reasonable persuasion – a Christian Antigone; and so she was martyred. Her relics began to work miracles, and in the eleventh century one of them was so famous that it aroused much jealousy and Bernard of Angers was sent to investigate it and report to the Bishop of Chartres. It seemed that a man had had his eyes put out by a jealous priest. He had become a *jongleur*, a blind acrobat. After a year he went to the shrine of St Foy and his eyes were restored. The man was still alive. He said that at first he had suffered from terrible headaches, but now they had passed and he could see perfectly. There *was* a difficulty: witnesses said that after his eyes had been put out they had been taken up to heaven, some said by a dove, others by a magpie. That was the only point of doubt. However, the report was favourable, a fine Romanesque church was built at Conques, and in it was placed a strange eastern-looking figure to contain the relics of St Foy [5, facing p. 44]. A golden idol! The face is perhaps the golden mask of some late Roman emperor. How ironical that this little girl, who was put to death for refusing to worship idols, should have been turned into one herself. Well, that's the medieval mind. They cared passionately about the truth, but their sense of evidence was different from ours. From our point of view nearly all the relics in the world depend on unhistorical assertions; and yet they, as much as any factor, led to that movement and diffusion of ideas from which western civilisation derives part of its momentum.

Of course the most important place of pilgrimage was Jerusalem. After the tenth century, when a strong Byzantine empire made the journey practicable, pilgrims used to go in parties of 7,000 at a time. This is the background of that extraordinary episode in history, the First Crusade. Although other factors may have determined its course – Norman restlessness, the ambitions of younger sons, economic depression, all the factors that make for a goldrush, there can be no doubt that the majority of people joined the crusade in a spirit of pilgrimage.

What was the effect of the crusades on western civilisation? I simply don't know. But its effect on art was considerable. It explains a great deal that would otherwise be mysterious in the style we call Romanesque. The first attempts at monumental sculpture in the eleventh century, based on Roman remains, are dull and dead. Then about ten years later this stiff antiquarian style is animated by a turbine of creative energy. The

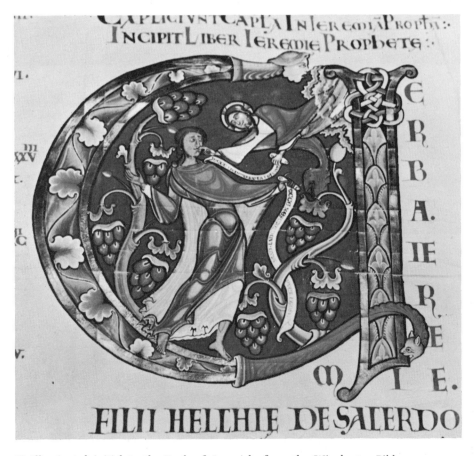

30 Illuminated initial to the Book of Jeremiah, from the Winchester Bible

31 Abbey church, Vézelay

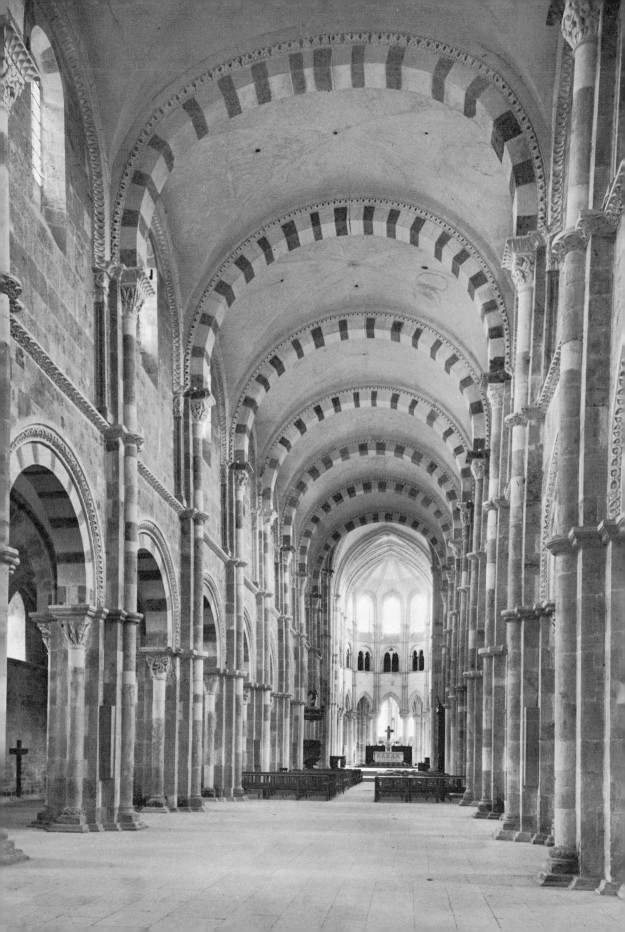

new style was transmitted by manuscripts, and it arose from a conjunction of northern rhythms and oriental motives. I see them as two fierce beasts tugging at the carcass of Graeco-Roman art. Very often one can trace a figure back to a Classical original, but it has been entirely tugged out of shape – or perhaps one could say into shape – by these two new forces [30].

This feeling of tugging, of pulling everything to bits and re-shaping it, was characteristic of twelfth-century art, and was somehow complementary to the massive stability of its architecture. And I find rather the same situation in the realm of ideas. The main structure, the Christian faith, was unshakable. But round it was a play of minds, a tugging and a tension, that has hardly existed since and was, I think, one of the things that prevented Western Europe from growing rigid, as so many other civilisations have done. It was an age of intense intellectual activity. To read what was going on in Paris about the year 1130 makes one's head spin. At the centre of it was the brilliant, enigmatic figure of Peter Abelard, the invincible arguer, the magnetic teacher. Abelard was a star. Like a great prize-fighter, he expressed his contempt for anyone who met him in the ring of open discussion. The older medieval philosophers like Anselm had said: 'I must believe in order that I may understand.' Abelard took the opposite course: 'I must understand in order that I may believe.' He said: 'By doubting we come to questioning, and by questioning we perceive the truth.' Strange words to have been written in the year 1122. Of course they got him into trouble. Only the strength and wisdom of Cluny saved him from excommunication. He ended his days calmly, in a Cluniac house, and after his death Peter the Venerable, Abbot of Cluny, wrote to Heloise saying that she and Abelard would be reunited 'where, beyond these voices, there is peace'.

I am in the Cluniac Abbey of Vézelay, standing in the covered portico. Above my head the relief on the main door shows Christ in glory [32], no longer the Judge as at Moissac, but the Redeemer. His saving grace streams from his finger-tips and inspires his apostles, who will preach his Gospel to all the nations of the world. These are represented in the panels that surround the tympanum, and in the long frieze below – and a queer lot they are, including pygmies, wolf-headed men, and various other experiments that the Creator made before arriving at the solution known as man, whose likenesses had been transmitted to the Middle Ages in a late antique manuscript.

Vézelay is full of sculpture on the doors and capitals. But fascinating as it is, one forgets about it when one looks through the door at the architecture of the interior [31]. It is so harmonious that surely St Bernard, who preached the Second Crusade here, must have felt it to be an expression of the Divine Law and an aid to worship and contemplation. It certainly has that effect on

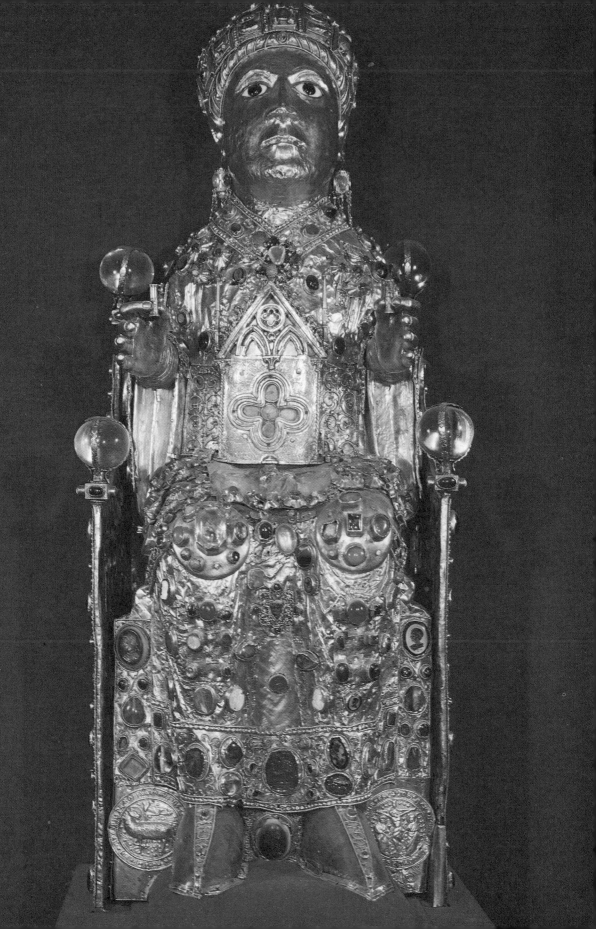

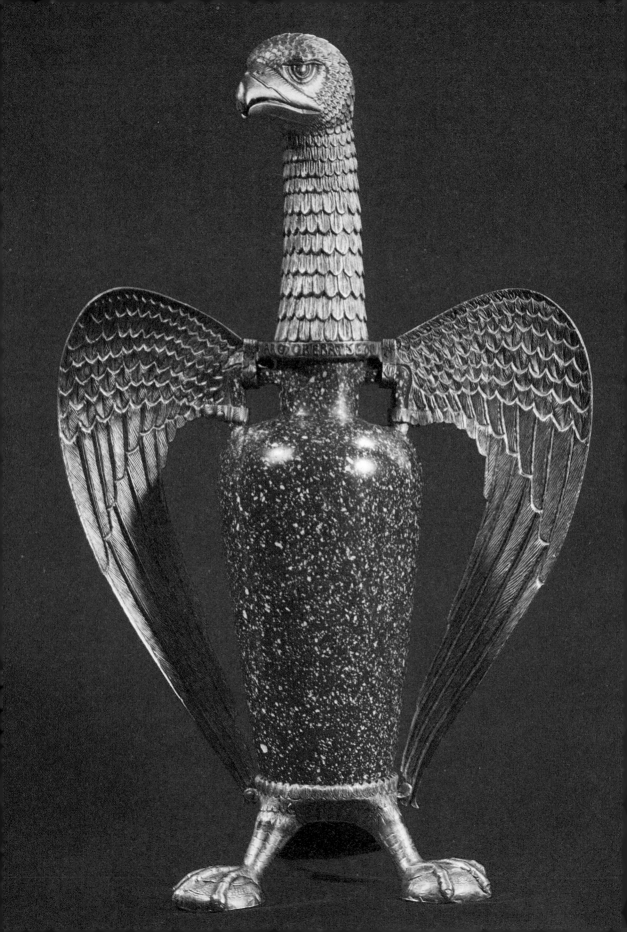

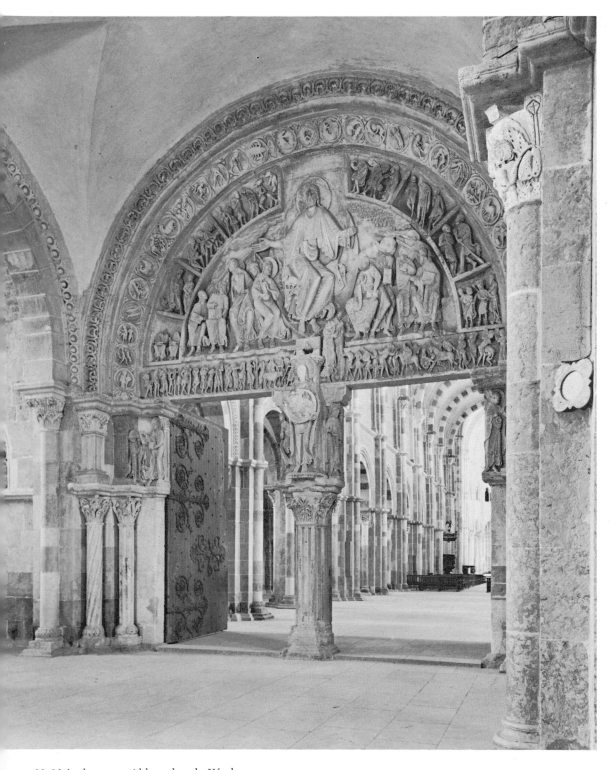

32 Main doorway, Abbey church, Vézelay

6 Porphyry jar transformed into an eagle for Abbot Suger

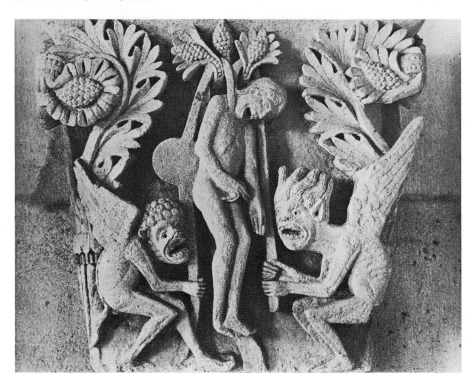

me. Indeed, I can think of no other Romanesque interior that has this quality of lightness, this feeling of Divine Reason. And it seems inevitable that this Romanesque should emerge into a beautiful early Gothic.

We don't know the name of the architect of Vézelay, nor of the highly individual sculptors of Moissac and Toulouse. This used to be taken as a proof of Christian humility in the artists – or alternatively as a sign of their low status. I think it was just an accident, because in fact we do know the names of a good many medieval builders, including the architect of Cluny, and the form of their inscriptions does not at all suggest excessive modesty. One of the most famous is bang in the middle of the main portal of the cathedral at Autun, under the feet of Christ. *Gislebertus hoc fecit*. One of the Blessed looks up at the name of Gislebertus with admiration. He must have been considered a very important man for his name to have been permitted in such a prominent place. At a later date it would have been, not the artist's name, but the patron's. And in fact Gislebertus was important to Autun because he did something unique in the Middle Ages and very rare at any time, he carried out the whole decoration of the cathedral himself. As a rule the master-mason did the relief over the main portal and some of the principal figures, and left the rest to assistants. Gislebertus seems to have carved the whole thing, including nearly all the capitals of the interior, with his own hand.

This extraordinary feat was in keeping with his character as an artist. He wasn't an inward-looking visionary like the Moissac master, not a perfectionist, like the master of St Etienne at Toulouse. He was an extrovert. He loves to tell a story, and his strength lies in his dramatic force. The row of the Damned under the feet of their Judge in the predella of the tympanum forms a crescendo of despair. They are reduced to essentials in a way that brings them very close to the art of our time: a likeness terrifyingly confirmed by the gigantic hands that carry up the head of a sinner as if it were a piece of rubble on a building-site. The same is true of the capitals. They haven't the compulsive rhythm of the finest Cluniac art; but, on the other hand, they are not so open to the objections of St Bernard. Of course they contain rich and splendid pieces of ornament, but in the end it's the human narrative that counts. Even in the abstract-looking design of the Three Kings asleep under their magnificent counterpane [34], what matters is the angel's gesture, the gentle way he places one finger on the hand of the sleeping king. Like all story-tellers, Gislebertus had a taste for horrors, and went out of his way to depict them. He dwells with relish on the repulsive suicide of Judas [33]. But he also did a figure of Eve which is the first female nude since antiquity to give a sense of the pleasures of the body.

Gislebertus had probably been employed at Cluny and he certainly

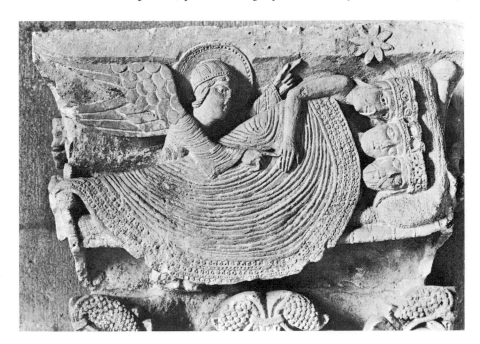

34 Gislebertus, The Three Kings, Autun

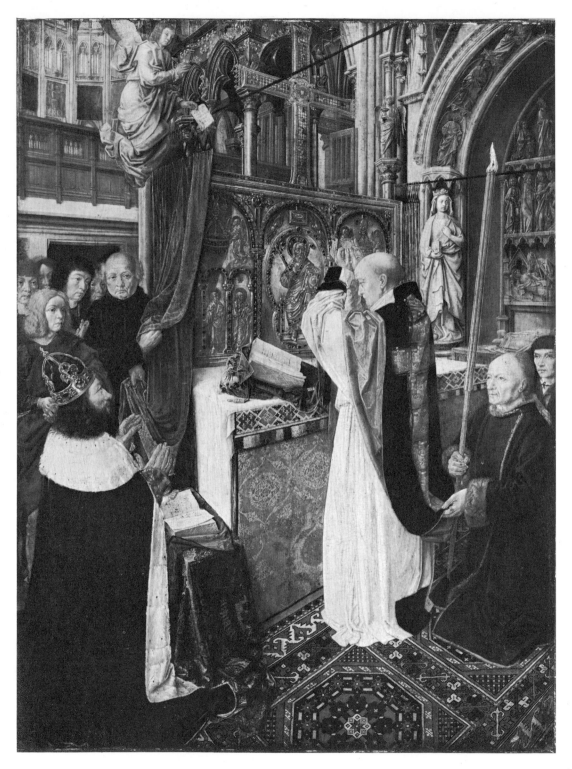

35 Master of St Gilles, *Mass of St Gilles*

worked at Vézelay. When he came to Autun, in about 1125, he was a mature man whose style was set; it was the crowning work of his career, hence the prominent inscription. By the time it was finished, say 1135, a new force had appeared in European art: the Abbey of St Denis.

The royal Abbey of St Denis had been famous enough in earlier times, but the part it played in western civilisation was due to the abilities of one extraordinary individual, the Abbot Suger. He was one of the first men of the Middle Ages whom one can think of in modern, I might almost say in transatlantic, terms. His origins were completely obscure and he was extremely small, but his vitality was overwhelming. It extended to everything that he undertook – organisation, building, statesmanship. He was Regent of France for seven years and a great patriot; indeed he seems to have been the first to pronounce those now familiar words: 'The English are destined by moral and natural law to be subjected to the French and not contrariwise.' He loved to talk about himself without any false modesty, and he tells the story of how his builders assured him that beams of the length he needed for a certain roof could never be found because trees just weren't as tall as that. Whereupon he took his carpenters into the forests ('they smiled,' he says, 'and would have laughed if they had dared'), and in the course of the day he had discovered twelve trees of the necessary size, had them felled and brought back. You see why I used the word transatlantic.

Like several of the pioneers of the new world, for example Van Horne, the builder of the Canadian-Pacific Railway, Suger had a passionate love of art. One of the most fascinating documents of the Middle Ages is the account he wrote of the works carried out at St Denis under his administration – the gold altar, the crosses, the precious crystals. Suger's great gold cross was twenty-four feet high; it was studded with jewels and inlaid with enamels made by one of the finest craftsmen of the age, Godfroix de Claire. It was all destroyed in the Revolution. We can form some idea of an altar in St Denis from a fifteenth-century picture by the master of St Gilles in the National Gallery [35]; and a few of the sacred vessels have survived, most of them made out of semi-precious materials from the East like an Egyptian porphyry jar [6, facing p. 45] now in the Louvre, which, Suger tells us, he found forgotten in a cupboard and, inspired perhaps by a piece of Byzantine silk, made into an eagle.

Suger's feeling for all these objects was partly that of a great collector – love of brightness and splendour and antiquity – and a love of acquisition. He describes how some Cistercians (who didn't believe in display) brought him a lot of gems – hyacinths, sapphires, rubies, topazes, emeralds – which had belonged to the feckless King Stephen of England, and how he was able to get them for £400 (thanks be to God) although they were worth much more. But as usual the analogy with a modern collector breaks down because everything Suger did was genuinely done to the glory of God. And he was not merely a collector – he was a creator. His work had a philosophic basis that is very important to western civilisation.

It arose out of a typical medieval muddle. St Denis, the patron saint of the abbey, was confused with an Athenian named Denis who was converted by St Paul, and this Greek Denis was, quite wrongly, believed to be the author of a philosophical treatise called *The Heavenly Hierarchies*. Suger had this treatise translated from the Greek, and it was from this that he was able to give a theoretical justification of his love of beauty. He argued that we could only come to understand absolute beauty, which is God, through the effect of precious and beautiful things on our senses. He said : 'The dull mind rises to truth through that which is material.' This was really a revolutionary concept in the Middle Ages. It was the intellectual background of all the sublime works of art of the next century and in fact has remained the basis of our belief in the value of art until today.

In addition to this revolution in theory, Suger's St Denis was also the beginning of many new developments in practice – in architecture, in sculpture, in painted glass. Owing to its connection with royalty the church was a good deal knocked about during the French Revolution, and then all too thoroughly restored. But one can still see that Suger introduced, perhaps really invented, the Gothic style of architecture, not only the pointed arch, but the lightness of high windows – what we call the clerestory and triforium. 'Bright,' he says, 'is the noble edifice that is pervaded by new light,' and in these words anticipates all the architectural aspirations of the next two hundred years. One knows that he introduced the idea of the rose window, and a few pieces of his painted glass are still to be seen at St Denis. The most striking (much restored, I fear) shows the ancestry of Christ in the form of a tree growing from the side of Jesse; and like so many symbolic-historical subjects of Gothic art, this too seems to have been invented by Suger. Many of his other innovations have disappeared from St Denis: for example his porticos with rows of standing figures, now all replaced by columns. And the whole exterior, in its squalid Parisian suburb, stained by the fumes of factories, makes no impression of sanctity. To form any notion of its first effect on the mind one must go to Chartres [36].

In some miraculous way Chartres has survived. Fire and war, revolution and restoration, have attacked it in vain. Even the tourists have not destroyed its atmosphere, as they have in so many temples of the human spirit from the Sistine Chapel to Elephanta. One can still climb the hill to the

36 West Front, Chartres Cathedral

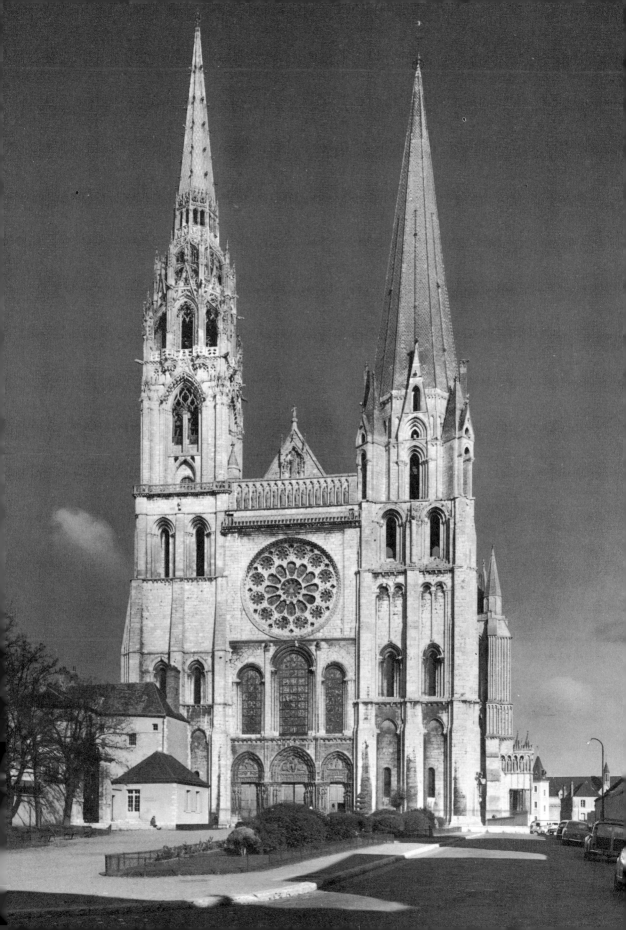

52

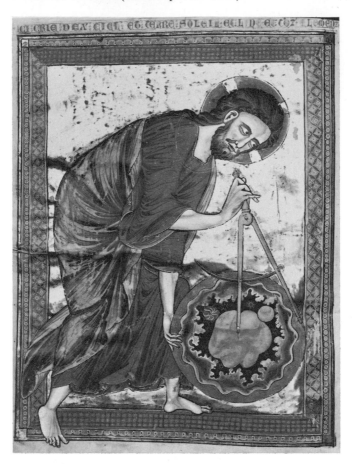

cathedral in the spirit of a pilgrim; and the south tower is still more or less as it was when it was completed in 1164. It is a masterpiece of harmonious proportion. Was this harmony calculated mathematically? Ingenious scholars have produced a system of proportions based on measurements: it's so complex that I find it very hard to credit. However, one must remember that to medieval man geometry was a divine activity. God was the great geometer [37], and this concept inspired the architect. Moreover, Chartres was the centre of a school of philosophy devoted to Plato, and in particular to his mysterious book called the *Timaeus*, from which it was thought that the whole universe could be interpreted as a form of measurable harmony. So perhaps the proportions of Chartres reflect a more complex mathematics than one is inclined to believe.

One proportion certainly wasn't calculated, and that was the relation of the west front to the towers. It was originally much further back, but soon after it was built the foundations became unsteady, so it was taken down,

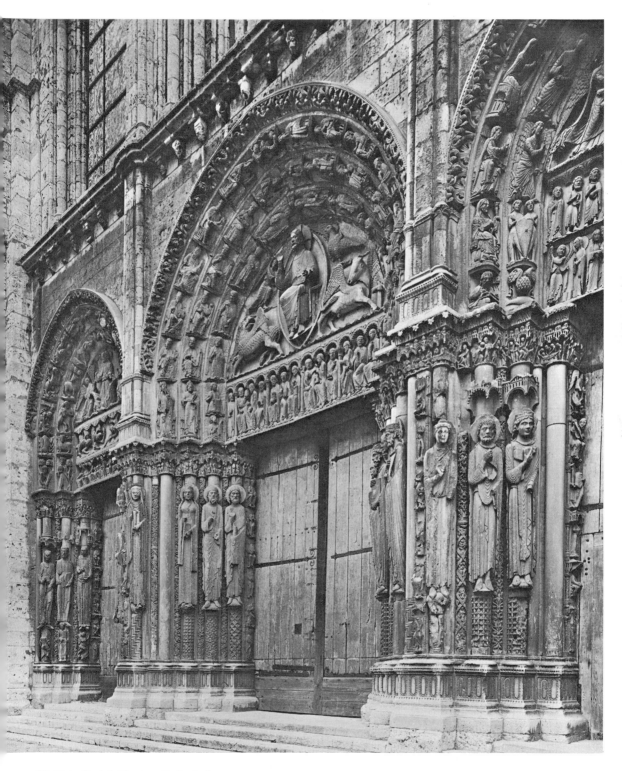

38 Main Portal, Chartres Cathedral

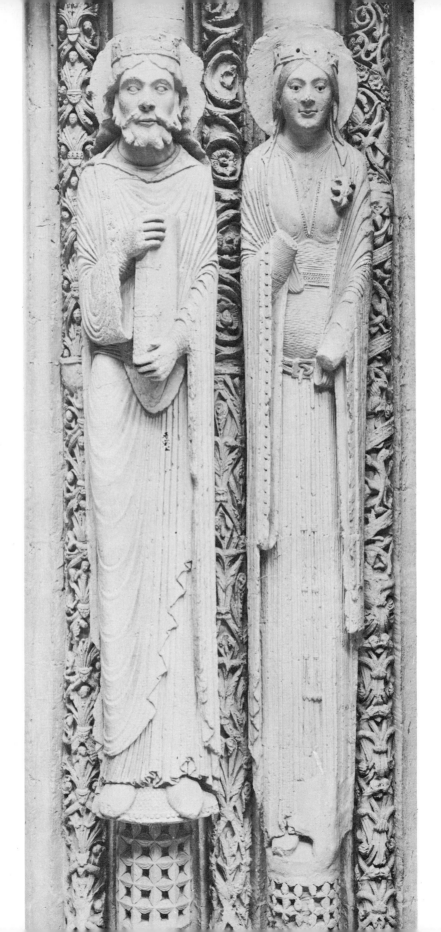

stone by stone, and moved forwards. This accounts for a certain flatness in the famous façade which always worries me. But in the event it was one of the many miracles that have preserved Chartres, because when the cathedral was burnt down in 1194, there was a sort of vestibule that formed a fire-gap between the nave and the west front, and this saved it.

The main portal of Chartres is one of the most beautiful congregations of carved figures in the world [38]. The longer you look at it, the more moving incidents, the more vivid details you discover. I suppose the first thing that strikes anyone is the row of pillar people. In naturalistic terms, as bodies, they are impossible, and the fact that one believes in them is a triumph of art. Figures had been made into columns since the Cnidian treasury at Delphi, but never so narrowly compressed and elongated as they are here – except perhaps at St Denis, because there is evidence that the master who carved them had worked for Suger before he came on to Chartres. He was not only a sculptor of genius, but one of great originality. He must have begun carving when style was dominated by the violent twisting rhythms of Cluny and Toulouse; and he has created a style as still and restrained and classical as the Greek sculptors of the sixth century.

The man who carved the pillar of Souillac, although a great artist, cannot be called a representative of civilisation. We have no such doubts about the master-mason of Chartres. One can see that his classic style was a personal creation when one compares the figures by the master himself – all of them are in the central door – with those of his assistants who worked on the doors either side. They could follow the outline of his columnar figures, but when it came to draperies they reverted to the curls and spirals of southern Romanesque, which are meaningless in their new context, whereas the chief master's style is absolutely Greek in the simplicity and precision of every fold. Was it really Greek – I mean Greek in derivation? Were these reed-like draperies, the thin straight lines of the fluted folds, the zigzag hems, and the whole play of texture which so obviously recall a Greek archaic figure, arrived at independently? Or had the Chartres master seen some fragments of early Greek sculpture in the south of France? For various reasons I am quite certain that he had.

There was far more Greek sculpture visible in the twelfth century than anyone used to realise. One can find dozens of examples of its being imitated. It even reached England: Henry of Blois, Bishop of Winchester, had a shipload of antiques sent to him. And this style was particularly appropriate to Chartres, because it was there that men first began seriously to study the two founders of Greek philosophy, Plato and Aristotle. John of Salisbury, Bishop of Chartres just after the west portal was finished, was a real humanist,

39 Kings and Queens, Chartres Cathedral

comparable to Erasmus. In the arch of the right-hand door the Greek philosophers are represented with their attributes: Aristotle, with the severe figure of Dialectic; Pythagoras, who discovered that the musical scale could be stated mathematically, with Music striking the bells; and so forth, all round the arch. Music meant a great deal to the men of the twelfth century, and round the arch of the central doorway a really extraordinary artist – perhaps the head master himself, cutting more sharply in harder stone – has shown the elders of the book of Revelation, with musical instruments, each so accurately depicted that one could reconstruct it and play it.

These figures give one an idea of the incomparable richness of the west portal, and the thought that underlies the whole scheme. But from the point of view of civilisation, the most important thing about the central doorway, more important even than its Greek derivation, is the character of the heads of the so-called kings and queens – no one knows exactly who they are [39]. Think of the people we encountered in the ninth and tenth centuries: vigorous, passionate, earnestly striving towards some kind of intellectual light, but fundamentally still barbarians; that is to say, embodiments of will, their features moulded by the need to survive. Do not the kings and queens of Chartres show a new stage in the ascent of western man? Indeed I believe that the refinement, the look of selfless detachment and the spirituality of these heads is something entirely new in art. Beside them the gods and heroes of ancient Greece look arrogant, soulless and even slightly brutal. I fancy that the faces which look out at us from the past are the surest indication we have of the meaning of an epoch. Of course something depends on the insight of the artist who portrays them. If you pass from the heads of the master-mason to those of his more old-fashioned colleagues you are back in the slightly woozy world of Moissac. But good faces evoke good artists – and conversely a decline of portraiture usually means a decline of the face, a theory which can now be illustrated by photographs in the daily papers. The faces on the west portal of Chartres are amongst the most sincere and, in a true sense, the most aristocratic that Western Europe ever produced.

We know from the old chronicles something about the men whose state of mind these faces reveal. In the year 1144, they say, when the towers seemed to be rising as if by magic, the faithful harnessed themselves to the carts which were bringing stone, and dragged them from the quarry to the cathedral. The enthusiasm spread throughout France. Men and women came from far away carrying heavy burdens of provisions for the workmen – wine, oil, corn. Amongst them were lords and ladies, pulling carts with the rest. There was perfect discipline, and a most profound silence. All hearts were united and each man forgave his enemies. This feeling of dedication

40 Interior, Chartres Cathedral

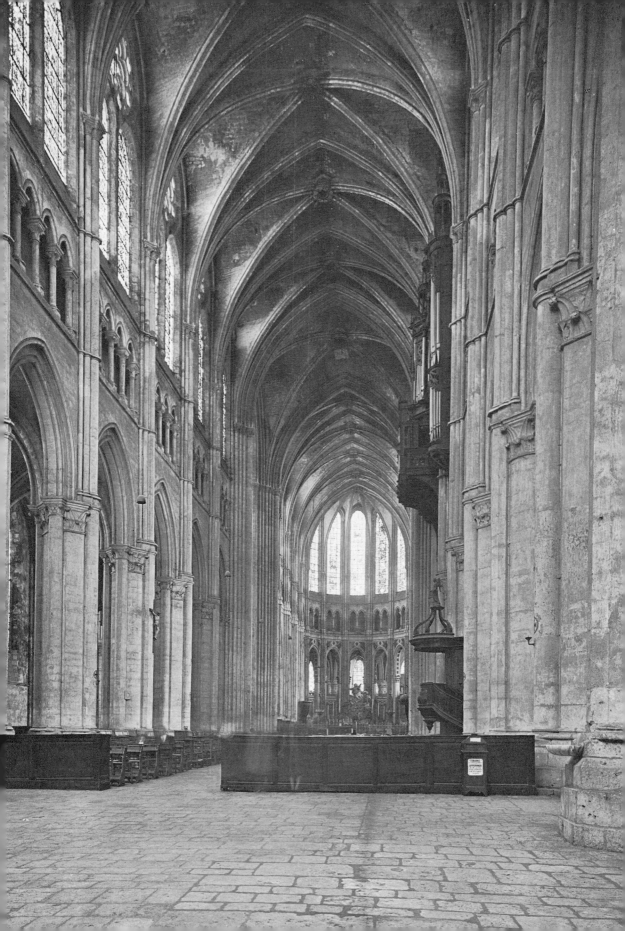

to a great civilising ideal is even more overwhelming when we pass through the portal into the interior [40]. This is not only one of the two most beautiful covered spaces in the world (the other is St Sophia in Constantinople), but it is one that has a peculiar effect on the mind; and the men who built it would have said that this was because it was the favourite earthly abode of the Virgin Mary.

Chartres contained the most famous of all relics of the Virgin, the actual tunic she had worn at the time of the Annunciation, which had been presented to Chartres by Charles the Bald in the year 876. From the first this relic had worked miracles, but only in the twelfth century did the cult of the Virgin appeal to the popular imagination. I suppose that in earlier centuries life was simply too rough. At any rate, if art is any guide, and in this series I am taking it as my guide, the Virgin played a very small part in the minds of men during the ninth and tenth centuries. She appears, of course, in incidents like the Annunciation and the Adoration of the Magi, but representations of the Virgin and Child as objects of special devotion are extremely rare in Ottonian art. The earliest cult figure of the Virgin and Child of any size is a painted wooden statue in St Denis which must date from about 1130. The great Romanesque churches were dedicated to the saints whose relics they contained – St Sernin, St Etienne, St Lazarus, St Denis, St Mary Magdalene – none of them to the Virgin. Then, after Chartres the greatest churches in France were dedicated to her – Paris, Amiens, Laon, Rouen, Rheims.

What was the reason for this sudden change? I used to think that it must have been a result of the crusades: that the returning warriors brought back an admiration for the womanly virtues of gentleness and compassion, as opposed to the male virtues of courage and physical strength which they themselves represented. I am not so sure about this now; but it does seem to be confirmed by the fact that the first representations of the Virgin as an object of devotion are in a markedly Byzantine style, for example on a page of a manuscript from Citeaux, the community of St Bernard. St Bernard was one of the first men to speak of the Virgin as an ideal of beauty and a mediator between man and God. Dante was right to put into his mouth at the close of the *Paradiso* a hymn to the Virgin which I think one of the most beautiful pieces of poetry ever written.

But whatever the effect of St Bernard, a strong influence in spreading the cult of the Virgin was certainly the beauty and splendour of Chartres Cathedral. Its very construction was a kind of miracle. The old Romanesque church had been destroyed by a terrible fire in 1194: only the towers and the west front remained, and the people of Chartres feared that they had lost their precious relic. Then, when the debris was cleared away, it was found intact in the crypt. The Virgin's intention became clear – that a new church should be built, even more splendid than the last. Once more the chroniclers describe how people came from all over France to join in the work, how whole villages moved in order to help provide for the workmen; and of course there must have been many more of them this time, because the building was bigger and more elaborate, and required hundreds of masons, not to mention a small army of glass-makers who were to provide the hundred and seventy huge windows with stained glass. Perhaps it sounds sentimental, but I can't help feeling that this faith has given the interior of Chartres a unity and a spirit of devotion that exceeds even the other great churches of France, like Bourges and Le Mans.

However, one must add that all the faith in France couldn't have rebuilt the cathedral if the see of Chartres hadn't been extremely rich. After the fire, the Dean and Chapter decided to put aside three years' income for the re-building; and their income in modern terms has been reckoned to be about £750,000 a year. The Dean's personal income was £250,000 a year. Add to this that the see of Chartres was closely connected with the royal house of France, and one sees that, like most miracles, this one can be explained in material terms which, in fact, do not explain it at all.

The building is in the new architectural style to which Suger had given the impress of his authority at St Denis: what we call Gothic. Only at Chartres the architect was told to follow the foundations of the old Roman-esque cathedral, and this meant that the Gothic vaulting had to cover a space far wider than ever before. It was a formidable problem of construc-tion, and in order to solve it the architect has used the device known as flying buttresses – one of those happy strokes where necessity has led to an architectural invention of marvellous and fantastic beauty. Inside there is no trace of difficulty or calculation: the whole harmonious space seems to have grown up out of the earth according to some natural law of harmony.

So much has been written about the Gothic style that one feels inclined to take it for granted. But it remains one of the most remarkable of human achievements. Since the first expression of civilised life in architecture, say the pyramid of Sakara, man had thought of buildings as a weight on the ground. He had accepted their material nature and although he had tried to make them transcend it by means of proportion or by the colour of precious marbles, he had always found himself limited by problems of stability and weight. In the end it kept him down to the earth. Now by the devices of the Gothic style – the shaft with its cluster of columns, passing without interruption into the vault and the pointed arch – he could make stone seem weightless: the weightless expression of his spirit.

By the same means he could surround his space with glass. Suger said that he did this in order to get more light, but he found that these areas of glass could be made into an ideal means of impressing and instructing the faithful – far better than wall-painting because with a resonance, an effect on the senses, that the matt surface of a wall-painting could never have. 'Man may rise to the contemplation of the divine through the senses.' Well, nowhere else, I think, is this saying of the old pseudo-St Denis so wonderfully illustrated as it is in Chartres Cathedral. As one looks at the painted glass which completely surrounds one [7, on facing page], it seems almost to set up a vibration in the air. It is primarily a sensuous-emotional impact. As a matter of experience it is quite hard to find out what is going on in the various windows, even when one goes round with a crib prepared by some learned student of iconography; and whether the faithful of the early thirteenth century were well enough informed to follow all these stories seems to me extremely doubtful. But then we know that the frieze of the Parthenon was almost invisible when it was in its original position, and we must accept that in a non-utilitarian age people under the stress of some powerful emotion are prepared to make and do things for their own sakes or, as they would have said, to the glory of God.

Chartres is the epitome of the first great awakening in European civilisation. It is also the bridge between Romanesque and Gothic, between the world of Abelard and the world of St Thomas Aquinas, the world of restless curiosity and the world of system and order. Great things were to be done in the next centuries of high Gothic, great feats of construction, both in architecture and in thought. But they all rested on the foundations of the twelfth century. That was the age which gave European civilisation its impetus. Our intellectual energy, our contact with the great minds of Greece, our ability to move and change, our belief that God may be approached through beauty, our feeling of compassion, our sense of the unity of Christendom – all this, and much more, appeared in those hundred marvellous years between the consecration of Cluny and the rebuilding of Chartres.

7 *Death of the Virgin*, from a window of Chartres Cathedral

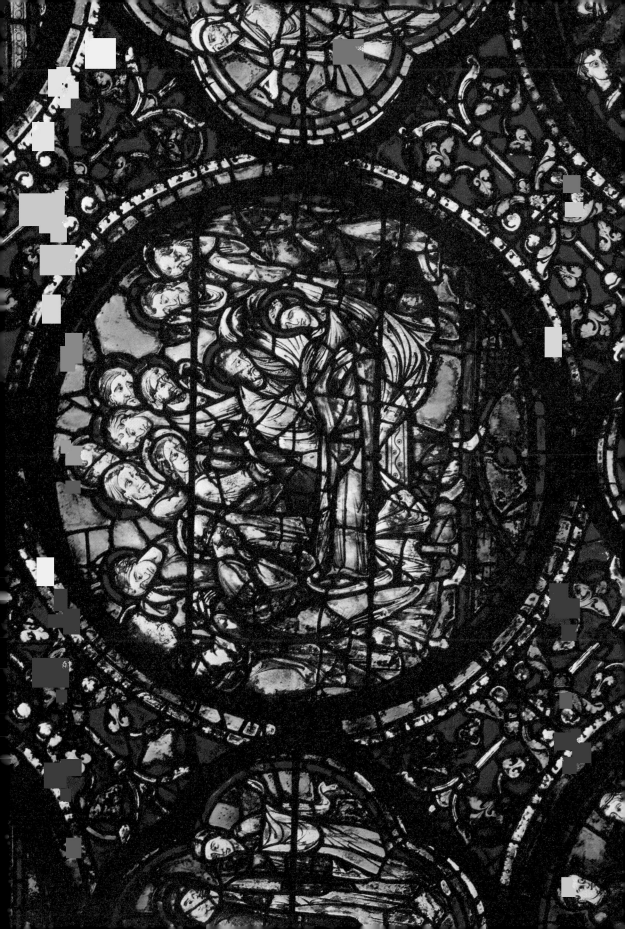

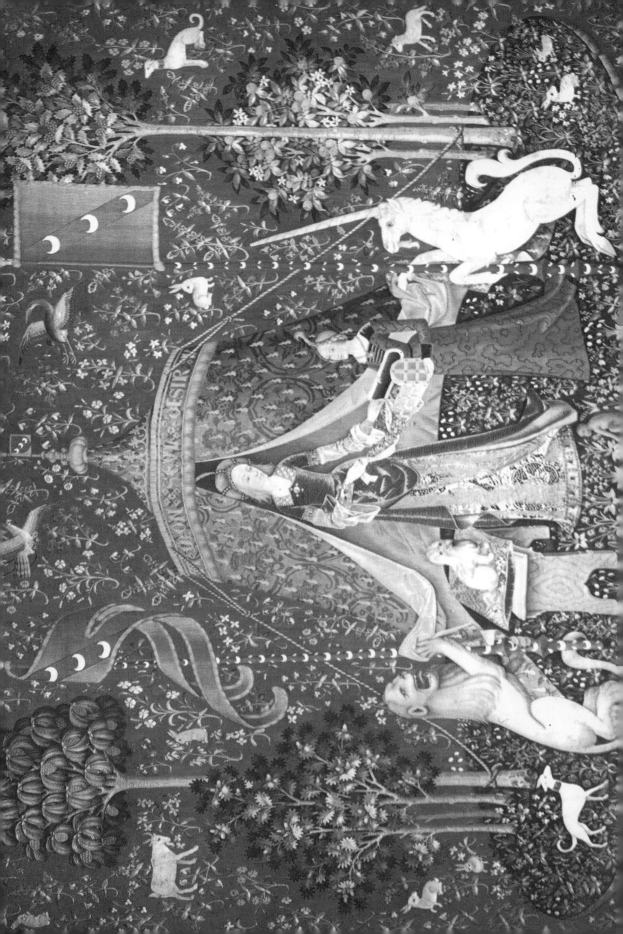

3 Romance and Reality

I am in the Gothic world, the world of chivalry, courtesy and romance; a world in which serious things were done with a sense of play – where even war and theology could become a sort of game; and when architecture reached a point of extravagance unequalled in history. After all the great unifying convictions of the twelfth century, High Gothic art can look fantastic and luxurious – what Marxists call conspicuous waste. And yet these centuries produced some of the greatest spirits in the history of man, amongst them St Francis of Assisi and Dante. Behind all the fantasy of the Gothic imagination there remained, on two different planes, a sharp sense of reality. Medieval man could see things very clearly, but he believed that these appearances should be considered as nothing more than symbols or tokens of an ideal order, which was the only true reality.

The fantasy strikes us first, and last; and one can see it in the room in the Cluny Museum in Paris hung with a series of tapestries known as *The Lady with the Unicorn*, one of the most seductive examples of the Gothic spirit [**8**, on facing page]. It is poetical, fanciful and profane. Its ostensible subject is the four senses. But its real subject is the power of love which can enlist and subdue all the forces of nature, including those two emblems of lust and ferocity, the unicorn and the lion. They kneel before this embodiment of chastity, and hold up the corners of her cloak. These wild animals have become, in the heraldic sense, her supporters. And all round this allegorical scene is what the medieval philosophers used to call *natura naturans* – nature naturing – trees, flowers, leaves galore, birds, monkeys, and those rather obvious symbols of nature naturing, rabbits. There is even nature domesticated, a little dog, sitting on a cushion. It is an image of worldly happiness at its most refined, what the French call the *douceur de vivre*, which is often confused with civilisation.

We have come a long way from the powerful conviction that induced knights and ladies to draw carts of stone up the hill for the building of Chartres Cathedral. And yet the notion of ideal love, and the irresistible power of gentleness and beauty, which is emblematically conveyed by the homage of these two fierce beasts, can be traced back for three centuries; we may even begin to look for it in the north portal of Chartres.

This portal was decorated in about the year 1220, and seems to have been paid for by that formidable lady, Blanche of Castile, the mother of St Louis.

8 *The Lady with the Unicorn*: A mon seul désir (tapestry: detail)

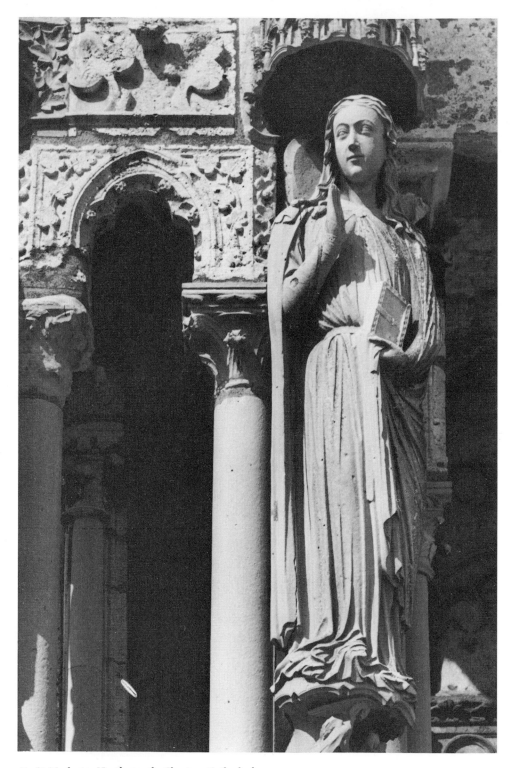

41 St Modeste, North porch, Chartres Cathedral

Perhaps for that reason, or perhaps simply because it was dedicated to the Virgin, many of the figures are women. Several of the stories depicted in the arches concern Old Testament heroines; and at the corner of the portico is one of the first consciously graceful women in western art [41]. Only a very few years before, women were thought of as the squat, bad-tempered viragos that we see on the font of Winchester Cathedral: these were the women who accompanied the Norsemen to Iceland [42]. Now look at this embodiment of chastity, lifting her mantle, raising her hand, turning her head with a movement of self-conscious refinement that was to become mannered but here is genuinely modest. She might be Dante's Beatrice. In fact she represents a saint called St Modeste. She is still a little austere. And when one looks at the details of the portal – those marvellous details which reflect the whole imaginative life of the century – one finds figures of women whose femininity is warmer and more accessible: Judith kneeling in her oratory and covering her head with ashes, and Esther throwing herself at the feet of King Holofernes. There, for almost the first time in visual art, one gets a sense of human rapport between man and woman.

These feelings had of course long been the theme of the wandering poets of Provence, the *jongleurs* and troubadours, and of that dream-like romance, *Aucassin and Nicolette*. Of the two or three faculties that have been added to the European mind since the civilisation of Greece and Rome, none seems

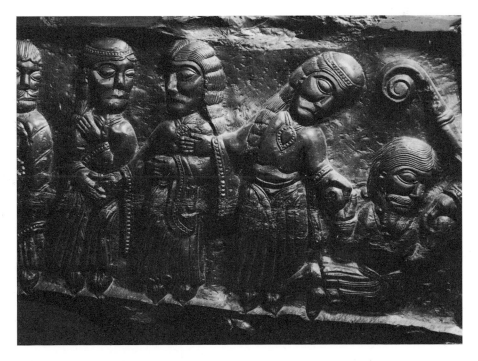

42 The Font, Winchester Cathedral

to me stranger and more inexplicable than the sentiment of ideal or courtly love. It was entirely unknown to antiquity. Passion, yes; desire, yes of course; steady affection, yes. But this state of utter subjection to the will of an almost unapproachable woman; this belief that no sacrifice was too great, that a whole lifetime might properly be spent in paying court to some exacting lady or suffering on her behalf – this would have seemed to the Romans or to the Vikings not only absurd but unbelievable; and yet for hundreds of years it passed unquestioned. It inspired a vast literature – from Chrétien de Troyes to Shelley – most of which I find unreadable; and even up to 1945 we still retained a number of chivalrous gestures; we raised our hats to ladies, and let them pass first through doors, and, in America, pushed in their seats at table. And we still subscribed to the fantasy that they were chaste and pure beings, in whose presence we couldn't tell certain stories or pronounce certain words.

Well, that's all over now, but it had a long run, and there was something to be said for it. How did it begin? The truth is that nobody knows. Most people think that, with the pointed arch, it came from the east; that pilgrims and crusaders found in the Moslem world a tradition of Persian literature in which women were the subject of extravagant compliment and devotion. I don't know enough about Persian literature to say if this is true; but I do think the crusades had another, less direct influence on the concept of courtly love. The lady of a castle must have had a peculiar position with so many unoccupied young men who couldn't spend all their time hunting, and who of course never did a stroke of what we call work; and when the lord was away for a year or two, the lady was left in charge. She took on his functions and received the kind of homage that was accepted in a feudal society; and the wandering knight who visited her did so with the mixture of deference and hope that one gets in the troubadour poems. The numerous ivory mirror cases and other domestic objects of the fourteenth century support this theory. They are a repertoire of flirtation, and culminate in a scene known as the Siege of the Castle of Love [43], in which the ladies leaning on the battlements put up a weak defence as young gallants climb up on rope ladders. The hilarious scenes in Rossini's *Comte d'Ory* are not as unhistorical as one might suppose. I ought perhaps to add that the idea of marriage doesn't come into the question any more than it would today. A 'love match' is almost an invention of the late eighteenth century. Medieval marriages were entirely a matter of property, and, as everybody knows, marriage without love means love without marriage.

Then I suppose one must admit that the cult of the Virgin had something to do with it. In this context it sounds rather blasphemous, but the fact remains that one often hardly knows if a medieval love lyric is addressed to the poet's mistress or to the Virgin Mary. The greatest of all writings about ideal love, Dante's *Vita Nuova*, is a quasi-religious work, and in the end it is Beatrice who introduces Dante to Paradise.

For all these reasons I think it is permissible to associate the cult of ideal love with the ravishing beauty and delicacy that one finds in the madonnas of the thirteenth century [44]. Were there ever more delicate creatures than the ladies on Gothic ivories? How gross, compared to them, are the great

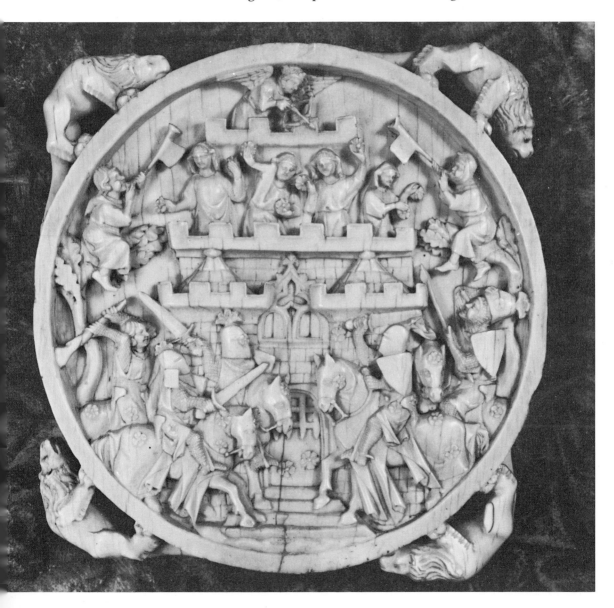

43 *Siege of the Castle of Love* (ivory)

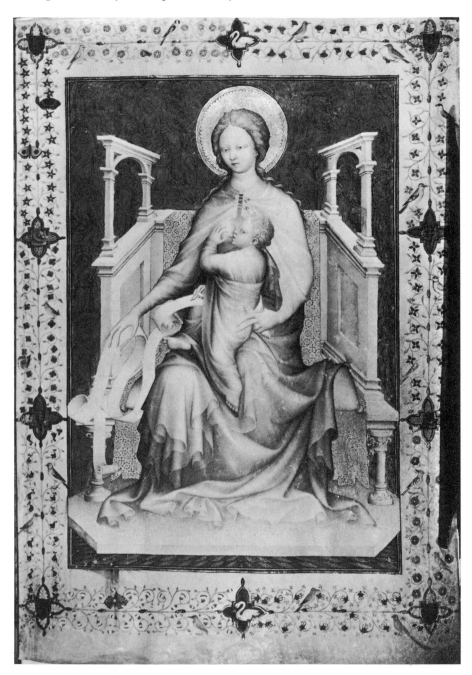

beauties of other woman-worshipping epochs – of the sixteenth-century Venetians for example. Perhaps only Botticelli and Watteau can compete. This subtle physical beauty was accompanied by a new rhythm – the sweet new style. People have suggested that the graceful curve of a Gothic Virgin

[9, facing page 68] was due to the curve of the elephant's tusk out of which it was carved. Not impossible: but this flowing rhythm spread far beyond material necessities. In the ivory plaque of the *Maries at the Sepulchre* [45], the figures have a musical relationship to one another.

Did the ladies of the fourteenth century really look like this? It's hard to say, because the notion of portraiture was not fully developed before the end of the century. But it's certain that this is what their admirers, even their husbands, wanted them to look like. So it is all the more surprising to learn that these exquisite creatures got terribly knocked about. It must be true, because there is a manual on how to treat women – actually how to bring up daughters – by a character called the Knight of the Tower of Landry, written

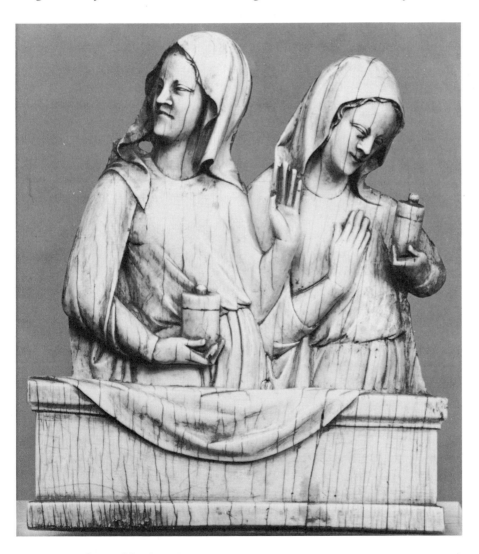

45 *Maries at the Sepulchre* (ivory)

in 1370 and so successful that it went on being read as a sort of textbook right up to the sixteenth century – in fact an edition was published with illustrations by Dürer. In it the knight, who is known to have been an exceptionally kind man, describes how disobedient women must be beaten and starved and dragged around by the hair of the head. I dare say they got their own back – one has the impression, from their confident smiles, that Gothic women were well able to look after themselves.

Courtly love was not only the subject of lyrics, but of long – very long – stories in prose and verse. And this reminds me of something else that the Gothic centuries added to the European consciousness: that cluster of ideas and sentiments which surrounds the words 'romantic' and 'romance'. One can't put it more precisely than this, because it is in the nature of romanticism to evade definition. One can't even say that romance was a Gothic invention: I suppose that, as the word suggests, it was really Romanesque, and grew up in those southern districts of France where the memories of Roman civilisation had not been quite obliterated when they were overlaid by the more fantastic imagery of the Saracens. But the chivalrous romances of the Gothic time, from Chrétien de Troyes in the thirteenth century to Malory in the fifteenth, with their allegories and personifications, their endless journeys and night-long vigils, their spells and mysteries, all hung on the thread of courtly love, were a speciality of the medieval mind [10, facing p. 69]. For two hundred years the *Roman de la Rose* was with Boethius and the Bible the most read book in Europe. I don't know many people who have read it through today, except in pursuit of a degree. But of course the effect of these romances on nineteenth-century literature was decisive, whether as a quarry or an escape, especially in England: 'The Eve of St Agnes', 'La Belle Dame sans Merci', *The Idylls of the King*, to say nothing of that crucial masterpiece of the late nineteenth century, Wagner's *Tristan and Isolde*. We may not read the Gothic romances, but they still play a part in our imaginative lives.

The greatest patrons of art and learning of the Gothic world were four brothers: Charles V, King of France, whose long nose is one of the first royal features to reach us unidealised; the Duke of Burgundy, the slyest and most ambitious – ultimately the most powerful – of the brothers; Louis d'Anjou; and the Duke of Berry. They were all patrons of art – builders, bibliophiles and collectors – but the Duke of Berry was peculiar in that the arts were his whole life. He was an amiably self-indulgent man whose feelings about women were not much influenced by ideals of chivalry. He is reported to have said: 'The more the merrier, and never tell the truth.' In an illustration to one of his books St Peter seems to be admitting him to heaven without

9 *Virgin and Child* (ivory)

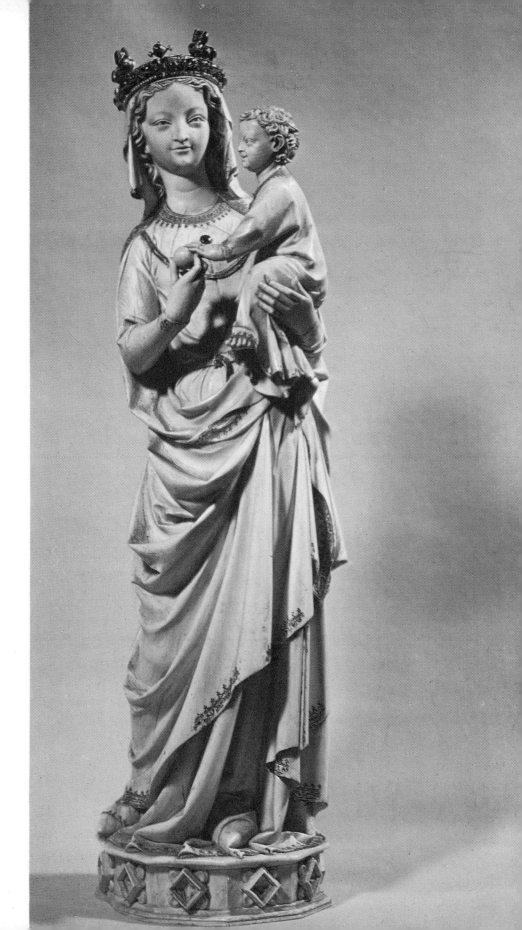

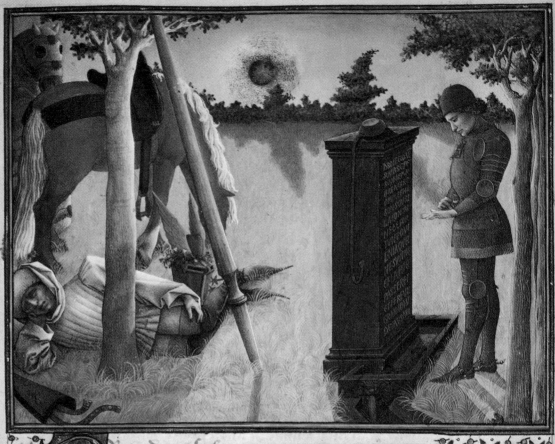

Doit et devant soubz ce perron
De marbre noir comme charbon
Sourt la fontaine de fortune
Ou il n'y a quelle neshne
Et la fist compasser et faire
Vng grant Joyant de sauls assaire

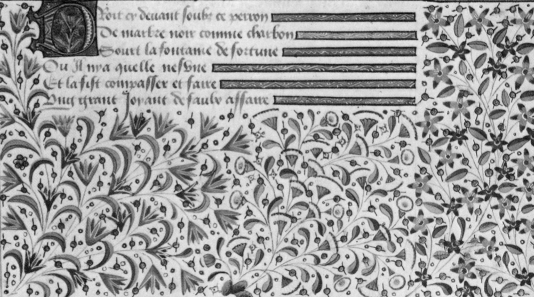

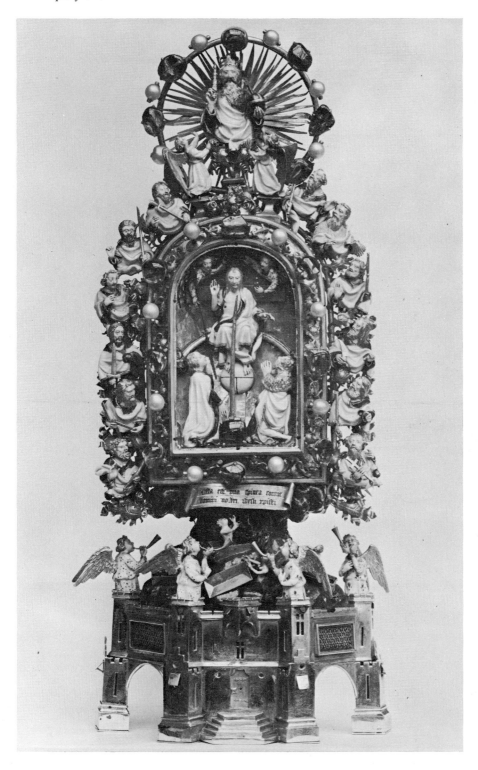

the usual formalities, but his subjects, whom he taxed mercilessly, might not have agreed. He built a series of fabulous filigree castles, of which the painter Paul de Limbourg has left us an accurate record, and filled them with pictures and tapestries, jewels and jewelled contraptions – to say nothing of a famous collection of bears and dogs: he had 1,500 dogs, which is too many, even for me. The castles have vanished with the dogs and bears, and moths have eaten all the tapestries, except a set at Angers, made for Louis d'Anjou. But a few of the treasures remain, nominally reliquaries, but actually charming, extravagant toys, and from them one can still catch the flavour of this fanciful luxurious world [46].

Above all we have a good many of his books, and they show him to have been what can properly be called a creative patron – that is to say, he not only discovered the most gifted artists of his time, but he encouraged them to follow new paths. His brother, Charles V, had a large library, but his books were chosen for their instructive texts, and the painters who illustrated them were the ordinary court craftsmen. But the Duke of Berry's artists were the most perceptive spirits of the age. What do they tell us about civilisation in the late fourteenth century? First of all, that the delicacy and refinement of the thirteenth century lasted over one hundred years. It survived the Black Death and the Hundred Years War and the economic revolution of the first enclosures, and became completely international. The sweet new style of the Gothic ivories became sweeter and softer and (may one still say?) rather effeminate. There is a spring and tension in the early fourteenth century which is lost after 1380: in compensation there is an increase in subtlety. How many layers of feeling are discernible in Jaquemard de Hesdin's picture of the fool [**12**, facing p. 77]? In this vein the Duke left us his self-portrait kneeling before the Virgin. He does not pretend to be anything but a worldling; and the Virgin, occupied in her own reverie, pays no attention to him. Her softly curling draperies are like an emblem of her gentle, complex, inward-turning thoughts.

As luck would have it, this type of composition has come down to us in an English royal portrait – the so-called Wilton Diptych [47]. It shows Richard II with his patron saints, who are recommending him to the Virgin. The Queen of Heaven is taking a little more interest in him than she did in the Duke of Berry, and in fact all her attendant angels are wearing the king's badge, the white hart and peascod collar. How exquisite it is; and how gross, by comparison, are all subsequent royal portraits! And yet, as we all know, Richard II was brutally murdered and his love of art certainly did not count in his favour: one more example of how, in the Middle Ages, civilisation seems to fly in at one window and out at another.

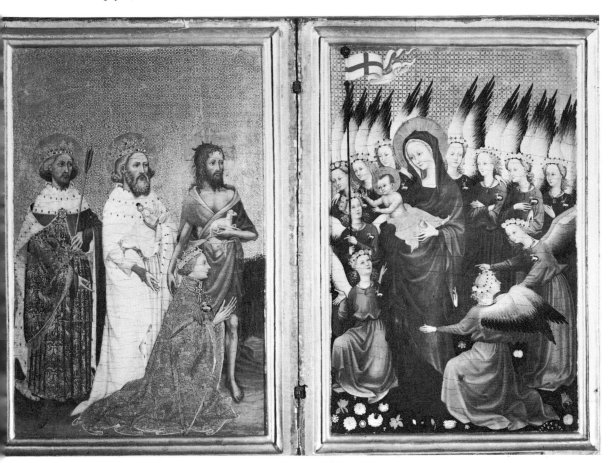

The Duke of Berry's manuscripts illustrate another capacity of the human mind which had grown up in the preceding century: the delighted observation of natural objects – leaves and flowers, animals and birds. The odd thing about the medieval response to nature was that it saw all those things in isolation. It quite literally couldn't see the wood for the trees. As early as the mid-thirteenth century Gothic sculptors had begun to take pleasure in leaves and flowers, and one finds astonishing accuracy and intensity of observation on the capitals outside the chapter-house at Southwell. As for birds, they were a medieval obsession. They are the subject of one of the earliest medieval sketch-books [48], and they fill the borders of manuscripts. If you had asked a fourteenth-century cleric to account for all these birds he would probably have said that they represented souls, because they can fly up to God; but this doesn't really explain why artists drew them with such obsessive accuracy, and I think the reason is that they had become symbols of freedom. Under feudalism men and animals were tied to the land:

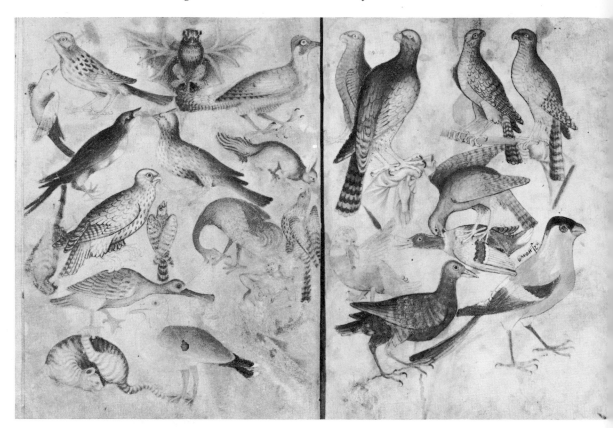

very few people could move about – only artists and birds. Birds were cheerful, hopeful, impudent and mobile – and in addition had the kind of markings that fitted in with medieval heraldry.

The earlier manuscripts in Jean de Berry's library show this isolating and symbolising approach to nature, in which flowers and trees are put side by side on a flat surface. But in the middle of his career as a patron the Duke discovered an artist – or a group of artists – called de Limbourg, who by some stroke of original genius saw nature as we see it, as part of a complete visual experience. No doubt much of their work has been lost, but at least one book remains, *The Very Rich Hours*, and it is one of the miracles of art history [11, facing p. 76]. Here are men and women cultivating the fields, scything, harrowing, sowing, with a scarecrow in the background – and suddenly we realise that all this had been going on in the same places, and with the same tools, all through the Dark Ages (because, after all, people had continued to eat bread), and went on without a change right up to the last war.

In addition to showing the country life of medieval France these illustrations give a vivid account of court life. They begin with a picture of the

Duke at dinner. Here he is, with his famous gold salt-cellar, mentioned in the inventories, and two of his little dogs beside it on the table [49]. Behind him his chamberlain is saying to some bashful suitor, *'approche, approche'*, and his courtiers, including a cardinal, are raising their hands in astonishment at such condescension. The war-like scene in the background is only a tapestry – the Duke wasn't fond of war. The ladies are not present at this

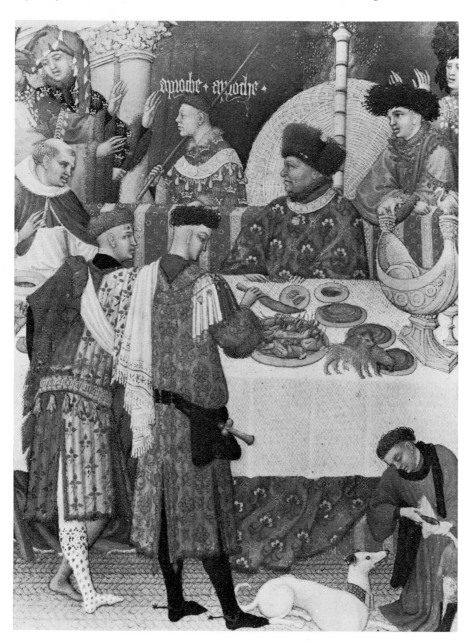

49 *Les Très Riches Heures du Duc de Berry*: The Duke at dinner (detail)

grand dinner; but in April they put on their Easter bonnets and indulge in a little mild courtship, so-called because it was only in courts that one had time for those agreeable preliminaries. In May everyone puts on crowns of leaves and goes out riding. What a dream! No society has ever been more elegant, more debonair, more dainty.

Those French and Burgundian courts were the model of fashion and good manners all over Europe. The concept lasted a long time: 'In courtesy I'd have her chiefly learned' was still Mr Yeats's prayer for his daughter in 1916. And many people when you mention the word 'civilisation' think of something like this. Well, it isn't to be sneezed at. But it isn't enough to keep a civilisation alive, because it exists solely in the present. It depends on a small static society that never looks outside or beyond, and we know from many examples that such societies can become entirely petrified – anxious only to hold on to their own social order. The great, indeed the unique, merit of European civilisation has been that it has never ceased to develop and change. It has not been based on a stationary perfection, but on ideas and inspiration; and even the ideal of courtesy can take an unexpected form.

In the years when the north portal of Chartres was being built, a rich young dandy named Francesco Bernadone suffered a change of heart. He was, and always remained, the most courteous of men, deeply influenced by French ideals of chivalry. And one day when he had fitted himself up in his best clothes in preparation for some chivalrous campaign, he met a poor gentleman whose need seemed to be greater than his own, and gave him his cloak [51]. That night he dreamed that he should rebuild the Celestial City. Later he gave away his possessions so liberally that his father, who was a rich businessman in the Italian town of Assisi, was moved to disown him; whereupon Francesco took off his remaining clothes and said that he would possess nothing, absolutely nothing. The Bishop of Assisi hid his nakedness, and afterwards gave him a cloak; and Francesco went off into the woods, singing a French song.

The next three years he spent in abject poverty, looking after lepers, who were very much in evidence in the Middle Ages, and rebuilding with his own hands (for he had taken his dream literally) abandoned churches. One day at Mass he heard the words 'Carry neither gold nor silver, nor money in your girdle, nor bag, nor two coats, nor sandals, nor staff'. I suppose he had often heard them before, but this time they spoke directly to his heart. He threw away his staff and his sandals and went out bare-footed onto the hills. In all his actions he took the words of the Gospels literally and he translated them into the language of chivalric poetry and of those *jongleur* songs that were always on his lips. He said that he had taken poverty for his Lady, and

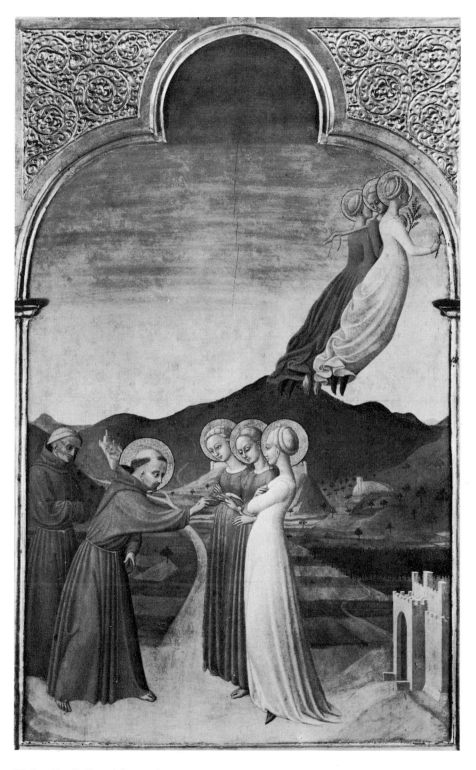

50 Sasetta, *St Francis's marriage to poverty*

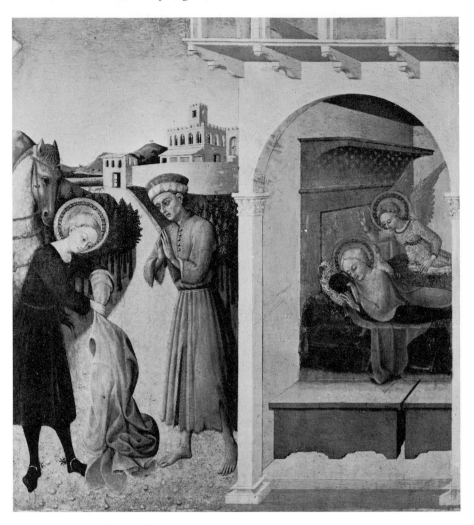

when he achieved some still more drastic act of self-denial, he said that it was to do her a courtesy. It was partly because he saw that wealth corrupts; partly because he felt that it was discourteous to be in the company of any-one poorer than oneself.

From the first everyone recognised that St Francis (as we may now call him) was a religious genius – the greatest, I believe, that Europe has ever produced; and when, with his first twelve disciples, he managed to gain access to Innocent III, the toughest politician in Europe (who was also a great Christian), the Pope gave him permission to found an order. It was an extraordinary piece of insight, because St Francis was not only a layman with no theological training, but he and his poor, ragged companions were so excited when they went to see the Pope that they began to dance. What a

11 de Limbourg, 'August', from *Les Très Riches Heures du Duc de Berry*

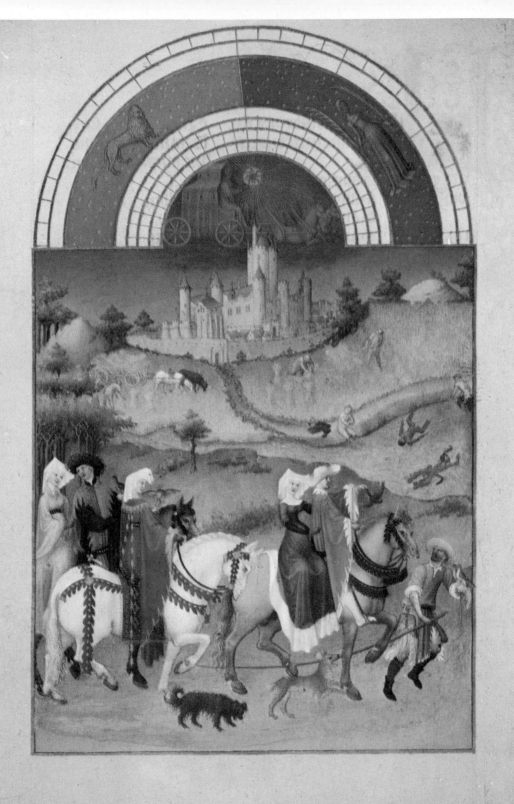

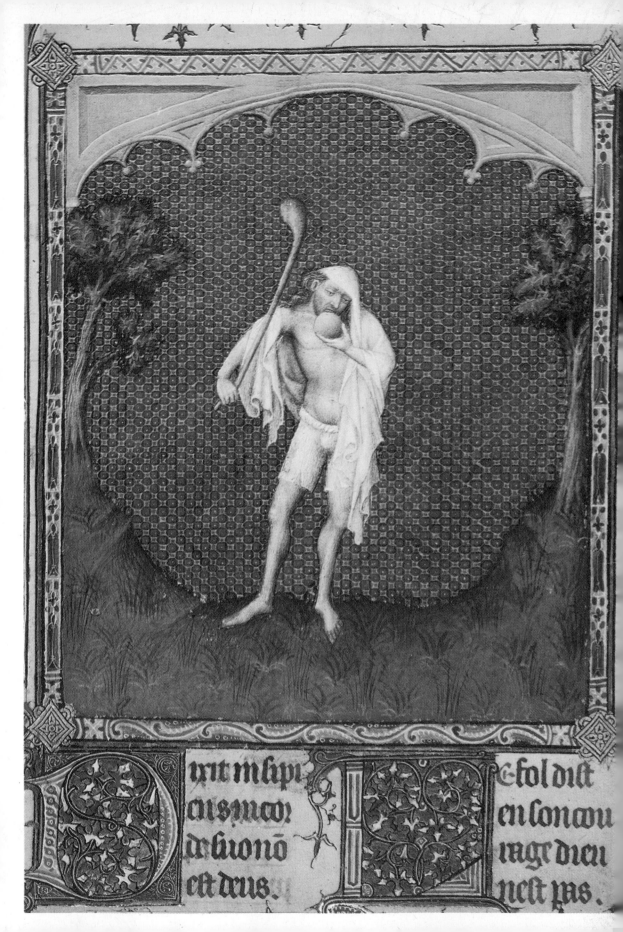

ixit m̃ sapi
ens m cor
de suo nõ
est deus.

e fol dist
en con cou
rage dieu
nest pas.

picture! Unfortunately the early painters of the Franciscan legend do not reproduce it.

The most convincing illustrations of the story of St Francis [50 and 51] are the work of the Sienese painter Sasetta, although he painted so much later, because the chivalric, Gothic tradition lingered on in Siena as nowhere else in Italy, and gave to Sasetta's sprightly images a lyric, even a visionary quality more Franciscan than the ponderous images of Giotto. But they have more authority, not only because Giotto was working almost a hundred and fifty years nearer to the time of St Francis, but because he, and his circle, were chosen to decorate the great church dedicated to St Francis in Assisi. And when it comes to the later and – how shall I say it? – less lyrical episodes in the saint's life, Giotto's frescoes have a fullness of humanity that was beyond Sasetta. Where they seem to me to fail is in their image of the saint himself. They make him too grave and commanding. They don't show a spark of the joy that he valued almost as highly as courtesy. Incidentally we don't know at all what he looked like. The earliest representation which must date from just after his death is (appropriately enough) on a French enamel box. The best known early painting is attributed to the first famous Italian painter, Cimabue. It looks quite convincing, but I'm afraid that it is entirely repainted, and only shows us what the nineteenth century thought St Francis ought to have been like.

St Francis died in 1226 at the age of forty-three worn out by his austerities. On his deathbed he asked forgiveness of 'poor brother donkey, my body' for the hardships he had made it suffer. He had seen his group of humble companions grow into a great institution, and in 1220 he had, with perfect simplicity, relinquished control of the order. He recognised that he was no administrator. Two years after his death he was canonised and almost immediately his followers began to build a great basilica in his memory [52]. With its upper and lower church, jammed onto the side of a steep hill, it is both an extraordinary feat of engineering and a masterpiece of Gothic architecture. It was decorated by all the chief Italian painters of the thirteenth and fourteenth centuries, from Cimabue onwards, so that it became the richest and most evocative church in Italy. A strange memorial to the little poor man, whose favourite saying was, 'Foxes have holes and the birds of the air have nests: but the Son of Man hath not where to lay his head'. But of course, St Francis's cult of poverty could not survive him – it did not even last his lifetime. It was officially rejected by the Church; for the Church had already become part of the international banking system that originated in thirteenth-century Italy. Those of Francis's disciples, called Fraticelli, who clung to his doctrine of poverty were denounced as heretics and burnt at

12 Jacquemard de Hesdin, *The Fool*

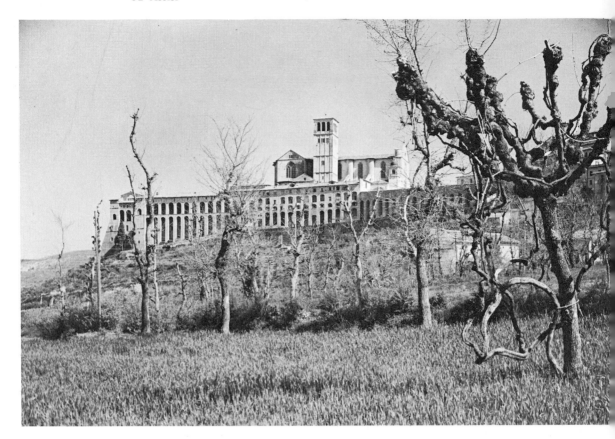

the stake. And for seven hundred years capitalism has continued to grow to its present monstrous proportions. It may seem that St Francis has had no influence at all, because even those humane reformers of the nineteenth century who sometimes invoked him did not wish to exalt or sanctify poverty but to abolish it.

And yet his belief that in order to free the spirit we must shed all our earthly goods is the belief that all great religious teachers have had in common – eastern and western, without exception. It is an ideal to which, however impossible it may be in practice, the finest spirits will always return. By enacting that truth with such simplicity and grace, St Francis made it part of the European consciousness. And by freeing himself from the pull of possessions, he achieved a state of mind which gained a new meaning in the late eighteenth century through the philosophy of Rousseau and Wordsworth. It was only because he possessed nothing that St Francis could feel sincerely a brotherhood with all created things, not only living creatures, but brother fire and sister wind.

This philosophy inspired his hymn to the unity of creation, the 'Canticle of the Sun'; and it is expressed with irresistible naivety in a collection of legends known as the *Fioretti*, 'The Little Flowers'. Not many people can make their way through the arguments of Abelard or the *Summa* of St Thomas Aquinas, but everyone can enjoy these holy folk-tales, which, after all, may not be completely untrue. They are, in contemporary jargon, among the first examples of popular communication – at any rate since the Gospels. They tell us, for instance, how St Francis persuades a fierce wolf that terrified the people of Gubbio to make a pact by which, in return for regular meals, he will leave the citizens alone. 'Give me your paw', said St Francis, and the wolf gave his paw. Most famous of all is the sermon to the birds – those creatures which seemed to the Gothic mind singularly privileged. Seven centuries have not impaired the naive beauty of that episode, either in the text of the *Fioretti* or in Giotto's fresco.

St Francis is a figure of the pure Gothic time – the time of crusades and castles and the great cathedrals. Although he interpreted it in a curious way, he belonged to the age of chivalry. Well, however much one loves that world, it must, I think, remain for us today infinitely strange and remote. It is as enchanting, as luminous, as transcendental as the stained glass that is its glory – and, in the ordinary meaning of the word, as unreal. But already during the lifetime of St Francis another world was growing up, which, for better or worse, is the ancestor of our own, the world of trade and of banking, of cities full of hard-headed men whose aim in life was to grow rich without ceasing to appear respectable.

Cities, citizen, civilian, civic life: I suppose that all this ought to have a direct bearing on what we mean by civilisation. Nineteenth-century historians, who loved word-games of this sort, believed that it had, and even maintained that civilisation began with the Italian republics of the fourteenth century. Well, civilisation as I understand it can be created in a monastery or a court just as well as in a city – perhaps rather better. But all the same, the social and economic system that grew up in Italian towns, particularly in Florence in the thirteenth century, had a point. As opposed to the system of chivalry, it was realistic: and the proof is that it has survived. Industrial and banking conditions in Florence at the time of Dante were surprisingly similar to those that exist in Lombard Street today, except that double entry wasn't invented till the fourteenth century. Of course, the Italian republics weren't in the least democratic, as those pre-Marxist innocents, the liberal historians, used to think they were. The power of exploitation was in the hands of a few families who managed to operate within the framework of a guild system in which the workers had no say at all.

The Italian merchant of the fourteenth century isn't a sympathetic figure – less so really than that old reprobate Jean de Berry. The stories of Florentine thrift are like the stories that Jews used to tell about each other. But – and here the parallel with Lombard Street is not so close – the new merchant classes, as patrons of the art of their own time, were at least as intelligent as the aristocracy. And just as their economic system was capable of an expansion that has lasted till today, so the painting they commissioned had a kind of solid reality that was to be the dominant aim of western art up to the time of Cézanne. It continued to grow because it involved a third dimension. Two-dimensional art – tapestry art – is enchanting. It creates its own world of suspended belief. It allows the artist to free his fancy and to decorate his surfaces. But for some reason it can't develop. It arrives at a limited perfection and there it sticks. But the moment you introduce a third dimension – space, solidity – then the possibilities of expansion and development are limitless.

To anyone whose eye has been conditioned by realism as it existed in European art from the Renaissance till the cubists, Giotto's frescoes in the Arena Chapel in Padua [13, facing p. 92] do not look very realistic – perhaps no more so than the Gothic tapestry. But this much is clear: instead of a decorative jumble, he concentrates on a few simple, solid-looking forms arranged in space. This allowed Giotto to appeal to us through two different but complementary means, our sense of solidity and our interest in humanity. For some reason that isn't hard to understand, we believe more thoroughly in our sense of touch than in sight, hearing or smell. When Dr Johnson wished to refute a philosopher who said that matter didn't exist, he kicked a stone and thought he had proved the point. Giotto had, more than any artist before him, the ability to make his figures look solid. He manages to simplify them into large, comprehensible, apprehensible shapes; and it gives one a profound satisfaction to feel that one can grasp them so completely. He makes his figures more vividly credible because he wishes us to feel more intensely the human drama in which they are involved. Once we have, so to say, learnt Giotto's language, we can recognise him as one of the greatest masters of painted drama that has ever lived.

How did Giotto evolve this very personal and original style? When he was a young man – he was born near Florence in about 1265 – Italian painting was really only a less polished form of Byzantine painting. It was a flat, flowing linear style based on traditional concepts which had changed very little for five hundred years. For Giotto to break away from it and evolve this solid, space-conscious style was one of those feats of inspired originality that have occurred only two or three times in the history of art. When such drastic changes do take place, one can usually find certain points of departure, models or predecessors. But not with Giotto. We know absolutely nothing about him till the year 1304, when he decorated a small, plain building in Padua known as the Arena Chapel, and made it, to anyone who cares for painting, one of the holy places of the world.

It was commissioned by a money-lender named Enrico Scrovegni whose father had been imprisoned for usury – that is to say, for charging an extortionate rate of interest, because moderate rates of interest were unofficially countenanced; and it's one of the first instances of the new rich commissioning works of art as a kind of atonement, a practice that has benefited the world almost as much as vanity and self-indulgence. Here he is [53], in perhaps the earliest painted portrait that is obviously a genuine likeness, presenting a model of his chapel to three angels, and for that reason placed among the Blessed in the Last Judgement.

Giotto's other great works were also painted for bankers, the two chief financial families in Florence, the Bardi and the Peruzzi. These hard-headed men were later to make a disastrous mistake: they failed to recognise the gulf that separated their bourgeois economy from the irresponsible aristocracy of the north, and lent millions of pounds to King Edward III to carry on his war against France. In 1339 he calmly defaulted – what were money-lenders to the father of the Black Prince? The result was one of the first classic crashes in the history of capitalism.

Twenty years before that catastrophe Giotto had decorated two chapels side by side in Santa Croce, which are evidence that his mastery of his art continued to develop. I put it in this roundabout way because both chapels were much repainted in the nineteenth century, one of them completely, the other in great part. The compositions remain and are masterpieces of pictorial architecture, but making all allowance for restoration, I think they must always have been – how shall I say? – almost too well worked out. The more elaborate groups are the foundation of European academism at its best, the basis of Raphael, Poussin or even David. In the better preserved of the two scenes Giotto reverted to the story of St Francis. Strange that those financial potentates should have chosen the subject of the *poverello*; but of course by this time his unfortunate association with my Lady Poverty had been hushed up. Giotto's frescoes represent the official version of the Franciscan legend, and there is something almost official in their style. Admirable as they are, they give me the feeling that Giotto had already become the grand old man of Florentine painting; and in his last years, like many grand old men, he ceased to produce anything at all. To discover his real qualities one must return to the Arena Chapel.

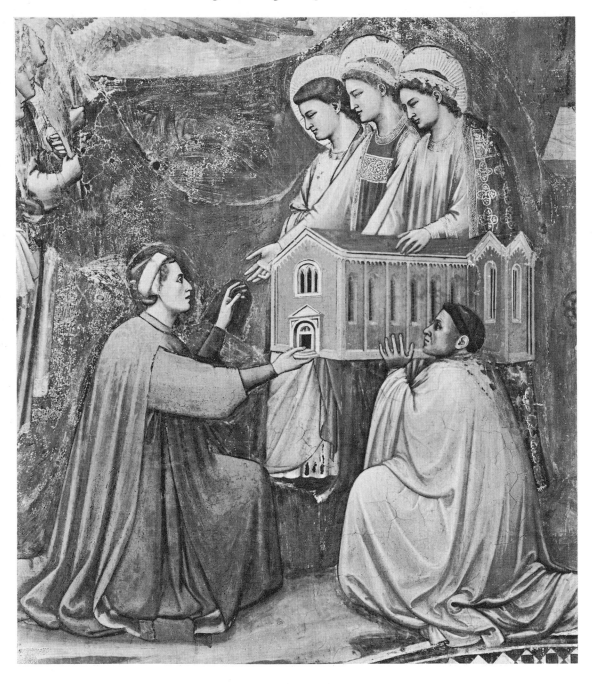

As I have said, he is the supreme dramatist of human life in all its diversity. His range extends from the Chaucerian scene of the *Marriage at Cana*, with the pot-bellied host standing behind his pots and tasting with astonishment the wine that has been created out of water, to the lyrical beauty of the

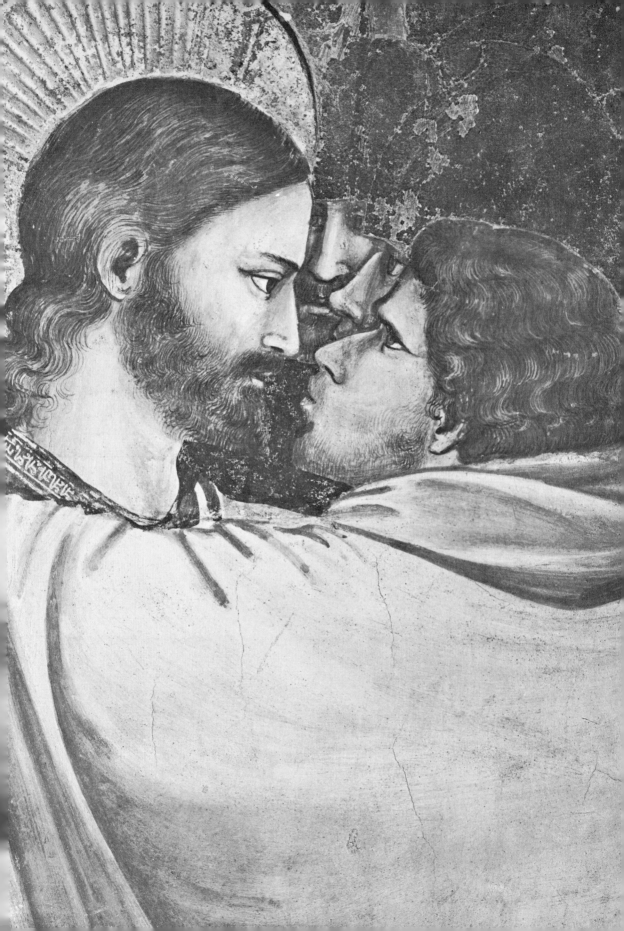

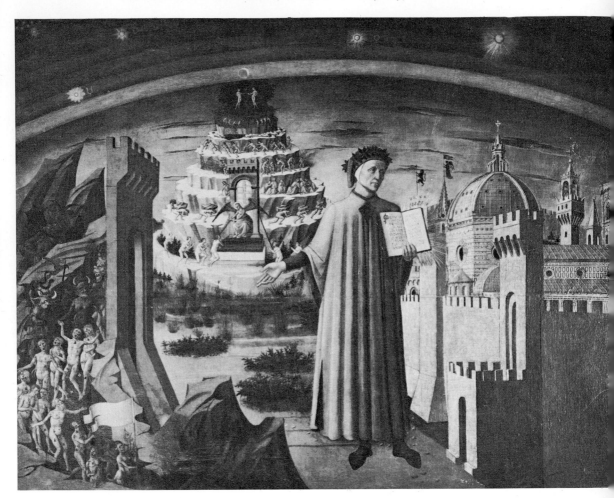

Virgin's *Wedding Procession* and the tenderness of the *Noli Me Tangere*. He is greatest when the human drama is greatest, as in the scene of the betrayal in the garden of Gethsemane [54]. What a marvellous invention that Judas should put his cloak round Our Lord! Finally the *Lamentation over Christ* [13, facing p. 92] – which foreshadows the carefully constructed compositions of the later Giotto, but is still painted with a passion and spontaneity that they seem to lack.

Although I think that Giotto was one of the greatest of painters, he has equals. But in almost the same year that he was born, and in the same part of Italy, was born a man who is unequalled – the greatest philosophic poet that has ever lived, Dante [55]. Since they were contemporaries and compatriots, one feels that it should be possible to illustrate Dante by Giotto. They seem to have known each other and Giotto may have painted Dante's portrait.

But in fact their imaginations moved on very different planes. Giotto was, above all, interested in humanity: he sympathised with human beings and his figures, by their very solidity, remain on earth. Of course there is humanity in Dante – there's everything in Dante. But he also had certain qualities that Giotto lacked: philosophic power, a grasp of abstract ideas, moral indignation, that heroic contempt for baseness that was to come again in Michelangelo; and, above all, a sense of the *un*earthly, a vision of heavenly radiance.

In a way, Giotto and Dante stand at the junction of two worlds. Giotto belonged to the new world of solid realities, the world created by the bankers and wool merchants for whom he worked. Dante belonged to the earlier Gothic world, the world of St Thomas Aquinas and the great cathedrals. One comes closer to Dante in the masterpieces of Gothic sculpture, like the west portal at Bourges, than in the Arena Chapel. And in Italian art the man who approaches most nearly to the Dantesque spirit is in fact a sculptor deeply influenced by Gothic art, Giovanni Pisano.

Giovanni Pisano was one of the great tragic dramatists of sculpture, as one may see in the sculptured panels of two pulpits, one in Pisa, the other in Pistoia [56]. Like Dante's *Inferno*, they depict a terrible world. There is hatred, cruelty and suffering. But they differ from Dante in that the figures are more generalised. Dante filled his poem with the people he had known: all the characters he had pitied, hated or admired when he was in the thick of Florentine politics are vividly present in the incredible surroundings of Hell. No one had a sharper eye, and it reached beyond men to nature – to flowers, animals and birds. But Giovanni's stage is as bare as the stage of Greek drama. There is no sign of nature, no attempt to please the eye, no relaxation. I can think of no more moving representation of grief than Giovanni Pisano's relief in Pistoia of the Massacre of the Innocents.

> *Io no piangeva; si dentro impietrai*
> *Piangevar elli.*
> I did not weep, so much of stone had I become within.
> They wept.

But Giovanni Pisano's feeling of tragic indignation was only one side of Dante; the second half of his poem – from the middle of the *Purgatorio* onwards – contains moments of disembodied bliss to which no artist of the time did justice. Nor were painters of the fourteenth century ready to reflect Dante's feeling for light. Like all the heroes of this series, Dante thought of light as a symbol of the spiritual life, and in his great poem he describes, accurately and economically, light in its varying effects – the light of dawn, light on the sea, the light on leaves in spring. But all these beautiful descrip-

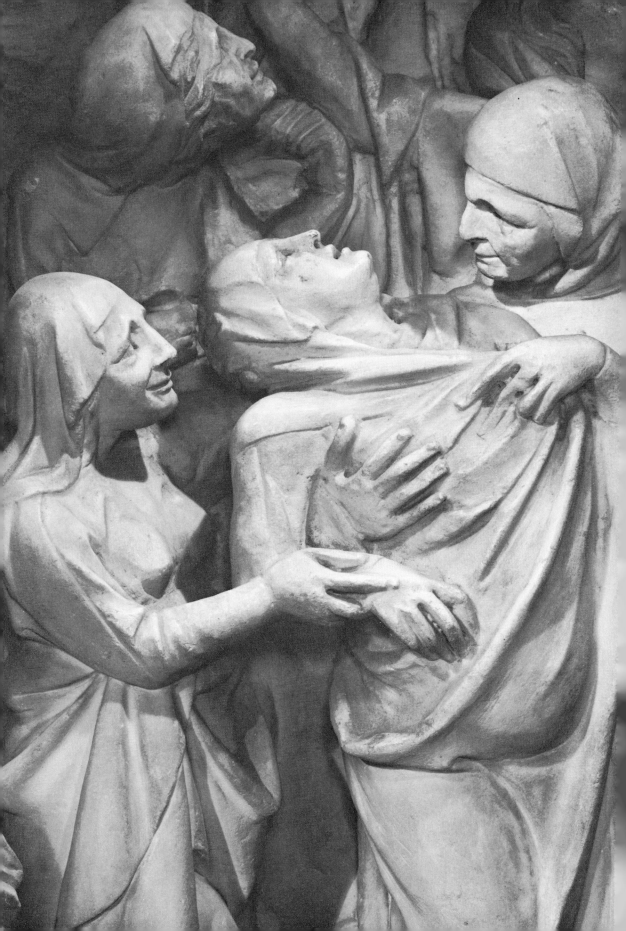

tions, which are the part of Dante that many of us like best, are similes: they are introduced by the words 'as when'. They are intended only to illustrate and make comprehensible to our earth-bound senses a vision of divine order and heavenly beauty.

56 Giovanni Pisano, Pulpit, Pistoia

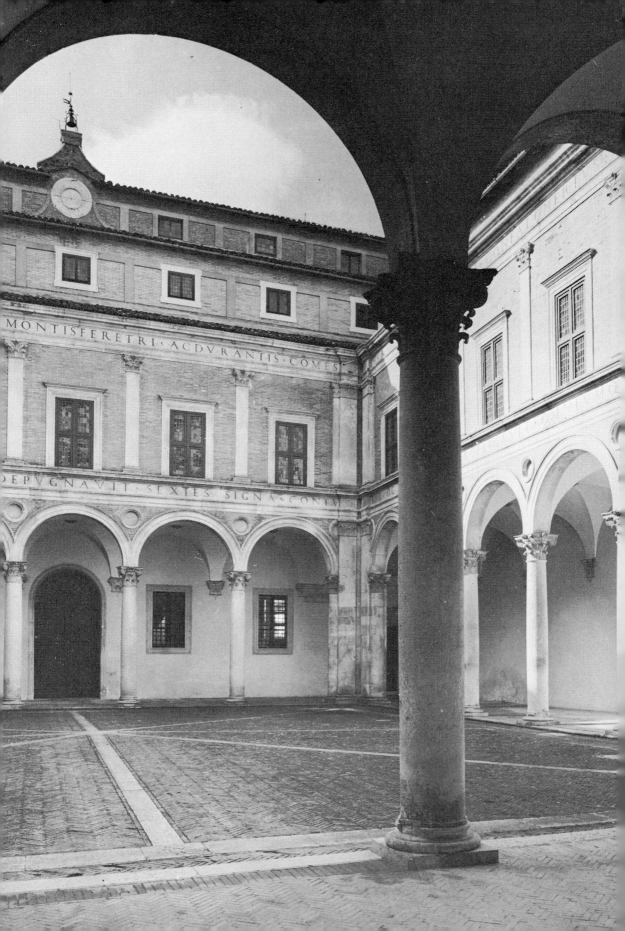

4 Man – the Measure of all Things

The men who had made Florence the richest city in Europe, the bankers and wool-merchants, the pious realists, lived in grim defensive houses strong enough to withstand party feuds and popular riots. They don't foreshadow in any way the extraordinary episode in the history of civilisation known as the Renaissance. There seems to be no reason why suddenly out of the dark, narrow streets there arose these light, sunny arcades with their round arches 'running races in their mirth' under their straight cornices. By their rhythms and proportions and their open, welcoming character they totally contradict the dark Gothic style that preceded, and, to some extent, still surrounds them. What has happened? The answer is contained in one sentence by the Greek philosopher Protagoras, 'Man is the measure of all things'. The Pazzi Chapel [58], built by the great Florentine Brunellesco in about 1430, is in a style that has been called the architecture of humanism. His friend and fellow-architect, Leon Battista Alberti, addressed man in these words: 'To you is given a body more graceful than other animals, to you power of apt and various movements, to you most sharp and delicate senses, to you wit, reason, memory like an immortal god.' Well, it is certainly incorrect to say that we are more graceful than other animals, and we don't feel much like immortal gods at the moment. But in 1400 the Florentines did. There is no better instance of how a burst of civilisation depends on confidence than the Florentine state of mind in the early fifteenth century. For thirty years the fortunes of the republic, which in a material sense had declined, were directed by a group of the most intelligent individuals who have ever been elected to power by a democratic government. From Salutati onwards the Florentine chancellors were scholars, believers in the *studia humanitatis*, in which learning could be used to achieve a happy life, believers in the application of free intelligence to public affairs, and believers, above all, in Florence.

The second and greatest of these humanist chancellors, Leonardo Bruni, compared the civic virtues of republican Florence with those of republican Rome. Later he went even further and compared her to Athens in the age of Pericles. Medieval philosophers, insofar as they thought of their own times in the context of history, were inclined to be gloomy. 'We are dwarfs,' said John of Salisbury, 'standing on the shoulders of giants.' But Bruni saw the Florentine republic as reviving the virtues of Greece and Rome. And on his

57 Courtyard, Ducal Palace, Urbino

58 Pazzi Chapel, Florence

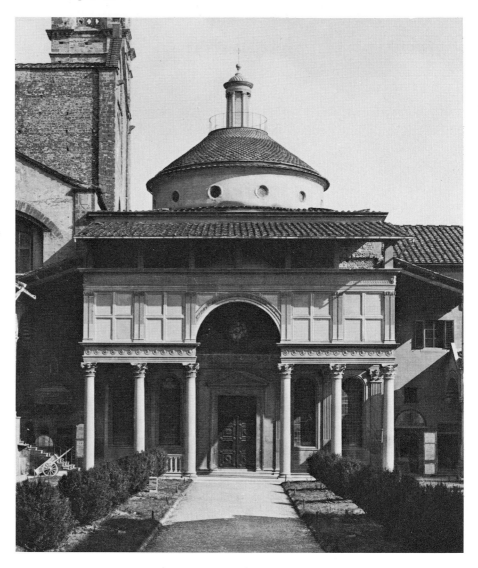

tomb in the church of Santa Croce are the words, 'History is in mourning' [59]. This inscription is supported by two winged figures which, since they are in a church, one may call angels, but are in fact victories from a Roman triumphal arch; and above them, supporting Bruni's bier, are imperial eagles. It's true that in the lunette there is a Madonna, but the important part of the tomb is furnished entirely with Classical symbols, and expresses an ideal that, in fifteenth-century Florence, was to supplant the idea of chivalry – fame; the ultimate reward of the outstanding individual.

Bruni and his friends had derived these ideals from the authors of Greece and Rome. Much as one would like to say something new about the Renais-

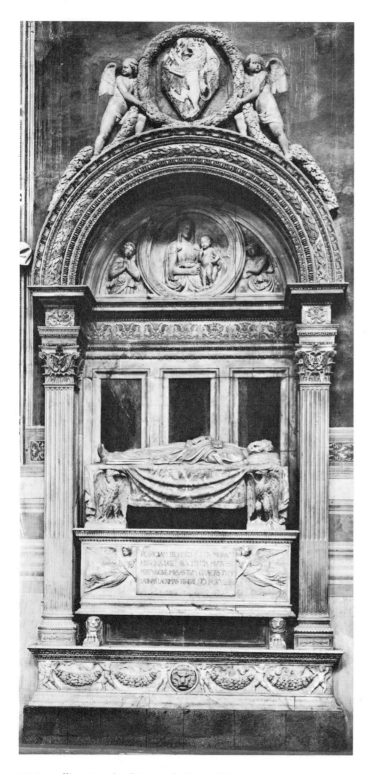

59 Rossellino, Tomb of Leonardo Bruni, Florence

sance, the old belief that it was largely based on the study of antique literature remains true. Of course the Middle Ages derived a good deal more from Classical antiquity than used to be supposed. But their sources were limited, their texts corrupt, and their interpretations often fanciful. Almost the first man to read Classical authors with real insight was Petrarch, that complex figure of the fourteenth century, that false dawn of humanism, whose love of opposites, of fame and solitude, of nature and politics, of rhetoric and self-revelation, makes us think of him as the first modern man – until we begin to read his works. Petrarch never learnt Greek, but his younger contemporary Boccaccio did, and so there entered into Florentine thought a new, regenerating force and a new example. When Bruni compared Florence to Athens, he *had* read Thucydides. In Florence the first thirty years of the fifteenth century were the heroic age of scholarship when

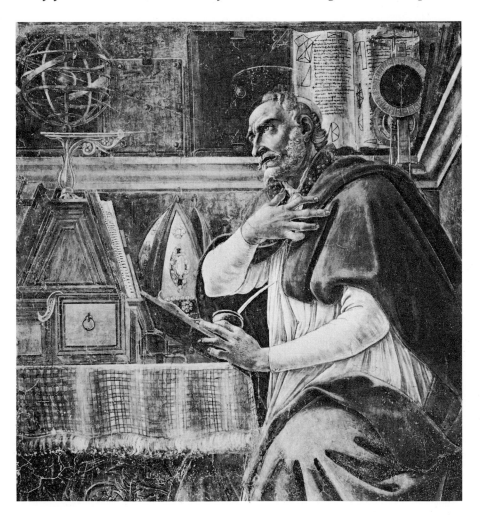

60 Botticelli, *St Augustine*

13 Giotto, *Lamentation over Christ*

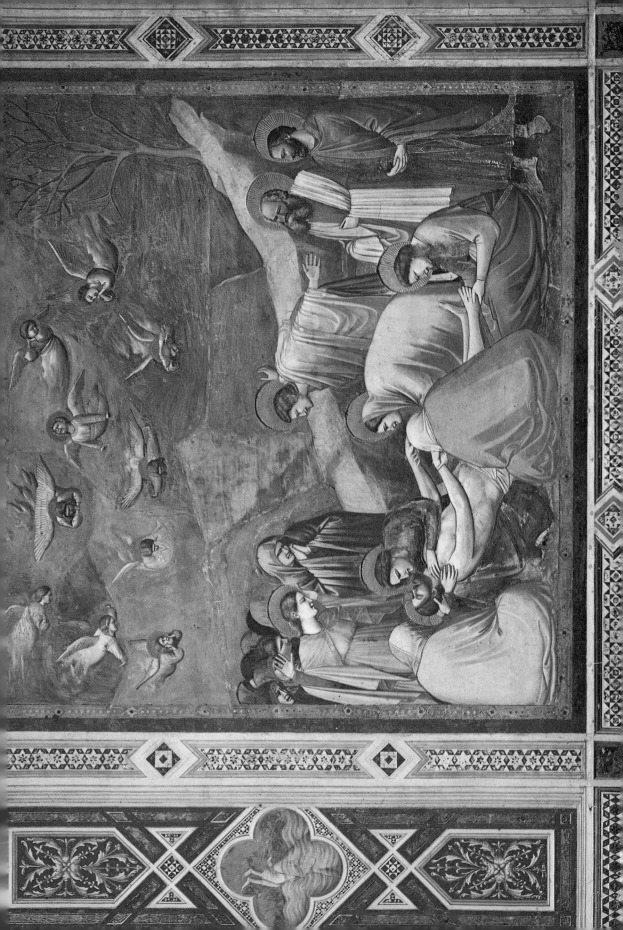

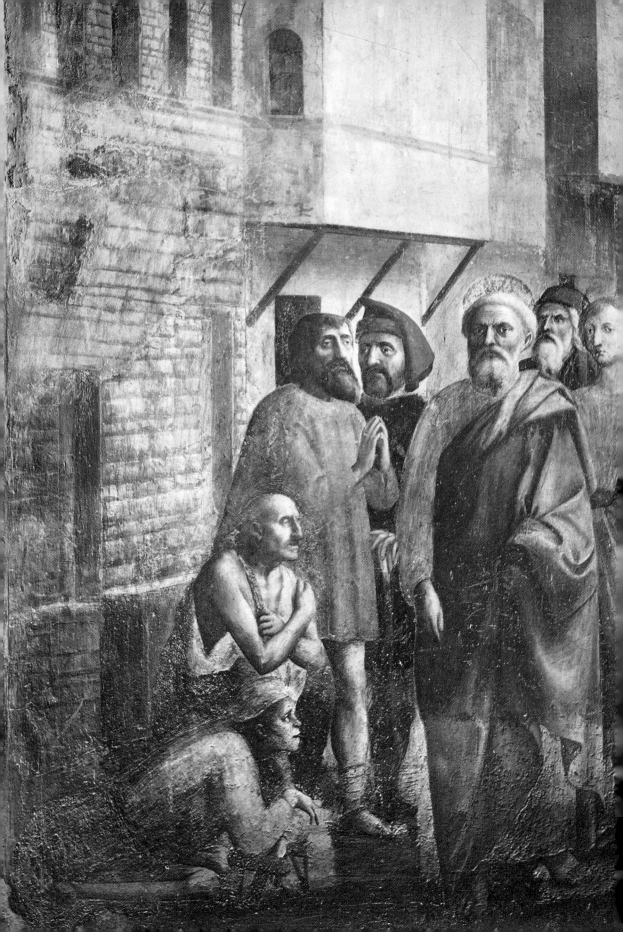

new texts were discovered and old texts edited, when scholars were
teachers and rulers and moral leaders. There are plenty of Renaissance
pictures of scholars in their studies, usually represented as one of the
Church Fathers, Jerome or Augustine. They look fairly snug in their
well-furnished studies, their books piled on the shelves, their texts propped
before them, their contemplation of the universe assisted by a celestial
sphere. The passionate earnestness of Botticelli's St Augustine [60] was no
doubt directed towards the contemplation of God. But the scholar searching
for truth in Classical texts was scarcely less intense.

It was to house these precious texts, any one of which might contain
some new revelation that might alter the course of human thought, that
Cosimo de Medici built the library of San Marco [61]. It looks to us peaceful
and remote – but the first studies that took place there were not remote from
life at all. It was the humanist equivalent of the Cavendish Laboratory. The

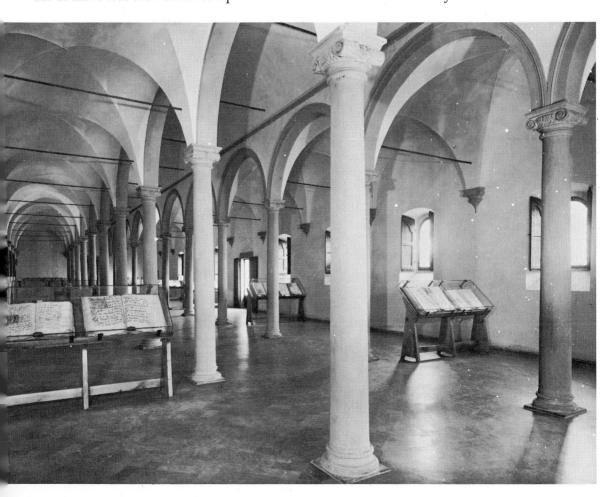

61 Library of San Marco, Florence

14 Masaccio, *St Peter healing the sick*

manuscripts unpacked and studied under these harmonious vaults could alter the course of history with an explosion, not of matter, but of mind.

But although the study of Greek and Latin influenced the thought and style and moral judgements of the Florentines, its influence on their art was not very far-reaching – it consisted chiefly of isolated quotations. And their architecture, as one sees it in the Pazzi Chapel, isn't antique at all. Where did it come from, this light, economical style which is unlike anything before or since? I think that it was really the invention of an individual – Brunellesco. But of course, an architectural style cannot take root unless it satisfies some need of the time. Brunellesco's style satisfied the need of the clear-headed, bright-minded men who appeared on the Florentine scene at the moment when the discipline of trade and banking, in its most austere form, was beginning to be relaxed, and life – a full use of the human faculties – became more important than making money.

People sometimes feel disappointed the first time they see the famous beginnings of Renaissance architecture – the Pazzi Chapel and the Old Sacristy of San Lorenzo – because they seem so small. Well, so they are, after the great monuments of Romanesque and Gothic architecture. They don't try to impress us or crush us by size and weight, as all God-directed architecture does. Everything is adjusted to the scale of reasonable human necessity. They are intended to make each individual more conscious of his powers, as a complete moral and intellectual being. They are an assertion of the dignity of man.

The dignity of man. Today those words die on our lips. But in fifteenth-century Florence their meaning was still a fresh and invigorating belief. Gianozzo Manetti, a humanist man of action, who had seen the seamy side of politics, nevertheless wrote a book entitled *On the Dignity and Excellence of Man*. And this is the concept that Brunellesco's friends were making visible. Round the merchants' church of Orsanmichele are life-size figures of the saints: Donatello's St Mark, of whom Michelangelo said: 'No one could fail to believe the word of such a sincere man'; and that 1914 soldier, Donatello's St George [62]. They show the ideal of humanity that presided over these mundane activities. The grandest of all testimonies to the dignity of man is by another member of the same group, Masaccio, in the series of frescoes he painted in the church of the Carmine. What characters they are: morally and intellectually men of weight [63], the least frivolous of men, infinitely remote from the gay courtiers of Jean de Berry – who were only thirty years older. They have the air of contained vitality and confidence that one often sees in the founding fathers of a civilisation – the ones that come first to my mind are the Egyptians of the first four dynasties.

62 Donatello, *St George*

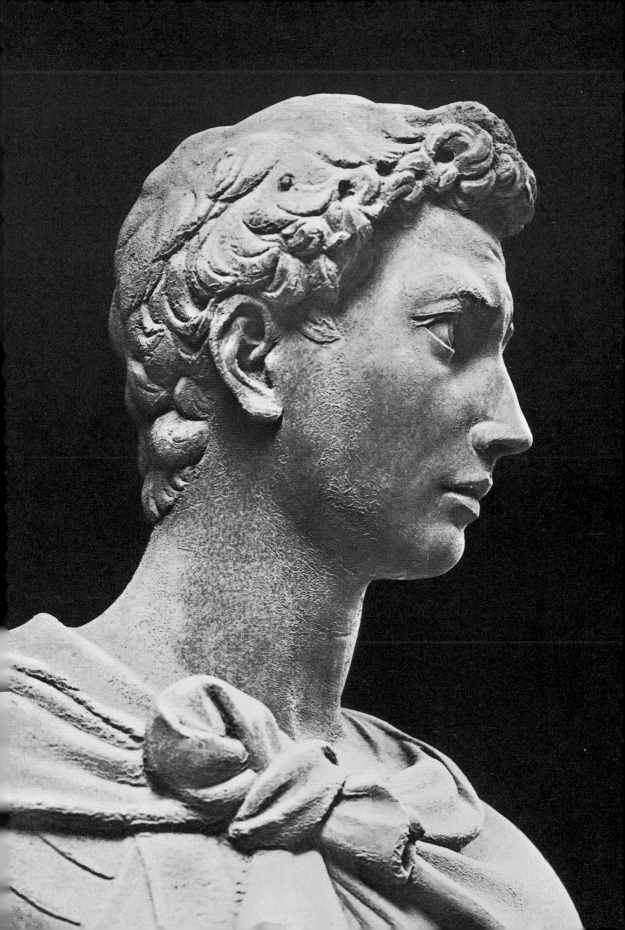

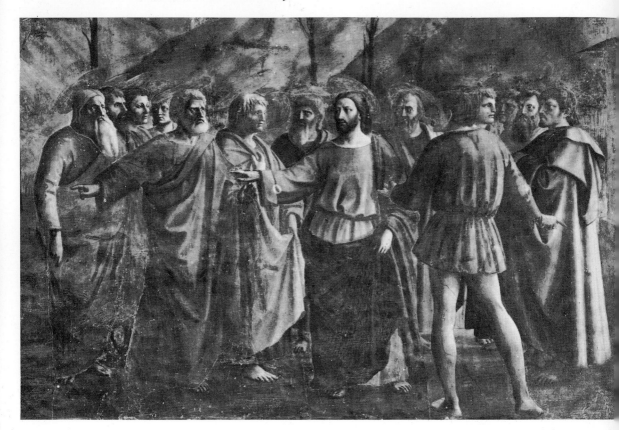

But these men are also moved by the concept of Christian charity. As St Peter moves gravely through the streets, his shadow cures the sick [**14,** facing p. 93]. In the balancing fresco Peter and his disciples give alms to a poor woman who is one of the great sculptural creations in painting.

Gravitas, the heavy tread of moral earnestness, becomes a bore if it is not accompanied by the light step of intelligence. Next to the Pazzi Chapel are the cloisters of Santa Croce, also built by Brunellesco. I said that the Gothic cathedrals were hymns to the divine light. These cloisters happily celebrate the light of human intelligence, and sitting in them I find it quite easy to believe in man. They have the qualities that give distinction to a mathematical theorem: clarity, economy, elegance. And no doubt early Renaissance architecture is based on a passion for mathematics, particularly for geometry. Of course medieval architects had designed on a mathematical basis, but it seems to have been of immense complexity, as elaborate as scholastic philosophy. The Renaissance architects used much simpler geometrical figures – the square, the circle, forms which they believed to have some ultimate perfection – and they entertained the idea that these forms must be applicable to the human body: that each, so to say, guaranteed the perfection of the other. This idea occurs in the ancient architectural theorist Vitruvius, and it was therefore known to the medieval builders (there was a manuscript of Vitruvius in the library at Cluny), but they had interpreted it differently. There are dozens of drawings and en-

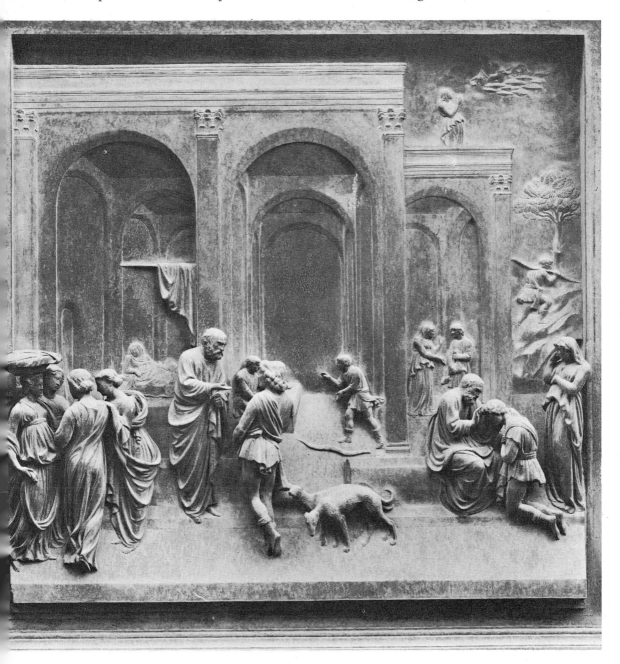

64 Ghiberti, *Jacob and Esau*, from the Baptistry doors, Florence

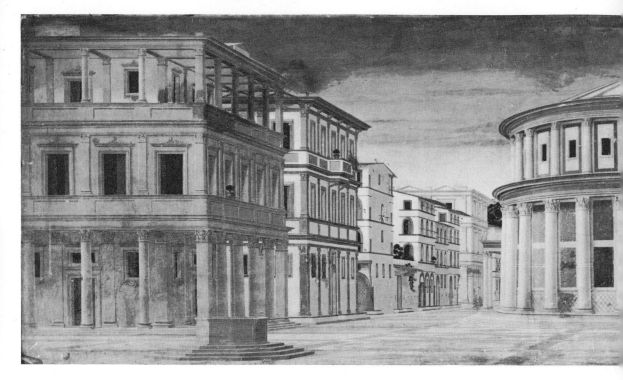

gravings to demonstrate this proposition, of which the most famous is by
Leonardo da Vinci. Mathematically I'm afraid it's really a cheat; but
aesthetically it has some meaning, because the symmetry of the human
body, and to some extent the relation of one part of it to another, do
influence our sense of a normal proportion. And philosophically it contains
the germ of an idea which might save us – if we could believe in it: that
through proportion we can reconcile the two parts of our being, the
physical and the intellectual.

The same approach was applied to painting, in the system known as
perspective, by which it was thought that with mathematical calculation
one could render on a flat surface the precise position of a figure in space.
This too seems to have been invented by Brunellesco, but we can see it best
in the works of his two friends, Ghiberti and Donatello, whose low-relief
sculpture is really a kind of painting. Ghiberti's Jacob and Esau [64] on the
famous Baptistry doors in Florence shows perspective used to achieve a
spatial harmony that has almost a musical effect. Donatello's relief of St
Antony of Padua curing a boy's leg shows the other use of perspective: to
heighten emotion by a more intense awareness of space. The Florentines
were extremely proud of this invention, which they thought (wrongly as it
turns out) was unknown to antiquity, and it remained part of an artist's train-

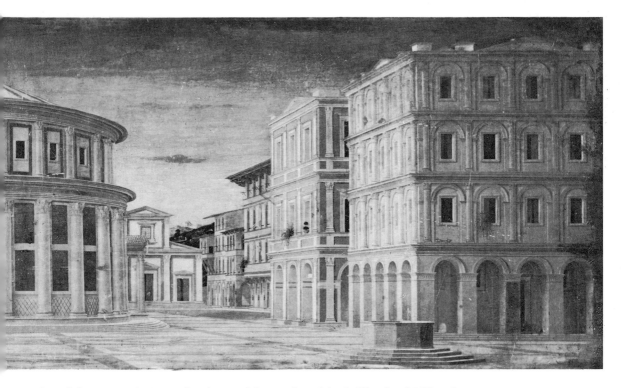

ing right up to 1945. But has it anything to do with civilisation? When it was first invented I think it had. The belief that one could represent a man in a real setting and calculate his position and arrange figures in a demonstrably harmonious order, expressed symbolically a new idea about man's place in the scheme of things and man's control over his own destiny.

Perspective was concerned with the representation of towns, if only because it was by the paved floor and receding arcades that the system could show to advantage. Brunellesco's original exercise represented the piazza in front of the cathedral of Florence, with the Baptistry in the middle, but the pure perspectives which have survived represent imaginary towns, architectural harmonies, the perfect setting for social man. Alberti, in his great book on building, describes the necessity of a public square 'where young men may be diverted from the mischievousness and folly natural to their age; and, under handsome porticos, old men may spend the heat of the day, and be mutually serviceable to one another'. I think that Piero della Francesca, who derived so much from Alberti, may well have had this and similar passages in mind when he painted the most harmonious of ideal cities [65]. The early Florentine Renaissance was an urban culture, bourgeois properly so-called. Men spent their time in the streets and squares, and in the shops. A good Florentine, says one of their moralists, *sta sempre a*

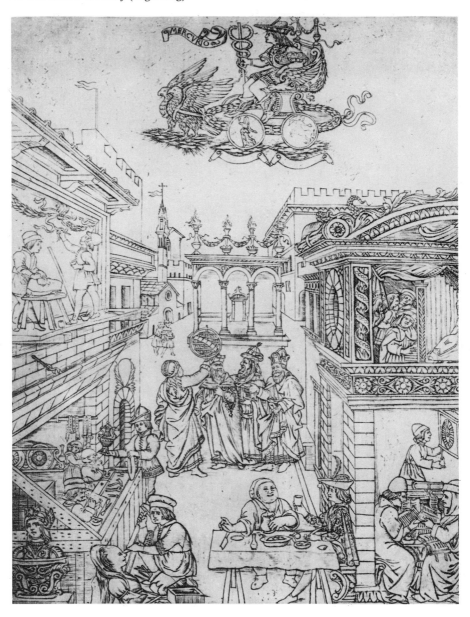

bottega, 'is always in the shop'. And these shops were completely public. A fifteenth-century engraving [66], representing the activities influenced by the planet Mercury, shows a craftsman's workshop open to the street, so that passers-by could see what was being done, and rival artists make scathing comments.

The Renaissance historian of art, Vasari, when he asked himself (characteristically) why it was in Florence and not elsewhere that men became perfect in the arts, gave as his first answer: 'The spirit of criticism: the air of Florence making minds naturally free, and not content with mediocrity.' And this harsh, outspoken competition between Florentine craftsmen not only screwed up technical standards, but also meant that there was no gap of incomprehension between the intelligent patron and the artist. Our contemporary attitude of pretending to understand works of art in order not to appear philistines would have seemed absurd to the Florentines. They were a tough lot. Many people since Bruni in 1428 have compared them with the Athenians. But the Florentines were more realistic. Whereas the Athenians loved philosophical argument, the Florentines were chiefly interested in making money and playing appalling practical jokes on stupid men. However, they had a good deal in common with the Greeks. They were curious, they were extremely intelligent, and they had, to a supreme degree, the power of making their thoughts visible. I hesitate to pronounce the much abused word 'beauty', but I can't think of a substitute. Like the Athenians, the Florentines loved beauty. This is a constant source of surprise to anyone who knows them. I suppose that market day in fifteenth-century Florence was much the same as it is today – the same arguments, the same harsh

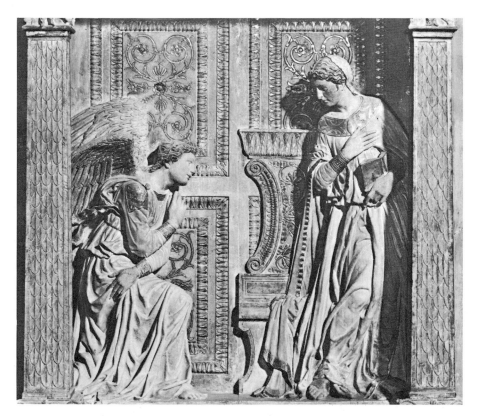

67 Donatello, *Annunciation*

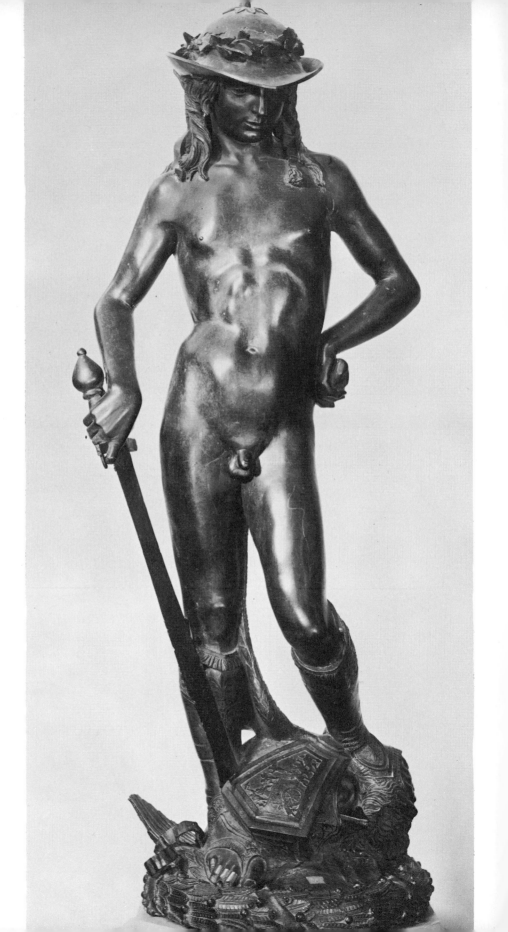

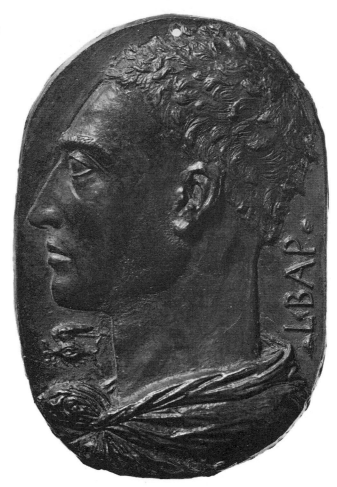

accents. But just above the heads of these shouting, bargaining farmers, on their church of Orsanmichele, is Luca della Robbia's *Virgin and Child*, the quintessence of milky sweetness. Next to the Bruni monument in Santa Croce is a stone relief of the Annunciation by Donatello [67]. That great master of character and human drama, who loved to portray the scholar's furrowed brow, also has the Florentine sense of beauty: his Virgin's head reminds us of an Athenian grave relief of the fifth century BC, and the shape of her chair proves that this resemblance is not accidental. Donatello paid an even more direct tribute to the antique concept of physical beauty in his bronze David [68], whose head is derived from that of the Emperor Hadrian's beloved Antinous, although with a sharper Florentine accent that makes it far more attractive.

One of the best places to get the flavour of fifteenth-century Florence is the old prison and hall of justice, the Bargello, because it not only contains great works of the Florentine imagination, like the David, but also the portraits of famous Florentines. These proudly individual characters wished to record for posterity exactly what they were like. There had been a few likenesses of individuals in the fourteenth century – Dante, Petrarch, Charles V of France, Jean de Berry. But they were exceptional. As a rule, medieval people were presented to the eye as figures that symbolised their status: the painter of the Spanish chapel in Santa Maria Novella, although he included so much lively detail, made his popes, kings, bishops, into stereotypes – their status would have been recognised all over the Gothic world. To take another example, we know nothing about the lives of the men who built the great cathedrals, but Brunellesco is the subject of a long, detailed biography written by a friend, and we have a replica of his death-mask which, following the example of ancient Rome, Florentines had begun to make in the late fourteenth century. Alberti, the quintessential early Renaissance man, left us his self-portrait [69] on two bronze reliefs. What a face! Proud and alert, like a wilful, intelligent race-horse. Alberti also wrote an autobiography and, as we should expect, he is not inhibited by false modesty. He tells us how the strongest horses trembled under him, how he could throw further, and jump higher, and work harder than any man. He describes how he conquered every weakness, for 'a man can do all things if he will'. It could be the motto of the early Renaissance.

Realistic portraiture, the use of the accidents of each individual face to reveal inner life, was not a Florentine, nor even an Italian invention. It was invented in Flanders, and came to an immediate perfection in the work of Jan van Eyck. No one has looked at the human face with a more dispassionate eye and recorded his findings with a more delicate hand. But in fact many of his sitters were Italians – Arnolfini [70], Albergati – part of the international world of the wool-trade, banking and papal diplomacy; and perhaps it was only in such a society that these evolved and subtle characters could have accepted the revelation of their personalities. Van Eyck's exploration of personality extended beyond the face. He shows people in their setting and in his double portrait of Arnolfini and his wife he lovingly records the details of their daily life; their wooden pattens for walking in the muddy streets of Bruges, their little dog of nameless breed, their convex mirror and, above all, their splendid brass chandelier. By a miracle that defies the laws of art-history, he was able to show them to us enveloped in daylight as close to experience as if it had been observed by Vermeer of Delft.

This sensibility to atmosphere the Florentines never attempted – they were a sculpture-minded people. But in their portrait busts they came to achieve an almost Flemish realism. How like these Florentine worthies are to the confident faces that we see in Victorian photographs! Antonio

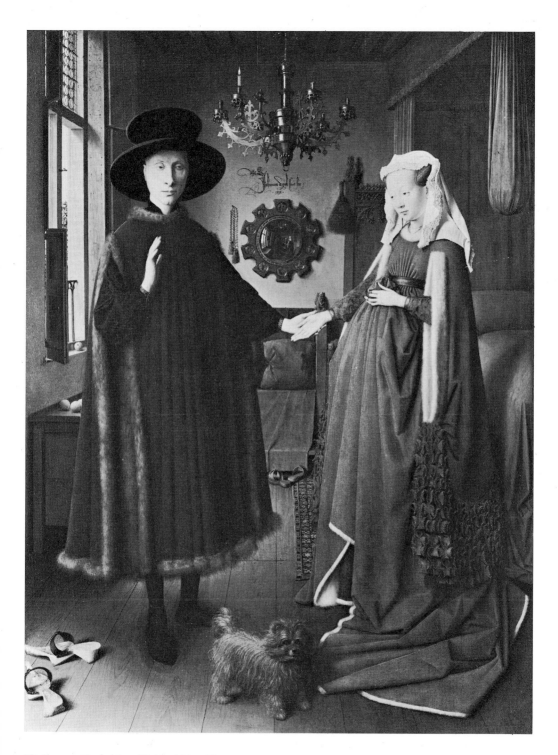

70 Jan van Eyck, *Arnolfini and his wife*

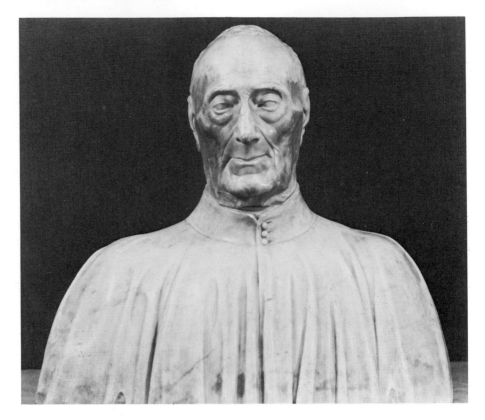

Rossellino's bust of Giovanni Chellini [71] is the professional man: a doctor, his face lined with the wisdom of experience – in fact he was Donatello's doctor and saved his life; Benedetto da Maiano's portrait of Pietro Mellini is the business man of any age. A character in one of Alberti's dialogues says: 'A man cannot set his hand to more liberal work than making money, for what we sell is our labour – the goods are merely transferred.' Yes: that was really written in 1434, not in 1850; and contrariwise, if you dressed Mellini in nineteenth-century clothes, he would look perfectly convincing.

But this atmosphere of liberal materialism is less than half the story. After the middle of the fifteenth century the intellectual life of Florence took a new direction, very different from the robust civic humanism of the 1430s. Florence had ceased to be a republic in anything but name, and for almost thirty years it was virtually ruled by that extraordinary character Lorenzo de' Medici. His father and grandfather had prepared the way for him by their activities as bankers. He himself was no financier – he lost a great part of the family fortunes. But he was a politician of genius who could distinguish between the reality of power and its outward trappings. The frontispiece [72] to his book of poems shows him in the streets of Florence, dressed as a

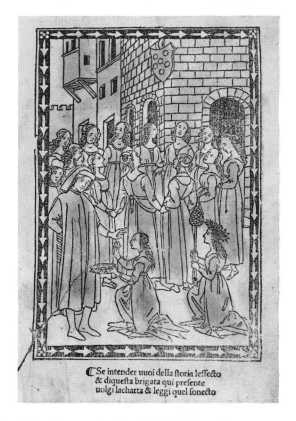

Se intender uuoi della ftoria leffecto
& diquefta brigata qui prefente
uolgi lacharta & leggi quel fonecto

simple citizen, surrounded by girls who are singing his ballads. What a contrast is this modest printed page to the rich manuscripts of the Duke of Berry! In fact Lorenzo was a good poet and a most admirable patron of other poets; also of scholars and philosophers. He was not much interested in the visual arts: the paintings by which his period is remembered were commissioned by his cousin Lorenzino. And it was for Lorenzino that Botticelli painted the works in which the Florentine sense of beauty appears in its most evolved and peculiar form: the *Spring* [15, facing p. 124] and the *Birth of Venus*. In the *Spring*, the subject is derived from Ovid, but this Classical inspiration is given a new complexity by memories of the Middle Ages. The pagan divinities sway before a background of leaves like a Gothic tapestry. What a marvellous feat of the reconciling imagination. As for the heads, they are a discovery of beauty that means much more to us today than the full, smooth oval of antiquity. The subject of Botticelli's other great allegory, the *Birth of Venus*, is taken from a contemporary poet, Poliziano. He was one of a group of subtle Florentines who were inspired by the late Greek philosophers known as neo-Platonists. It was their ambition to reconcile these pagan philosophers with Christianity, and so Botticelli's Venus, not at all

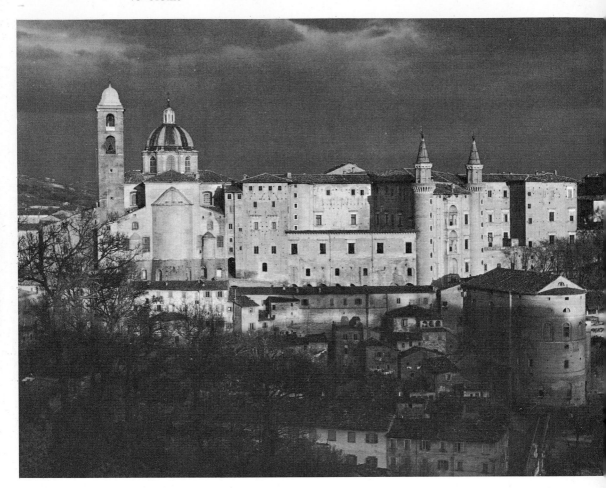

the amorous strumpet of paganism, but pale and withdrawn, dissolves into his image of the Virgin Mary.

The discovery of the individual was made in early fifteenth-century Florence. Nothing can alter that fact. But in the last quarter of the century the Renaissance owed almost as much to the small courts of northern Italy – Ferrara, Mantua and, above all, Urbino [73], a small remote town on the eastern perimeter of the Apennines. It could be argued that life in the court of Urbino was one of the high-water marks of western civilisation. The reason is that the first Duke of Urbino, Federigo Montefeltro, was not only a highly cultivated and intelligent man, but also the greatest general of his day who could defend his dominions from the surrounding ruffians. He was a passionate book collector; and the portrait he had painted for his precious library shows him reading one of his manuscripts. But he is dressed in full armour, the garter (which he received from Edward IV) on his leg, and his

15 Botticelli, *The Three Graces* (detail from *Spring*)

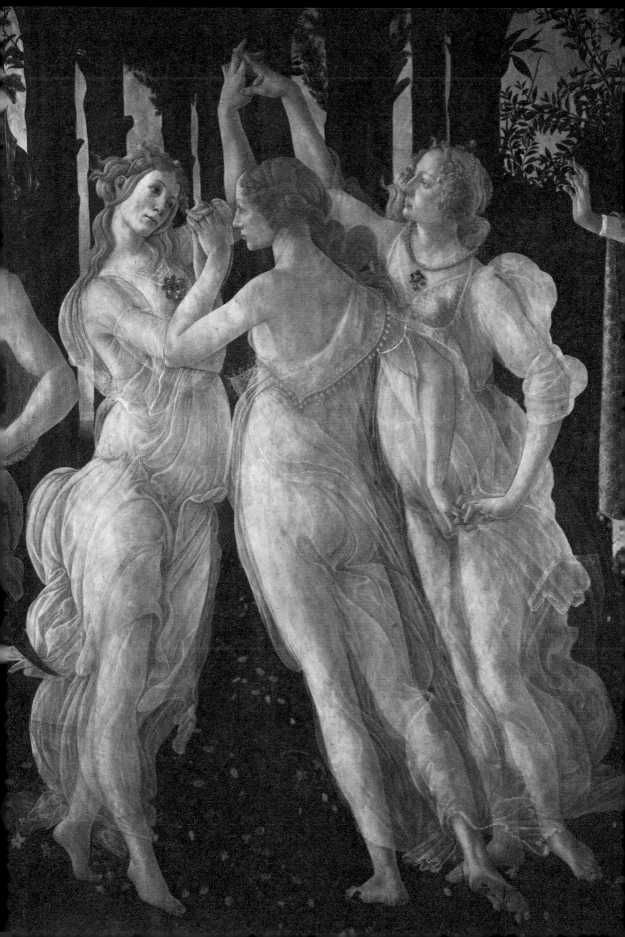

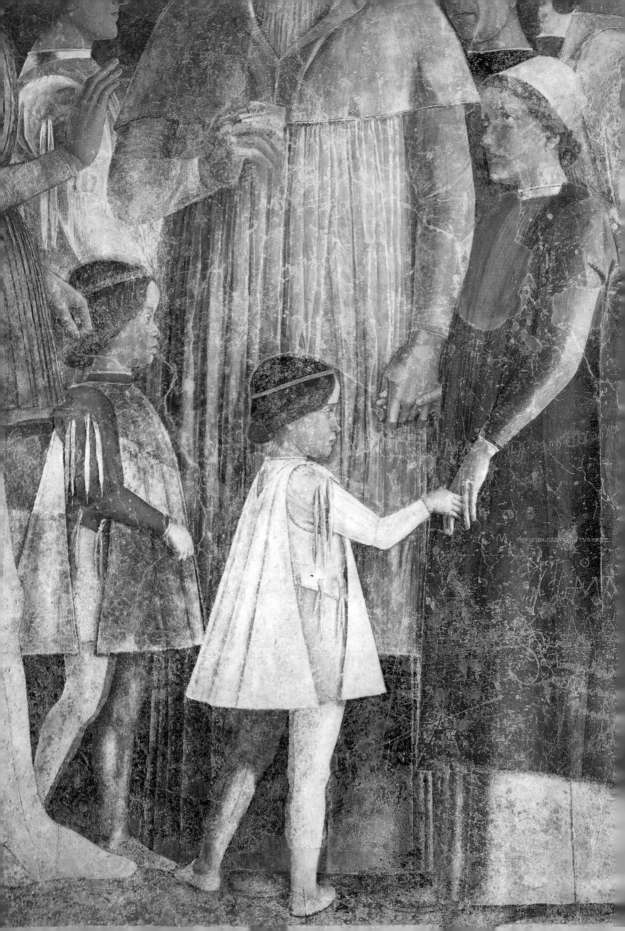

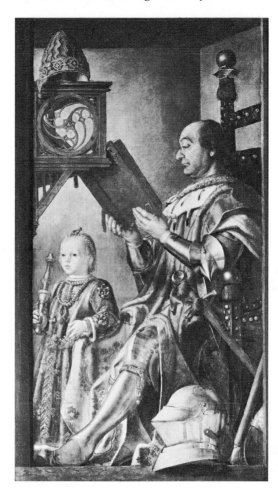

helmet at his feet [74]. His palace began as a fortress built on an almost im-
pregnable rock and only when he had fought his way to security could he
afford to give it the sweet and delicate form which makes it one of the most
beautiful pieces of architecture in the world.

The palace of Urbino has a style of its own. The arcaded courtyard [57]
isn't swift and springy, like Brunellesco's cloister, but calm and timeless.
The rooms [75] are light and airy, and so perfectly proportioned that it
exhilarates one to walk through them: in fact it's the only palace in the
world I can go round without feeling oppressed and exhausted. Curiously
enough, we don't know who designed it. A famous fortress-builder named
Laurana did the substructure, but left Urbino before the lived-in part of the
palace was begun. All we can say is that the Duke's own character seems to
permeate the whole building – and this we know from a life of him written by
his bookseller, Vespasiano di Bistici, the man who furnished his library. Again

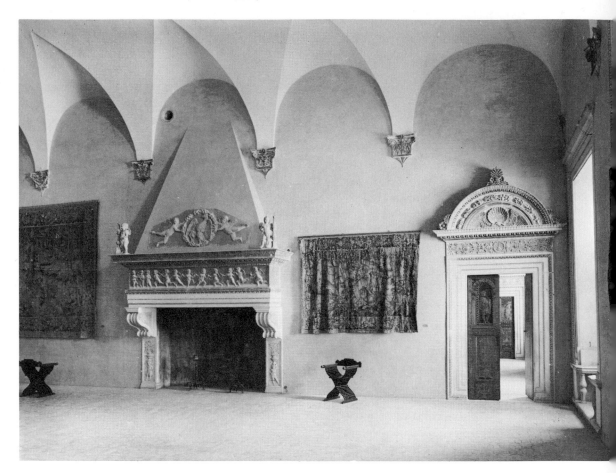

and again he refers to the Duke's humanity. He asked the Duke what is necessary in ruling a kingdom; the Duke replied: *essere umano* – 'to be human'. Whoever invented the style, this is the spirit that pervades the palace of Urbino.

As a part of civilisation the palace of Urbino extended beyond the fifteenth century. The chief architect of the High Renaissance, Bramante, was a native of Urbino and may have worked on the palace when it was being completed. The court painter was a silly old creature named Giovanni Santi, the sort of obliging mediocrity who is always welcome in courts, even in the court of Urbino. No doubt the ladies, when they were in need of a design for embroidery, used to say, 'Let's send for dear old Mr Santi' – and when he came he brought with him his beautiful little son, Raffaelo. And so Raphael, one of the civilising forces of the western imagination, found his earliest impressions of harmony and proportion and good manners in the court of Urbino.

Good manners; that was another product of Urbino. In common with other Italian courts – Ferrara and Mantua – young men went there to finish their education. They learnt to read the classics, to walk gracefully, speak quietly, play games without cheating or kicking each other on the shins; in short, to behave like gentlemen. Under Federigo's son and successor, Guidobaldo, the notion of a gentleman was given classic expression in a book called *Il Cortegiano* – 'The Courtier' – by Baldassare Castiglione. It had an immense influence. The Emperor Charles V had only three books beside his bed: the Bible, Macchiavelli's *Prince* and Castiglione's *Cortegiano*. For over a hundred years it formed everybody's notion of good manners. Actually it is very much more than a handbook on polite behaviour, because Castiglione's ideal of a gentleman is based on real human values. He must not hurt people's feelings or make them feel inferior by showing off. He must be easy and natural, yet he must not be a mere worldling; and *Il Cortegiano* ends with a moving discourse on the subject of love. Just as Botticelli's *Spring* unites the tapestry world of the Middle Ages with pagan mythology, so Castiglione's *Courtier* unites the medieval concept of chivalry with the ideal love of Plato.

There is no doubt that the court of Urbino, under both Federigo and Guidobaldo, was a high point in the history of civilisation. The same is true, in a lesser degree, of the court of Mantua. The palace of Mantua lacks the exhilarating lightness and lucidity of the palace of Urbino. Yet it contains a room in which more than anywhere else, perhaps, one can get an idea of civilised life in an Italian court. It was decorated by the court painter, Andrea Mantegna. On the ceiling are painted busts of the Roman emperors, but the scenes below are not all archaeological. They show the Gonzaga family as large as life (perhaps the first life-size portraits in art), their dogs, their old retainers and one of their famous collection of dwarfs. In spite of the frontal formality of the Marchioness, the spirit of the whole group is remarkably natural [76]. The little girl asks if she may eat an apple, but her mother is interested to know what news the Marquess has just received from his secretary – in fact it is good news: that their son has been made a cardinal. In another scene the Marquess goes to greet him, accompanied by his younger sons. What an agreeably informal reception! One of the younger children holds his father's hand and the little boy takes the hand of his elder brother [16, facing p. 109]. It is still without the odious pomposity that was to grow up in Europe during the next century, and reach its zenith at Versailles. I am bound to say that even Mantegna has not been able to make the newly created cardinal look a very spiritual type. Which reminds one of the obvious fact – that this kind of social organisation depended entirely on the individual characters of the rulers. In one state was Federigo Montefeltro, the God-fearing father of his people; in the neighbouring state was Sigismondo Malatesta, the wolf of Rimini, who did things that even the most advanced theatrical producer would hesitate to put on the stage. And yet both of them employed Alberti and were painted by Piero della Francesca.

This was one of the weaknesses of Renaissance civilisation. And the other, no less obviously, was that it depended on a very small minority. Even in republican Florence, the Renaissance touched relatively few people, and in places like Urbino and Mantua it was practically confined to the court. This is contrary to our modern sense of equality, but one can't help wondering how far civilisation would have evolved if it had been entirely dependent on the popular will. Yeats actually used the example of Urbino when he addressed a poem to 'A wealthy man who promised a subscription to Dublin Municipal Gallery if it were proved that people wanted pictures'.

> And Guidobaldo, when he made
> That mirror-school of courtesies
> Where wit and beauty learned their trade
> Upon Urbino's windy hill,
> Had sent no runners to and fro
> That he might learn the shepherds' will.

One may not like courts, but at a certain stage it is only in a court that a man may do something extravagant for its own sake, because he wants to, because it seems to him worth doing. And it is sometimes through the wilful, superfluous actions of individuals that societies discover their powers. I have often thought that the lath-and-plaster architecture, which men of the fifteenth and sixteenth centuries used to erect for the funerals or betrothals of prominent citizens, gave architects that chance to experiment and fantasticate that is so gloomily lacking in the carefully costed buildings of today.

All the same, as one walks through the splendidly extravagant rooms of the palace at Urbino, one can't help thinking, 'What about the people in the fields, or those shepherds whom Mr Yeats rightly supposed that Guidobaldo did not consult on matters of taste and good manners? Could they not have had a kind of civilisation of their own?' Well, there is such a thing as civilised countryside. Looking at the Tuscan landscape with its terraces of vines and olives and the dark vertical accents of the cypresses, one has the impression of timeless order. There must have been a time when it was all forest and swamp – shapeless, formless; and to bring order out of chaos is a process of civilisation. But of this ancient, rustic civilisation we have no record beyond the farmhouses themselves, whose noble proportions seem to be the basis of Italian architecture; and when the men of the Renaissance

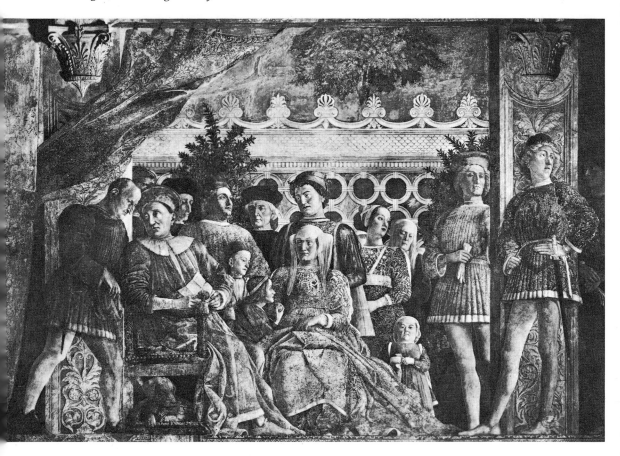

looked at the countryside it was not as a place of ploughing and digging, but as a kind of earthly paradise.

This is how it appears in the first evolved landscape in European painting, the background of van Eyck's *Adoration of the Lamb* [17, facing p. 116]. The foreground is painted with a medieval sharpness of detail, but our eyes, passing over the dense greenery of laurel and ilex, float into a gleaming distance. Already awareness of nature is associated with the desire to escape and with hope of a better life, and in the late Middle Ages painters had shown elegant company, even the Virgin herself, sitting on the ground among flowers and grasses. Then, in the first years of the sixteenth century, the Venetian painter Giorgione transformed this happy contact with nature into something more openly sensual. The ladies who, in the Gothic gardens, had been protected by voluminous draperies, are now naked; and, as a result, his *Fête Champêtre* [77] opens a new chapter in European art. Giorgione was, indeed, one of the inspired, unpredictable innovators who disturb the course of history; and in this picture he has illustrated one of the comforting illusions of civilised man, the myth of Arcadia which had been popularised some twenty years earlier by the poet Sannazaro. Of course, it's only a myth. Country life isn't at all like this, and even on a picnic ants attack the sandwiches and wasps buzz round the wine-glasses. But the pastoral fallacy had inspired Theocritus and Virgil, and had not been unknown in the Middle Ages. Giorgione has seen how fundamentally pagan it is. The pleasant contrast of sun and shade, the flapping leaves, the sound of water trickling from a well, mixed with the sound of a lute, all these are sensual pleasures, and require for their fulfilment the forms and rhythms of antique sculpture. This arcadia is as much a tribute to antiquity as were the republican virtues of the Florentine humanists, and as much a part of the rediscovery of man: but in his sensual rather than his intellectual nature.

With Giorgione's picnic the balance and enjoyment of our human faculties seems to achieve perfection. But in history all points of supposed per-

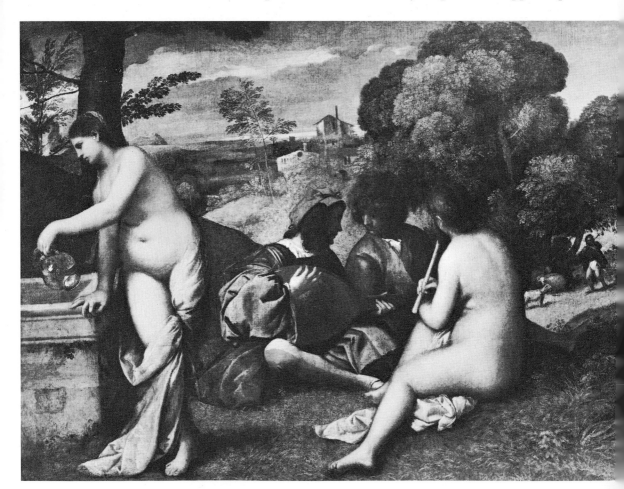

77 Giorgione, *Fête Champêtre*

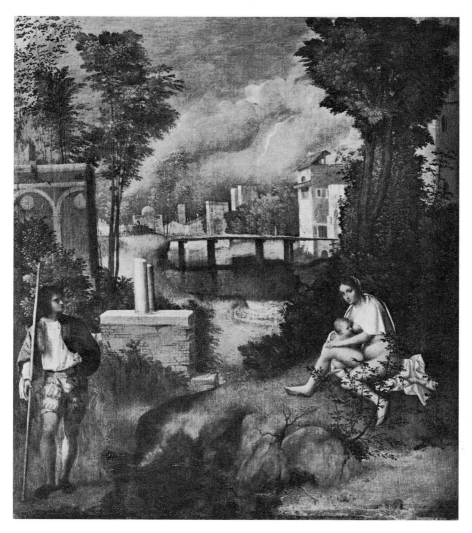

fection have a hint of menace; and Giorgione himself discovers it in that mysterious picture known as the *Tempesta* [78]. What on earth is going on? What is the meaning of this half-naked woman suckling a baby, this flash of lightning, this broken column? Nobody knows; nobody has ever known. It was described in Giorgione's own time as 'a soldier and a gypsy'. Well, whatever it means, it certainly doesn't show any confidence in the light of human reason.

'A man can do all things if he will.' How naive Alberti's statement seems when one thinks of that great bundle of fears and memories that every individual carries around with him; to say nothing of the external forces which are totally beyond his control. Giorgione, the passionate lover of physical beauty, painted a picture of an old woman [79] and called it *col*

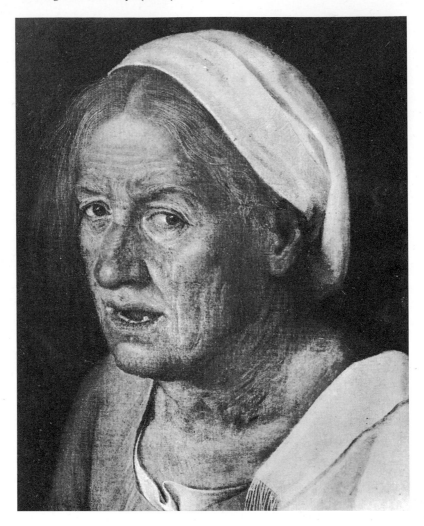

tempo – 'with time'. One can see that she must have once been a beauty. It is one of the first masterpieces of the new pessimism – new, because without the comfort of religion – that was to be given final expression by Hamlet.

The truth is, I suppose, that the civilisation of the early Italian Renaissance was not broadly enough based. The few had gone too far away from the many, not only in knowledge and intelligence – this they always do – but in basic assumptions. When the first two generations of humanists were dead their movement had no real weight behind it, and there was a reaction away from the human scale of values. Fortunately, they left in sculpture, painting, architecture, a message to every generation that values reason, clarity and harmonious proportion, and believes in the individual.

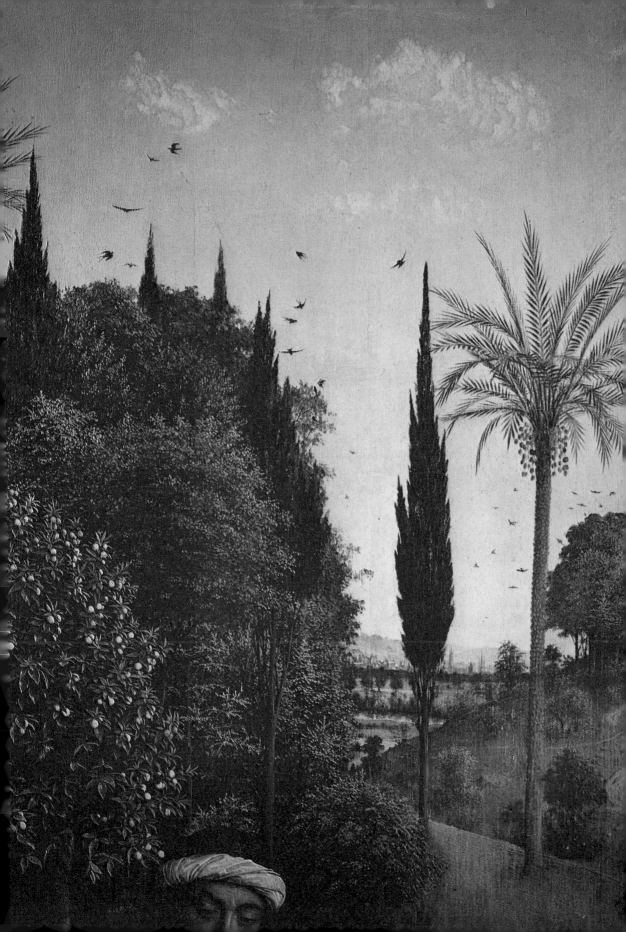

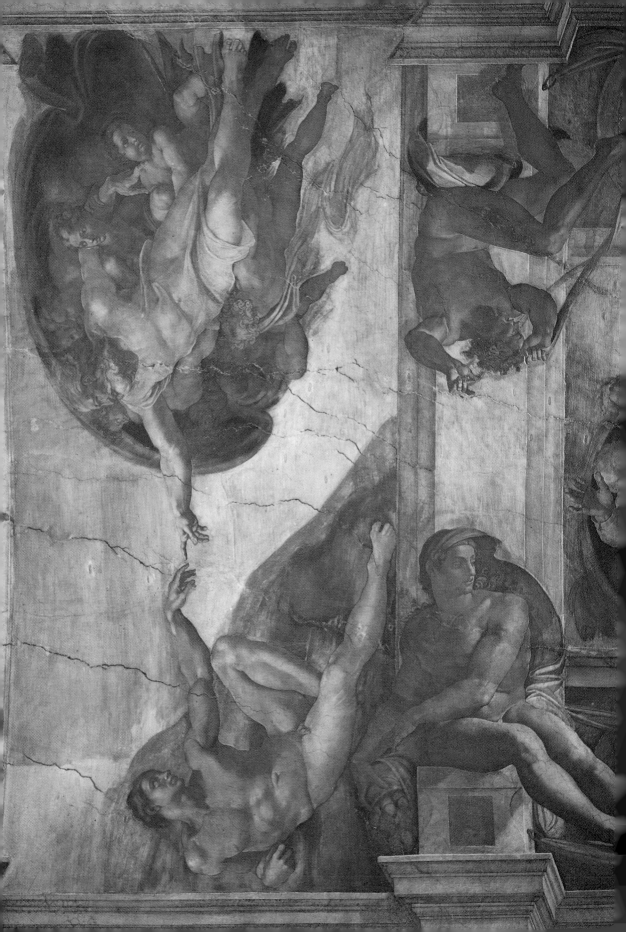

5 The Hero as Artist

The scene has changed from Florence to Rome, from the city of hard heads, sharp wits, light feet, graceful movement, to a city of weight, a city that is like a huge compost-heap of human hopes and ambitions, despoiled of its ornament, almost indecipherable, a wilderness of imperial splendour, with only one ancient emperor, Marcus Aurelius, above ground in the sunshine through the centuries. The scale has changed. I am standing in the court-yard of the Vatican, at the end of which the architect Bramante has built a sun-trap, known as the Belvedere, from which the Pope could enjoy the view of the ancient city. It is in the form of a niche, but instead of being designed to hold a life-size statue it is enormous – in fact it has always been known as *il nicchione*, 'the monster niche'. It is the outward and visible sign of the great change that overcame the civilisation of the Renaissance in about the year 1500. This is no longer a world of free and active men, but a world of giants and heroes.

In the niche is a bronze pine-cone big enough to contain a man. It came from that earlier world of giants, antiquity, and was probably the finial of Hadrian's tomb. But in the Middle Ages it was thought to have marked the point at which the chariots turned in their races round the hippodrome, and since in that hippodrome many Christian martyrs were put to death, it was here that the Christian Church elected to make its headquarters. Huge, cloudy concepts, compared to the sharp focus of Florence. But in Rome they were not so cloudy after all, because the huge buildings of antiquity were there [80] – and very much more of them than we have today. Even after three centuries in which they were used as quarries, and in which our sense of scale has expanded, they still are surprisingly big. In the Middle Ages men had been crushed by this gigantic scale. They said that these buildings must be the work of demons, or at best they treated them simply as natural phenomena – like mountains – and built their huts in them, as who should take advantage of a ravine or sheltering escarpment. Rome was a city of cowherds and stray goats in which nothing was built except a few fortified towers from which the ancient families carried out their pointless and interminable feuds – literally interminable, because they are still quarrelling today.

But by 1500 the Romans had begun to realise that they had been built by men. The lively and intelligent individuals who created the Renaissance,

18 Michelangelo, *Creation of Man*

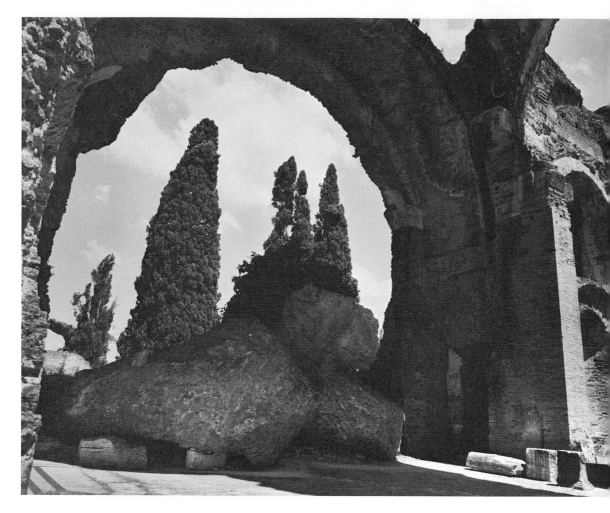

bursting with vitality and confidence, were not in a mood to be crushed by antiquity. They meant to absorb it, to equal it, to master it. They were going to produce their own race of giants and heroes.

The scene has changed to Rome also for political reasons. After years of exile and adversity, the sovereign pontiff has returned to his seat of temporal power. In what is commonly described as the decadence of the papacy, the Popes were men of unusual ability who used their international contacts, their great civil service and their increasing wealth in the interests of civilisation. Nicholas V, the friend of Alberti and the humanists, was the first man who saw that papal Rome could revive the grandeurs of pagan Rome. Pius II, a poet, a lover of nature and of beauty in all its forms, yet gave up his life in an attempt to save Christendom from the Turks. Even Sixtus IV, who was as brutal and cunning as he looks in the wall-painting by Melozzo da

Forli [81], founded the Vatican library and made the great humanist, Platina, its first prefect. In the same wall-painting we see for the first time the splendid head of the young cardinal who, more than any man, was destined to give the High Renaissance its heroic direction, Giuliano della Rovere. What a lion he looks compared to the donkeys of the papal secretariat! And when he became Pope Julius II he was able by magnanimity and strength of will to inspire and bully three men of genius – Bramante, Michelangelo and Raphael. Without him Michelangelo would not have painted the Sistine Ceiling, nor Raphael decorated the papal apartments; and so we should have been without two of the greatest visible expressions of spiritual power and humanist philosophy.

This splendidly over-life-size character conceived a project so audacious, so extravagant, that to this day the very thought of it makes me feel slightly jumpy. He decided to pull down old St Peter's [82]. It was one of the largest and most ancient churches in the western world; and certainly the most venerable, for it stood on the place where St Peter was supposed to have

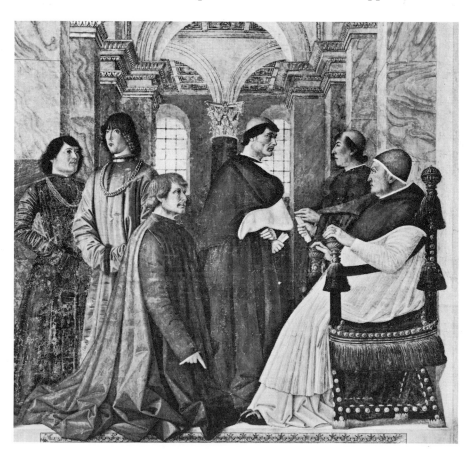

81 Melozzo da Forli, *Platina, Julius II and Sixtus IV*

82 Interior of Old St Peter's (16th-century fresco)

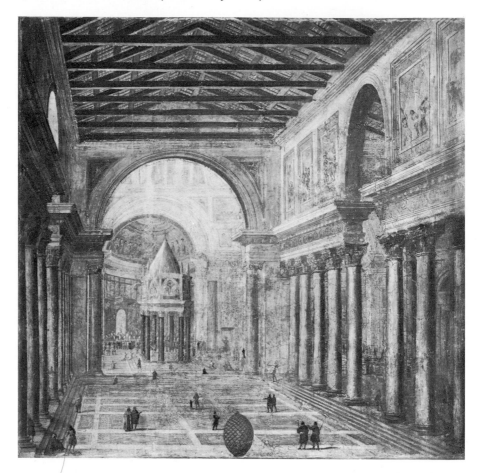

been martyred. Julius decided to pull it down and put something far more splendid in its place. In his thoughts for the new building he was influenced by two Renaissance ideals. It must be based on 'perfect' forms – the square and the circle; and it must be on a scale, and in a style, that surpassed the grandiose ruins of antiquity. And he called on Bramante to provide a plan. He did not get very far with it. Great movements in the arts, like revolutions, don't last for more than about fifteen years. After that the flame dies down, and people prefer a cosy glow. Julius II was Pope for only ten years – from 1503 to 1513; St Peter's wasn't completed till almost a century after his death, and by that time it was expressive of quite a different philosophy. But the first step in this visible alliance between Christianity and antiquity was taken when Julius decided to pull down the old basilica.

Antiquity: the men of fifteenth-century Florence had looked back eagerly to the civilisation of Greece and Rome. They sought for ancient authors and read them with passion, and wrote to each other in Latin. Their greatest source of pride was to write prose like Cicero. But although their minds were full of antique literature, their imaginations remained entirely Gothic. It's true, of course, that Donatello and Ghiberti included in their work a great many quotations from antique sculpture. But when the average painter set out to depict a scene from antique literature he did so in the costume of his own time, with dainty fantastical movements which show not the slightest consciousness of the physical weight and the flowing

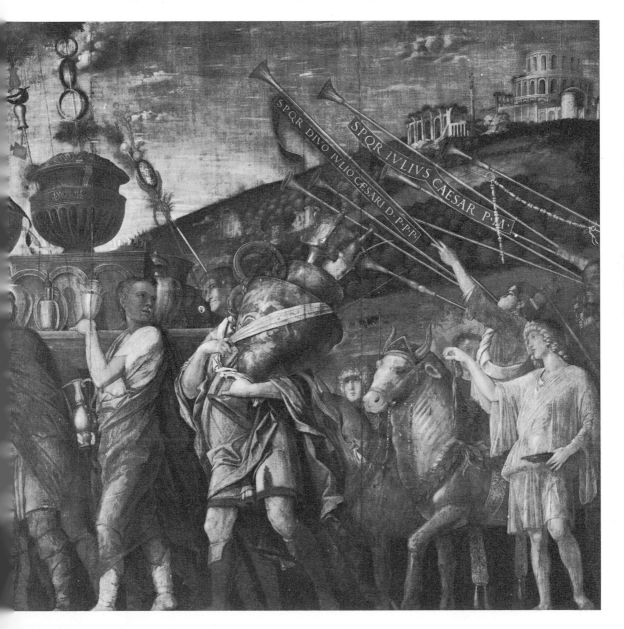

83 Mantegna, *The Triumph of Caesar — the vase-bearers*

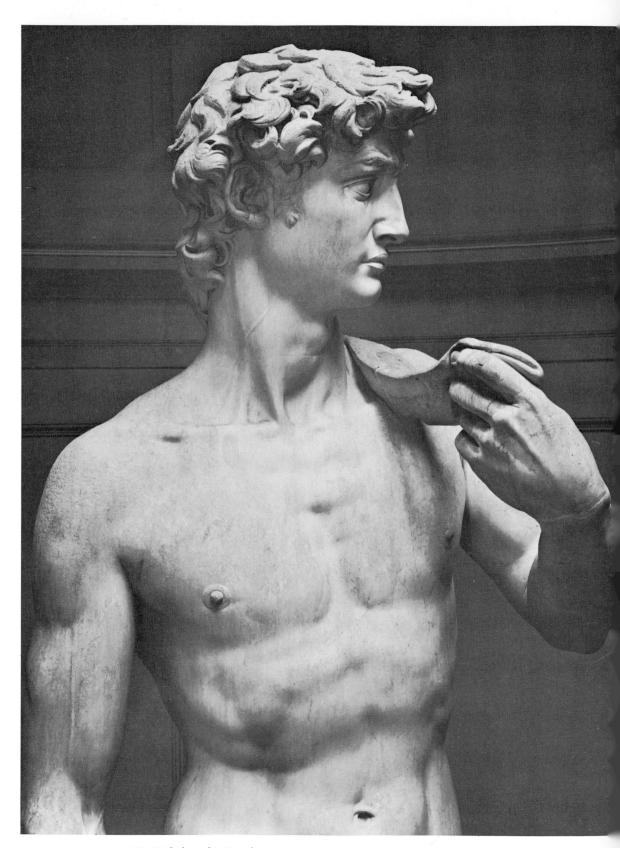

84 Michelangelo, *David*

rhythms of antiquity. And the curious thing is that the humanists, who took so much trouble about the text of an author like Livy, accepted, as a correct representation of the event, a picture of the death of Julius Caesar in which the figures are obviously dressed like fifteenth-century dandies. As long as there was this rather comical discrepancy between the written word and the image, antiquity could not exert its humanising power on the imagination.

I suppose that the first occasion in which the dream of antiquity is given a more or less accurate visible form is the series of decorations representing the *Triumph of Caesar* [83] done for the court of Mantua by Mantegna in about 1480. It is the first piece of romantic archaeology. Mantegna has rummaged passionately in the ruins of ancient Roman towns to find evidence for the shape of every vase and trumpet and he has subordinated his antiquarian knowledge to a feeling for the drive and discipline of Rome. But the man who really assimilated antique art and recreated it, with all its expressive power made more vital and more intense, was Michelangelo. He went to Rome in 1496, and was so overcome by what he saw that he made imitations of Graeco-Roman sculpture, one of which (now lost) was actually sold as an antique – the first recorded fake.

In 1501 Michelangelo returned to Florence. I said that the gigantic and the heroic spirit of the High Renaissance belongs to Rome. But there was a sort of prelude in Florence. The Medici, who had been the rulers of Florence for the last sixty years, had been kicked out in 1494, and the Florentines, under the influence of Savonarola, had established a republic, with all the noble, puritanical sentiments which pre-Marxist revolutionaries used to dig up out of Plutarch and Livy. To symbolise their achievement, the republic commissioned various works of art on heroic-patriotic themes. One of them was for a gigantic figure of David, the tyrant-slayer. The commission was given to the alarming young man who had just returned from Rome. Only twenty-five years separate Michelangelo's marble hero [84] from the dapper little figure, which had been the last word in Medician elegance, the *David* of Verrocchio: and one sees that there really has been a turning-point in the human spirit. The Verrocchio is light, nimble, smiling – and clothed. The Michelangelo is vast, defiant and nude. It's rather the same as the progression that we shall find in music between Mozart and Beethoven.

Seen by itself the *David*'s body might be some unusually taut and vivid work of antiquity; it is only when we come to the head that we are aware of a spiritual force that the ancient world never knew. I suppose that this quality, which I may call heroic, is not a part of most people's idea of civilisation. It involves a contempt for convenience and a sacrifice of all those pleasures that contribute to what we call civilised life. It is the enemy of

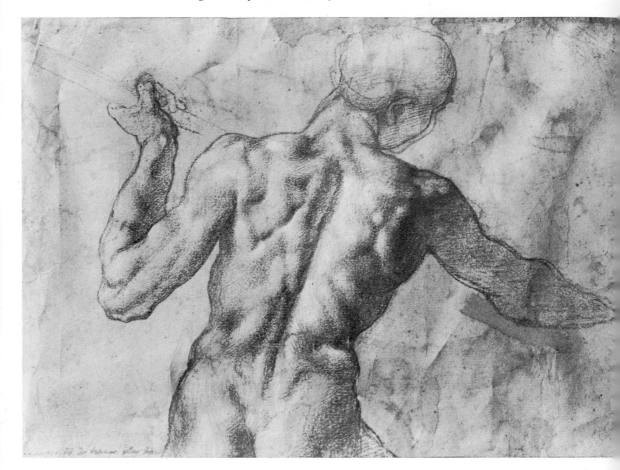

happiness. And yet we recognise that to despise material obstacles, and even to defy the blind forces of fate, is man's supreme achievement; and since, in the end, civilisation depends on man extending his powers of mind and spirit to the utmost, we must reckon the emergence of Michelangelo as one of the great events in the history of western man.

In the same moment of republican zeal Michelangelo was commissioned to paint a decoration in the hall of the great council which had been set up at the summit of the new democratic system. It was intended to represent some heroic episode in Florentine history. Actually Michelangelo's subject was rather discreditable, a group of Florentine soldiers taken by surprise: he chose it simply because these bathing soldiers gave him the opportunity of depicting the nude. He only got as far as the full-size drawing (what is called the cartoon) and even that is lost, but it had an immense influence, and surviving studies for it show why [85]. It was the first authoritative statement that the human body — that body which, in Gothic times, had been the

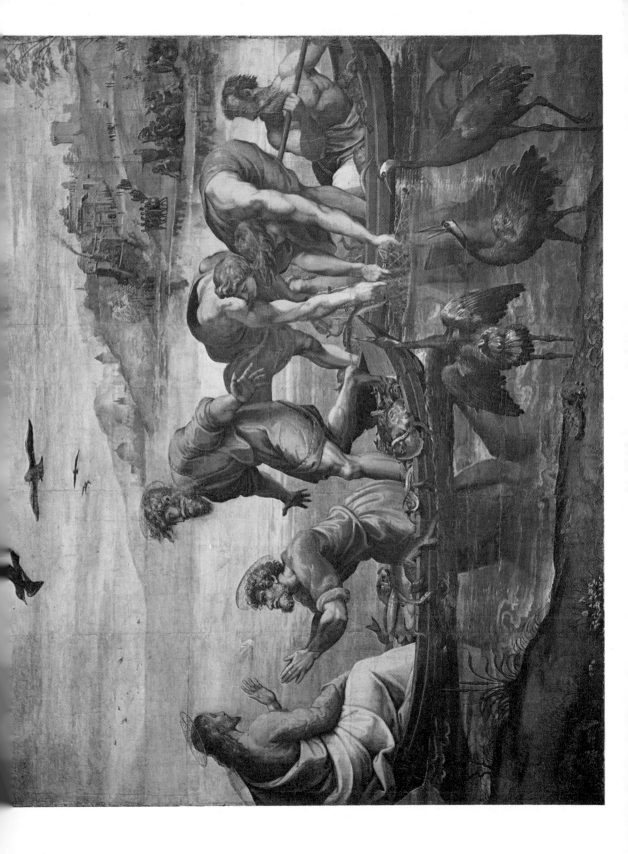

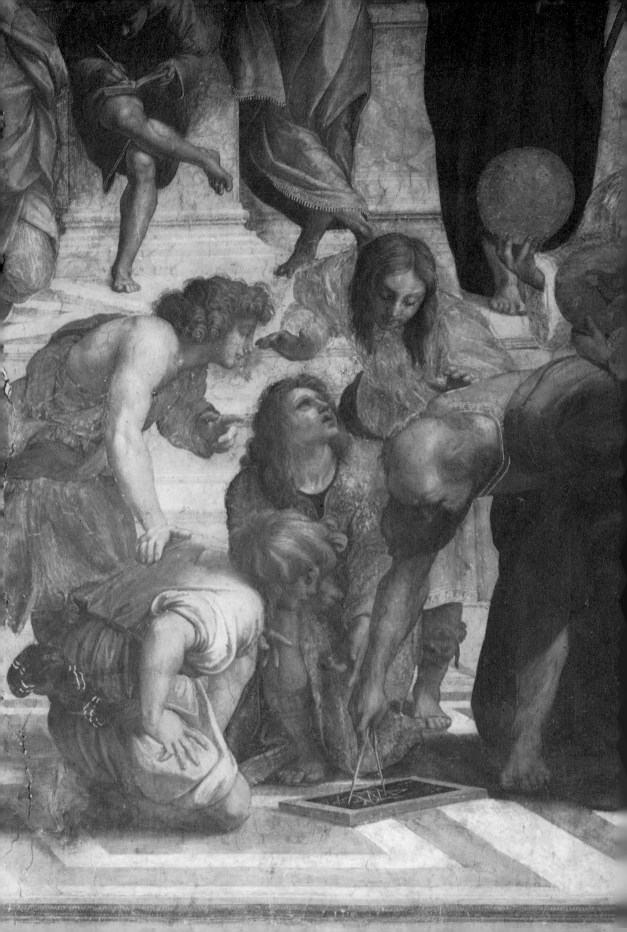

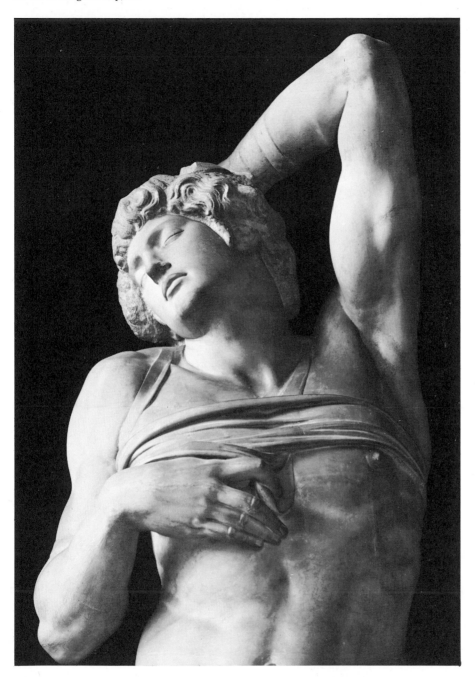

subject of shame and concealment, that body which Alberti had praised so extravagantly – could be made the means of expressing noble sentiments, life-giving energy and God-like perfection. It was an idea that was to have an incalculable influence on the human mind for four hundred years – perhaps we may say until Picasso's *Demoiselles d'Avignon*. Of course it was ultimately a Greek idea: and at first Michelangelo was directly inspired by antique fragments. But not for long. What I might call the Beethoven element – the spirit of the *David*'s head – was soon extended to the body as well.

And this brings us back to Rome, and to the terrible Pope. Julius II was not only ambitious for the Catholic Church: he was ambitious for Julius II, and in his new temple he planned to erect the greatest tomb of any ruler since the time of Hadrian. It was a staggering example of *superbia*; and Michelangelo at that time was not without the same characteristic. I need not go into the question of why the tomb was never built. There was a quarrel – heroes do not easily tolerate the company of other heroes. Nor does it matter to us what the tomb was going to look like. All that matters is that some of the figures made for it survive, and they add something new to the European spirit – something that neither antiquity nor the great civilisations of India and China had ever dreamed of. As a matter of fact the two most finished of them were derived from antiques, but Michelangelo has turned them from athletes into captives, one of them struggling to be free – from mortality? – and the other sensuously resigned [86], 'half in love with easeful death'. Michelangelo had in mind a Greek figure of a dying son of Niobe. These two are carved out in the round, but the others, which are usually assumed to be part of the same set, are unfinished [87]. Their bodies emerge from the marble with the kind of premonitory rumbling that one gets in the Ninth Symphony, and then sink back into it. To some extent the rough marble is like shadow in a Rembrandt – a means of concentrating on the parts that are felt most intensely; but it also seems to imprison the figures – in fact they are always known as the prisoners, although there is no sign of bonds or shackles. As with the finished captives one feels that they express Michelangelo's deepest preoccupation: the struggle of the soul to free itself from matter.

People sometimes wonder why the Renaissance Italians, with their intelligent curiosity, didn't make more of a contribution to the history of thought. The reason is that the most profound thought of the time was not expressed in words, but in visual imagery. Two sublime examples of this truism were produced in the same building in Rome, not more than one hundred yards from each other, and during exactly the same years: Michelangelo's ceiling of the Sistine Chapel and Raphael's frescoes in the room known as the Stanza della Segnatura. Both of them we owe entirely to Julius II. For centuries writers on Michelangelo have criticised Julius for taking him off the tomb, on which he had set his heart, and putting him to work on the painting of the Sistine Ceiling, although he always said he

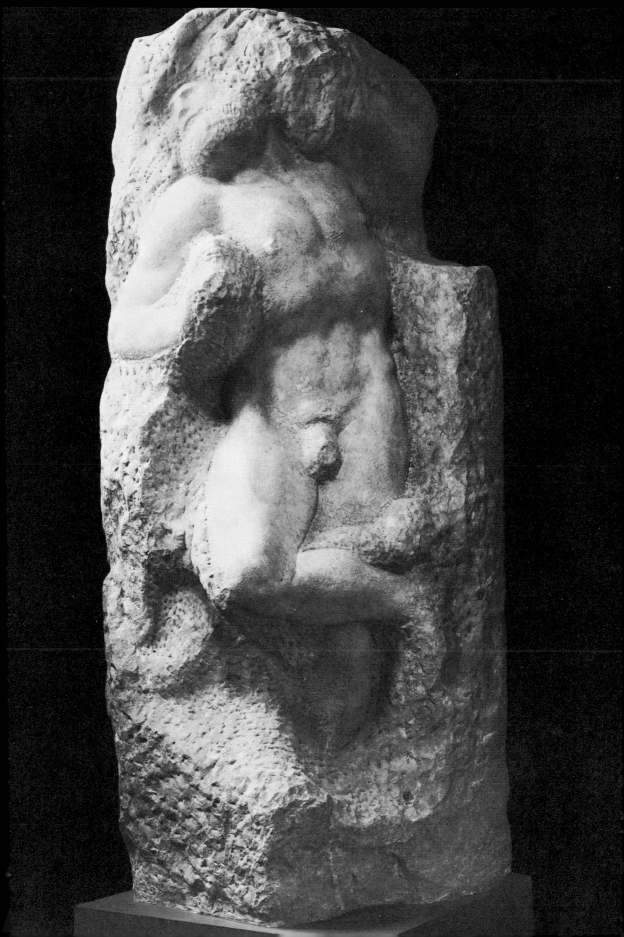

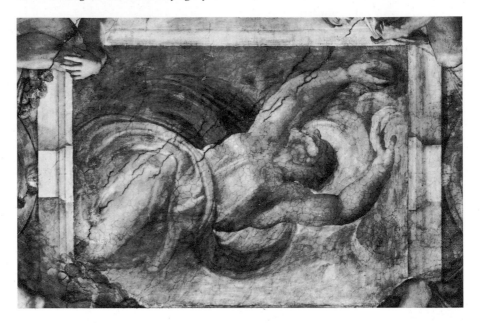

hated the act of painting. I think it was a stroke of inspiration. The original project for the tomb included almost forty marble figures, over life-size. How could Michelangelo ever have completed it? We know that he carved marble faster than any mason, but even with his heroic energy the tomb would have taken twenty years, during which time his mind was changing and developing. And the very fact that, on the Ceiling, he decided to illustrate themes, not simply to concentrate on single figures, freed him to extend his thoughts about human relationships and human destiny. Were they *his* thoughts? In most of the great philosophical paintings of the Renaissance the ideas were suggested by poets and theologians. But in one of Michelangelo's letters he says that the Pope told him to do what he liked, so I suppose that the subject of the Ceiling was largely his own idea: or rather, his own composition from theological sources. This is one reason why it is difficult to interpret. All writers on Michelangelo have given different interpretations, none of which is quite convincing. But one thing is certain. The Sistine Ceiling passionately asserts the unity of man's body, mind and spirit. You can admire it from the point of view of the body – as nineteenth-century critics used to do, who looked first at the so-called athletes; or from the point of view of the mind, as one does when one looks at those great embodiments of intellectual energy, the Prophets and Sibyls. But when one looks at the sequence of stories from Genesis, I think one feels that Michelangelo was chiefly concerned with the spirit. As narrative they begin with the Creation and end with the drunkenness of

Noah. But Michelangelo compels us to read them in reverse order – and indeed they were painted in the reverse order. Over our head as we enter is the figure of Noah, where the body has taken complete possession. At the other end, over the altar, is the Almighty dividing light from darkness [88]: the body has been transformed into a symbol of the spirit, and even the head, with its too evident human associations, has become indistinct.

In between these two scenes comes the central episode, the creation of man [18, facing p. 117]. It is one of those rare works which are both supremely great and wholly accessible, even to those who do not normally respond to works of art. Its meaning is clear and impressive at first sight, and yet the longer one knows it, the deeper it strikes. Man, with a body of unprecedented splendour, is reclining on the ground in the pose of all those river gods and wine gods of the ancient world who belonged to the earth and did not aspire to leave it. He stretches out his hand so that it almost touches the hand of God and an electric charge seems to pass between their fingers. Out of this glorious physical specimen God has created a human soul; and it is possible to interpret the whole of the Sistine Ceiling as a poem on the subject of creation, that god-like gift which so much occupied the thoughts of Renaissance man. Behind the Almighty, in the shadow of his cloak, is the figure of Eve, already in the Creator's thoughts and already, one feels, a potential source of trouble.

After God has brought Adam to life (still reading the sequence in reverse) come scenes of the Almighty in the earlier acts of creation. They form a sort of crescendo, with the movement accelerating from one scene to the next. First of all, God dividing the waters from the earth. 'And the spirit of God moved upon the face of the waters.' I don't know why these words give one such a feeling of peace, but they do, and Michelangelo has conveyed it by a tranquil movement and a gesture of benediction. In the next scene, the creation of sun and moon, he does not bless or evoke, but commands, as if dealing with these fiery elements required all his authority and speed, and to the left he swishes off the scene to create the planets. Finally we are back at the separation of light and darkness. Of all the attempts of finite man to set down an image of infinite energy, this seems to me the most convincing; one might even say the most realistic, because photographs of the formation of stellar nuclei show very much the same swirling movement.

Michelangelo's power of prophetic insight gives one the feeling that he belongs to every epoch, and most of all, perhaps, to the epoch of the great Romantics, of which we are still the almost bankrupt heirs. It is the attribute that distinguishes him most sharply from his brilliant rival. Raphael was a man of his age. He absorbed and combined all that was being felt or

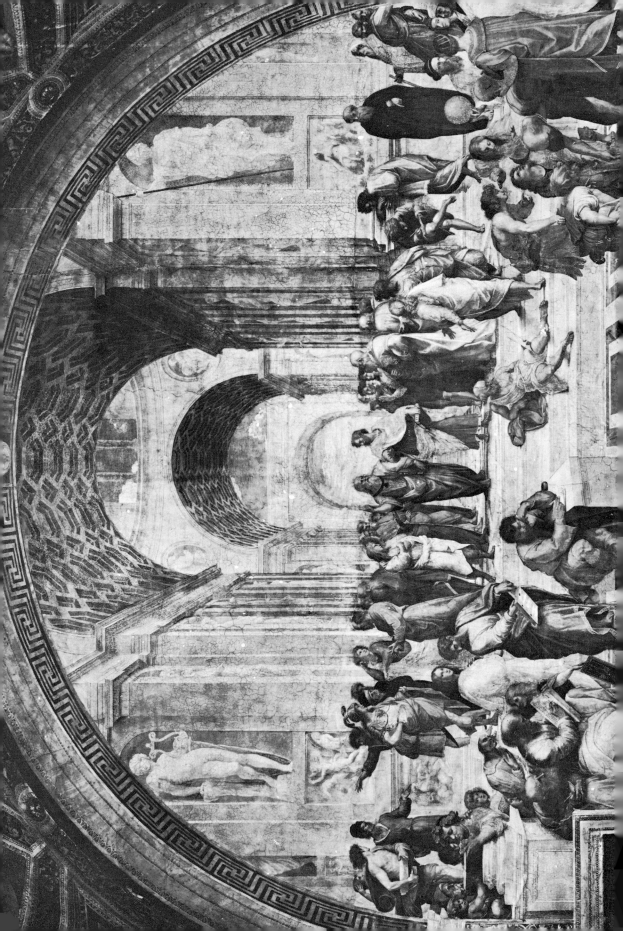

thought by the finest spirits of his time. He is the supreme harmoniser – that's why he is out of favour today. But in an attempt to describe European civilisation he must come right at the top. The thoughts to which he gave visible expression in the papal apartments were a synthesis as all-inclusive as the summaries of the great medieval theologians.

It is reasonable to suppose that Raphael was introduced to the papal service by his fellow townsman, Bramante, who seems to have been on relatively intimate terms with Julius II. The sight of one of Raphael's drawings would have been enough to show Julius that God had presented him with another genius. All the same, it was a bold stroke to take a young man of twenty-seven, who had only once tried his hand at mural painting, and shown no evidence at all that he could cope pictorially with great ideas, and commission him to decorate the rooms which were to be the centre of the Pope's life, his decisions and his meditations.

The Stanza della Segnatura was to be the Pope's private library. Raphael knew the library at Urbino where paintings of poets, philosophers and theologians were placed above the shelves containing their books, and he determined to carry the same idea much further. He would not only portray the figures whose books were in the shelves below, but would relate them to each other and to the whole discipline of which they formed a part. He must have had advice from the learned and cultivated men who made up about a third of the papal curia. But this sublime company wasn't assembled by a committee. Everything in the groups is thought out. For example, of the two central figures in the *School of Athens* [89], Plato the idealist is on the left, and he points upwards to divine inspiration. Beyond him to the left are the philosophers who appealed to intuition and the emotions. They are nearer the figure of Apollo – and they lead on to the wall of the *Parnassus*. To the right is Aristotle, the man of good sense, holding out a moderating hand; and beyond him are the representatives of rational activities – logic, grammar and geometry. Curiously enough, Raphael has put his own portrait in this group, next to that of Leonardo da Vinci. Below them is a geometer [20, facing p. 125] – Euclid, I suppose. This is certainly a portrait of Bramante; and it is fitting that Bramante should be there, because the building in which these representatives of human reason are assembled represents Bramante's dream of the new St Peter's. Raphael was later to become an architect – and a very fine architect – but in 1510 he couldn't possibly have conceived a building like this: one of the most life-enhancing effects of space in art. It may have been designed by Bramante, but Raphael has made it his own. Like all great artists he was a borrower and he absorbed his borrowings more than most. One has a vague feeling that his poses are

89 Raphael, *School of Athens*

inspired by Hellenistic sculpture, but every figure in the Stanze is pure Raphael – or every figure but one. The morose philosopher seated alone in the foreground does not come into the full-size drawing for the fresco (which by a miracle has survived); we can see where he comes from – the Sistine ceiling. Michelangelo would not let anyone in while he was at work there, but Bramante had the key and one day when Michelangelo was away, he took Raphael in with him. Who cares. The great artist takes what he needs.

While Human Reason is rooted to the earth, on the opposite wall Divine Wisdom floats in the sky above the heads of those philosophers, theologians and Church Fathers who have tried to interpret it. In these two flowing groups the seekers after revealed truth are arranged with the same regard for their relations with each other, and with the philosophic scheme of the whole room, that exists in the *School of Athens*. In so far as civilisation consists in grasping imaginatively all that is best in the thought of a time, these two walls represent a summit of civilisation. On the third wall, the fresco of *Parnassus* reveals another side of Raphael's character. Michelangelo took no interest in the opposite sex; Leonardo thought of women solely as reproductive mechanisms. But Raphael loved the girls as much as any

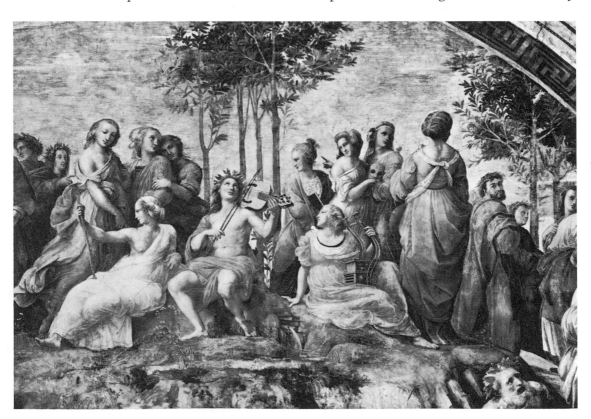

90 Raphaël, *Parnassus* (detail)

Venetian, and his Muses [90] embody a vein of sensuous poetry which, in its way, is as civilising as his intellectual abstractions.

While the rooms of the Vatican were still unfinished, in 1513 Julius II died and his successor, Leo X, was far from being a hero. Michelangelo returned to Florence. Raphael remained in Rome, overstretching his powers of execution and even his matchless powers of invention, handing out drawings and projects to a group of brilliant young men, who turned them into wall-paintings and architectural decorations – the rest of the Stanze, the lunettes in the Farnesina, the Loggie, the Villa Madama, and a very pagan bathroom for the Cardinal Bibiena, to say nothing of the *Transfiguration*, a prophetic work of seventeenth-century academism, which he must have worked on himself: half a century of work in three years. Among them were masterpieces that have added to European imagination, including the greatest evocation of paganism of the Renaissance – the *Galatea* [91] in the Villa Farnesina. Only fifteen years earlier pagan antiquity was still handled awkwardly, with timid, angular gesture: now it is perfectly understood. When Renaissance poets came to write Latin verse (very beautiful Latin verse, too), they had plenty of models. But what wonderful imaginative insight it required for Raphael to recreate from scraps and fragments of sarcophagi a scene that must be very like the great lost paintings of antiquity.

Raphael's other achievement in these years is more questionable, although its influence on the European mind was incomparably greater. One sees it most clearly in the designs [**19**, facing p. 124] he made for a set of tapestries of the Sistine Chapel, representing episodes in the lives of the apostles. The apostles were poor men, their hearers a cross-section of common humanity. Raphael has made them uniformly handsome and noble. It may be good for us to leave our daily chores and inhabit this high plateau for a short time. But the convention by which the great events in biblical or secular history could be enacted only by magnificent physical specimens, handsome and well-groomed, went on for a long time – till the middle of the nineteenth century. Only a very few artists – perhaps only Rembrandt and Caravaggio in the first rank – were independent enough to stand against it. And I think that this convention, which was an element in the so-called grand manner, became a deadening influence on the European mind. It deadened our sense of truth, even our sense of moral responsibility; and led, as we now see, to a hideous reaction.

In the autumn of 1513, soon after the death of Julius, there arrived, to stay in the Belvedere of the Vatican, one more giant – Leonardo da Vinci. Historians used to speak of him as a typical Renaissance man. This is a

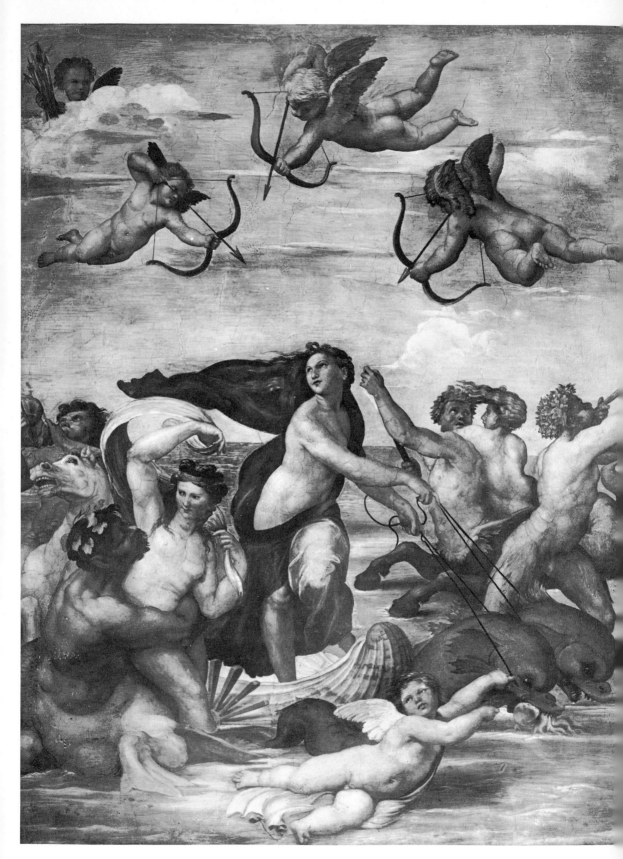

91 Raphael, *Galatea*

mistake. If Leonardo belongs in any epoch it is in the later seventeenth century; but in fact he belongs to no epoch, he fits into no category, and the more you know about him, the more mysterious he becomes. Of course, he had certain Renaissance characteristics. He loved beauty and graceful movement. He shared or even anticipated the megalomania of the early sixteenth century: the horse that he modelled as a memorial to Francesco Sforza was to be twenty-six feet high; he made schemes for diverting the River Arno that even modern technology could not accomplish. And then, of course, he had, to a supreme degree, the gift of his time for recording and condensing whatever took his eye.

But all these gifts were dominated by one ruling passion which was not a Renaissance characteristic – curiosity. He was the most relentlessly curious man in history. Everything he saw made him ask why and how. Why does one find sea-shells in the mountains? How do they build locks in Flanders? How does a bird fly? What accounts for cracks in walls? What is the origin of wind and clouds? How does one stream of water deflect another? Find out; write it down; if you can see it, draw it. Copy it out. Ask the same question again and again and again. Leonardo's curiosity was matched by an incredible mental energy. Reading the thousands of words in Leonardo's note-books, one is absolutely worn out by this energy. He won't take yes for an answer. He can't leave anything alone – he worries it, re-states it, answers imaginary antagonists. Of all these questions, the one he asks most insistently is about man: not the man of Alberti's invocation, with 'wit, reason and memory like an immortal God', but man as a mechanism. How does he walk? He describes how to draw a foot in ten ways, each of which should reveal some different components in its structure. How does the heart pump blood? What happens when he yawns and sneezes? How does a child live in the womb? Finally, why does he die of old age? Leonardo discovered a centenarian in a hospital in Florence, and waited gleefully for his demise so that he could examine his veins. Every question demanded dissection and every dissection was drawn with marvellous precision [92]. At the end, what does he find? That man, although remarkable as a mechanism, is not at all like an immortal god. He is not only cruel and superstitious, but feeble compared to the forces of nature. If Michelangelo's defiance of fate was superb, there is something almost more heroic in the way that Leonardo, that great hero of the intellect, confronts the inexplicable, ungovernable forces of nature. In Rome, in the very year that Raphael was celebrating the god-like human intelligence, Leonardo did a series of drawings of the world overwhelmed by water [93]. The way in which he depicts this disaster shows a strange mixture of relish and defiance. On the one hand he is the

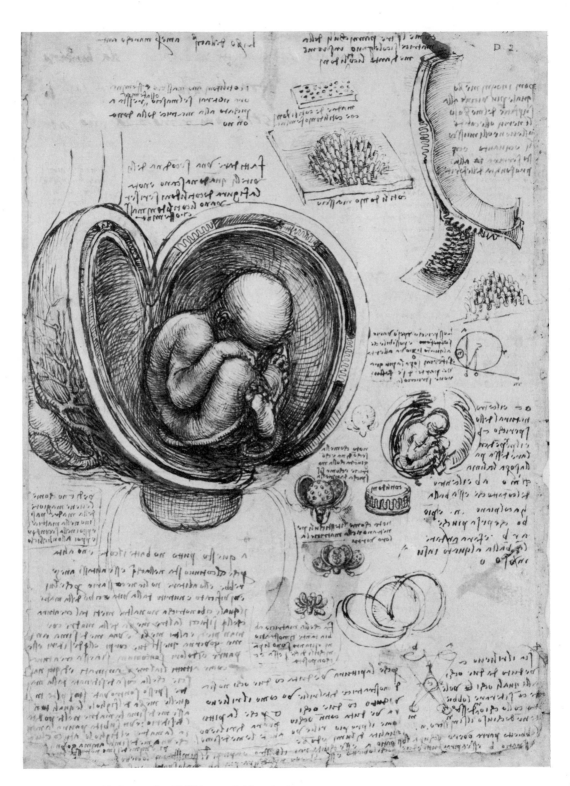

92 Leonardo, *Child in womb* (drawing)

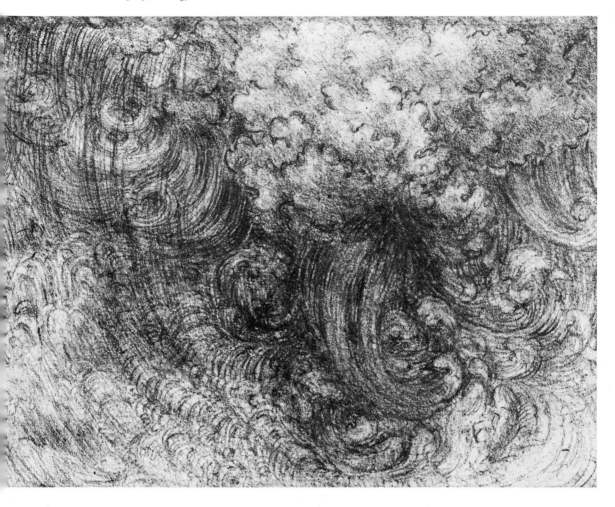

patient observer of hydrodynamics; on the other hand he is King Lear addressing the deluge:

> Blow, winds, and crack your cheeks! rage! blow!
> You cataracts and hurricanoes, spout
> Till you have drench'd our steeples, drown'd the cocks!

We are used to catastrophes; we see them every day on television. But coming from a perfectly endowed man of the Renaissance, these extraordinary drawings are prophetic. The golden moment is almost over. But while it lasted man achieved a stature that he has hardly ever achieved before or since. To the humanist virtues of intelligence was added the quality of heroic will. For a few years it seemed that there was nothing which the human mind could not master and harmonise.

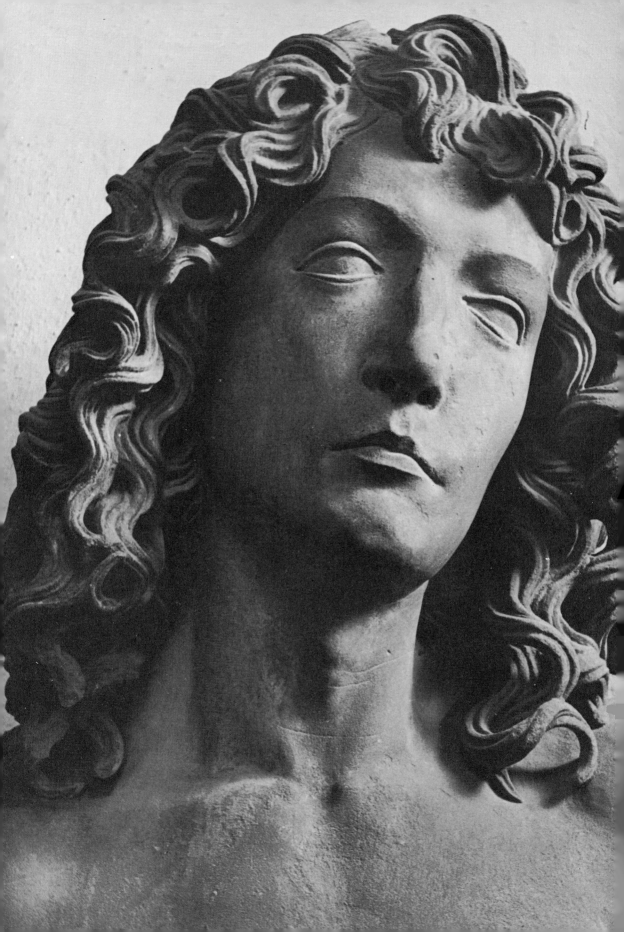

6 Protest and Communication

The dazzling summit of human achievement represented by Michelangelo, Raphael and Leonardo da Vinci lasted for less than twenty years. It was followed (except in Venice) by a time of uneasiness often ending in disaster. For the first time since the great thaw civilised values were questioned and defied, and for some years it looked as if the footholds won by the Renaissance – the discovery of the individual, the belief in human genius, the sense of harmony between man and his surroundings – had been lost. Yet this was an inevitable process, and out of the confusion and brutality of sixteenth-century Europe, man emerged with new faculties and expanded powers of thought and expression.

In this room in the castle of Würzburg are the carvings of Tilman Riemenschneider, one – perhaps the best – of many German carvers in the late Gothic style. The Church was rich in fifteenth-century Germany, and the landowners were rich, and the merchants of the Hanseatic League were rich; and so, from Bergen right down to Bavaria, sculptors were kept busy doing huge, elaborate shrines and altars and monuments like the famous group of St George in the old church at Stockholm: a supreme example of the late Gothic craftsman deploying his fancy and his almost irritating skill of hand.

The Riemenschneider figures [94] show very clearly the character of northern man at the end of the fifteenth century. First of all, a serious personal piety – a quality quite different from the bland conventional piety that one finds, say, in a Perugino. And then a serious approach to life itself. These men (although of course they were unswerving Catholics) were not to be fobbed off by forms and ceremonies – what at the time were, rather misleadingly, called 'works'. They believed that there was such a thing as truth, and they wanted to get at it. What they heard from Papal legates, who did a lot of travelling in Germany at this time, did not convince them that there was the same desire for truth in Rome, and they had a rough, raw-boned peasant tenacity of purpose. Many of these earnest men would have heard about the numerous councils that had tried throughout the fifteenth century to reform the organisation of the Church. I am reminded of them when I attend a meeting of UNO: the time spent on points of procedure, the speeches made for home consumption, the result a foregone conclusion. These grave northern men wanted something more substantial.

94 Riemenschneider, *Adam*

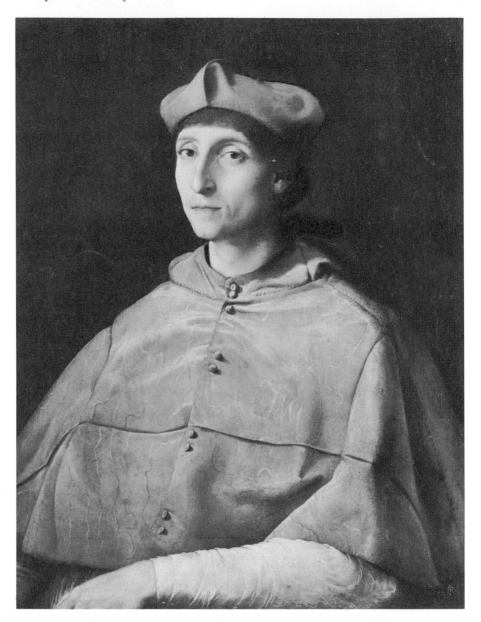

So far so good. But these faces reveal a more dangerous characteristic, a vein of hysteria. The fifteenth century had been the century of revivalism – religious movements on the fringe of the Catholic Church. They had, in fact, begun in the late fourteenth century, when the followers of John Huss almost succeeded in wiping out the courtly civilisation of Bohemia. Even in Italy Savonarola had persuaded his hearers to make a bonfire of their so-called vanities, including pictures by Botticelli: a heavy price to pay for religious conviction. The Germans were much more easily excited. Comparisons are sometimes an over-simplification; but I think it is fair to compare one of the most famous of German portraits, Dürer's Oswald Krell [21, facing p. 156], with Raphael's portrait of a cardinal in the Prado [95]. The cardinal is not only a man of the highest culture but balanced and self-contained. Oswald Krell is on the verge of hysteria. Those staring eyes, that look of self-conscious introspection, that uneasiness, marvellously conveyed by Dürer through the uneasiness of the planes in the modelling — how German it is; and what a nuisance it has been for the rest of the world.

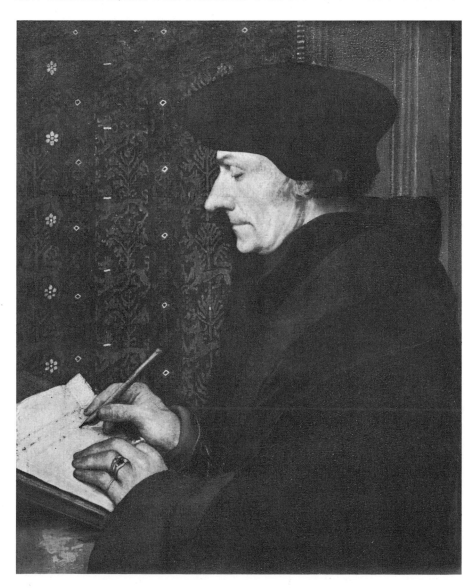

96 Holbein, *Erasmus*

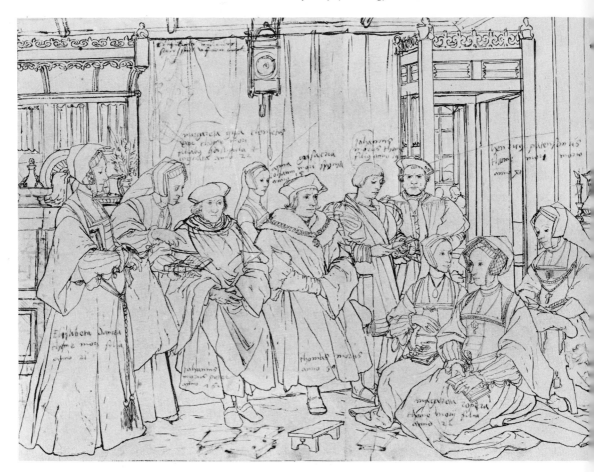

However, in the 1490s these destructive national characteristics had not shown themselves. It was still an age of internationalism. The German printers were working in Italy; Dürer was in Venice; and in 1498 there arrived in Oxford a poor scholar who was destined to become the spokesman of northern civilisation and the greatest internationalist of his day, Erasmus. Erasmus was a Dutchman – he came from Rotterdam – but he never went back to live in Holland, partly because he had been in a monastery there and had hated it, and partly (as he said repeatedly) because people drank too much: he himself had a delicate digestion and would drink only a special kind of Burgundy. All his life he moved from place to place, partly to avoid the plague (that King of Terrors kept all free men on the move throughout the early sixteenth century) and partly due to a restlessness that overcame him if he stayed anywhere too long. However, in his earlier life he seems to have liked England, and so for the first time this country makes a brief appearance in our survey of civilisation. Considering the barbarous and disorderly state of England in the fifteenth century the colleges of Oxford and Cambridge are surprising creations; and I suppose that the Oxford which welcomed Erasmus contained a few (not very many) pious and enlightened men. Of course, the atmosphere must have been somewhat provincial and unsophisticated compared to Florence or even Padua; and yet, in about the year 1500, this kind of naivety had its value, and Erasmus, who was anything but naive, recognised it.

Erasmus had seen enough of the religious life to know that the Church must be reformed, not only in its institutions but in its teachings. The great civiliser of Europe was aground, stranded on forms and vested interests. And he knew that there was more hope of reform from the teachings of a man like Colet, who simply wanted people to read the Bible as if it were true, than from the fine wits of Florence. There were good reasons why Erasmus should admire Colet. But why did Colet and his friends pay such honour to the poor, invalidish, crotchety young scholar from Rotterdam? Well, clearly Erasmus was an intellectual charmer. His charm comes through in his letters and must have been irresistible in his company. By great good fortune we can supplement Erasmus's letters by visible evidence, because he was the friend of the greatest portrait painter of the time, Hans Holbein. His portraits [96] show Erasmus when he had become famous and elderly, but they are so penetrating that we can imagine him at every age. Like all humanists, I might almost say like all civilised men, Erasmus set a high value on friendship, and he was anxious that Holbein should paint pictures of his English friends. So in 1526 Holbein went to London, and was introduced into the circle of Sir Thomas More. The brilliant youth with whom, twenty years earlier, Erasmus had fallen in love, was now Lord Chancellor; he was also author of the *Utopia*, where, in rather a quaint style, the author recommends almost everything that was believed in by the Fabians in the 1890s.

Holbein painted a large picture of Sir Thomas More and his family. Alas, it was burnt, but the original drawing [97] remains, and studies for many of the heads. Erasmus used to say that More's family was like the academy of Plato. They don't look oppressively intellectual, but alert, sensible people of any epoch. Thomas More himself was a noble idealist, too good for the world of action where he sometimes lost his way. It shows how quickly civilisation can appear and disappear that the author of the *Utopia* should have flourished – should have become, against his will, First Minister of the Crown – half way between the death of Richard III and the judicial murders of Henry VIII, of which he, of course, was to be the most distinguished victim.

98 Grünewald, *Isenheim Altar* (detail)

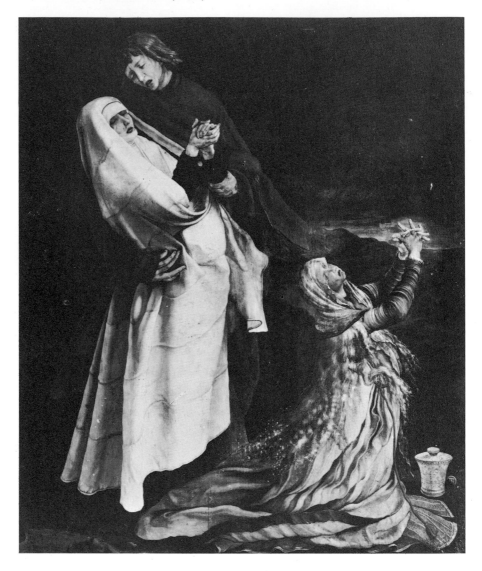

Holbein depicted other members of Erasmus's circle in England, and I'm bound to say that some of them, like the Archbishops Warham and Fisher, look as if they had no illusions about the transitory nature of civilisation in the court of Henry VIII. They look defeated, and they were defeated. Holbein found more placid faces when he returned to Switzerland. Is there a picture in the world that gives a more intimate feeling of family life than the portrait of his wife and children at Basle? No wonder it was such a favourite with the Victorians. The same is true of his masterpiece, the Madonna of Burgomaster Meyer [**22**, facing p. 157]. In the nineteenth century it was considered the greatest picture of the northern Renaissance. Now I suppose everyone would prefer Grünewald's *Isenheim Altar* [98], where the sense of tragedy makes the very word civilisation falter on our lips. But if one is looking for a reasonable god-fearing society, one finds it reflected in the Holbein; and when one stands before the original picture in Darmstadt one is slowly penetrated by a spirit of devotion that goes far beyond the need for material stability.

In 1506 Erasmus went to Italy. He was in Bologna at the exact time of Julius II's famous quarrel with Michelangelo; he was in Rome when Raphael began work on the Papal apartments. But none of this seems to have made any impression on him. His chief interest was in the publication of his works by the famous Venetian printer and pioneer of finely printed popular editions, Aldus Manutius. Whereas in the last chapter I was concerned with the enlargement of man's spirit through the visual image, in this one I am chiefly concerned with the extension of his mind through the word. And this was made possible by the invention of printing. In the nineteenth century people used to think of the invention of printing as the lynchpin in the history of civilisation. Well, fifth-century Greece and twelfth-century Chartres and early fifteenth-century Florence got on very well without it, and who shall say that they were less civilised than we are. Still, on balance I suppose that printing has done more good than harm, and early presses, like those that survive in the Plantin house in Antwerp, do give the impression of instruments of civilisation. Perhaps one's doubts are due to a later development of the craft.

Printing, of course, had been invented long before the time of Erasmus. Gutenberg's Bible was printed in 1455. But the first printed books were large, sumptuous and expensive. The printers still thought of themselves as competing with the scribes of manuscripts. Many of them were printed on vellum and had illuminations, like manuscripts. It took preachers and persuaders almost thirty years to recognise what a formidable new instrument had come into their hands, just as it took politicians twenty years to recognise the value of television. The first man to take full advantage of the printing press was Erasmus. It made him, and unmade him, because in a way he became the first journalist. He had all the qualifications: a clear, elegant style (in Latin, of course, which meant that he could be read everywhere, but not by everyone), opinions on every subject, even the gift of putting things so that they could be interpreted in different ways. He poured out pamphlets and anthologies and introductions; and so in a few years did everyone who had views on anything.

Early in his journalistic career he produced a masterpiece – the *Praise of Folly*. He wrote it staying with his friend Thomas More; he said it took him a week, and I dare say it's true. He had an amazing fluency, and this time his whole being was engaged. It's not unlike Voltaire's *Candide*. To an intelligent man, human beings and human institutions really are intolerably stupid and there are times when his pent-up feelings of impatience and annoyance can't be contained any longer. Erasmus's *Praise of Folly* was a dam-burst of this kind; it washed away everything: popes, kings, monks (of course), scholars, war, theology – the whole lot. On one page there is a marginal drawing [99] by Holbein, showing Erasmus at his desk; Erasmus has written over the drawing that if he was really as handsome as this he wouldn't lack a wife. Not quite convincing. He goes very far – one wonders that it was tolerated; and it's interesting to see certain similarities with Leonardo as when Erasmus mocks those philosophers who 'speak with confidence about the creation of innumerable worlds, measuring sun, moon and stars, and never hesitating for a moment, as though they had been admitted into the secrets of creation: with whom and with whose conjectures nature is mightily amused'. In the ordinary way satire is a negative activity; but there are times in the history of civilisation when it has a positive value, times when a glutinous mixture of conformism and complacency holds the free spirit down. This was the first time in history that a bright-minded intellectual exercise – something to make people stretch their

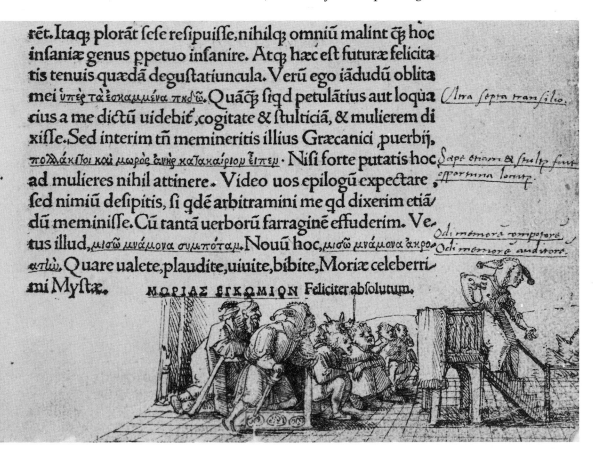

minds, and think for themselves, and question everything – was made available to thousands of readers all over Europe.

However, it was not Erasmus's wit and satire that made him, for ten years, the most famous man in Europe, but rather his appeal to the earnest, pious, truth-seeking state of mind exemplified by the Riemenschneider apostles. After the *Praise of Folly* he devoted himself to theological matters, and did a translation of the New Testament from the original Greek (up to then, of course, it was known only from the Latin of the Vulgate which contained a certain number of mistakes). To thousands of serious men – not only in the north, but in Spain – he seemed to offer a reasonable solution to all their perplexities. Through his scholarship, through his intelligence and through the clarity of his style, he was going to tell them the truth.

During the period in which Erasmus was spreading enlightenment and information through the word, another development of the art of printing was nourishing the imagination: the woodcut. Of course, the illiterate faithful had for centuries been instructed by wall-paintings and

100 Holbein, Drawing from Erasmus's copy of *In Praise of Folly*

stained glass, but the vast multiplication of images that was made possible by the printed woodcut put this form of communication on quite a different footing, at once more widespread and more intimate. As usual the invention coincided with the man. The man was Albrecht Dürer. He was a very strange character. Although born and brought up in the *Meistersingers'* town of Nuremberg, his father was a Hungarian and Dürer was not at all the pious German craftsman figure he was once supposed to be. For one thing he was intensely self-conscious and inordinately vain. His self-portrait [102], now in Madrid, with its ringlets of hair framing a face that insists on its sensibility, is a masterpiece of self-love; and two years later he went even further, by portraying himself in the traditional pose and likeness of Christ. This seems to us rather blasphemous, and Dürer's admirers do not make it much better by explaining that he thought creative power was a divine quality and that he wished to pay homage to his own genius by depicting himself as God. It is true that this belief in the artist as inspired creator was part of the

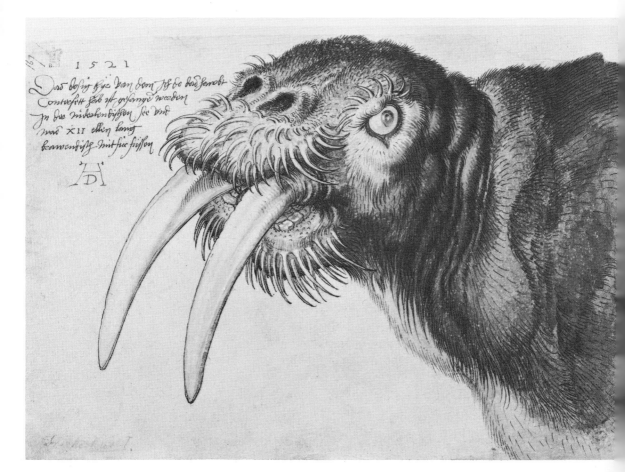

101 Dürer, *Walrus* (watercolour)

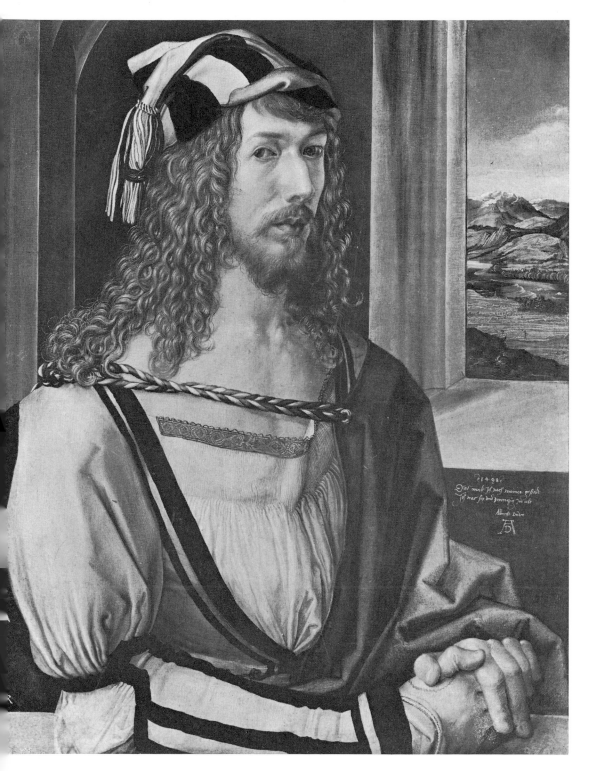

102 Dürer, *Self-portrait*

103 Dürer, *Grasses* (watercolour)

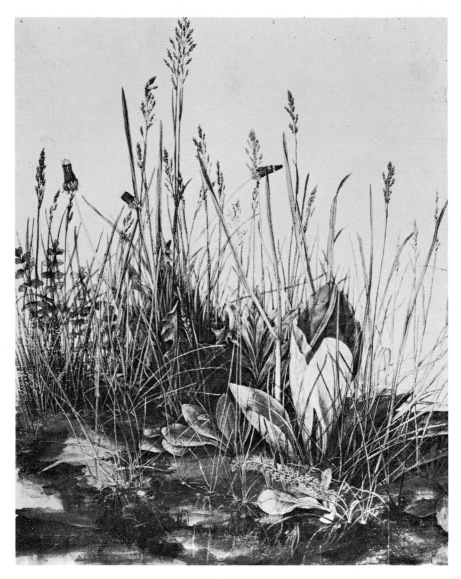

Renaissance spirit and had been invented by the Florentine philosophers. Leonardo talks a lot about it in his treatise on painting; but one can't imagine Leonardo painting himself as Christ.

However Dürer had certain qualities in common with Leonardo. For one thing Dürer also had a vision of a deluge that would wipe out mankind, although his response to it was not defiance, but timid prayer. And then Dürer shared Leonardo's curiosity, although not Leonardo's determination to find out how things worked. He collected all kinds of rarities and oddities, the kind of curiosities which a hundred years later were to lead to the first

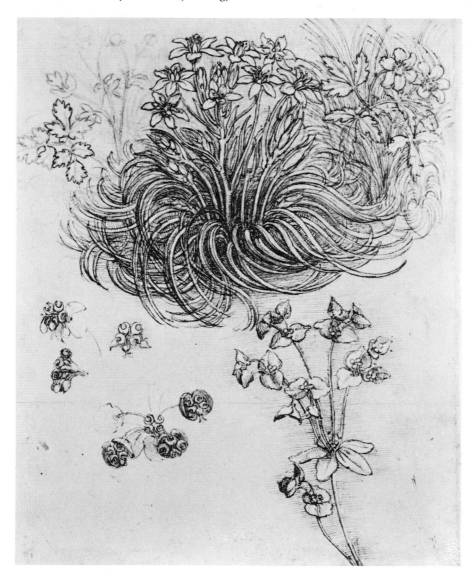

museums. He would go anywhere to see them, and actually died as the result of an expedition to see a stranded whale in Zeeland (he never saw it: it disintegrated before he got there). However, he did see a walrus [101], whose spiny snout delighted him. No man has ever described natural objects, flowers and grasses and animals, more minutely; and yet, to my mind something is missing – the inner life. Compare his famous watercolour of grass [103] with a drawing by Leonardo [104]: how lacking it is in concentration of purpose and in the sense of organic life; it is like the back of a case containing a stuffed animal.

But if Dürer did not try to peer so deeply into the inner life of nature, as Leonardo did, nor feel its appalling independence, he was deeply engaged by the mystery of the human psyche. His obsession with his own personality was part of a passionate interest in psychology in general, and this led him to produce one of the great prophetic documents of western man, the engraving he entitled *Melancholia I* [105]. In the Middle Ages melancholia meant a simple combination of sloth, boredom and despondency that must

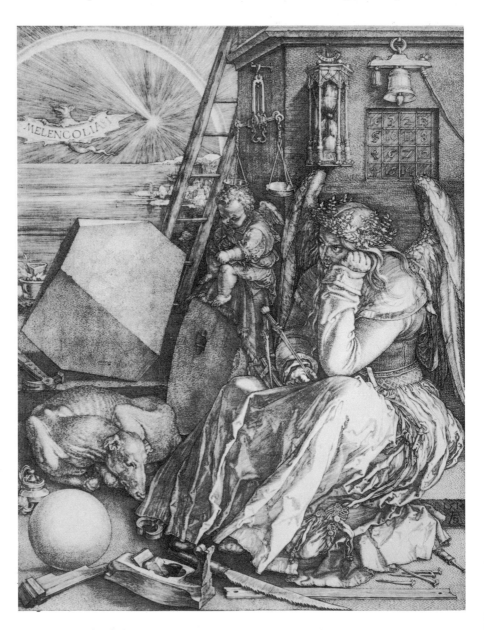

105 Dürer, *Melancholia I* (engraving)

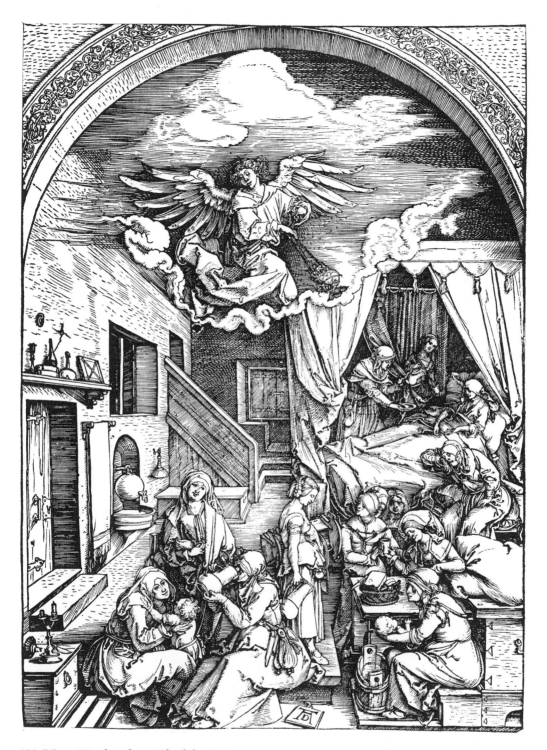

106 Dürer, Woodcut from *Life of the Virgin*

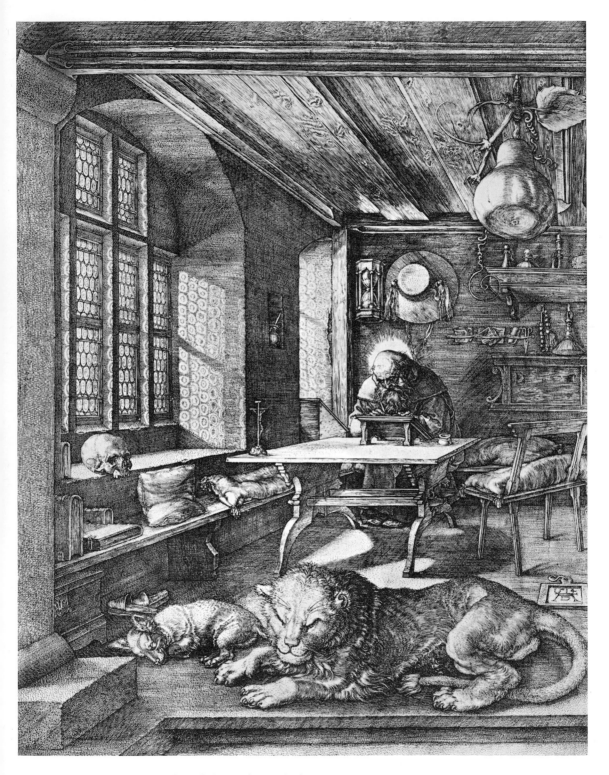

107 Dürer, *St Jerome* (engraving)

have been common in an illiterate society. But Dürer's application is far from simple. This figure is humanity at its most evolved, with wings to carry her upwards. She sits in the attitude of Rodin's *Penseur*, and still holds in her hands the compasses, symbols of measurement by which science will conquer the world. Around her are all the emblems of constructive action: a saw, a plane, pincers, scales, a hammer, a melting pot, and two elements in solid geometry, a polyhedron and sphere. Yet all these aids to construction are discarded and she sits there brooding on the futility of human effort. Her obsessive stare reflects some deep psychic disturbance. The German mind that produced Dürer and the Reformation also produced psychoanalysis. I began by mentioning the enemies of civilisation: well, here, in Dürer's prophetic vision, is one more way in which it can be destroyed, from within.

However, what made Dürer so important in his own age was that he combined an iron grip on the facts of appearance with an extremely fertile invention. His woodcuts and engravings of sacred subjects carried absolute conviction. Also, as time went on, he became absolute master of all the techniques of his day, and in particular the science of perspective, which he used not simply as an intellectual game, as the early Florentines had done, but in order to increase the sense of reality. His woodcuts diffused a new way of looking at art, not as something magical or symbolic, but as something accurate and factual. I don't doubt that the many simple people who bought his woodcuts of the life of the Virgin [106] accepted them as a correct record.

Dürer was immersed in the intellectual life of his time. In the same year that Erasmus completed his translation of St Jerome's letters, Dürer did an engraving of the saint at work [107] in a typically Erasmian room, clear, sunny, orderly, and with lots of cushions, which they don't give you in monasteries. An even more striking reference to Erasmus is in the engraving of *The Knight, Death and the Devil* [108]. One of Erasmus's most widely read books, *Manual of the Christian Knight*, was almost certainly in Dürer's mind when he did the engraving because he writes in a diary that refers to the engraving: 'O Erasmus of Rotterdam, where wilt thou take thy stand. Hark, thou knight of Christ, ride forth at the side of Christ our Lord, protect the truth, obtain the martyr's crown.' Well, that wasn't Erasmus's line: and the grimly determined knight in his heavy Gothic armour, forging ahead, oblivious of the two rather grotesque terrors that accost him, is as far removed as possible from the agile intelligence, the nervous side-glances of the great scholar.

For fifteen years Dürer's cry to Erasmus was echoed by his contempor-

108 Dürer, *The Knight, Death and the Devil* (engraving)

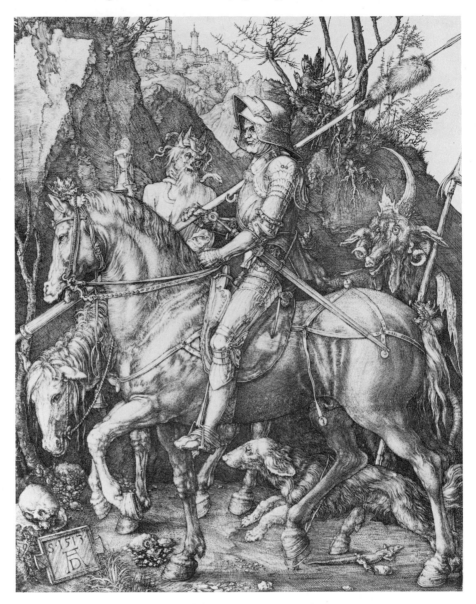

aries all over Europe, and it still appears in old-fashioned history books. Why didn't Erasmus intervene? He would have answered that he wanted above all to avoid a violent split down the middle of the civilised world. He didn't think a revolution would make people any happier – and in fact revolutions seldom do. In one of his letters written soon after Dürer had done his portrait, he says of the Protestants: 'I have seen them return from hearing a sermon as if inspired by an evil spirit. The faces of all showed a curious wrath and ferocity.' Although he seems to us so modern, he actually

21 Dürer, *Oswald Krell*

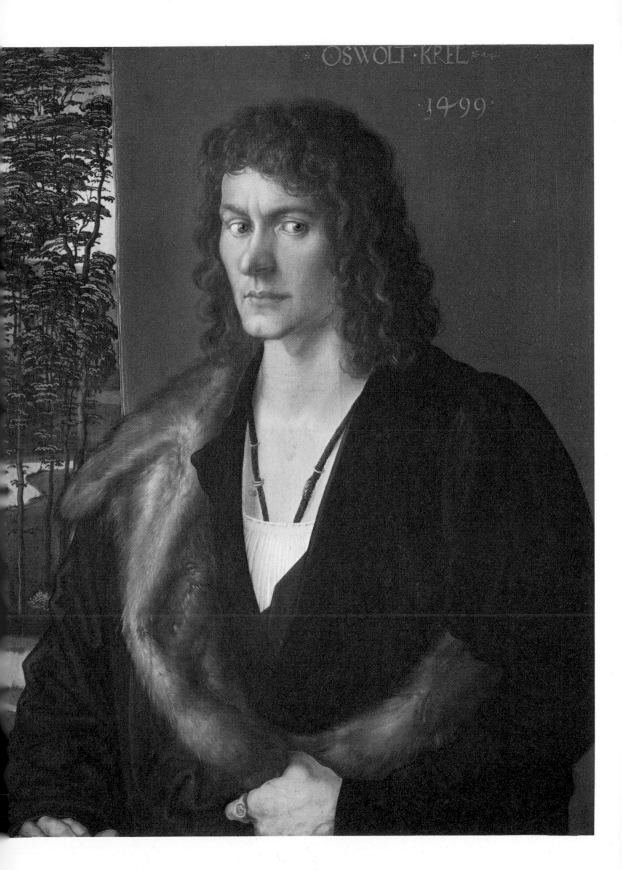

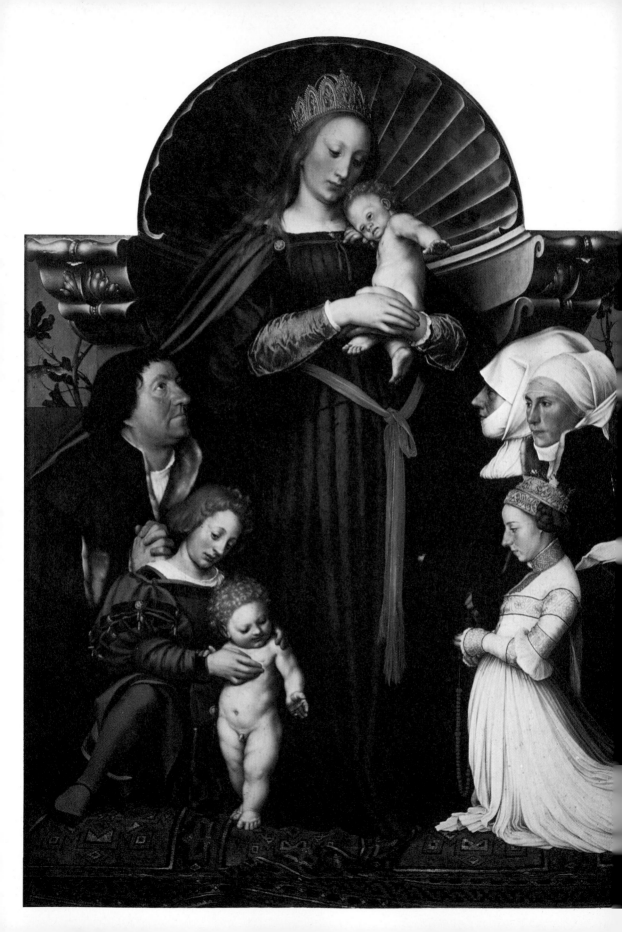

lived beyond his time. He was by nature a man of the preceding century – a humanist in the wider sense, like Pius II. The heroic world that came to birth in Florence in the year 1500 was not his climate. To my mind the extraordinary thing is what a huge following he had and how close Erasmus, or the Erasmian point of view, came to success. It shows that many people, even in a time of crisis, yearn for tolerance and reason and simplicity of life – in fact for civilisation. But on the tide of fierce emotional and biological impulses they are powerless. So almost twenty years after the heroic spirit was made visible in the work of Michelangelo, it appeared in Germany in the words and actions of Luther.

Whatever else he may have been, Luther was a hero; and after all the doubts and hesitations of the humanists, and the hovering flight of Erasmus, it is with a real sense of emotional relief that we hear Luther say: 'Here I stand.' We can see what this burning spirit was like, because the local painter of Wittenberg, Lucas Cranach, was one of Luther's most trusted friends. It was a much closer friendship than that of Erasmus and Holbein. They were godfathers to each other's children, and Cranach portrayed Luther in all his changing aspects – the tense spiritually struggling monk; the great theologian with the coarse peasant's jaw and the brow of Michelangelo [109]; the emancipated layman, painted at the time of his marriage

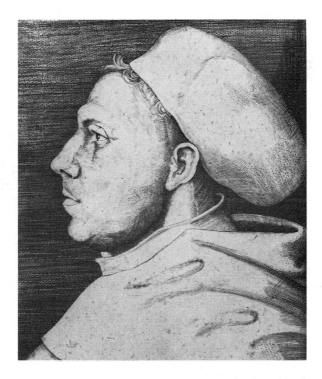

109 Cranach, *Martin Luther* (engraving)

22 Holbein, *Madonna of Burgomaster Meyer*

to an admirable and intelligent nun (Cranach was a witness); even in the disguise he wore when he escaped incognito to Wittenberg. No doubt he was extremely impressive, the leader for which the earnest German people is always waiting.

Unfortunately for civilisation he not only settled their doubts and gave them the courage of their convictions: he also released that latent violence and hysteria that I mentioned earlier. And beyond this was another northern characteristic that was fundamentally opposed to civilisation: an earthy, animal hostility to reason and decorum that Nordic man seems to have retained from his days in the primeval forest. Look at this old Troll King [110], who seems to have grown out of the earth: that's Luther's

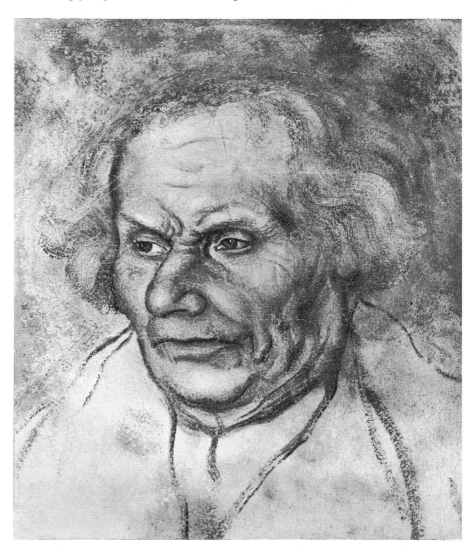

110 Cranach, *Luther's father*

father (in fact he did come up out of the earth – he was a miner), painted by Cranach.

H. G. Wells once made a distinction between communities of obedience and communities of will; he thought that the first produced the stable societies like Egypt and Mesopotamia, the original homes of civilisation, and that the second produced the restless nomads of the north. He may have been right, in so far as any generalisation of this kind can be right. The community of will which we call the Reformation was basically a popular movement. At the end of Erasmus's letter in which he describes the surly Protestants coming out of church, he adds that none of them, except one old man, raised his hat. Erasmus was against forms and ceremonies in religion, but when it came to society he felt differently; and so, strangely enough, did Luther. The great popular uprising, known as the Peasants' Revolt, filled him with horror and he urged his princely patrons to put it down with the utmost ferocity. Luther didn't approve of destruction, not even the destruction of images. But most of his followers were men who owed nothing to the past – to whom it meant no more than an intolerable servitude. And so Protestantism became destructive, and, from the point of view of those who love what they see, was an unmitigated disaster.

We all know about the destruction of images – what we nowadays call works of art; how commissioners went round to even the humblest parish church and smashed everything of beauty it contained, not only images, but carved font-covers, reredoses – anything within reach, because it didn't pay them to stay too long on a single job. You can see the results in almost every old church and cathedral in England, and a good many in France. For example, in the Lady Chapel at Ely, all the glass was smashed, and as the beautiful series of carvings of the life of the Virgin was in reach they knocked off every head – made a thorough job of it. I suppose the motive wasn't so much religious as an instinct to destroy anything comely, anything that reflected a state of mind that an unevolved man couldn't share. The existence of these incomprehensible values enraged them. But it had to happen. If civilisation was not to wither, or petrify, like the society of ancient Egypt, it had to draw life from deeper roots than those which had nourished the intellectual and artistic triumphs of the Renaissance. And ultimately a new civilisation was created – but it was a civilisation not of the image, but of the word.

There can be no thought without words. Luther gave his countrymen words. Erasmus had written solely in Latin. Luther translated the Bible into German – noble German, too, as far as I can judge – and so gave people not only a chance to read Holy Writ for themselves, but the tools of thought.

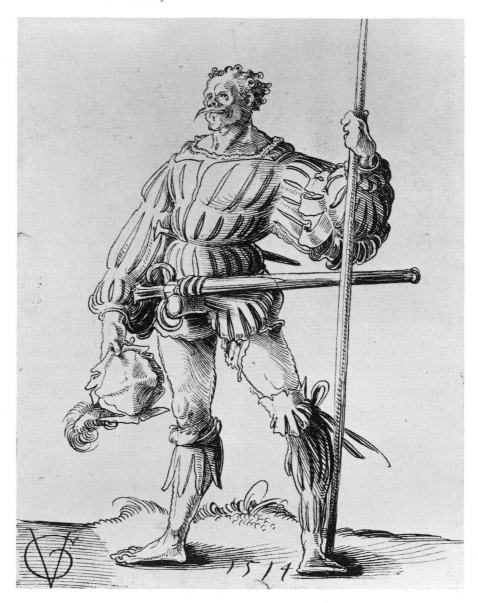

And the medium of printing was there to make it accessible. The translations of the Bible, by Calvin into French, by Tyndale and Coverdale into English, were crucial in the development of the western mind; and if I hesitate to say to the development of civilisation, it is because they were also a stage in the growth of nationalism, and as I have said, and shall go on saying, nearly all the steps upward in civilisation have been made in periods of internationalism. But whatever the long-term effects of Protestantism, the immediate results were very bad: not only bad for art, but bad for life. The North was full of bully boys who rampaged about the country and took any excuse to beat people up. They appear frequently in sixteenth-century German art [111], very pleased with themselves and apparently much admired. All the elements of destruction were let loose. Thirty years earlier Dürer had done a series of woodcuts illustrating the Apocalypse [112].You can say that they express the Gothic side of his nature – because the Apocalypse had been a favourite work of the Middle Ages. Or you can regard them as prophetic, because they show with terrifying precision the horrors that were to descend on Western Europe, both sides proclaiming themselves as the instruments of God's wrath. Fire rains down from heaven on kings, popes, monks and poor families; and those who escape the fire fall victim to the avenging sword. It's a terrible thought that so-called wars of religion, religion of course being used as a pretext for political ambitions, but still providing a sort of emotional dynamo, went on for one hundred and twenty years, and were accompanied by such revolting episodes as the massacre of St Bartholomew. No wonder that the art of the time, which has recently and ominously come back into fashion under the catch-penny title of Mannerism, should have abandoned all that belief in the decency and high destiny of man that had been achieved in the Renaissance. Play it for kicks: that is the mannerist motto, and like all forms of indecency, it's irresistible.

What could an intelligent, open-minded man do in mid-sixteenth-century Europe? Keep quiet, work in solitude, outwardly conform, inwardly remain free. The wars of religion evoked a figure new to European civilisation, although familiar in the great ages of China: the intellectual recluse. Petrarch and Erasmus had used their brains at the highest level of politics. They had been the advisers of princes. Their successor, the greatest humanist of the mid-sixteenth century, retreated into his tower (it was a real tower, not the 'ivory tower' of cliché language). This was Michel de Montaigne. He was a fairly conscientious mayor of Bordeaux; but he refused to go any nearer to the centre of power. He had no illusions about the effect of the religious convictions released by the Reformation. 'In trying to make themselves angels,' he said, 'men transform themselves into beasts.'

He was born in southern France in 1533. His mother was a Jewish Protestant, his father a Catholic who achieved wide culture as well as a considerable fortune. But Montaigne was not only detached from the two religious factions: he was completely sceptical about the Christian religion altogether. He said: 'I would willingly carry a candle in one hand for St Michael and a candle for his Dragon in the other.' His essays are as crammed with quotations as are the tracts of the warring priests, but instead of being texts from the Bible they are quotations from the authors of Greece and Rome, whose

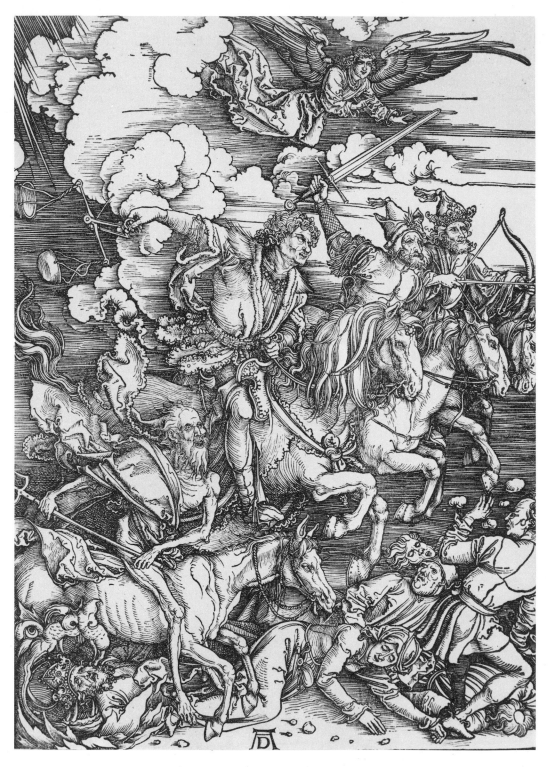

112 Dürer, *Apocalypse* (woodcut)

works he seems to have known almost by heart. But far more important than this Classical learning was his unequalled detachment. Only two emotions had stirred his heart, his love of his father, and his friendship, like that of Tennyson for Hallam, for a man named La Boétie; and when they had both died, he retired into himself. Only one thing engaged his mind – to tell the truth. But it was a concept of truth very different from that which serious men had sought in Colet's sermons or Erasmus's New Testament. It involved always looking at the other side of every question, however shocking, by conventional standards, that other side might be. And it was a truth that depended on the testimony of the only person he could examine without shame or scruple, himself. In the past, self-examination had been painful and penetential. To Montaigne it was a pleasure, and as he says: 'No pleasure hath any savour unless I can communicate it.' In order to do so he invented the essay, which was to remain the accepted form of humanist communication for three centuries, from Bacon to Hazlitt.

These self-searchings really mark the end of the heroic spirit of the Renaissance. As Montaigne says, 'Sit we upon the highest throne in the world, yet sit we only upon our own tail.' The strange thing is that people on high thrones didn't resent Montaigne: on the contrary, they sought his company. Had he lived, his friend Henry IV might have forced him to become Chancellor of France. But he preferred to remain in his tower.

Such was the egocentric isolation that the wars of religion forced on the most civilised man in late sixteenth-century Europe. But there was one country in which, after 1570, men could live without fear of civil war or sudden revenge (unless they happened to be Jesuit priests) – England. I suppose it is debatable how far Elizabethan England can be called civilised. Certainly it does not provide a reproducible pattern of civilisation as does, for example, eighteenth-century France. It was brutal, unscrupulous and disorderly. But if the first requisites of civilisation are intellectual energy, freedom of mind, a sense of beauty and a craving for immortality, then the age of Marlowe and Spenser, of Dowland and Byrd, was a kind of civilisation. It also produced a fantastic architecture [113], palaces of glass and stone, rich embroideries of black and white [114], unmoated, vulnerable, intolerably draughty, but designed to give men a free relationship with nature and with each other, which architecture has tried to regain in our own day.

This is the background of Shakespeare. Of course I can't compress Shakespeare into the scale of these soliloquies. But I can't altogether omit him, because one of the first ways in which I would justify civilisation is that it can produce a genius on this scale. In his freedom of mind, in his power of

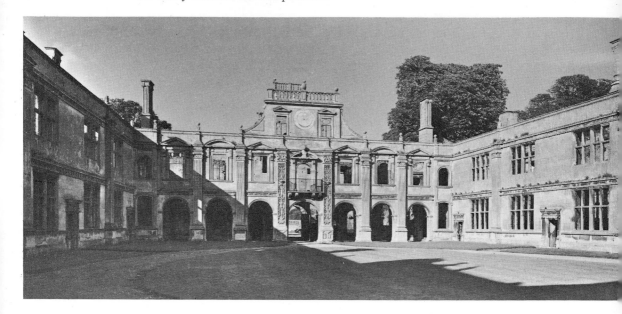

self-identification, in his complete absence of any dogma, Shakespeare sums up and illuminates the piece of history that I have just described. His mature plays are, amongst other things, the poetical fulfilment of Montaigne's intellectual honesty; in fact, we know that Florio's translation of Montaigne made a deep impression on Shakespeare. But Shakespeare's scepticism was more complete and more uncomfortable. Instead of Montaigne's detachment, there is a spirit of passionate engagement; and instead of the essay, there is the urgent communication of the stage.

> Thou rascal beadle, hold thy bloody hand!
> Why doest thou lash that whore?
> Strip thine own back;
> Thou hotly lust to use her in that kind
> For which thou whipst her . . .
> None does offend, none – I say none.

Pure Montaigne – with a difference. And then Shakespeare must be the first and may be the last supremely great poet to have been without a religious belief, even without the humanist's belief in man. In contrast to Alberti's invocation, quoted on p. 89, is Hamlet's soliloquy

What a piece of work is man! how noble in reason! how infinite in faculties! in form and moving how express and admirable! in action how like an angel! in apprehension how like a god! the beauty of the world! the paragon of animals! And yet, to me, what is this quintessence of dust? man delights not me.

There have been great pessimists since his time – Leopardi, Baudelaire – but
who else has felt so strongly the absolute meaninglessness of human life?

> Tomorrow and tomorrow and tomorrow
> Creeps in this petty pace from day to day,
> To the last syllable of recorded time,
> And all our yesterdays have lighted fools
> The way to dusty death. Out, out, brief candle;
> Life's but a walking shadow; a poor player
> That struts and frets his hour upon the stage
> And then is heard no more: it is a tale
> Told by an idiot; full of sound and fury,
> Signifying nothing.

How unthinkable before the break-up of Christendom, the tragic split that
followed the Reformation; and yet I feel that the human mind has gained a
new greatness by outstaring this emptiness.

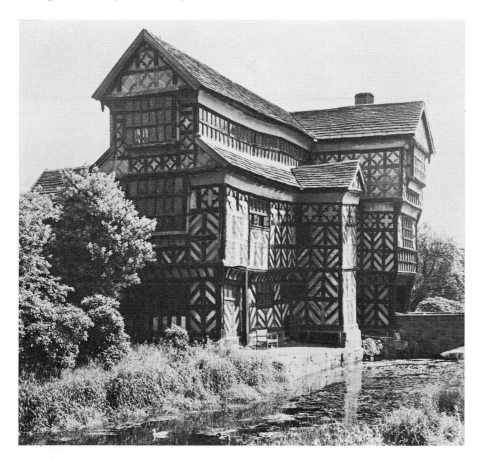

114 Little Moreton Hall, Cheshire

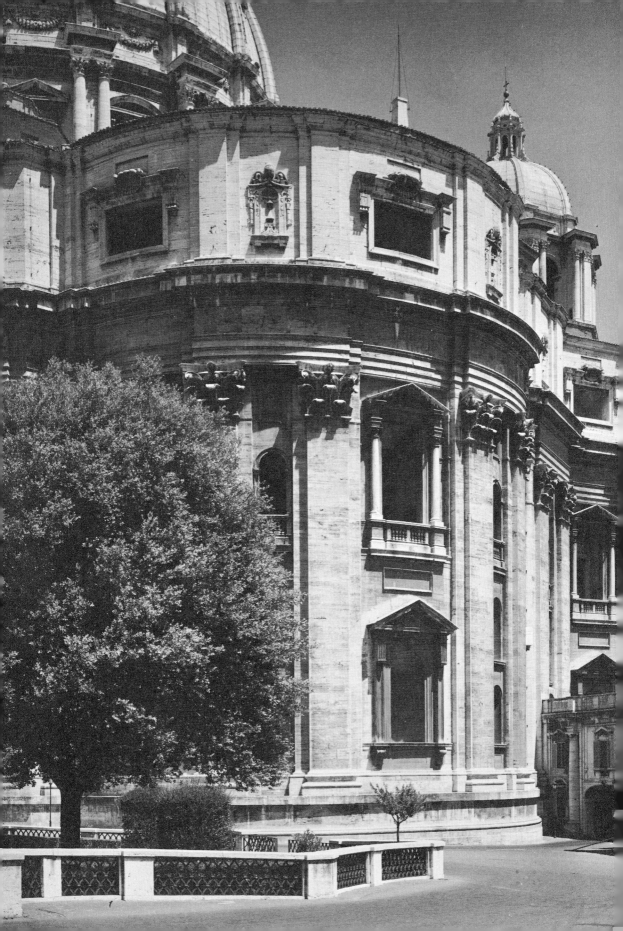

7 Grandeur and Obedience

I am back in Rome, standing on the steps of the ancient church of Santa Maria Maggiore. The hellish Roman traffic swirls all round it, but inside [116] are the original columns of the fifth-century basilica, and above them the mosaics of Old Testament stories that are almost the earliest illustrations of the Bible that exist. Since old St Peter's was pulled down and the Lateran disguised in stucco, there is nowhere else in Rome where one gets such a powerful impression of the Christian Church before the barbarian conquests. This is the grandeur that the Roman Church had once achieved and was to achieve again. If one climbs to the roof of Santa Maria Maggiore one can see long straight streets, stretching for miles up and down, and each ending in a piazza containing a famous church – the Lateran, the Trinità dei Monti, Santa Croce in Gerusalemme – and in the piazzas are Egyptian obelisks, symbols of the first civilisation and god-directed state which Rome had superseded. This is Papal Rome as it was to remain until the present century, the most grandiose piece of town planning ever attempted. The amazing thing is that it was done only fifty years after Rome had been (as it seemed) completely humiliated – almost wiped off the map. The city had been sacked and burnt, the people of Northern Europe were heretics, the Turks were threatening Vienna. It could have seemed to a far-sighted intellectual (like the French intellectuals in 1940) that the Papacy's only course was to face the facts, and accept its dependence on the gold of America, doled out through Spain.

Well, this didn't happen. Rome and the Church of Rome regained many of the territories it had lost, and, what is more important to us, became once more a great spiritual force. But was it a civilising force? In England we tend to answer no. We have been conditioned by generations of liberal, Protestant historians who tell us that no society based on obedience, repression and superstition can be really civilised. But no one with an ounce of historical feeling or philosophic detachment can be blind to the great ideals, to the passionate belief in sanctity, to the expenditure of human genius in the service of God, which are made triumphantly visible to us with every step we take in Baroque Rome. Whatever it is, it isn't barbarian or provincial. Add to this that the Catholic revival was a popular movement, that it gave ordinary people a means of satisfying, through ritual, images and symbols, their deepest impulses, so that their minds were at peace; and I

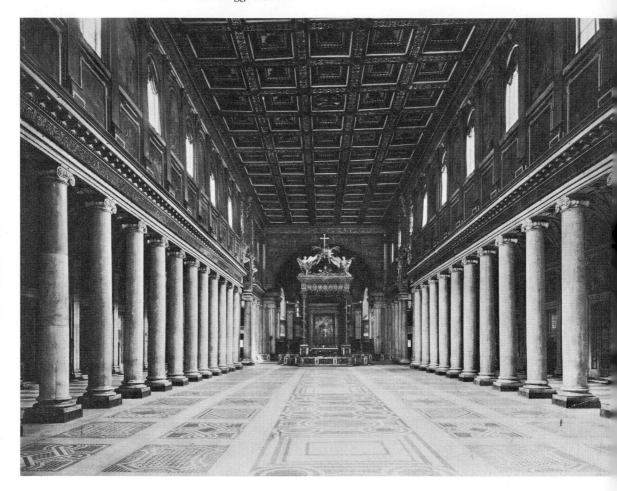

think one must agree to put off defining the word civilisation till we have looked at the Rome of the Popes.

The first thing that strikes one is that those who say the Renaissance had exhausted the Italian genius are very wide of the mark. After 1527 there was a failure of confidence; and no wonder. Historians may say that the Sack of Rome was more a symbol than a historically significant event: well, symbols sometimes feed the imagination more than facts – anyway the Sack was real enough to anyone who witnessed it. If you compare the lower part of Michelangelo's *Last Judgement* [117], which was commissioned by Clement VII as a kind of atonement for the Sack, with a group in Raphael's *Disputa* or with the *Creation of Adam*, you can see that something very drastic has happened to the imagination of Christendom.

Michelangelo had been reluctant to undertake the *Last Judgement*; under Clement's successor, Pope Paul III, Farnese, he was persuaded to continue it

117 Michelangelo, *Last Judgement* (detail)

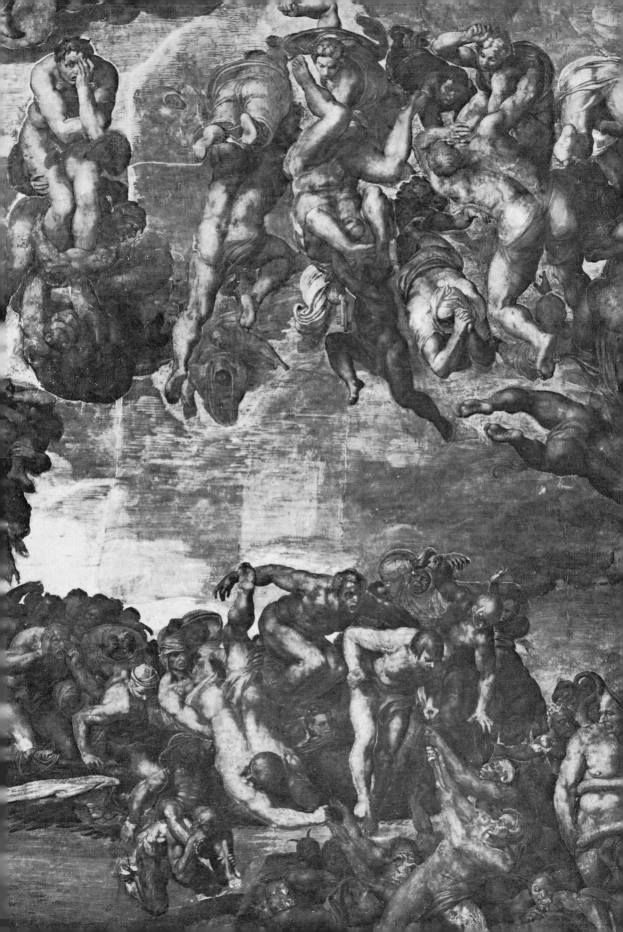

although with a rather different purpose. It ceased to be an act of atonement, or an attempt to externalise a bad dream, and became the first and greatest assertion of the Church's power, and of the fate that would befall heretics and schismatics. It belongs to a period of severity, when the Catholic Church was approaching its problems in rather the same puritanical spirit as the Protestants. It is curious that the period should have been inaugurated by Paul III because, in many ways, he was the last of the humanist Popes. He was cradled in corruption. He was made a cardinal because his sister, known as La Bella, had been the mistress of Alexander Borgia. In culture and sympathy he was a man of the Renaissance. At first sight he seems a crafty old fox, but if you look at Titian's portrait of him [23, facing p. 172] in Naples – one of the greatest portraits ever painted – it is a wise old head, and the longer you look, the more impressive it becomes. And he took the two decisions that were successfully to counter the Reformation: he sanctioned the Jesuit order and he instituted the Council of Trent.

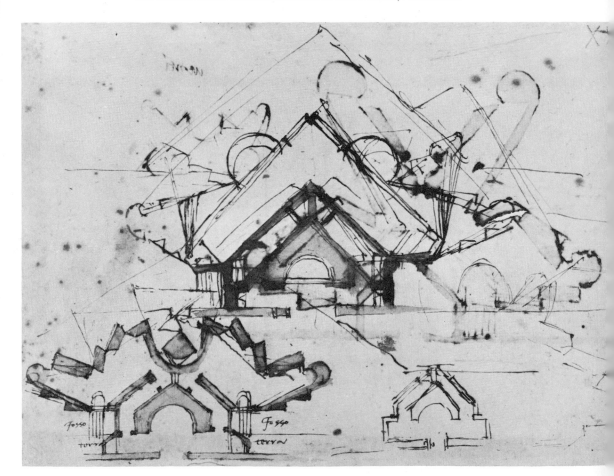

118 Michelangelo, *Plan of Fortifications*

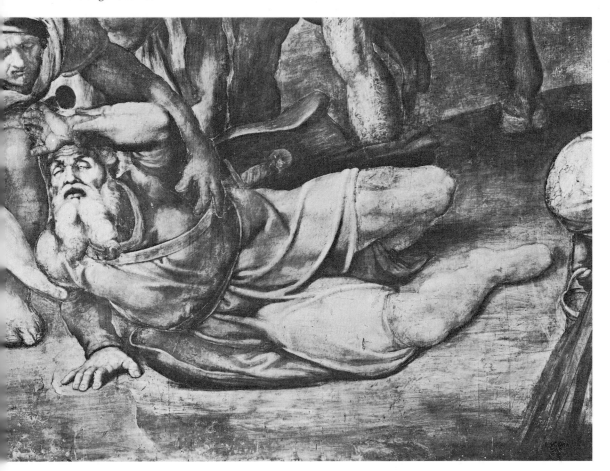

Michelangelo could refuse him nothing: he not only finished the *Last Judgement*, but also painted the mysterious, awe-inspiring frescoes in the Pauline Chapel [119], where, in the head of St Paul, he has shown the pain of spiritual sight and its antecedent blindness, made more moving by the fact that it is an idealised self-portrait. In 1546 he accepted from Pope Paul the post of overseer for the construction of St Peter's. Thus Michelangelo, by his longevity no less than by his genius, became the spiritual link between the Renaissance and the Counter-Reformation.

One of the reasons why medieval and Renaissance architecture is so much better than our own is that the architects were artists. The master masons of the Gothic cathedrals started as carvers working on the portals. In the Renaissance Brunellesco was originally a sculptor, Bramante a painter; Raphael, Peruzzi and Giulio Romano were all painters who became architects in middle life. Of the great architects of seventeenth-century Rome, Pietro da Cortona was a painter and Bernini was a sculptor; and this has

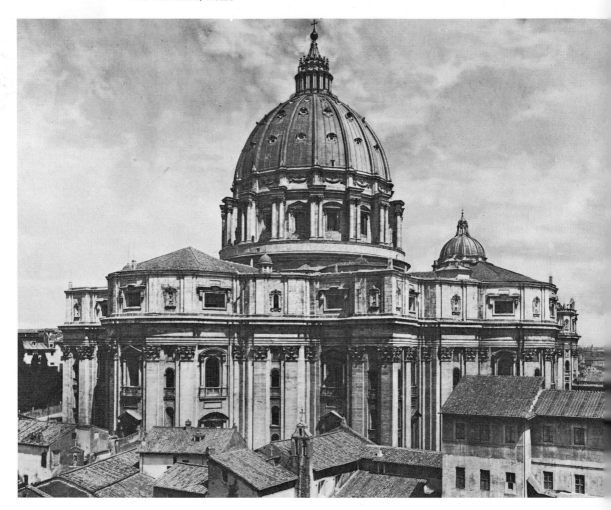

given to their work a power of plastic invention, a sense of proportion and an articulation based on the study of the human figure, which knowledge of the tensile strength of steel, and other requisites of modern building, do not always produce.

Of all non-professional architects Michelangelo was the most adventurous, the least constrained by either classicism or functional requirements. Not that he was unpractical – he did drawings for the fortification of Florence [118] which by standards of military necessity are most ingenious, and are also like the most superb abstract works of art. Perhaps only Michelangelo had the energy of spirit to pull together the vast inchoate mass of St Peter's. Four admirable architects had worked on it before him; the central piers were already built and part of the surrounding walls; but he was able

23 Titian, *Paul III*

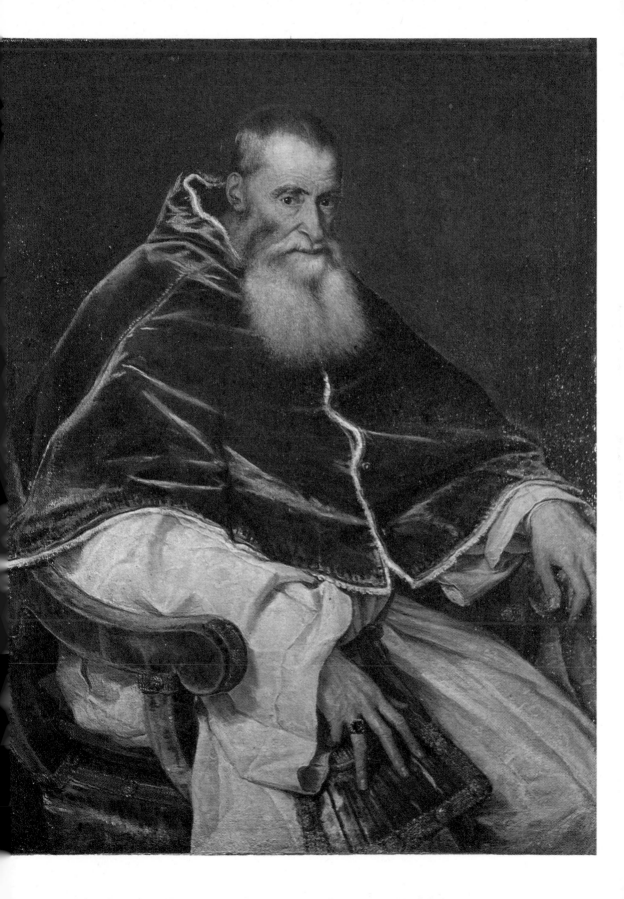

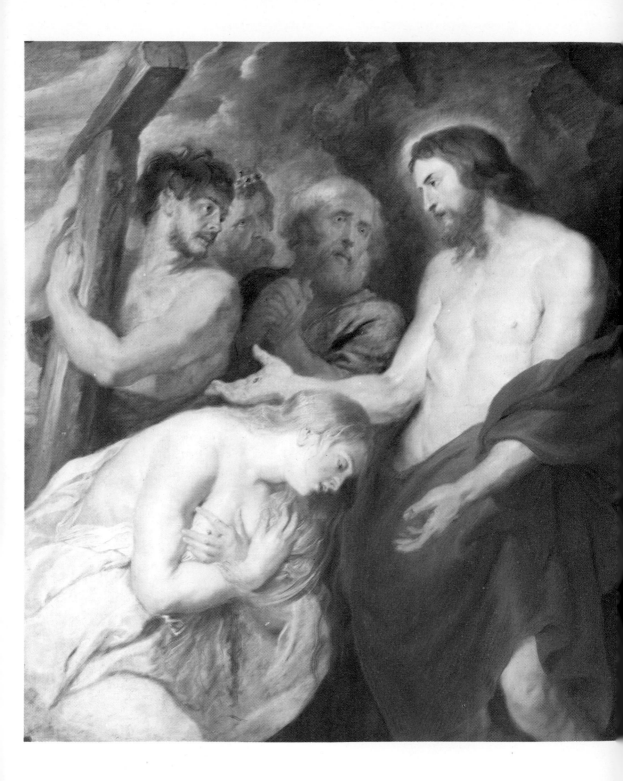

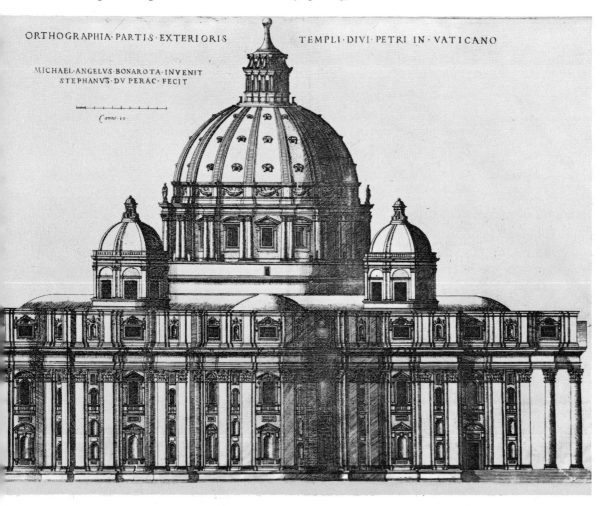

ORTHOGRAPHIA·PARTIS·EXTERIORIS   TEMPLI·DIVI·PETRI·IN·VATICANO

MICHAEL·ANGELVS·BONAROTA·INVENIT
STEPHANVS·DV·PERAC·FECIT

to give it the unifying stamp of his own character. It is the most sculptural of all his designs – a vast simple unit that carries the eye round as if it were the carving of a torso [115]. As for the dome: for centuries critics and lovers of art have gone into ecstasies about its noble energetic arc [120], expressive of Michelangelo's spiritual aspirations. It is perhaps the most commanding dome in the world, easily dominating the other Roman cupolas that one sees as one looks across the city. However, all the evidence suggests that it does not represent Michelangelo's final intention: he wanted it to be more spherical, less pointed [121]. It was designed by Della Porta after Michelangelo's death. Well, we can go on admiring it, and think rather more of Della Porta.

    Della Porta was, in fact, one of the few good architects in late sixteenth-century Rome. The men responsible for Sixtus V's grandiose plans – Domenico Fontana and the rest — were mediocre designers. For once an artistic revival didn't depend on individual artists of talent, but on the imagination and energy of their patrons. Painters were even worse — indeed, if I want to cheer myself up about the state of painting today I think of the feeble, mannered, self-conscious, repetitive painting that went on in Rome for about fifty years in the sixteenth century. It was a period of consolidation rather than an age of creation. It was also a period of austerity and restraint, typified by the leading spirit of the period, St Carlo Borromeo, whose legendary asceticism is commemorated in this picture [122]. But, such is the unpredictable nature of our subject, this period of heavy architecture and redundant painting produced a great musician, Palestrina. He was choir-master at the Lateran and later at St Peter's, and his music was thought to conform to the liturgical principles of the Council of Trent. St Carlo Borromeo was one of the men specially entrusted with the task of purifying the music at St Peter's; but he doesn't seem to have objected to the sensuous beauty of Palestrina's sound. The rebukes and restrictions that disturbed Shostakovich in the 1930s do not seem to have been levelled at Palestrina.

The last stone of the dome of St Peter's was put in place in 1590, a few months before the death of Sixtus V. The long period of austerity and consolidation was almost over, and in that decade were born the three men who were to make visible the victory of the Catholic Church: Bernini, Borromini and Pietro da Cortona.

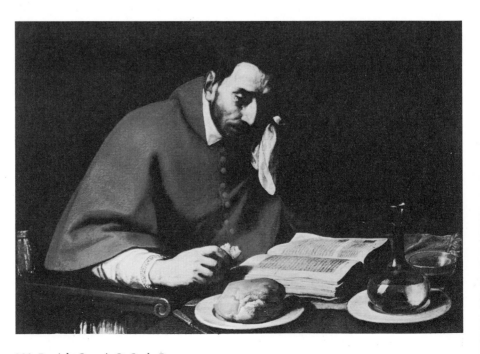

122 Daniele Crespi, *St Carlo Borromeo*

How had that victory been achieved? In England most of us were brought up to believe that it depended on the Inquisition, the Index and the Society of Jesus. I don't believe that a great outburst of creative energy such as took place in Rome between 1620 and 1660 can be the result of negative factors, but I admit that the civilisation of these years depended on certain assumptions that are out of favour in England and America today. The first of these, of course, was belief in authority, the absolute authority of the Catholic Church. This belief extended to sections of society which we now assume to be naturally rebellious. It comes as something of a shock to find that, with a single exception, the great artists of the time were all sincere, conforming Christians. Guercino spent much of his mornings in prayer; Bernini frequently went into retreats and practised the spiritual exercises of St Ignatius; Rubens attended Mass every morning before beginning work. The exception was Caravaggio, who was like the hero of a modern play, except that he happened to paint very well.

This conformism was not based on fear of the Inquisition, but on the perfectly simple belief that the faith which had inspired the great saints of the preceding generation was something by which a man should regulate his life. The mid-sixteenth century was a period of sanctity in the Roman Church almost equal to the twelfth. St John of the Cross, the great poet of mysticism; St Ignatius Loyola, the visionary soldier turned psychologist; St Theresa of Avila, the great headmistress, with her irresistible combination of mystical experience and common sense; and St Carlo Borromeo, the austere administrator – one does not need to be a practising Catholic to feel respect for a half-century that could produce these great spirits. Ignatius, Teresa, Filipo Neri and Francis Xavier were all canonised on the same day, 22 May 1622. It was like the baptism of a regenerated Rome.

However, I am not trying to pretend that this episode in the history of civilisation was of value chiefly because of its influence on artists or philosophers. On the contrary, I think that intellectual life developed more fully in the freer atmosphere of the north. The great achievements of the Catholic Church lay in harmonising, humanising, civilising the deepest impulses of ordinary, ignorant people. Take the cult of the Virgin. In the early twelfth century the Virgin had been the supreme protectress of civilisation. She had taught a race of tough and ruthless barbarians the virtues of tenderness and compassion. The great cathedrals of the Middle Ages were her dwelling places upon earth. In the Renaissance, while remaining the Queen of Heaven, she became also the human mother in whom everyone could recognise qualities of warmth and love and approachability [123]. Now imagine the feelings of a simple-hearted man or woman – a Spanish peasant, an Italian artisan –

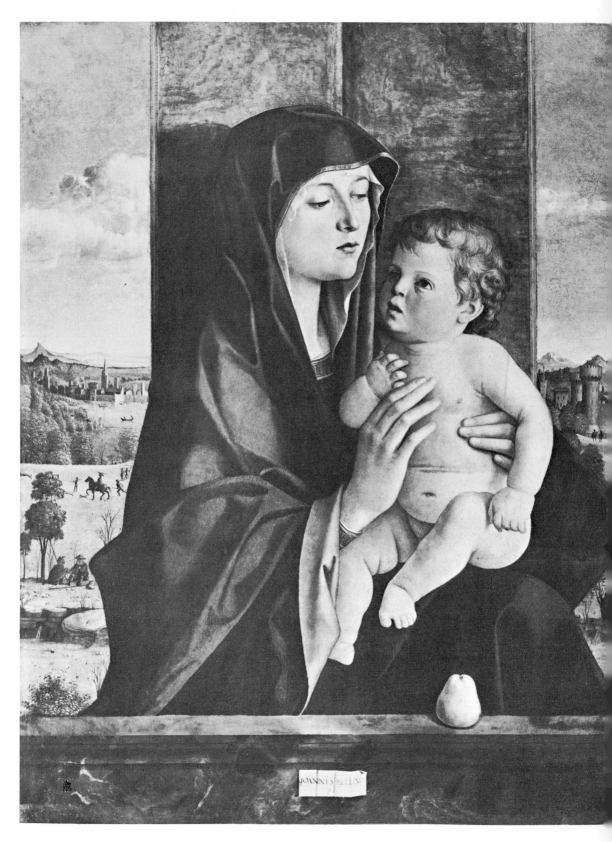

123 Bellini, *Madonna with the Pear*

on hearing that the northern heretics were insulting the Virgin, desecrating her sanctuaries, pulling down or decapitating her images. He must have felt something deeper than shock and indignation: he must have felt that some part of his whole emotional life was threatened. And he would have been right.

The stabilising, comprehensive religions of the world, the religions which penetrate to every part of a man's being – in Egypt, India or China – gave the female principle of creation at least as much importance as the male, and wouldn't have taken seriously a philosophy that failed to include them both. These were all what H. G. Wells called communities of obedience. The aggressive, nomadic societies – what he called communities of will – Israel, Islam, the Protestant North, conceived their gods as male. It's a curious fact that the all-male religions have produced no religious imagery – in most cases have positively forbidden it. The great religious art of the world is deeply involved with the female principle. Of course, the ordinary Catholic who prayed to the Virgin was not conscious of any of this; nor was he or she interested in the really baffling theological problems presented by the doctrine of the Immaculate Conception. He simply knew that the heretics wanted to deprive him of that sweet, compassionate, approachable being who would intercede for him, as his mother might have interceded with a hard master.

Take another human impulse that can be harmonised, but should not be suppressed: the impulse to confess. The historian cannot help observing how the need for confession has returned, even – or especially – in the land of the Pilgrim Fathers. The difference is that instead of confession being followed by a simple comforting rubric which has behind it the weight of divine authority, the modern confessor must grope his way into the labyrinth of the psyche, with all its false turnings and dissolving perspectives – a noble aim, but a terrifying responsibility. No wonder that psychoanalysts have the highest suicide rate of any vocation. And perhaps after all the old procedure had something to recommend it, because as a rule it is the act of confession that matters, not the attempted cure.

The leaders of the Catholic Restoration had made the inspired decision not to go half-way to meet Protestantism in any of its objections, but rather to glory in those very doctrines that the Protestants had most forcibly, and sometimes, it must be admitted, most logically, repudiated. Luther had repudiated the authority of the Pope: very well, no pains must be spared in making a giant assertion that St Peter, the first Bishop of Rome, had been divinely appointed as Christ's Vicar on earth. Ever since Erasmus, intelligent men in the north had spoken scornfully of relics: very well, their importance

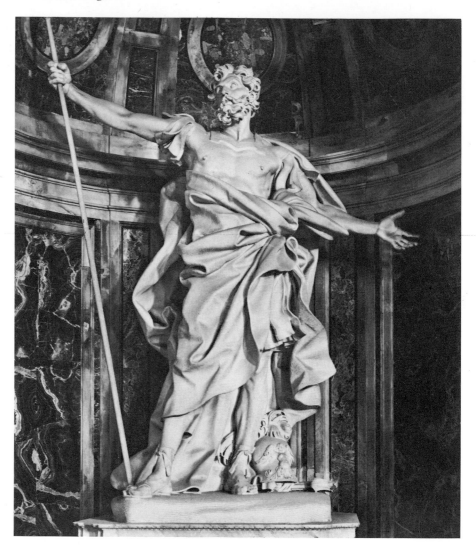

must be magnified, so that the four piers of St Peter's itself are gigantic reliquaries. One of them contained part of the lance that pierced Our Lord's side, and in front of it stands Bernini's figure of Longinus [124] looking up with a gesture of dazzled enlightenment. The veneration of relics was connected with the cult of the saints, and this had been equally condemned by the reformers. Very well, the saints should be made more insistently real to the imagination and in particular their sufferings and their ecstasies should be vividly recorded [125].

In all these ways the Church gave imaginative expression to deep-seated human impulses. And it had another great strength which one may say was part of Mediterranean civilisation – or at any rate a legacy from the pagan

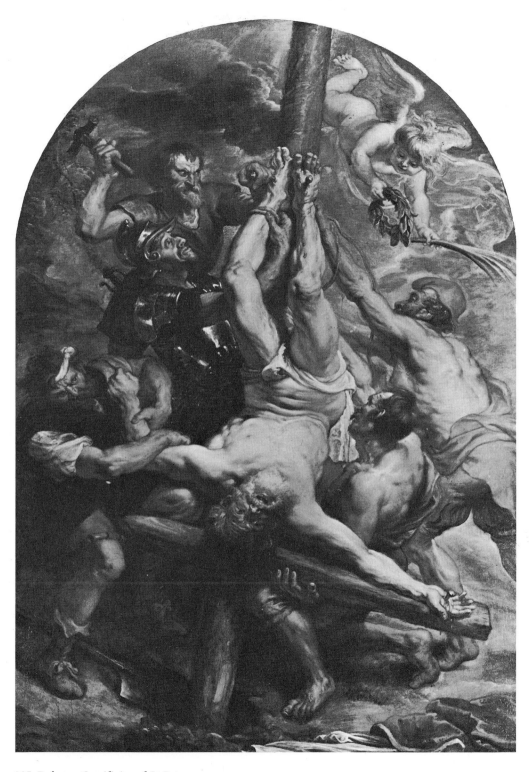

125 Rubens, *Crucifixion of St Peter*

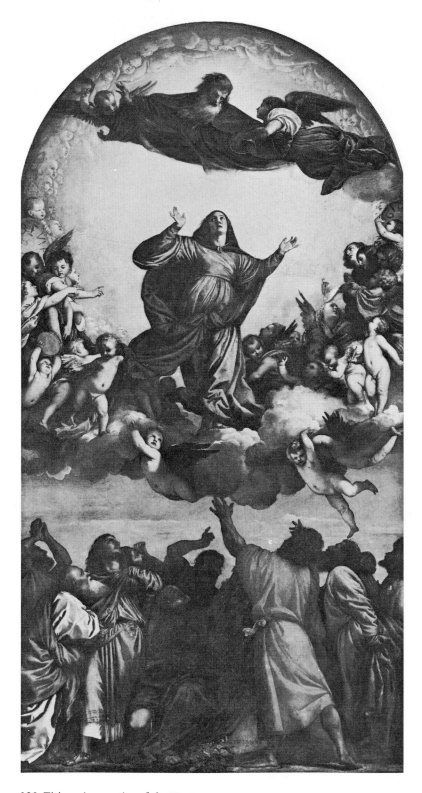

126 Titian, *Assumption of the Virgin*

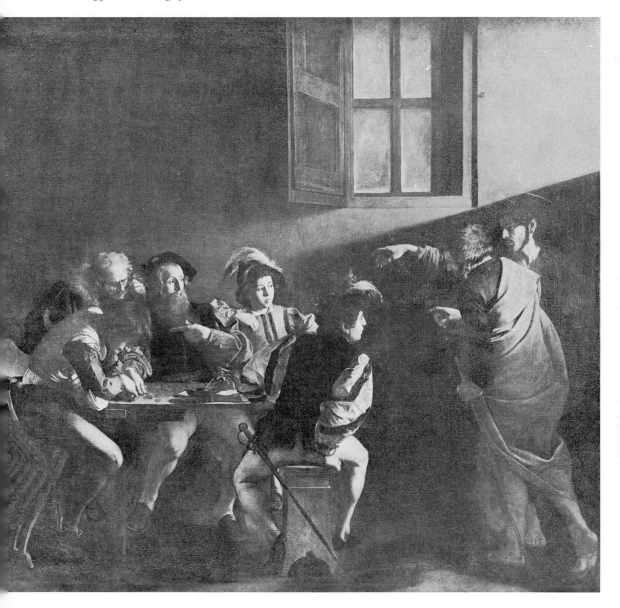

Renaissance: it was not afraid of the human body. Titian's *Assumption of the Virgin* [126], a Baroque picture almost one hundred years before its time, was painted in the same period as his great celebrations of paganism. Early in the sixteenth century Titian had given his immense authority to this union of dogma and sensuality; and when the first puritan influence of the Council of Trent was over, Titian's work was there to inspire both Rubens (who made superb copies of it) and Bernini. In their work the conflict between flesh and spirit is gloriously resolved. It would be hard to imagine a more comfortingly physical presence than the figure of Charity on Bernini's tomb of Urban VIII. And in Rubens's picture of that extremely un-Protestant subject *Sinners saved by Penitence* [**24**, facing p. 173], he has achieved in the repentant Magdalene, and even in the figure of Christ himself, a noble sensuality, perfectly at one with an unquestioning faith.

For all these reasons the art we call Baroque was a popular art. The art of the Renaissance had appealed through intellectual means – geometry, perspective, knowledge of antiquity – to a small group of humanists. The Baroque appealed through the emotions to the widest possible audience. The subjects were often obscure, thought out by some theologian: but the means of communication were popular, and even remind one of the films. Caravaggio, the earliest and, on the whole, the greatest Italian painter of the period, experimented with the kind of lighting fashionable in highbrow films of the 1920s, and gained thereby a new dramatic impact [127]. Later Baroque artists delighted in emotive close-ups with open lips and glistening tears. The huge scale, the restless movement, the shifting lights and dissolves – all these devices were to be rediscovered in the movies. The extraordinary thing is that the Baroque artists did it in bronze and marble, not on celluloid. In a way it is a frivolous comparison, because however much one admires the films, one must admit that they are often vulgar and ephemeral: whereas the work of Bernini is ideal and eternal. He was a very great artist, and although his work may seem to lack the awe-inspiring seriousness and concentration of Michelangelo, it was in its century even more pervasive and influential. He not only gave Baroque Rome its character, but he was the chief source of an international style that spread all over Europe, as Gothic had done, and as the Renaissance style never did.

Bernini was dazzlingly precocious. At the age of sixteen one of his carvings was bought by the Borghese family, and by the time he was twenty he was already commissioned to do a portrait of the Borghese Pope, Paul V. In the next three years he became more skilful in the carving of marble than any sculptor has ever been, before or since. His *David* [128], in contrast with the static *David* of Michelangelo, catches the sudden twist of action; and the vehement expression of the head is almost overdone – actually it is a self-portrait of the young Bernini, who made a face in a mirror, a mirror said to have been held for him by his patron, the Cardinal Scipione Borghese. The *Apollo and Daphne* [129] is an even more extraordinary example of how marble can be made into something fluid and fleeting, because it represents the moment when Daphne, crying for help to her father, is changed into a laurel tree. Her fingers are becoming leaves already. It is just beginning to dawn

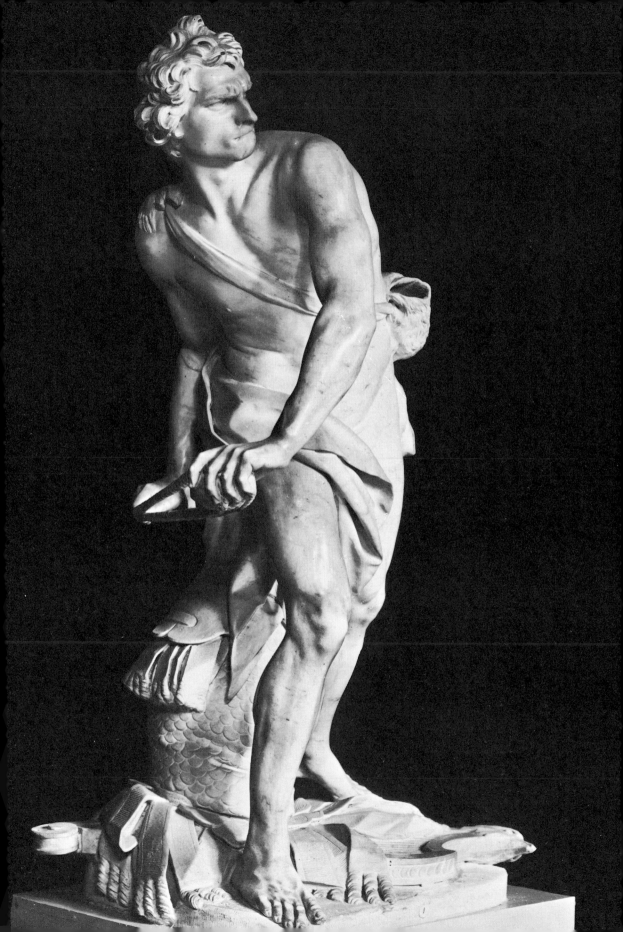

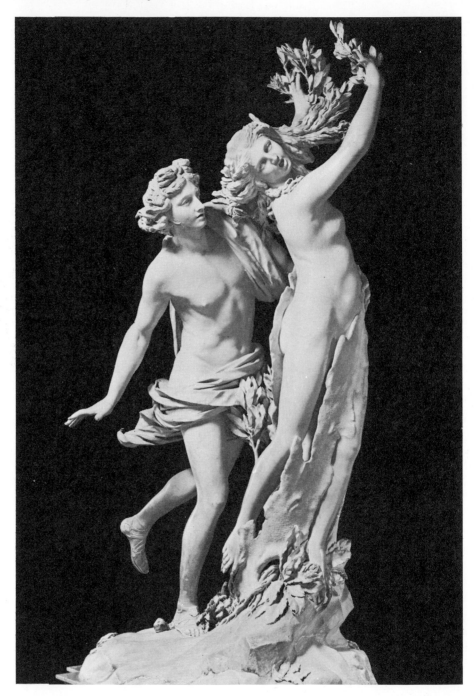

on Apollo that he has lost her, and if he could look down he would see that her beautiful legs are turning into a tree trunk and her toes are becoming roots and tendrils.

These brilliant works were done for the Borghese family, and the commissioning of them from so young a man was a remarkable feat of patronage. But by 1620 the rich Roman families, who were in fact the families of successive Popes, had begun to compete as patrons and collectors, often in a somewhat piratical manner. One is reminded of the competition between the great American collectors of sixty years ago – Mr Frick, Mr Morgan, Mr Walters – with the difference that the Roman patrons competed for the work of living artists, not simply for certified 'old masters'. The leading families put painters under contract like athletes – and the painters really got paid, which they never did in the Renaissance. As

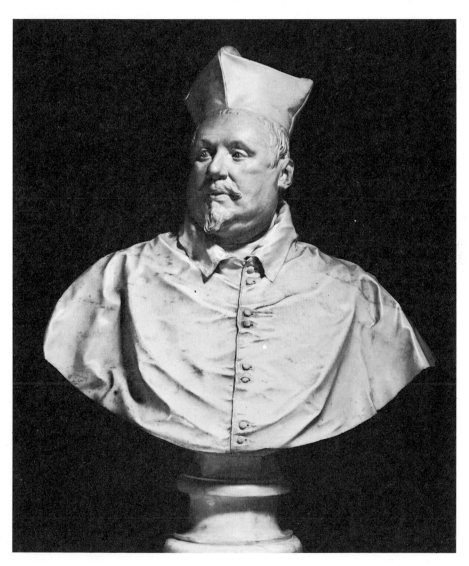

130 Bernini, *Scipione Borghese*

often happens, a sudden relaxation and affluence after a period of austerity produced an outburst of creative energy. The 1620s were relaxed all right, as one can see from Bernini's portrait of that most affluent cardinal, Scipione Borghese [130]. Of all these Papal families one easily outshone the rest – the Barberini. This was due to the pontificate of Matteo Barberini, who in 1623 became Pope Urban VIII. He was not only a genuine lover of art: he managed to survive as Pope for twenty years (it was always hoped that a Pope would last for about five years, so that a new lot of profiteers could move in to draw the benefits). It is said that one of Urban's first audiences was with Bernini, to whom he spoke the following words: 'It is your great good luck, Cavaliere, to see Matteo Barberini Pope, but We are even luckier that the Cavaliere Bernini lives at the time of Our pontificate.'

Bernini was then twenty-five. The next year he was made architect of St Peter's, and began work on that incredible feat of virtuosity, the bronze *baldacchino* over the high altar [131]. Yes, if one knows anything about bronze casting it really is incredible. It involved all kinds of engineering difficulties, and there was also a shortage of bronze. This was got over by the rather drastic decision to strip the roof from the most famous ancient building in Rome, the Pantheon – which led to the famous comment: 'What the Barbari dared not do was done by the Barberini.' Then there is the amazing richness and audacity of Bernini's invention and the perfection of craftsmanship, extending to every detail. More extraordinary still, Bernini seems already to have foreseen in his imagination what the whole development of St Peter's would be like, because this work, designed in 1642, is completely in harmony with the great progression of works executed over forty years later.

Bernini is perhaps the only artist in history who has been able to carry through a vast design over so long a period; and the result is a unity of impression that exists nowhere else on so large a scale. The pilgrim coming to Rome in 1600 would, it is true, have had the dome of St Peter's to encourage him. But otherwise his impressions would have been scrappy and disjointed. Now imagine his experiences after Bernini had done his work. He would cross the Ponte Sant' Angelo with its marble angels from Bernini's workshop, and make his way to the Piazza, where everything is calculated to overwhelm him [132]. The enormous colonnade throws out its arms to embrace him; he passes the Scala Regia, the entrance to the palace of Christ's Vicar on earth, and if he can put his head inside, sees Bernini's figure of the Conversion of Constantine, the first Christian emperor, who, he has been told, formally presented the city of Rome to the Popes. He climbs the steps of the Basilica, passes through the enormous façade, and at

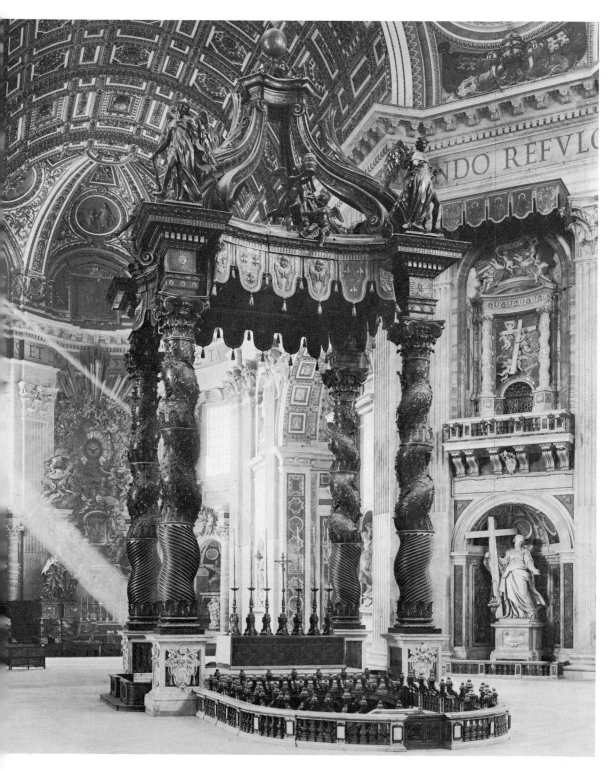

131 Bernini, *Baldacchino*

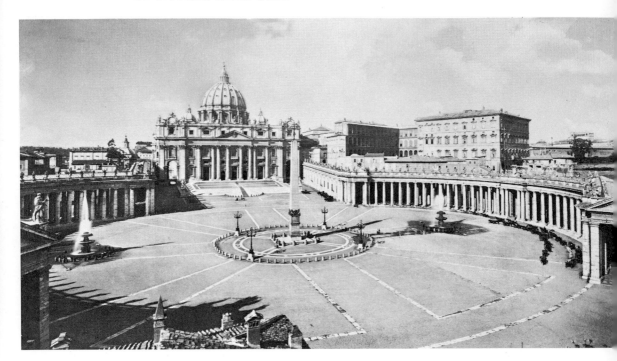

once receives a complete impression of unity [**25**, facing p. 192]. Not only is the decoration – which, whenever it was executed, was basically all conceived by Bernini – in a uniform style, but the eye passes without a break through the *baldacchino*, and as we finally come before the throne of St Peter, with its billowing bishops, weightless angels and trembling cherubs, we feel ourselves to be no longer weighed down by earthly things. We participate imaginatively, as we do at a ballet, in an ecstatic repudiation of the force of gravity.

But the word ballet puts us on our guard. It was no accident that Bernini was the greatest scene designer of his age. John Evelyn records how in 1644 he went to the opera in Rome, where Bernini 'painted the scenes, cut the statues, invented the engines, composed the music, wrote the comedy and built the theatre'. And other diarists record how, at Bernini's productions, people in the front row ran away, fearing that they would be drenched by water or burnt by fire, so powerful was the illusion he created. These creations have, of course, all vanished, but we have some evidence of what they were like in the fountain that Bernini designed for the Piazza Navona [133]. It is a breath-taking performance. A sizeable Egyptian obelisk is lifted up on a hollow rock as if it weighed no more than a ballerina. Round the rock are four gigantic figures symbolising the four great rivers of the world – the Danube, the Nile, the Ganges and the Plate. You can think of them as the four continents or the four rivers of Paradise – this muddle of symbolism was the way in which men thought in the seventeenth century. We don't think like that, but we can enjoy the extraordinary vigour of Bernini's invention. I say 'invention', because by this time his work was carried out by a small army of very skilful assistants, and the only part of the fountain said to have

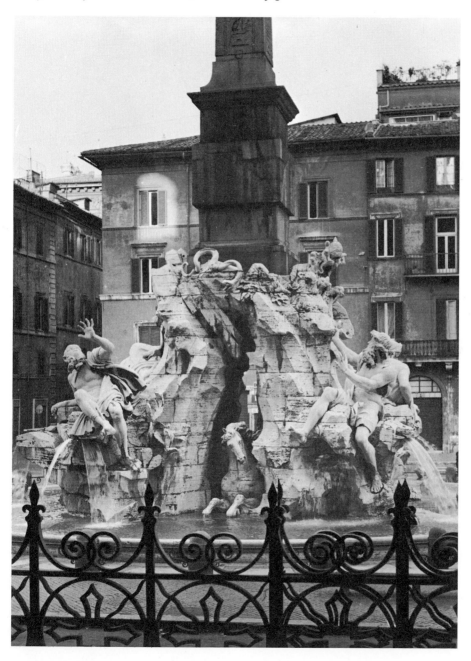

133 Bernini, Fountain, Piazza Navona, Rome

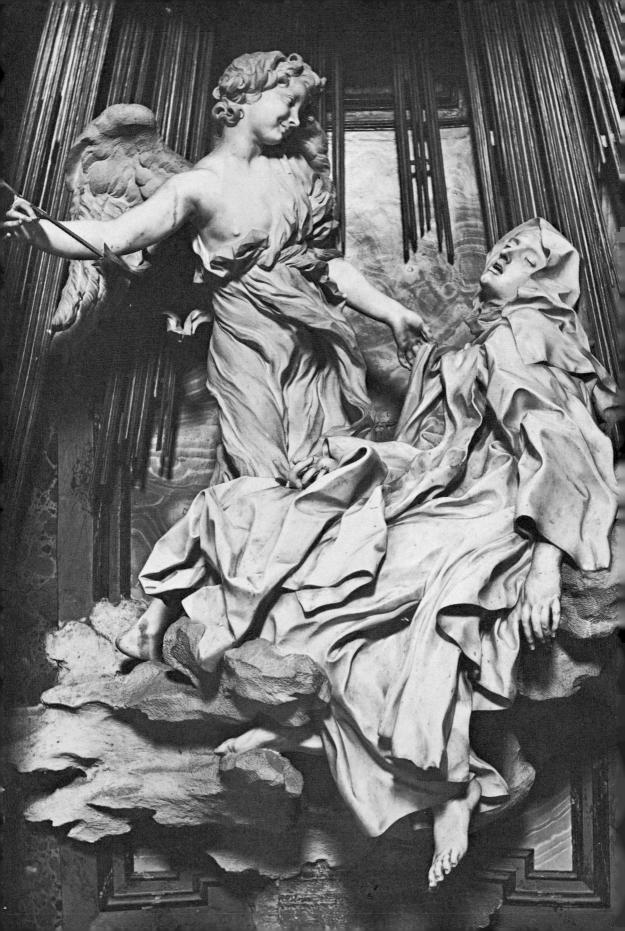

been carved by Bernini himself is the horse, symbolising the Danube (incidentally, the portrait of a real horse called Monte d'Oro), which surprisingly emerges from a watery grotto.

Of this theatrical element in Bernini a sublime example is the Cornaro Chapel in Santa Maria della Vittoria. To begin with, Bernini has represented the members of the Cornaro family on either side of the chapel looking as if they were in boxes waiting for the curtain to go up. And when we come to the drama itself, it is presented exactly as if it were on a small stage, with a spotlight falling on the protagonists. But at this point the theatrical parallel must be dropped because what we see, the *Ecstasy of St Teresa* [134], is one of the most deeply moving works in European art. Bernini's gift of sympathetic imagination, of entering into the emotions of others – a gift no doubt enhanced by his practice of St Ignatius' Spiritual Exercises – is used to convey the rarest and most precious of all emotional states, that of religious ecstasy. He has illustrated exactly the passage in the saint's auto-biography in which she describes the supreme moment of her life: how an angel with a flaming golden arrow pierced her heart repeatedly. 'The pain was so great that I screamed aloud, but simultaneously felt such infinite sweetness that I wished the pain to last eternally. It was the sweetest caressing of the soul by God.' Perhaps the closest parallel to the combination of deep feeling, sensuous involvement and marvellous technical control is to be found not in visual art but in music, particularly in the music of that great composer who was Bernini's older contemporary, Monteverdi.

I don't think that anyone can accuse me of underestimating the Catholic restoration, or its greatest image-maker, Gianlorenzo Bernini. So may I end by saying that this episode in the history of civilisation arouses in me certain misgivings? They may be summed up in the words 'illusion' and 'exploitation'. Of course, all art is to some extent an illusion. It transforms experience in order to satisfy some need of the imagination. But there are degrees of illusion, depending on how far from direct ex-perience the artist is prepared to go. Bernini went very far – just how far one realises when one remembers the historical St Teresa, with her plain, daunt-less, sensible face. The contrast with the swooning sensuous beauty of the Cornaro Chapel is almost shocking. One can't help feeling that affluent Baro-que, in its escape from the severities of the earlier fight against Protestantism, ended by escaping from reality into a world of illusion. Art creates its own momentum and once set on this course there was nothing it could do except become more and more sensational. And this is what happens in the aerial ballets that take place over our heads in the Churches of the Gesu and St Ignazio, or the Palazzo Barberini [135]. We feel that the stopper

134 Bernini, *Ecstasy of St Teresa*

is out. Imaginative energy is fizzing away, up into the clouds, and will soon evaporate.

As for my other misgivings, of course there was exploitation before the sixteenth century, but never on so vast a scale. In the Middle Ages it was usually accompanied by popular participation. Even in the Renaissance, palaces were to some extent seats of government and objects of local pride. But the colossal palaces of the Papal families were simply expressions of private greed and vanity. Farnese, Borghese, Barberini, Ludovisi, these rapacious parvenus spent their short years of power competing as to who should build the largest and most ornate saloons. In doing so, they commissioned some great works of art and one can't help admiring their shameless courage. At least they weren't mean and furtive, like some modern millionaires. But their contribution to civilisation was limited to this kind of visual exuberance. The sense of grandeur is no doubt a human instinct, but, carried too far, it becomes inhuman. I wonder if a single thought that has helped forward the human spirit has ever been conceived or written down in an enormous room: except, perhaps, in the reading room of the British Museum. *Karl Marx* ?

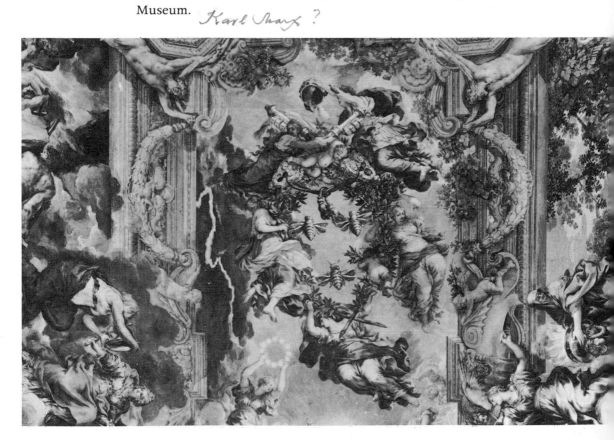

135 Pietro da Cortona, Ceiling, Palazzo Barberini, Rome (detail)

25 Pannini, *Interior of St Peter's*

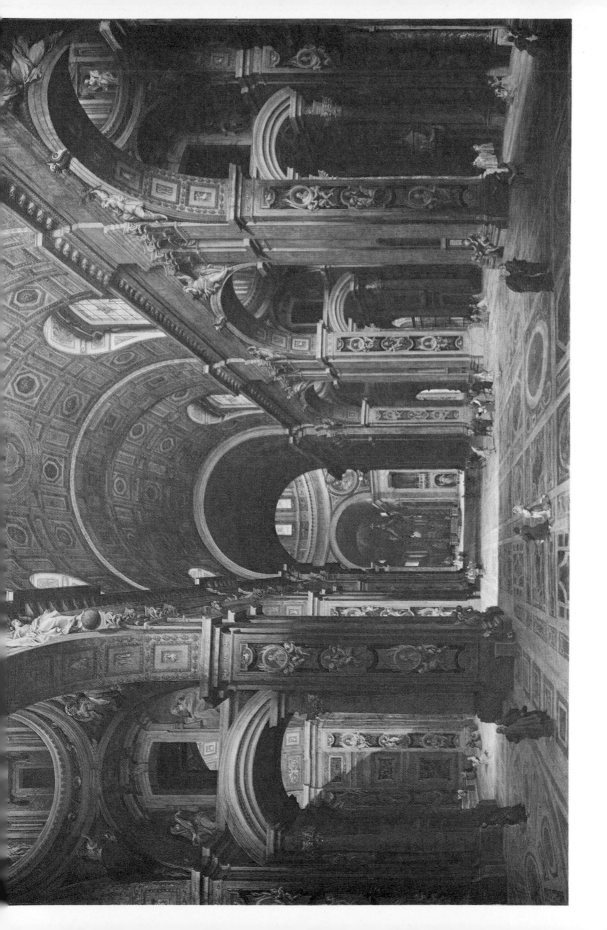

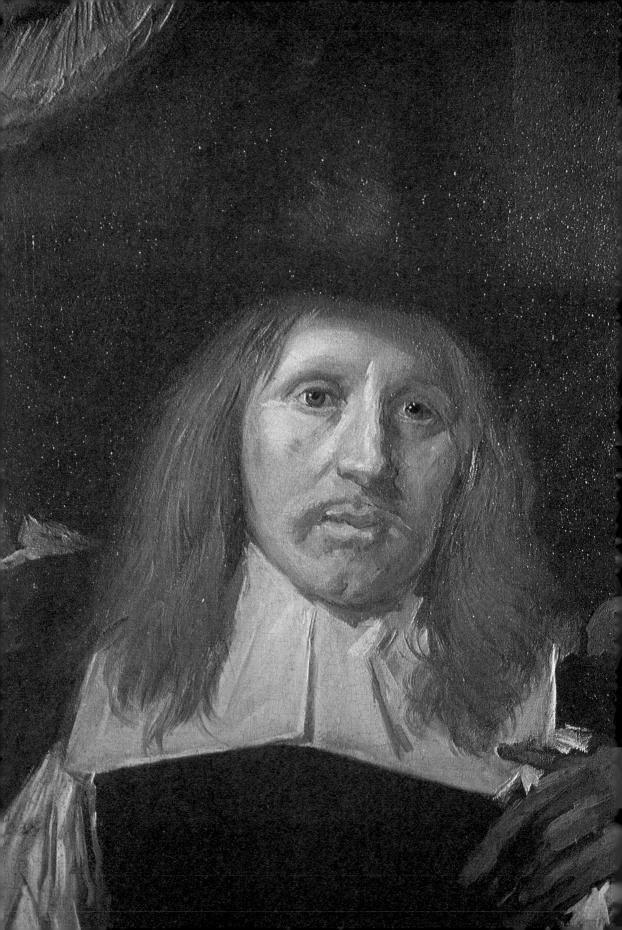

8 The Light of Experience

When Berckheyde painted his picture of the square at Haarlem [136] he appears to have seen almost exactly what we see, if we stand there today at about three o'clock on a sunny afternoon with the wind from the north-west. The architecture is relatively little changed, the sense of space is what we have come to regard as normal, the light is accurately observed. We feel that we could walk into that picture. Nothing strange in that; but like so many things we take for granted, it goes back to a revolutionary change in thought – the revolution that replaced Divine Authority by experience, experiment and observation.

I am in Holland not only because Dutch painting is a visible expression of this change of mind, but because Holland – economically and intellectually –

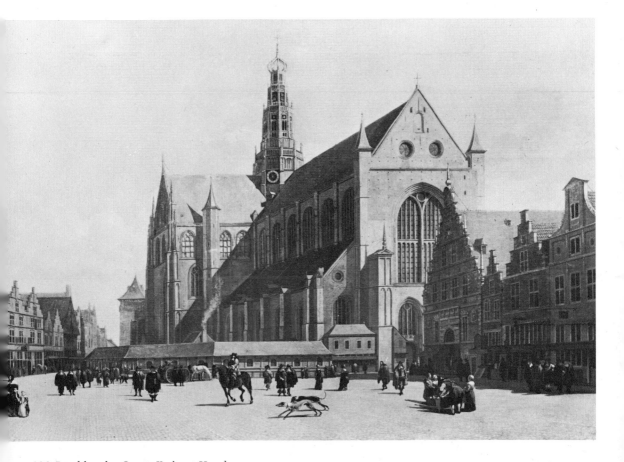

136 Berckheyde, *Groote Kerke at Haarlem*

26 Frans Hals, *Regents of the Old Men's Home* (detail)

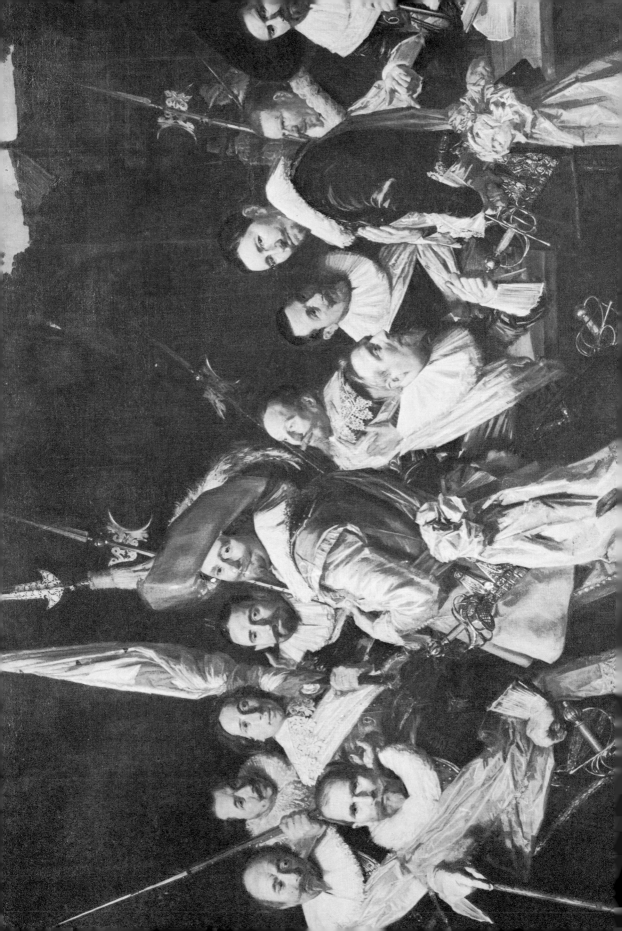

was the first country to profit from the change. When one begins to ask the question, 'does it work?' or even, 'does it pay?' instead of, 'is it God's will?' one gets a new set of answers, and one of the first of them is this: that to try to suppress opinions which one doesn't share is much less profitable than to tolerate them. This conclusion should have been reached during the Reformation – it was implicit in the writings of Erasmus who was, of course, a Dutchman. Alas, a belief in the divine authority of our own opinions afflicted the Protestants just as much as the Catholics – even in Holland. They continued to persecute each other right up to the middle of the seventeenth century; there was a revolting case of persecution of two intelligent Dutchmen called Koerbogh as late as 1668. And the Jews, who in Amsterdam were at last exempt from persecution by the Christians, began to persecute each other. Trials of witches positively increased in this age of reason. It seemed as if the spirit of persecution was like some kind of poison that couldn't be cured by the new philosophy, and had to work itself out of the system. Still, when all this is said, the spirit of Holland in the early seventeenth century was remarkably tolerant; and one proof is that nearly all the great books which revolutionised thought were first printed in Holland.

What sort of society was it that allowed these intellectual time-bombs to be set off in its midst? Inside the old almshouse in Haarlem, which is now a picture gallery, there is plenty of evidence. We know more about what the seventeenth-century Dutch looked like than we do about any other society, except perhaps the first-century Romans. Each individual wanted posterity to know exactly what he was like, even if he was a member of a corporate group. And the man who tells us all this most vividly was the Haarlem painter, Frans Hals. He is the supreme extrovert. I used to find his works [137] (all except the last) revoltingly cheerful and horribly skilful. Now I love their unthinking conviviality, and value skill more highly than I did. His sitters don't look like representatives of a new philosophy, but out of the all too numerous group-portraits of early seventeenth-century Holland, something does emerge which has a bearing on civilisation: these are individuals who are prepared to join in a corporate effort for the public good [26, facing p. 193]. For the most part they are solid, commonplace people, as they would be today, and they were portrayed by commonplace artists; but from this dead level of group portraiture there arose one of the summits of European painting, Rembrandt's *Syndics* [138]. One can't imagine groups like this being produced in Spain or seventeenth-century Italy, even in Venice. They are the first visual evidence of bourgeois democracy. Dreadful words – so debased by propaganda that I hesitate to use them. Yet in the context of

137 Frans Hals, *Civil Guard* (detail)

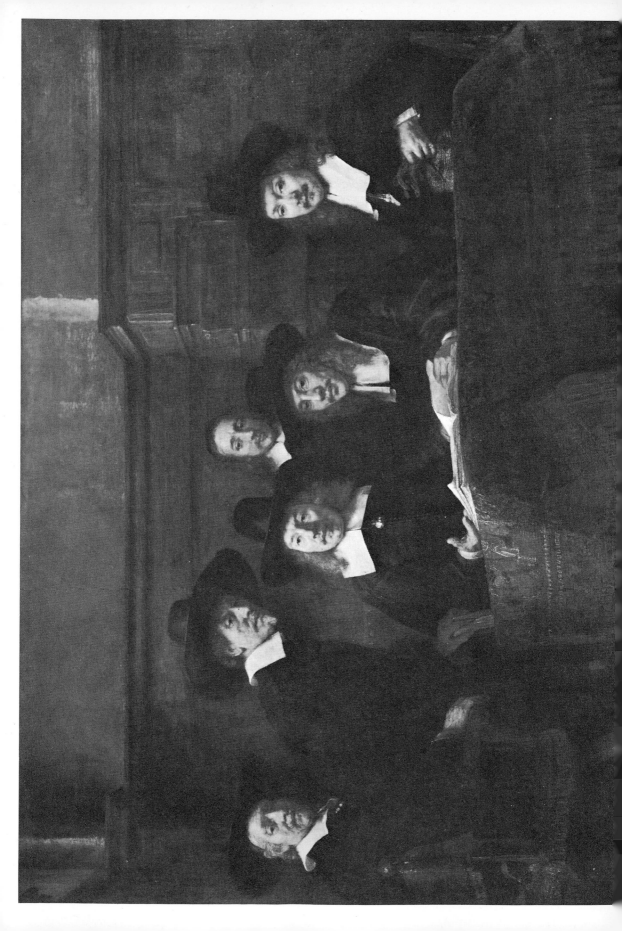

civilisation they really have a meaning. They mean that a group of individuals can come together and take corporate responsibility; that they can afford to do so because they have some leisure; and that they have some leisure because they have money in the bank. This is the society which you see in the portrait groups. They might be of meetings of local government committees or hospital governors today. They represent the practical, social application of the philosophy that things must be made to work.

Amsterdam was the first centre of bourgeois capitalism. It had become, since the decline of Antwerp and the Hanseatic League, the great international port of the north and the chief banking centre of Europe. Drifting through its leafy canals, lined with admirable houses, one may speculate on the economic system that produced this dignified, comfortable and harmonious architecture [141]. I don't say much about economics in this book chiefly because I don't understand them – and perhaps for that reason believe that their importance has been overrated by post-Marxist historians. But, of course, there is no doubt that at a certain stage in social development fluid capital is one of the chief causes of civilisation because it ensures three essential ingredients: leisure, movement and independence. It also allows that slight superfluity of wealth that can be spent on nobler proportions, a better door-frame or even a rarer and more extraordinary tulip. Please allow me two minutes' digression on the subject of tulips. It is really rather touching that the first classic example of boom and slump in capitalist economy should have been not sugar or railways or oil, but tulips. It shows how the seventeenth-century Dutch combined their two chief enthusiasms – scientific investigation and visual delight. The first tulip had been imported from Turkey in the sixteenth century, but it was a professor of botany at Leiden, the first botanical garden in the north, who discovered its attribute of variation which made it such an exciting gamble. By 1634 the Dutch were so bitten by this new craze that for a single bulb of a tulip called the Viceroy, one collector exchanged one thousand pounds of cheese, four oxen, eight pigs, twelve sheep, a bed and a suit of clothes. When the bottom fell out of the tulip market in 1637 the Dutch economy was shaken. However, it survived for another fifty years or so, and produced other superfluities of a most brilliant kind: silver cups and bottles; gold-stamped leather walls; and blue and white pottery, imitated from the Chinese with such technical skill that the Dutch were able to sell it back to China.

All this argues a high degree of civilisation in the purely material sense of the word, but unfortunately this kind of visual self-indulgence very soon leads to ostentation and this, in bourgeois democracy, means vulgarity. One can see this happening in Holland in the work of a single painter, Pieter de

138 Rembrandt, *Staalmeesters*

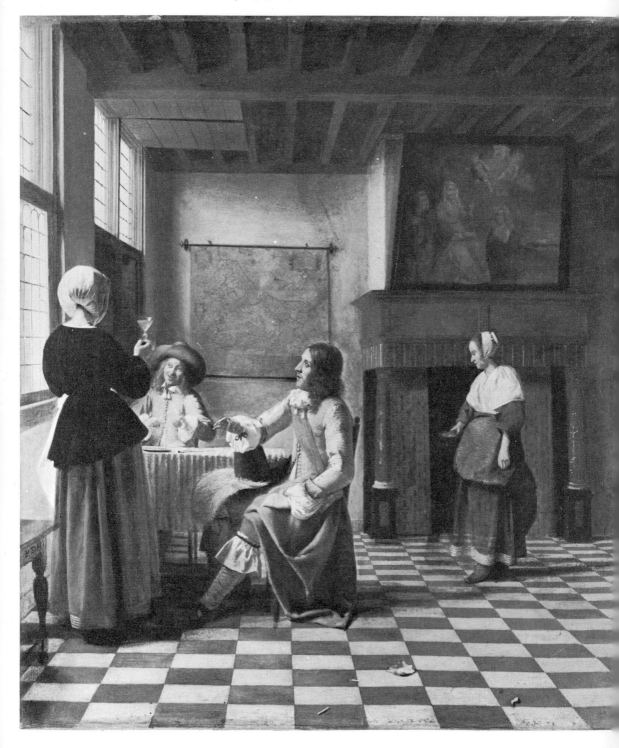

Hooch. In 1660 he was painting pictures of clean, simple interiors [139], their ordered space full of light. Ten years later his interiors were very elaborate, and instead of light whitewashed walls there was gold Spanish leather. The people are richer: and the pictures are much less beautiful [140]. Bourgeois capitalism led to a defensive smugness and sentimentality: no wonder that early Victorian painters imitated the genre pictures of Metsu and Terborch. Also the philosophy of observation involved a demand for realism in the most literal sense. In the nineteenth century Paul Potter's *Bull* was one of the most famous pictures in Holland. I must confess that I still find it irresistible. I am bored by abstractions, which so easily become vapid and repeti-

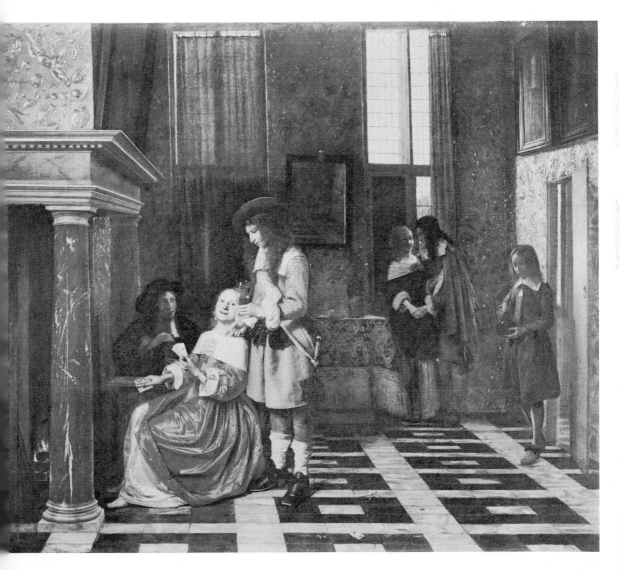

140 Pieter de Hooch, *The Card-players*

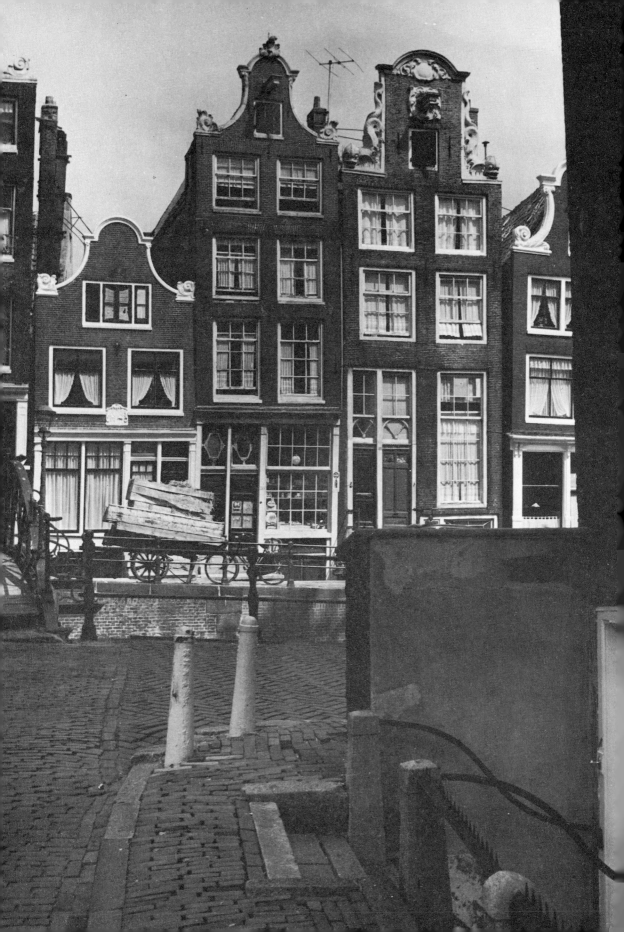

tive, but the uncanny realism of the sheep's head [142] keeps my eye occupied to the point of obsession, and there is something almost nightmarish about the way in which the young bull dominates this beautifully painted landscape. However, I must admit that bourgeois sentiment and realism can produce a vulgar trivial art, and the determinist historian, reviewing the social condition of seventeenth-century Holland, might say that this was what the Dutch were bound to get. Well – they also got Rembrandt [143].

In studying the history of civilisation one must try to keep a balance between individual genius and the moral or spiritual condition of a society. However irrational it may seem, I believe in genius. I believe that almost

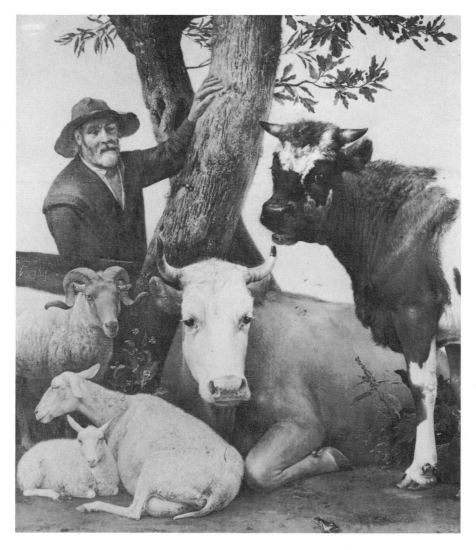

142 Paul Potter, *The Bull* (detail)

141 Amsterdam, seventeenth-century houses

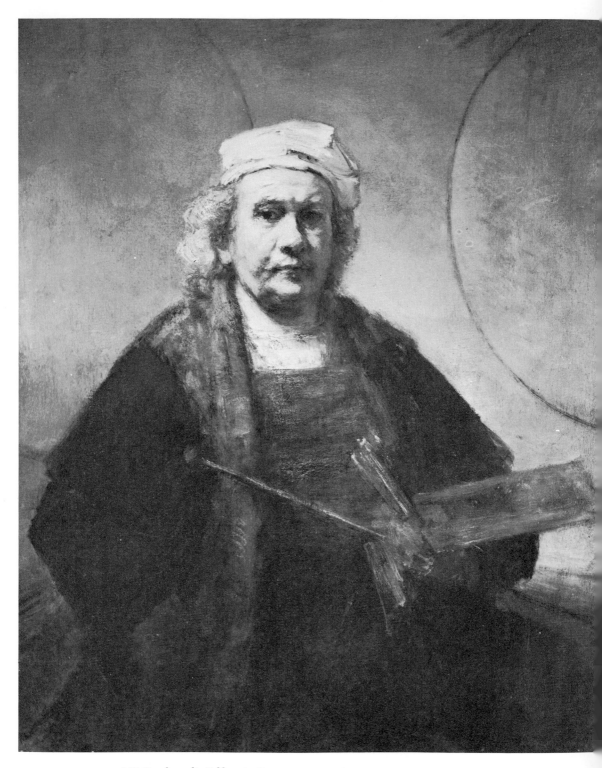

143 Rembrandt, *Self-portrait*

everything of value which has happened in the world has been due to individuals. Nevertheless, one can't help feeling that the supremely great figures in history – Dante, Michelangelo, Shakespeare, Newton, Goethe – must be to some extent a kind of summation of their times. They are too large, too all-embracing, to have developed in isolation. Rembrandt is a crucial instance of this conundrum. It is very easy – indeed rather more convenient for the historian – to imagine Dutch art without him; and there was no one else in Holland remotely comparable to him – nothing like the group of poets and dramatists who preceded and accompanied Shakespeare. Yet the very fact that Rembrandt was so immediately and overwhelmingly successful, and went on being successful – his etchings and drawings never went out of fashion – and that for twenty years almost every Dutch painter was his pupil, shows that the spiritual life of Holland needed him and so had, to some extent, created him.

Rembrandt was the great poet of that need for truth and that appeal to experience which had begun with the Reformation, had produced the first translations of the Bible, but had had to wait almost a century for visible expression. The most obvious link between Rembrandt and the intellectual life of Holland is the first commission he undertook when he had moved from Leiden to Amsterdam. It represents a demonstration given by the leading professor of anatomy, Dr Tulp [144]. The men surrounding him are not, of course, students, or even doctors, but members of the surgeons' guild. The first great modern anatomist, Van Wessel, usually known as Vesalius, had been a Dutchman, and Dr Tulp, who looks pretty pleased with himself, liked to be called Vesalius Reborn. I fancy he was a bit of a quack. He recommended his patients to drink fifty cups of tea a day. He was very successful – his son became an English baronet.

However, it was not in such external and quasi-official ways that Rembrandt associated himself with the intellectual life of his time, but by his illustrations to the Bible. One of the forms of authority that was bound to be upset by the appeal to experience was the authority of traditional iconography. Rembrandt, although in fact he was a profound student of the classical tradition, wanted to look at every episode as if it had never been depicted before, and to try to find an equivalent for it in his own experience. His mind was steeped in the Bible – he knew every story by heart down to the minutest detail, and, just as the early translators felt that they had to learn Hebrew so that no fragment of the truth should escape them, so Rembrandt made friends with the Jews in Amsterdam and frequented their synagogues in case he could learn something that would shed more light on the early history of the Jewish people. But in the end the evidence he used

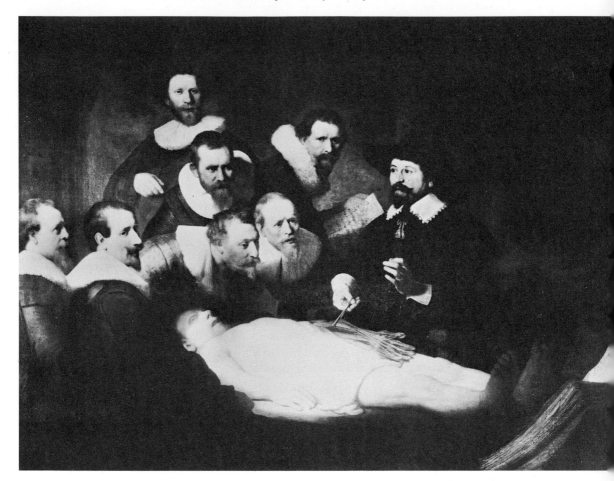

for interpreting the Bible was the life he saw around him [145]. In his drawings one often doesn't know if he is recording an observation or illustrating the scriptures, so much had the two experiences grown together in his mind.

Sometimes his interpretation of human life in Christian terms leads him to depict subjects that hardly exist in the Bible, but that he felt convinced must have existed. An example is the etching of Christ preaching the forgiveness of sins [146]. It is a classical composition – in fact it is based on two famous Raphaels which Rembrandt has completely assimilated. But how different is this small congregation from Raphael's ideal human specimens. They are a very mixed lot, some thoughtful, some half-hearted, some concerned only with keeping warm or keeping awake. And the child in the foreground, to whom the doctrine of the remission of sins is of no interest, is concentrating on drawing in the dust. If, as I suppose, sympathy with all sorts and conditions of men and tolerance of human diversity be an attribute of civilised life, then Rembrandt was one of the great prophets of civilisation.

The psychological truth in Rembrandt's paintings goes beyond that of any other artist who has ever lived. Of course they are masterpieces of sheer picture-making. In the *Bathsheba* [147] he makes use of studies from nature and from antique reliefs to achieve a perfectly balanced design. We may think we admire it as pure painting, but in the end we come back to the head. Bathsheba's thoughts and feelings as she ponders on David's letter are rendered with a subtlety and a human sympathy which a great novelist could scarcely achieve in many pages. We used to be told that painting shouldn't compete with literature. Well, perhaps not in its initial stages.

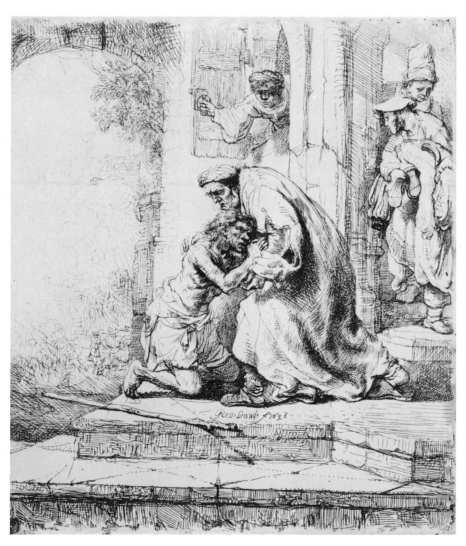

145 Rembrandt, *The Prodigal Son* (etching)

Or, rather, the literary element should not obtrude itself till it has taken the right shape. But when form and content are one, what a heavenly bonus this kind of human revelation can be.

To my mind the greatest example of this quality is the picture known as *The Jewish Bride* [**28**, facing p. 209]. Nobody knows exactly what its title should be – perhaps it was intended to represent some Old Testament characters such as Abraham and Rebecca. But its real subject is evident. It is a picture of grown-up love, a marvellous amalgam of richness, tenderness and trust, the richness symbolised by the actual painting of the sleeve, the tenderness by the hands, and the trust by the expression of the heads which, in their truth, have a spiritual glow that painters influenced by the classical ideal could never achieve.

Rembrandt reinterpreted sacred history and mythology in the light of human experience. But it is an emotional response based on a belief in the

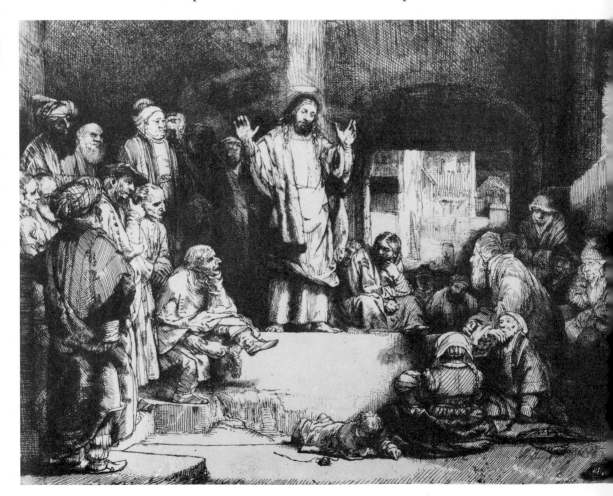

146 Rembrandt, *Christ preaching the forgiveness of sins* (etching)

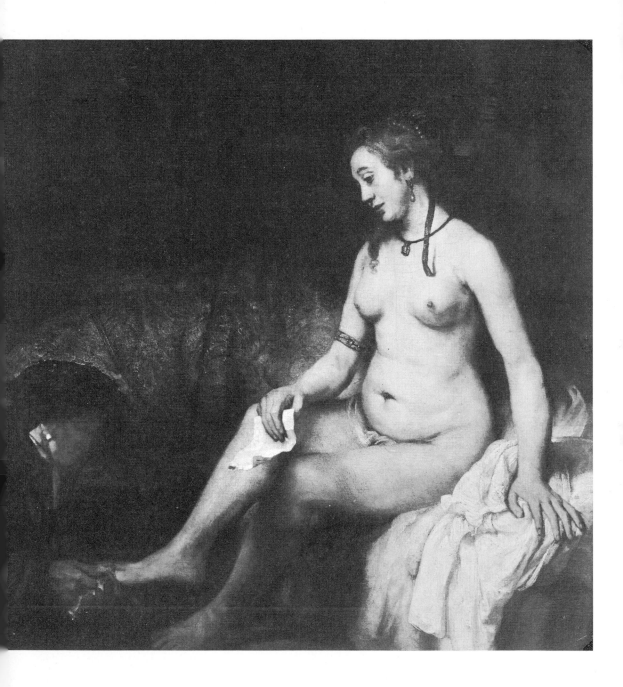

147 Rembrandt, *Bathsheba*

truth of revealed religion. The greatest of his contemporaries were looking for a different kind of truth – a truth that could be established by intellectual, not emotional means. This could be done either by the accumulation of observed evidence or by mathematics; and of the two, mathematics offered to the men of the seventeenth century the more attractive solution. Mathematics became, in fact, the religion of the finest minds of the time – the means of expressing a belief that experience could be united with reason. Bacon was the only philosopher of the period who was not a mathematician. He thought he could solve everything by material evidence, examined by an exceptionally sharp wit – and, my goodness, he was intelligent! The man who classified our fondest beliefs as Idols of the Tribe and Idols of the Market-Place has not lost his antiseptic value for the modern world. But

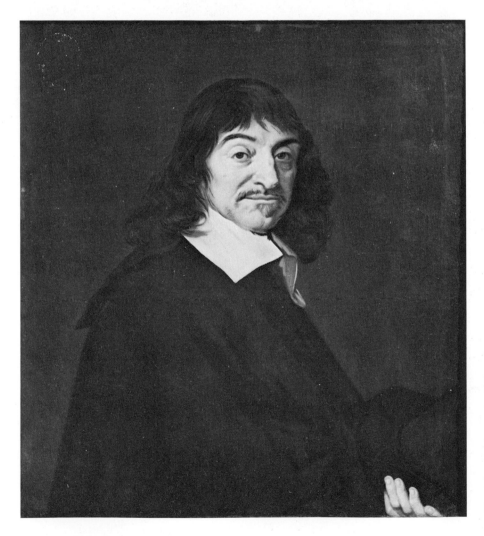

148 Frans Hals, *Descartes*

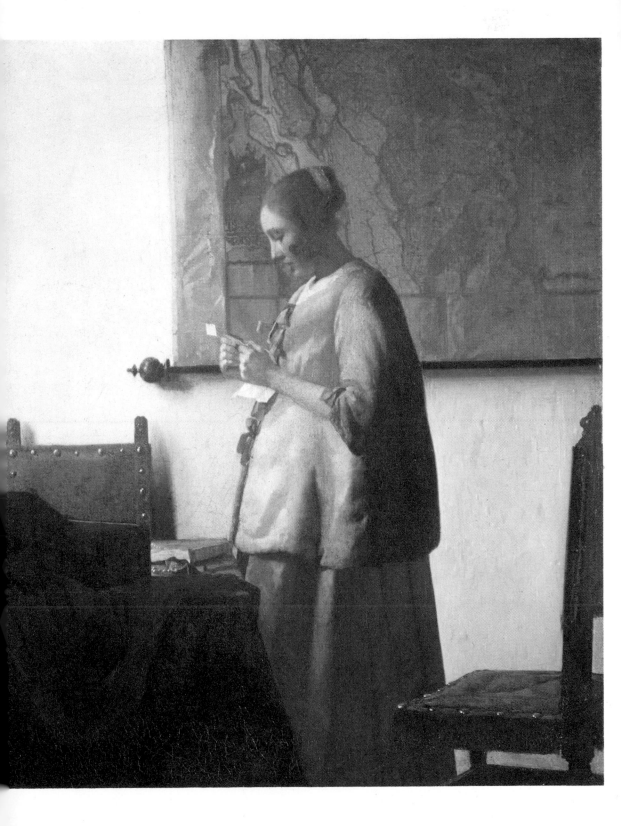

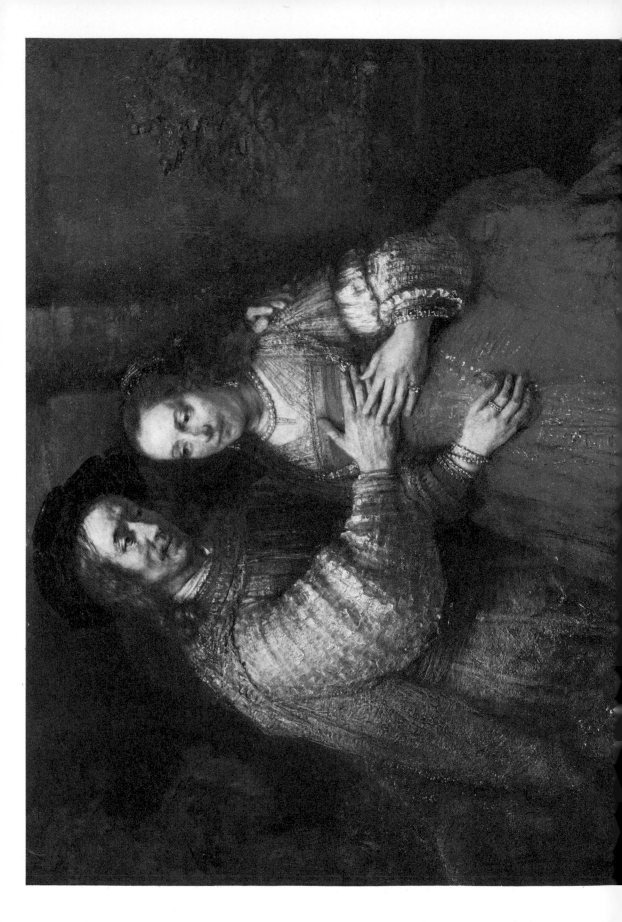

compared to the great thinkers who succeeded him – Descartes, Pascal, Spinoza – there is something faintly disreputable about Bacon, not because of his politics, but because he lacked the dominating faith of the seventeenth century – the faith in mathematics.

Descartes, on the other hand, is an extremely sympathetic figure. He started life as a soldier – he wrote a book on fencing – but he soon discovered that all he wanted to do was to think – very, very rare, and most unpopular. Some friends came to call on him at eleven o'clock in the morning and found him in bed. They said: 'What are you doing?' He replied: 'Thinking.' They were furious. To escape interference he went to live in Holland. He said that the people of Amsterdam were so much occupied with making money that they would leave him alone. However, he continued to be the victim of interruptions, so he moved about from place to place: he moved house in Holland twenty-four times, and at some point he evidently lived near Haarlem, where he was painted by Frans Hals [148]. He examined everything, rather as Leonardo da Vinci had done – the foetus, the refraction of light, whirlpools, all Leonardo's subjects. He thought that all matter consisted of whirlpools, with an outer ring of large curving vortices, and an inner core of small globules sucked into the centre; and whatever he meant by this (and perhaps he was thinking of Plato's *Timaeus*), it is odd that he should have described exactly Leonardo's drawings of whirlpools, which I suppose he had never seen. But in contrast to Leonardo's restless, insatiate curiosity, Descartes had, almost to excess, the French tidy-mindedness, and all his observations were made to contribute to a philosophic scheme. It was based on absolute scepticism – the inheritance of Montaigne's summing-up – *'que scais-je?'* 'what do I know?' Only Descartes arrived at an answer: 'I know that I think' – and turned it the other way round: 'I think, therefore I am.' His fundamental point was that he could doubt everything – except that he was doubting.

Descartes wanted to cut away all preconceptions and get back to the facts of direct experience, unaffected by custom and convention. Well, one needn't look far in Dutch art to illustrate this state of mind. There has never been a painter who has stuck so rigorously to what his optic nerve reported as Vermeer of Delft. His work is without a single *parti pris*, or a prejudice arising from knowledge, or the convenience of a style. It's really quite a shock to see a picture that has so little stylistic artifice as his View of Delft [149]. It looks like a coloured photograph, and yet we know that it is a work of extreme intellectual distinction. It not only shows the light of Holland, but what Descartes called 'the natural light of mind'. In fact Vermeer comes close to Descartes at many points. First of all in his detached, evasive

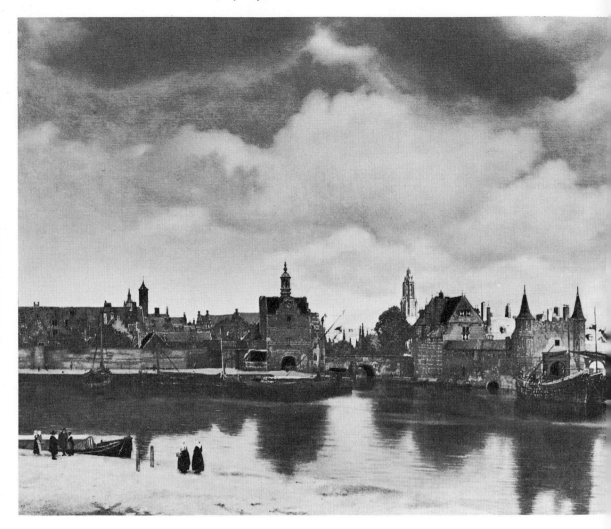

character. Vermeer didn't change house every three months; on the contrary, he loved his house in the square at Delft and painted it continually. His quiet interiors [**27**, facing p. 208] are all rooms in his own house. But he was equally suspicious of callers. He told one eminent collector who had made a special journey to visit him that he had no pictures to show him, which was just untrue because when he died his house contained unsold pictures of all periods. All he wanted was tranquility, in order to enjoy fine discrimination and discover the truth through a delicate balance.

'Study to be quiet'; ten years before Vermeer's interiors were painted Izaak Walton had inscribed these words on the title page of *The Compleat Angler*, and in the same period two religious sects had come into being, Quietism and the Quakers.

As far as I know, the first painter to feel Descartes' need to tidy up sensations by the use of reason was Pieter Saenredam, the scrupulous master of church interiors. He did drawings from nature in the 1630s, and often kept them ten or fifteen years until he could give them that stillness and finality which make them like ideal meeting places for the Society of Friends. The precision with which he places each accent, the small, black windows, the pews and the diamond-shaped hatchments, reminds one of Seurat [150]. In some of Saenredam's pictures the balance is too obviously tilted towards reason rather than experience. Vermeer always manages to preserve an illusion of complete naturalism. Yet what masterpieces of abstract design he created out of frames and windows and musical instruments [29, facing p. 220]. Are these intervals and proportions the result of calculation? Or did Vermeer discover them intuitively? No good asking such questions. Vermeer has a genius for evasion. All one can say is that as one looks into his work one is reminded of the most austerely geometrical of modern painters, his compatriot, Mondrian.

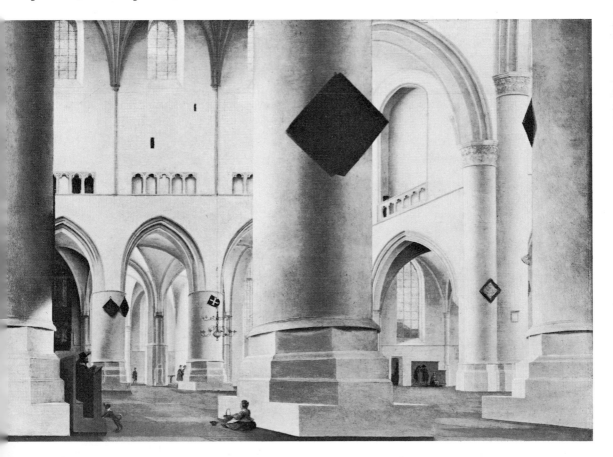

150 Saenredam, *Church interior*

But at the mention of Mondrian one remembers that one of Vermeer's characteristics separates him entirely from abstract modern painting – his passion for light. It is in this more than anything else that he is connected with the scientists and philosophers of his time. All the greatest exponents of civilisation, from Dante to Goethe, have been obsessed by light. But in the seventeenth century, light passed through a crucial stage. The invention of the lens was giving it a new range and power. The telescope (invented in Holland, although developed by Galileo) discovered new worlds in space; the microscope allowed a Dutch scientist named Van Leeuwenhoek to discover new worlds in a drop of water. And who polished the lenses that made these marvellous new observations possible? Spinoza, who, apart from being the greatest Dutch philosopher, was the finest lens-maker in Europe. Armed with these devices, philosophers attempted a new analysis of the nature of light itself. Descartes studied refraction, Huygens invented the wave theory – both in Holland. Finally Newton put forward his corpuscular theory, which was wrong, or at any rate less nearly right than Huygens's waves, but held the field till the nineteenth century.

Vermeer used the utmost ingenuity to make us feel the movement of light. He loved to show it passing over a white wall, and then, as if to make its progress more comprehensible, passing over a slightly crinkled map. At least four of these maps appear in his pictures, and, apart from their pleasantly light-transmitting surfaces, they remind us that the Dutch were the great cartographers of the age. Thus the mercantile sources of Vermeer's independence penetrate into the background of his quiet rooms.

In his determination to record exactly what he saw, Vermeer did not at all despise those mechanical devices of which his century was so proud. And in many of his pictures one finds the exaggerated proportions that one sees in photography, and the light is rendered by those little beads that one doesn't see with the naked eye, but which appear on the finder of an old-fashioned camera. Some people think he used the device known as the *camera obscura,* which projects an image onto a white sheet: but I fancy that he looked through a lens into a box with a piece of ground glass squared up, and painted exactly what he saw. Needless to say that Vermeer was also master of the science of perspective which had been revived in the 1650s with all the increased mathematical ardour of the time. And yet the scientific approach to experience ends in poetry, and I suppose that this is due to an almost mystical rapture in the perception of light. How else account for the joy that we feel when we look at the pewter jugs and white pots in Vermeer's pictures? This is partly a matter of his own sensibility; but it could hardly have existed without that specifically Dutch delight in material objects that produced their school of still-life painters, and often achieves what I can only call a spiritualisation of matter. It is the aesthetic equivalent of that passion for accurate observation that impelled their great scientists.

However, any attempt to relate art to society soon gets one into a false position. The greatest of all pictures based on the facts of vision wasn't painted in the scientific atmosphere of Holland, but in the superstitious, convention-ridden court of Philip IV of Spain: *Las Meninas*, 'The Ladies in Waiting', which was painted by Velasquez about five years before Vermeer's finest interiors. I draw no conclusions from this, except that although one may use works of art to illustrate the history of civilisation, one must not pretend that social conditions produce works of art or inevitably influence their form.

The enlightened tidiness of de Hooch and Vermeer and the rich imaginative experience of Rembrandt reached their zenith about 1660. Spinoza's *Tractatus* was printed in 1670. During that decade the leadership of intellectual life passed from Holland to England. The change began in 1660, when Charles II embarked from the Dutch beach at Scheveningen to return to England, and ended the isolation and austerity which had afflicted England for almost fifteen years. As so often happens, a new freedom of movement led to an outburst of pent-up energy. There are usually men of genius waiting for these moments of expansion, like ships waiting for a high tide; and on this occasion there was in England the brilliant group of natural philosophers who were to form the Royal Society – Robert Boyle, who used always to be described as the father of chemistry, Robert Hooke, the perfector of the microscope, Halley, the discoverer of comets, and Christopher Wren, the young geometer who at that date was a professor of astronomy.

Towering above all these remarkable scientists was Newton, one of the three or four Englishmen whose fame has transcended all national boundaries. I can't pretend that I have read the *Principia*, and if I did I wouldn't understand it any more than Samuel Pepys did when, as President of The Royal Society, it was handed to him for his approval. One must take on trust that it gave a mathematical account of the structure of the universe which for three hundred years seemed irrefutable. It was both the climax of the age of observation and the sacred book of the next century. Pope, who had probably not read as much of the *Principia* as I have, summed up the feelings of his contemporaries:

> Nature and Nature's laws lay hid in Night.
> God said, Let Newton be! and all was Light.

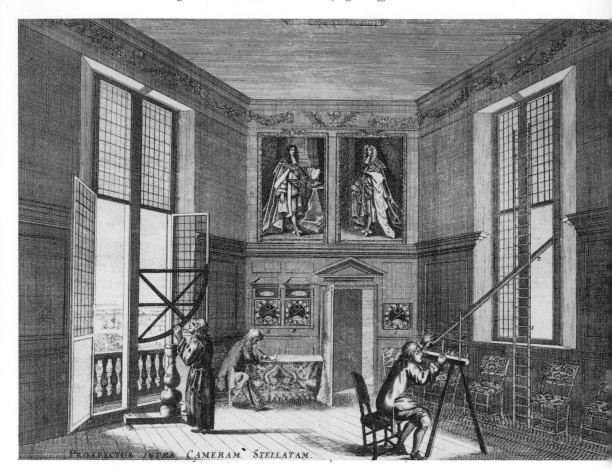

PROSPECTUS INTRA CAMERAM STELLATAM.

Parallel with the study of light was the study of the stars. In the Octagon Room of the Royal Observatory at Greenwich [151], founded, as Charles II's warrant puts it, 'in order to the finding out of the longitude of places, and for perfecting navigation and astronomy', one may draw together the threads of this chapter – light, lenses, observation, navigation and mathematics. And I can step into a print of the interior almost as I could step into the square at Haarlem. In this light, harmonious room one breathes the atmosphere of humanised science. Here is the quadrant that Flamsteed, the first Astronomer Royal, used to establish the meridian, and here is his telescope. This was the first great age of scientific instruments [152]: Huygens's clock, Van Leeuwenhoek's microscope. I must admit that they don't look very scientific by our standards: the telescopes look like something out of *Aurora's Wedding*, and these charming little globes and orreries still have style and the impress of human personality. Art and science have not yet drawn apart, and these instruments are not only means to an end, but symbols – symbols of hope that man might learn to master his environment and create a more humane and reasonable society. Such they remained until the end of the nineteenth century. When Tennyson was told that a Brahmin had destroyed a microscope because it revealed secrets that man should not know, he was profoundly shocked. Only in the last sixty years or so have we begun to feel that the descendants of these beautiful shining objects may be going to destroy us.

This room full of light, this shining enclosure of space, was designed by Sir Christopher Wren. It was built on the spur of a hill overlooking the old palace of Greenwich, and this too was rebuilt by Wren, transformed from a palace into a naval hospital [153]. How much of what we see is from his design is hard to say. By the time the buildings were going up he was prepared to leave their execution to his two very able assistants at the Board of Works, Sir John Vanbrugh and Nicholas Hawksmoor. But he certainly provided the plan; and the result is the greatest architectural unit built in England since the Middle Ages. It is sober without being dull, massive without being oppressive. What is civilisation? A state of mind where it is thought desirable for a naval hospital to look like this and for the inmates to dine in a splendidly decorated hall [154]. In fact the Painted Hall in Greenwich hospital is one of the finest rooms in England, and its ceiling, painted by Sir James Thornhill, is perhaps the best attempt made in England to imitate provincially the metropolitan glories of Roman Baroque.

By the time this room at Greenwich was built Wren had long been the most famous architect in England. But as a young man people had thought

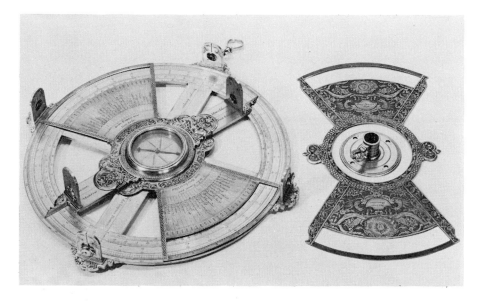

152 Circumferentor, mid-seventeenth century

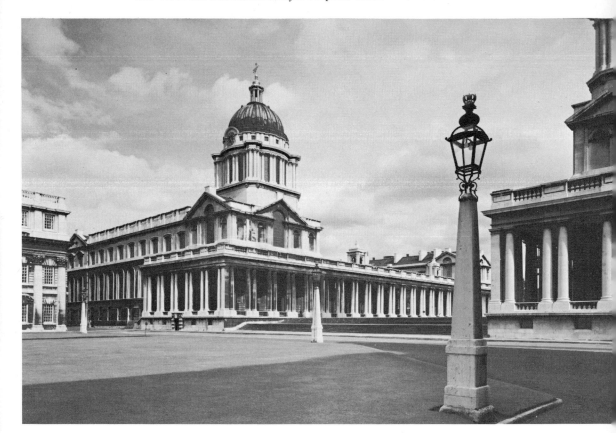

of him only as a mathematician and an astronomer. And why, at the age of thirty, he took up architecture, is not clear. I suppose he wanted to see his geometrical and mechanical solutions given shape. But he had to learn the rudiments of style; so he bought some books and went to France to draw the buildings and meet the leading architects. He even met Bernini, who was in Paris at the time, and saw his drawing for the Louvre. 'I would have given my skin for it,' he said, 'but the reserved old Italian gave me but a view.' On his return he was consulted, as an engineer, about old St Paul's, which was in danger of collapsing. He proposed replacing the tower by a dome. But before this questionable project could be considered, the Fire of London broke out. It ended on 5 September 1666. Six days later Wren submitted a plan for rebuilding the City. Only then was 'the ingenious Dr Wren' fully committed to architecture.

Ingenious is the word for the results that followed, the thirty new City churches. Each is the solution of a different problem, and Wren's power of invention never failed. But when he came to the crown and centre of the whole scheme, the new St Paul's [155], then he revealed something more

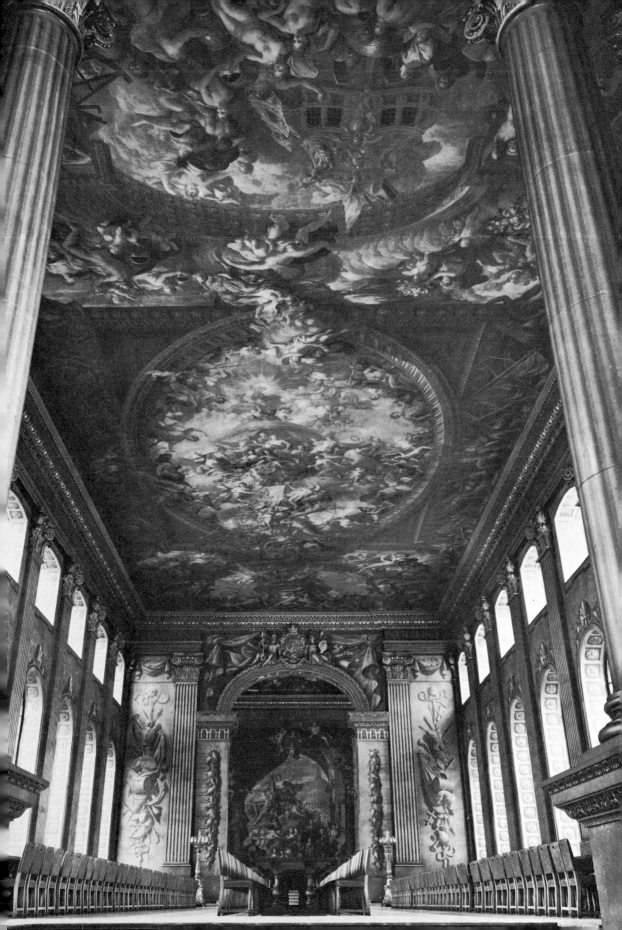

than ingenuity. In spite of the awkwardness of imposing a Roman elevation on to a Gothic plan, he has achieved areas of such refined and inventive detail as to make St Paul's Cathedral the chief monument of English classicism.

Wren's buildings show us that mathematics, measurement, observation – all that goes to make up the philosophy of science – were not hostile to architecture; nor to music, for this was the age of one of the greatest English composers, Henry Purcell. But what was the effect of the scientific attitude on poetry? At first I think it was harmless, even beneficial. When Vaughan wrote:

> I saw Eternity the other night,
> Like a great ring of pure and endless light,
> All calm, as it was bright;
> And round beneath it, Time in hours, days, years.
> Driv'n by the spheres
> Like a vast shadow mov'd; in which the world
> And all her train were hurl'd.

he was giving poetic expression to the same impulse that induced Flamsteed to look through his telescope. Milton called Galileo the 'Tuscan artist with his optic glass'. I believe he is the only contemporary mentioned in *Paradise Lost*; and without Galileo's discoveries Milton's universe would have taken a less grandiose form. Vaughan and Milton were writing as late as the 1660s, and by this time a change had come over the concept of poetry. Milton was to some extent an anachronism, a survivor from the belated English Renaissance. Intellectually he was closer to Inigo Jones than to Wren. It is a curious fact that in the same year that *Paradise Lost* was published, 1667, there appeared a book which can be quoted as the supreme example of anti-poetic rationalism – Sprat's *History of the Royal Society*. 'Poetry,' says Sprat, 'is the parent of superstition.' Indeed all products of the imagination are dangerous falsities and even ornaments of speech are a form of deceit. But from the time in which real philosophy has appeared, 'the course of things,' says Sprat, 'goes quietly along in its own true channel of natural causes and effects.'

I don't suppose that all the members of the Royal Society were quite so hostile to the imagination. After all, most of them remained professing Christians – in fact Newton spent (we would say, wasted) a lot of his time on Biblical studies. And they continued to use a celestial globe in which the constellations were grouped in the form of men and animals; they continued to accept the kind of personifications that one gets on the ceiling of the Painted Hall. But all the same, they recognised that all these were fancies, that reality lay elsewhere, in the realm of measurement and observation. And

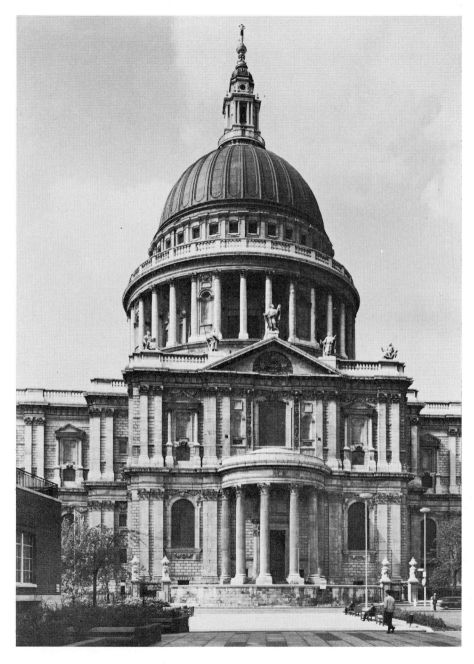

so began that division between scientific truth and the imagination which was to kill poetic drama, and give a feeling of artificiality to all poetry during the next hundred years.

However there was a compensation: the emergence of a clear, workable prose. Even then, of course, something was lost. Compare a piece of Thomas

Browne and Dryden. Here is the Browne, full of metaphor and allusion – an almost Shakespearean richness of language: 'Though Somnus in Homer be sent to rouse Agamemnon, I find no such effects in these drowsy approaches to sleep. To keep our eyes open longer were but to act our antipodes. The huntsmen are up in America, and they are already past their first sleep in Persia.' And here is the Dryden: 'If by the people you understand the multitude; 'tis no matter what they think; they are sometimes in the right, sometimes in the wrong: their judgment is a mere lottery.' Perfectly good sense, but the verbal magic, the incantation, of the Thomas Browne is on a higher plane. Still we must allow that what Dryden himself called 'the other harmony of prose' was a civilising force. It was a tool of the new philosophy almost as much as Stevins's decimal system was a tool of the new mathematics. This was particularly true of France. For about three hundred years French prose was the form in which the European intelligence shaped and communicated its thoughts about history, diplomacy, definition, criticism, human relationships – everything except metaphysics. It is arguable that the non-existence of a clear, concrete German prose has been one of the chief disasters to European civilisation.

There is no doubt that in its first glorious century the appeal to reason and experience was a triumph for the human intelligence. Between Descartes and Newton western man created those instruments of thought that set him apart from the other peoples of the world. And if you look at the average nineteenth-century historian you will find that to him European civilisation seems almost to begin with this achievement. The strange thing is that none of these mid-nineteenth-century writers (except for Carlyle and Ruskin) seemed to notice that the triumph of rational philosophy had resulted in a new form of barbarism. If, from the balcony of the Greenwich Observatory, I look beyond the order of Wren's hospital I see, stretching as far as the eye can reach, the squalid disorder of industrial society. It has grown up as a result of the same conditions that allowed the Dutch to build their beautiful towns and support their painters and print the works of philosophers: fluid capital, a free economy, a flow of exports and imports, a dislike of interference, a belief in cause and effect.

Every civilisation seems to have its nemesis, not only because the first bright impulses become tarnished by greed and laziness, but because of unpredictables – and in this case the unpredictable was the growth of population. The greedy became greedier, the ignorant lost touch with traditional skills, and the light of experience narrowed its beam so that a grand design like Greenwich would now be thought of as a waste of money that no accountant could condone.

29 Vermeer, *The Music Lesson* (detail)

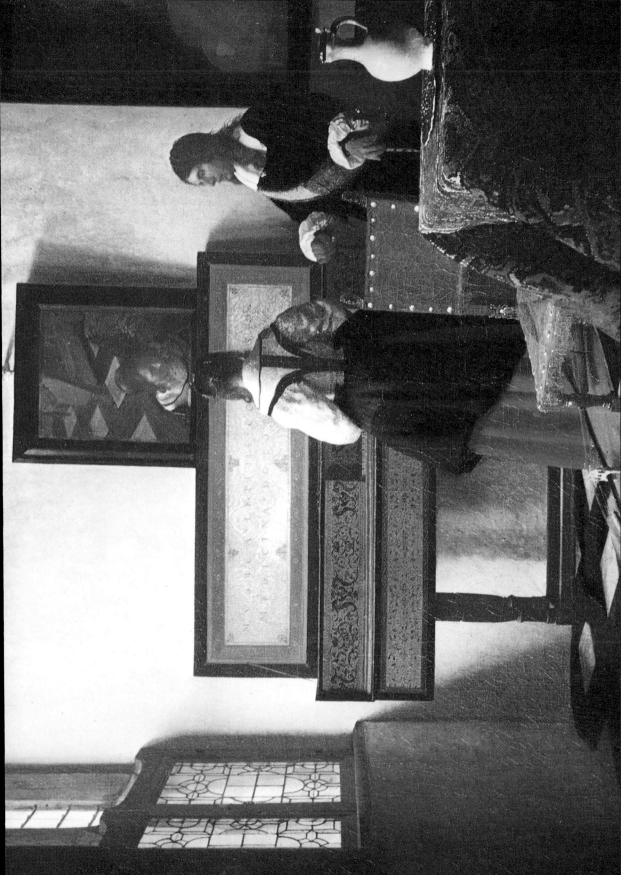

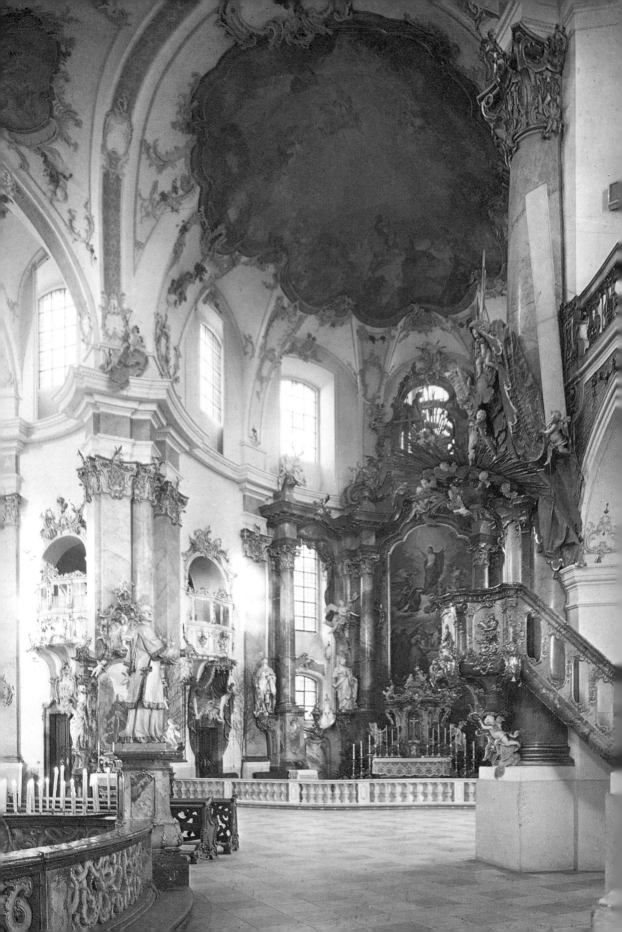

9 The Pursuit of Happiness

By the year 1700 the German-speaking countries have once more become articulate. For over a century the disorderly aftermath of the Reformation, followed by the dreary, interminable horrors of the Thirty Years War, had kept them from playing a part in the history of civilisation. Then peace, stability, the natural strength of the land, and a peculiar social organisation, allowed them to add to the sum of European experience two shining achievements, one in music, the other in architecture. Of course the music is more important to us. In a period when poetry was almost dead, when the visual arts were little more than a shadow of what they had been, when the emotional life seemed almost to have dried up, music expressed the most serious thoughts and intuitions of the time, just as painting had done in the early sixteenth century. This chapter is primarily about music; and some of the qualities of eighteenth-century music – its melodious flow, its complex symmetry, its decorative invention – are reflected in the architecture; but not its deeper appeal to the emotions. And yet the Rococo style has a place in civilisation. Serious-minded people used to call it shallow and corrupt, chiefly because it was intended to give pleasure; well, the founders of the American Constitution, who were far from frivolous, thought fit to mention the pursuit of happiness as a proper aim for mankind, and if ever this aim has been given visible form it is in Rococo architecture – the pursuit of happiness and the pursuit of love.

Before we plunge into the buoyant sea of Rococo I must say a word about the austere ideal that had preceded it. For sixty years France had dominated Europe, and this had meant a rigidly centralised, authoritarian government and a classic style. The classic discipline which the taste of Versailles applied to all the arts can be represented as one of the summits of European civilisation – *le grand siècle*. It produced two sublime dramatists, Corneille and Racine. Nowhere else in literature does one find, as one does in Racine, a subtle understanding of the human heart clothed in language of such sustained and flawless perfection. It produced a great and noble painter, Nicolas Poussin. Someone once said that to admire Poussin was the reward of civilisation, and although I would interpret the word in rather a wider sense, I see what was meant. It isn't only that Poussin was a learned artist who had studied and assimilated the poses of antique sculpture and the pictorial inventions of Raphael; it was that he brought to the profession of

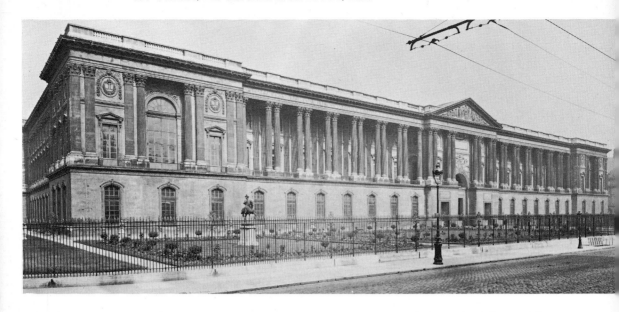

picture-making a mind stored with ancient literature and formed by stoic philosophy.

French Classicism also produced magnificent architecture. What could be more impressive than the south front of the Louvre – except perhaps the east side of the same building [156]. This is the architecture of a great metropolitan culture; and it expresses an ideal: not an ideal that appeals to me, but an ideal nonetheless – grandeur achieved through the authoritarian state. I often ask myself how Perrault's façade of the Louvre differs from the equally grandiose architecture of Rome, and the question is made more pertinent because Bernini actually did a design for the Louvre which was rejected. I think the answer is that Roman buildings – those of Bernini in particular – have a warmth of feeling that French Classicism lacks. In the end they appeal to the emotions, and give abstract form to the same popular sentiment that supported the Catholic revival; whereas Perrault's façade reflects the triumph of an authoritarian state, and of those logical solutions that Colbert, the greatest administrator of the seventeenth century, was imposing on politics, economics and every department of contemporary life, including, above all, the arts. This gives French Classical architecture a certain inhumanity. It was the work not of craftsmen, but of wonderfully gifted civil servants. As long as it reflects this grand comprehensive system, it is done with superb conviction. But when it has been attempted outside France it has usually looked as lifeless and pretentious as the dullest nineteenth-century town hall. French Classicism was eminently not exportable. But the High Baroque of Rome [157] was exactly what the north of

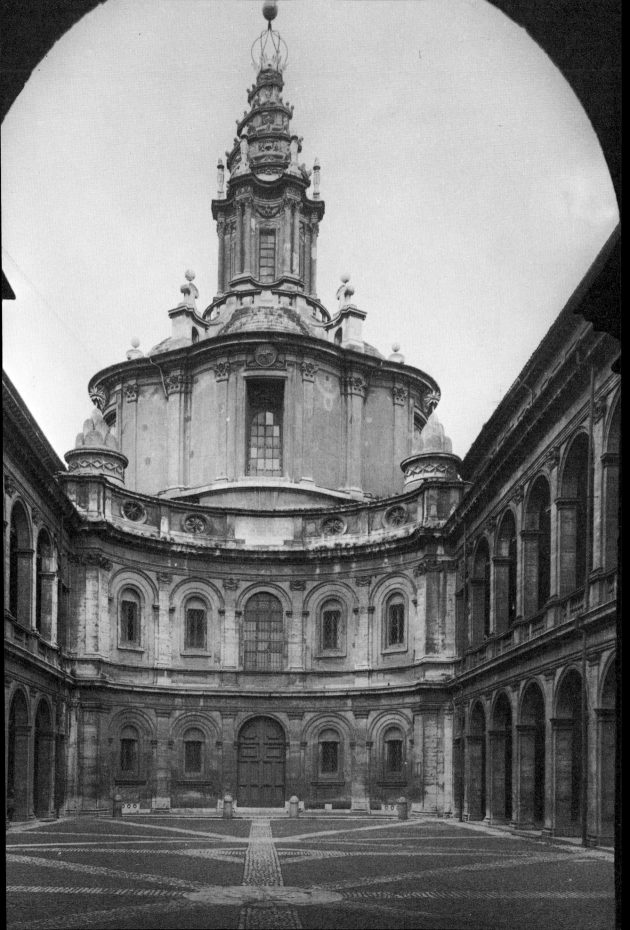

Europe needed, for a number of reasons. For one thing it was elastic and adaptable. Rules didn't exist for Borromini, and to this day he shocks the academically minded. And then I suppose one must say that the restless convolutions of Borromini's High Baroque often come very close to the swirls and twirls of late Gothic. All over Germany there are pieces of decorative architecture where at first one can hardly tell whether they are late fifteenth-century Gothic or mid-eighteenth-century Rococo.

So the architectural language in which northern Europe became articulate in the eighteenth century was Italian Baroque; and rather the same is true of music. Underlying much of the work of the German composers was the international style of the great Italians, in particular of Alessandro Scarlatti. With its mastery of long curving lines, its controlled elaborations, its perfection of detail, it is remarkably close to the architecture of Borromini. Borromini came from a land of stone-carvers – the Italian lakes that form a boundary with Switzerland – and his style could fit into the craftsman tradition of the Germanic north, a tradition serving a social order that was absolutely the reverse of the centralised bureaucracy of France. It's true that many of the German princes thought they would like to imitate Versailles. But the formative element in German art and German music didn't lie there, but in the multiplicity of regions and towns and abbeys – all competing for their architects and their choirmasters; and also relying on the talents of their local organists and plasterers. The creators of the German Baroque – the Assams and the Zimmermanns – were families of craftsmen: *zimmermann* is the German for carpenter. The finest buildings we shall look at are not palaces, but local pilgrimage churches, deep in the country, like the Vierzehnheiligen – the 'Fourteen Saints'. And, come to think of it, the Bachs were a family of local musical craftsmen out of which there suddenly emerged one of the great geniuses of Western Europe, Johann Sebastian.

The sound of Bach's music reminds me of a curious fact that people don't always remember when they talk about the eighteenth-century – that the great art of the time was religious art. The thought was anti-religious; the way of life ostentatiously profane; we are right to call the first half of the century the age of reason. But in the arts, what did this emancipated rationalism produce? One adorable painter – Watteau, some nice domestic architecture, some pretty furniture: but nothing to set beside the *Matthew Passion* or the *Messiah* or the abbeys and pilgrimage churches of Bavaria and Franconia. To some extent Bach's music grew out of the Italian style, just as northern Baroque grew out of Borromini. But there was another musical tradition in Germany which went back to the Reformation. Luther

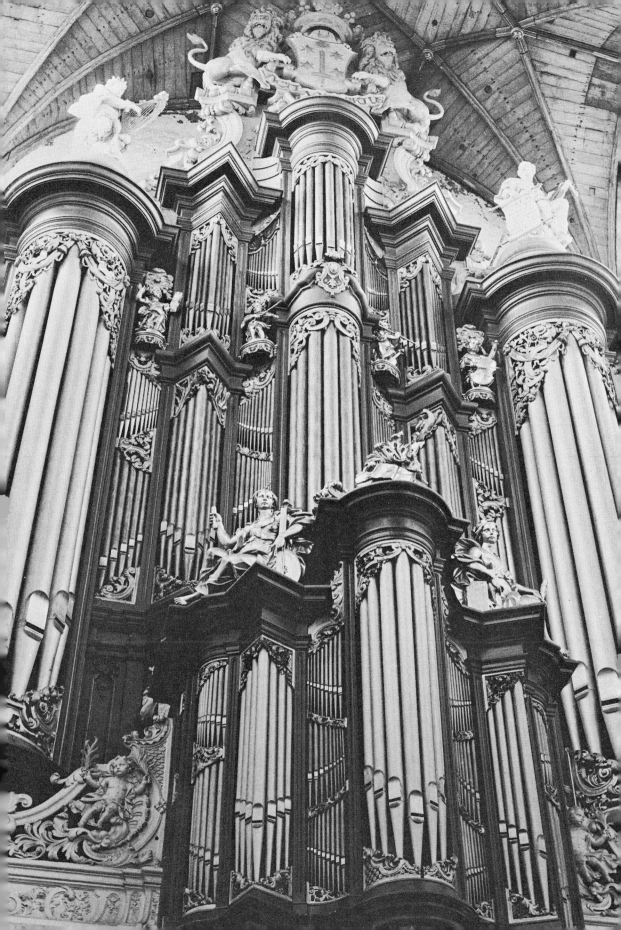

had been a fine musician – he wrote music and sang with (surprisingly enough) a sweet tenor voice. And although the Lutheran reform prohibited many of the arts that civilise our impulses, it encouraged church music. In small Dutch and German towns the choir and the organ became the only means through which men could enter the world of spiritualised emotion; when the Calvinists, in their still more resolute purification of the Christian rite, prohibited organs and destroyed them, they caused more distress than had ever been caused by the destruction of images. Organs have played a variable role in European civilisation. In the nineteenth century they were symbols of newly-won affluence, like billiard tables; but in the seventeenth and eighteenth centuries they were expressions of municipal pride and independence [158]. They were the work of the leading local craftsmen, often covered with decorative sculpture; and organists were respected members of the community.

Bourgeois democracy, which had provided a background to Dutch painting in the seventeenth century, became partly responsible for German music; and it was a society more earnest and more participating than the Dutch connoisseurs had been. This provincial society was the background of Bach. His universal genius rose out of the high plateau of competitive musical life in the Protestant cities of northern Germany. One can even say that it rose out of a family that had been professional musicians for one hundred years, so that in certain districts the very word 'Bach' meant a musician. And Johann Sebastian's life was that of a conscientious, somewhat obstinate, provincial organist and choirmaster. But he was universal. A great musical critic said of him: 'He is the spectator of all musical time and existence, to whom it is not of the smallest importance whether a thing be new or old, so long as it is true.'

Baroque elaboration is not the side of Bach that we value most. That severe head [159] belongs equally to the Renaissance or the late Middle Ages; take away the wig and it could easily come out of a Dürer, or even a Riemenschneider. And some of the great moments in Bach's oratorios of the Passion have the solemn simplicity and deep religious feeling of Giotto's frescoes. The towering polyphony has the quality of Gothic architecture. But then we remember how closely German Baroque, in its use of controlled space to work on our emotions, follows the traditions of Gothic architecture; and we find that we can illustrate Bach's music by a contemporary building. The pilgrimage church of the Vierzehnheiligen [30, facing p. 221] was built by an architect who was only two years younger than Bach. He was called Balthasar Neumann, and although his name is not well known in the English-speaking world, I think he was certainly one of the greatest architects of the

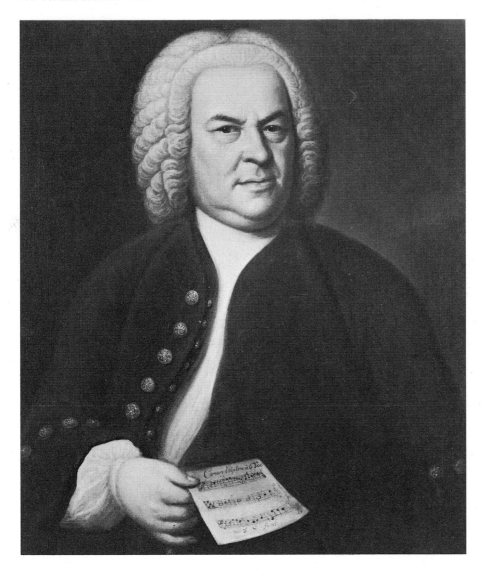

eighteenth century. Unlike the other builders of German Baroque, he was
not primarily a carver or plasterer, but an engineer. He made his name as a
master of town-planning and fortifications. Inside his buildings one is
conscious of a complex plan, worked out like the most intricate mathematical problem. But when occasion demanded it, he made use of ornament
as lavish and fanciful as that of the most ebullient Bavarian plasterers.

Balthasar Neumann [160] was fortunate in that the painted decorations in
his finest interiors were not the work of the amiable local ceiling painters
but of the greatest decorator of the age, the Venetian Giovanni Battista
Tiepolo; and it is in one of Neumann's great buildings, the Bishop's Palace

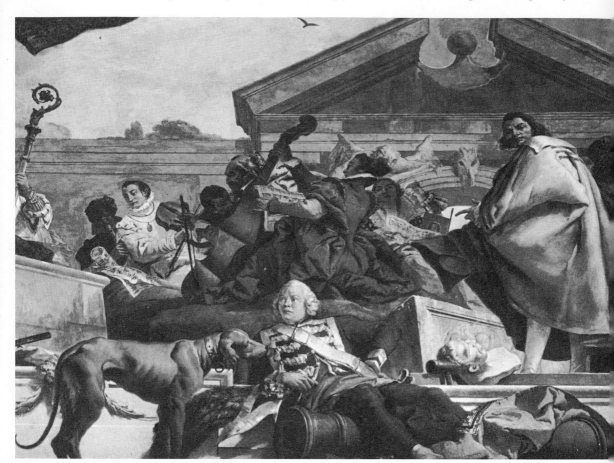

at Würzburg, that Tiepolo executed his masterpiece, the ceiling that covers the vast area of the staircase [161]. It represents the four continents, a theme for decorative art that had conveniently replaced the once-fashionable allegories of the Christian faith; and, looking at these brilliant inventions, one may happily argue which continent has proved the most inspiring: Africa with its ostriches, camels and disdainful negresses; America with ravishing girls in feathered head-dresses riding on crocodiles [31, facing p. 236]; or Asia with its tigers and elephants. Somewhere in the background of Asia is a bare hill with three empty crosses. I wonder if the Bishop ever noticed it. He had more gratifying things to look at, his Residenz being, in fact, about twice the size of Buckingham Palace and filled in every room of the *piano nobile* with splendid decoration. One can't help speculating on the tithes and taxes that the peasants of Franconia had to pay in order that their episcopal master should do himself so well. But one must admit that many of these rulers of small German principalities – bishops, dukes, electors — were in fact remarkably cultivated and intelligent men. Their competitive ambitions benefited architecture and music in a way that the democratic obscurity of the Hanoverians in England did not. The Schönborn family, one of whom was responsible for the Residenz, were really great patrons whose name should be remembered with the Medici.

I felt some scruples in comparing the music of Bach with a Baroque interior. No such hesitations need prevent me from invoking on the staircase of Würzburg the name of George Frideric Handel. Great men have a curious way of appearing in complementary pairs. This has happened so often in history that I don't think it can have been invented by symmetrically-minded historians, but must represent some need to keep human faculties in balance. However that may be, there is no doubt that the two great musicians of the early eighteenth century, Bach and Handel, fall into this pattern of contrasting and complementary personalities. They were born

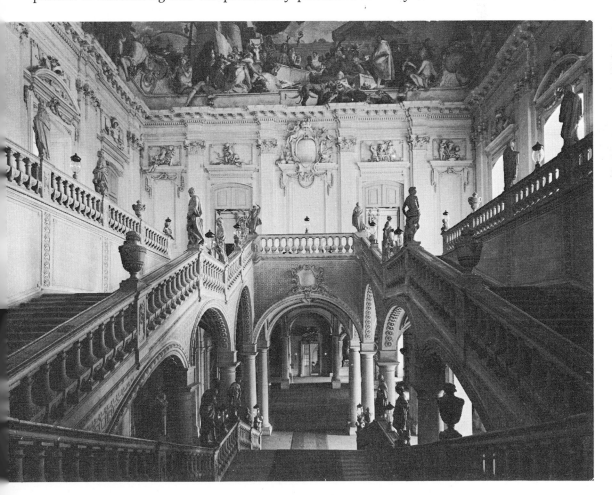

161 Balthasar Neumann, Staircase, Residenz, Würzburg

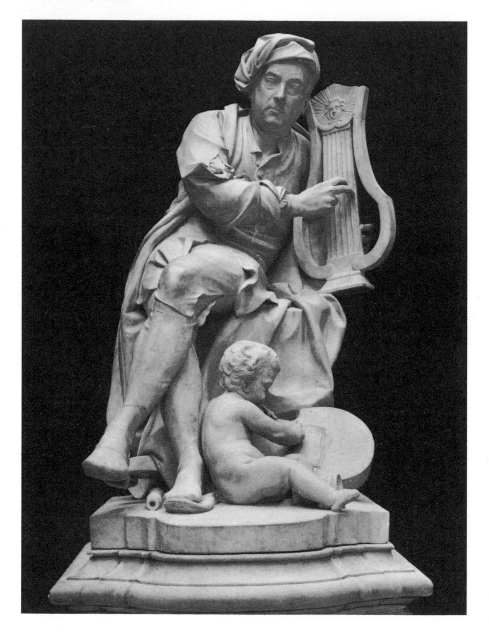

in the same year – 1685; they both went blind from copying musical scores and were operated on, unsuccessfully, by the same surgeon. But otherwise they were opposites.

In contrast to Bach's timeless universality, Handel was completely of his age. Instead of Bach's frugal, industrious career as an organist with numerous children, Handel made and lost several fortunes as a theatrical impresario. Roubillac's statue of him [162], now in the Victoria and Albert Museum, was erected by the grateful proprietors of an amusement park, Vauxhall, in which his music had been one of the attractions. There he sits in un-buttoned mood, one shoe off and one shoe on, not caring how much he snitched other people's tunes as long as he produced something effective. In his youth he must have been charming, because when he went to Rome as an unknown young virtuoso he was immediately taken up by society, and cardinals wrote libretti for him to set to music. There are remains of remark-able good looks in this head. Later in life, when he had settled in England and entered the world of operatic production, he became less anxious to please, and is traditionally said to have held one of his leading ladies out of the window and threatened to drop her if she did not sing in tune. He re-mained faithful throughout his life to the Italian Baroque style. In conse-quence his music goes well with the decorations of Tiepolo, which even have the romantic pseudo-historical subjects of his operas. The extra-ordinary thing is that this composer of flowing, florid airs and rousing choruses, when he turned from opera to oratorio – which was in fact a kind of sacred opera – wrote great religious music. *Saul, Samson, Israel in Egypt* not only contain wonderful melodic and polyphonic inventions, but show an understanding of the depths of the human spirit. As for the *Messiah*, it is, like Michelangelo's *Creation of Adam,* one of those rare works that appeal immediately to everyone, and yet is indisputably a masterpiece of the highest order.

I have called Handel a Baroque composer, and referred to the buildings of Neumann as northern Baroque. I could almost equally well have called them Rococo – in Würzburg the two terms overlap. But there is a real difference between them, which means something in the history of civilisation. Baroque, however modified in Germany and Austria, was an Italian inven-tion. Baroque first came into being as religious architecture, and expressed the emotional aspirations of the Catholic Church. Rococo was to some extent a Parisian invention, and provocatively secular. It was, superficially at any rate, a reaction against the heavy Classicism of Versailles. Instead of the static orders of antiquity, it drew inspiration from natural objects in which the line wandered freely – shells, flowers, seaweed – especially if it wandered in a double curve. Rococo was a reaction against the academic style; but it was not negative. It represented a real gain in sensibility. It achieved a new freedom of association and captured new and more delicate shades of feeling.

All this is expressed through the work of one exquisite artist, Watteau. He was born in 1684 – the year before Bach and Handel – in the Flemish town of Valenciennes, and he derived his technique from Rubens. But instead of a hearty Flemish acceptance of life, Watteau, who was a consumptive,

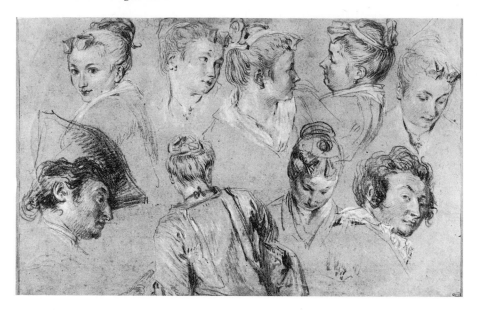

discovered something in himself that had hardly ever been seen in art before: a feeling of the transitoriness and, thus, the seriousness of pleasure. He had brilliant gifts – he could draw with the style and precision of a Renaissance artist – and used his skill to record his rapture at the sight of beautiful girls [163, 164]. What dreams of beauty they are! How happy all these exquisite people should be! But,

> Ay, in the very temple of Delight
> Veil'd Melancholy has her sovran shrine.
> Though seen of none save him whose strenuous tongue
> Can burst Joy's grape against his palate fine.

No one had a finer palate than Watteau. He can taste every delicate flavour in the open-air quadrille of *Fêtes Venitiennes* [32, facing p. 237], where glances suddenly meet. And he has depicted himself, not as one of the dancers, but as the bagpipe man, animating the scene with his humble, melancholy instrument. He was, his friend Caylus said, 'tender and perhaps something of a shepherd'. In this elegant company that he watched so discerningly he remained the odd man out, and Gilles, the simpleton, whose tall white figure rises in isolation above his fellow comedians, is a sort of idealised self-portrait – tender, simple and yet capable of love and of delicate intuitions [33, facing p. 252].

Watteau came on the scene at an incredibly early date in the eighteenth century. His masterpiece, the *Pilgrimage to Cythera*, was painted in 1712, when Louis XIV was still alive. It has the lightness and sharpness of a Mozart opera; also the sense of human drama. The delicate relationships between

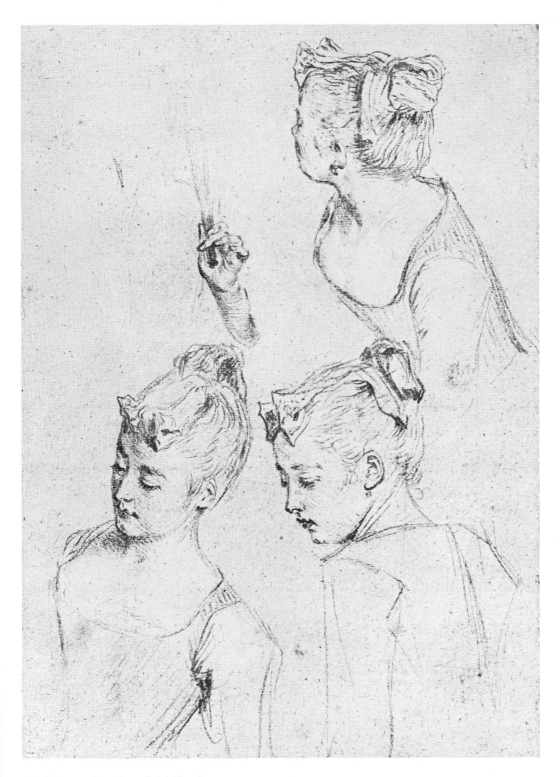

164 Watteau, Drawing of girls' heads

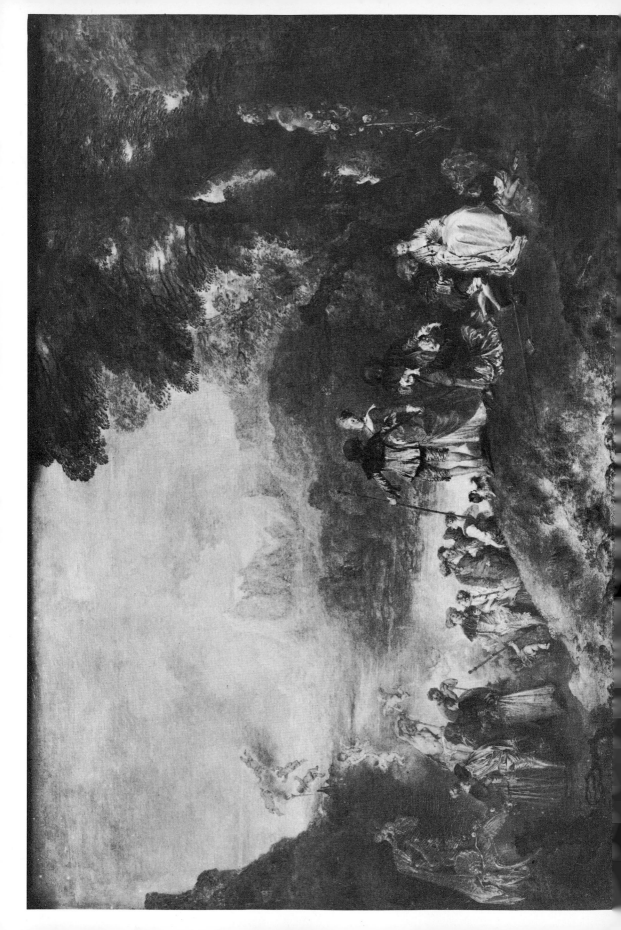

these men and women who have spent a few hours on the Island of Venus and must now return [165] reminds one of those rapturous stirrings that precede the departure of the confident lovers in *Così Fan Tutte*; and yet Mozart's opera was written over seventy years later.

The new sensibility, of which Watteau was the prophet, showed itself most of all in a more delicate understanding of the relations between men and women. Sentiment: the word has got into trouble, as words do but it was, in its day, a civilising word. Sterne, in his *Sentimental Journey*, that somewhat discredited work of Rococo prose, tells a fable about a town of Abdera, which was the vilest town in all Thrace.

The town of Abdera, notwithstanding Democritus lived there, trying all the powers of irony and laughter to reclaim it, was the vilest and most profligate town in all Thrace. What for poisons, conspiracies and assassinations, libels, pasquinades and tumults, there was no going there by day; 'twas worse by night.

Now, when things were at the worst, it came to pass that the Andromeda of Euripides being represented at Abdera, the whole orchestra was delighted with it: but of all the passages which delighted them nothing operated more upon their imaginations than the tender strokes of nature which the poet had wrought up in that pathetic speech of Perseus, 'O Cupid, prince of gods and men,' etc. Every man almost spoke pure iambics the next day, and talked of nothing but Perseus his pathetic address – 'O Cupid, prince of gods and men'; – in every street of Abdera, in every house – 'O Cupid! Cupid!' – in every mouth, like the natural notes of some sweet melody which drops from it, whether it will or no, nothing but 'Cupid! Cupid! prince of gods and men'. The fire caught, and the whole city, like the heart of one man, opened itself to Love.

No pharmacopolist could sell one grain of hellebore; not a single armourer had a heart to forge one instrument of death; Friendship and Virtue met together, and kissed each other in the street; the Golden Age returned, and hung over the town of Abdera; every Abderite took his oaten pipe, and every Abderitish woman left her purple web, and chastely sat her down, and listened to the song.

Next to love Watteau cared most about music for which, his friends tell us, he had a most delicate ear. Nearly all his scenes are enacted to the sound of music. In this he shows himself as part of a tradition going back to the Venetians, of whom Pater said that they painted the musical intervals of our existence when 'life itself is conceived as a kind of listening'. Giorgione's *Fête Champêtre* [77], which I described in an earlier chapter as the first picture in which man was content to do nothing, because he was perfectly in harmony with nature, is the direct ancestor of Watteau. And as with the Venetians, Watteau achieves this effect of music by translating experience into a different sensuous medium: colour. Watteau's colour has a shimmering iridescent quality which makes one think immediately of musical

165 Watteau, *The Pilgrimage to Cythera*

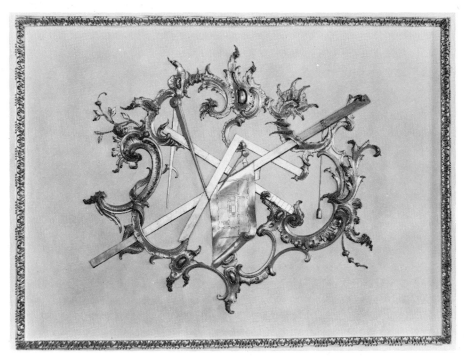

analogies. And yet the structure of every detail, for example the hands of his lutanists, is precise and articulate as a phrase of Mozart.

Watteau died in 1721 at the same age as Raphael, thirty-seven. By that date the Rococo style was beginning to affect decoration and architecture. Ten years later it had spread all over Europe, producing a style as international as early fifteenth-century Gothic; and not dissimilar in other ways. It was equally an art of small courts, an art of elegance rather than greatness, an art in which religious motives were treated with grace and sentiment rather than a solemn conviction. Rococo even spread to England, although the native good sense of a fox-hunting society prevented its more extravagant flights. I suppose that most of the plaster work, like most of the singing, was done by foreigners; but an Englishman named Mayhew did the decorations in the music room at Norfolk House [166], which is only a little less elegant than its Parisian counterparts. A true international style controls the shape of everything. It is an absolute compulsion which overrides convenience or what we used to call functionalism. No one supposed that Rococo knife-handles were easy to hold or Rococo soup tureens light to carry and easy to clean. They *had* to be like rocks and shells and seaweed, just as in late Gothic times they had to be like trees. Rococo, in spite of its love of sea-shells, was less descriptive than Gothic; and it made all the raw materials of its design dance to the same tune. Walter

31 Tiepolo, *America*, from the Staircase Ceiling

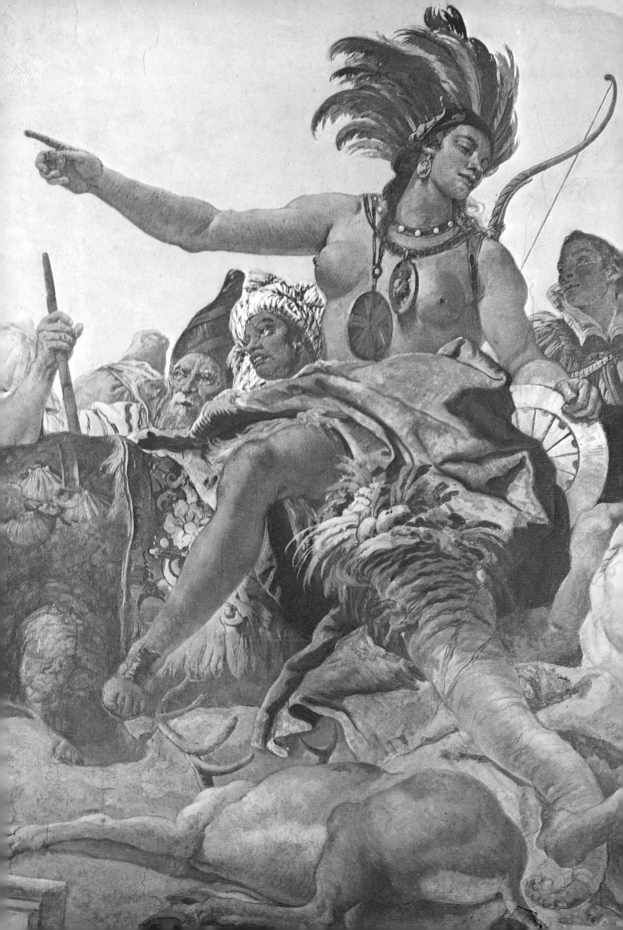

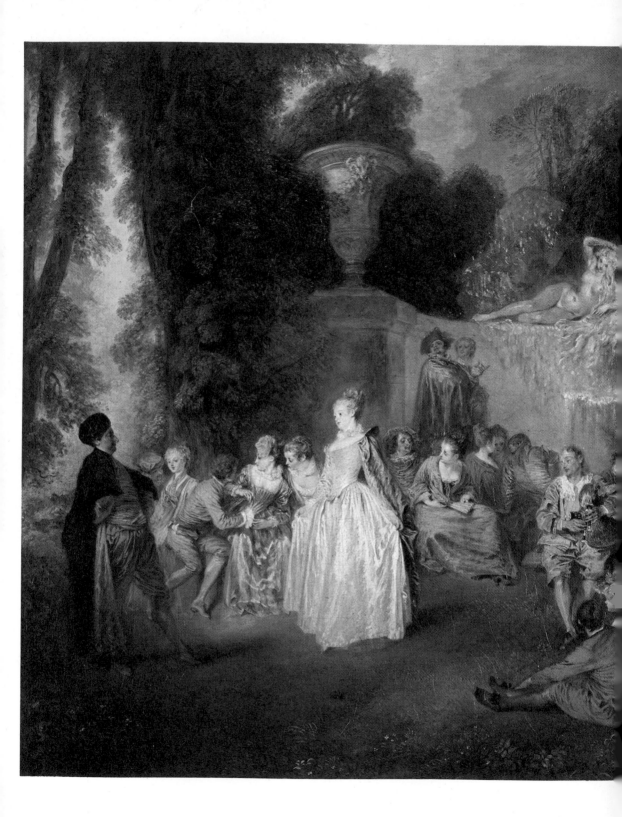

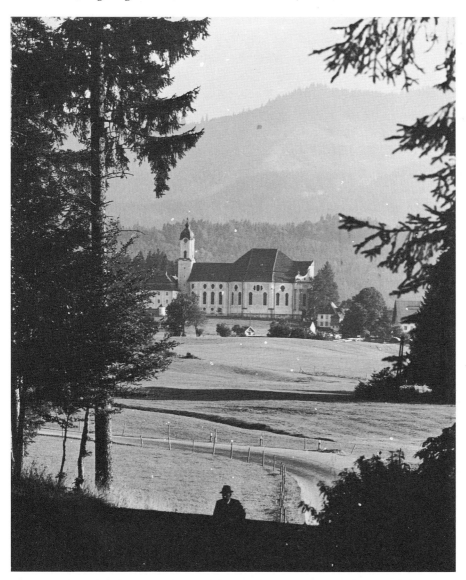

Pater said that all art aspired to the condition of music. I don't suppose he thought of extending this famous dictum to applied art. But it is true of the finest Rococo design. The rhythms, the assonances, the textures, have the effect of music, and seem to be echoed in the music of the next fifty years.

For a few bars it isn't always easy to tell the difference between Haydn and Mozart; and yet the two great musicians of the second half of the eighteenth century were very different characters and the difference comes through in their music. Haydn, who was twenty-four years older than Mozart, was born in a village, the son of a wheelwright, and was fundamentally a peaceful, spacious, soil-conscious man. He said that he wrote his music in order that 'the weary and worn or the men burdened with affairs might enjoy a few minutes of solace and refreshment'. And I think of this saying, as I approach the Bavarian pilgrimage church of the Wies [167]. It belongs to the countryside; in fact from a distance it might almost be the hall of a rustic manor. But enter it and the most incredible richness appears before your eyes. Heaven on earth. It is true that people entering the Gothic cathedrals left behind their life of material cares and seemed to pass into a different world. But it was a mysterious, awe-inspiring world in which hope of salvation was mixed with fear of death and judgement, and in simple communities the chief accent was on fear. Over the chancel arch in all parish churches was a scarifying representation of the Last Judgement, known as a Doom. In these Rococo churches the faithful are persuaded not by fear but by joy. To enter them [168] is a foretaste of paradise: sometimes, I admit, rather more like the Mohammedan paradise than the disembodied paradise of Christianity. One wonders what St Paul (or Ezekiel) would have thought of all those little *amorini* tumbling round the pulpit. 'O Cupid, Cupid, prince of gods and men.' Well, it's always been difficult, even for the saints, to represent spiritual love without having recourse to the symbols of physical love. Creation is the most mysterious of all God's acts. And it is Haydn's *Creation* that comes to my mind as I contemplate the rustic delights of the brothers Zimmermann. Of course the music of Haydn's *Creation* is what historians call Classical rather than Baroque – it was a late work written long after the building of the Wies. And yet I feel in Haydn's music very much the same naive joy in what I may call the dance of life that inspired the Bavarian craftsmen.

In Haydn's earlier works, particularly those for small orchestras and strings, his music does seem to be in exactly the same style as the Rococo rooms in which it was performed. For thirty years he was court musician to the Esterhazy family, one of the many enlightened patrons that emerged from the competitive patchwork of German principalities. Night after night dozens of pieces were performed in dimly glittering rooms. How bored the more bucolic courtiers must have been! But they had to stick it so long as the bishop or elector was amused and perhaps himself performed on the flute or 'cello. Haydn had to satisfy the inexhaustible princely appetite, and he wrote for Prince Esterhazy over forty quartets, over one hundred symphonies, and many hundreds of occasional pieces. They couldn't all be equally good, any more than Dickens's weekly instalments could all be equally good. But this is one way in which great things are done. Haydn said: 'Some of my children are well-bred, and some are ill-bred, but

168 Zimmermann, Die Wies, interior

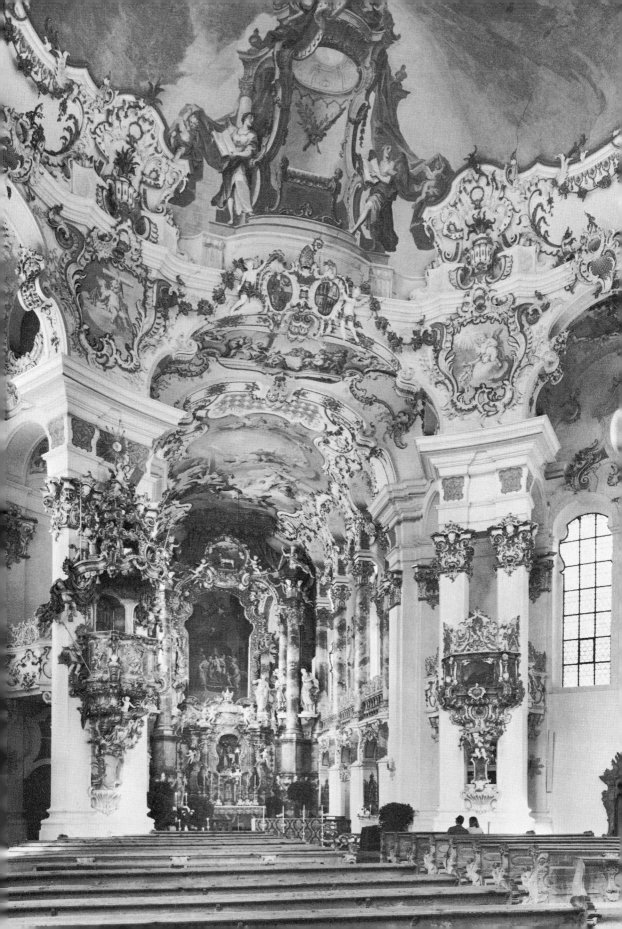

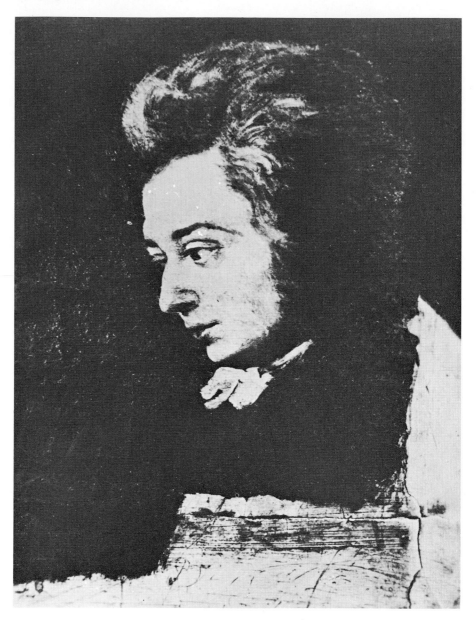

now and then there is a changeling among them.' Naturally we are interested in the changelings.

It's curious that in the present day we should have made such a cult of Rococo music when the Rococo style as a whole runs so strongly counter to our convictions. Many buildings of the eighteenth century were erected simply to give pleasure by people who believed that pleasure was important, and worth taking trouble about, and could be given some of the quality of art.

And we managed to destroy a good many of them during the war including the Zwinger at Dresden, the palace of Charlottenburg in Berlin, and the greater part of the Residenz at Würzburg. As I have said, it may be difficult to define civilisation, but it isn't so difficult to recognise barbarism. By chance we didn't hit the pleasure pavilions at Nymphenburg, a suburb of Munich (Munich itself we flattened out). They were built by an architect named Cuvilliés (who despite his French name came from Flanders). He had been the court dwarf of the Elector Max Emmanuel, who discovered that he was an architect of genius. His masterpiece, the Amalienburg [170], is the ultimate in Rococo decoration, and one might say that it bridges the gap between Watteau and Mozart.

And yet to pronounce the name of Mozart in the Amalienburg is dangerous. It gives colour – very pretty colour – to the notion that Mozart was merely a Rococo composer. Fifty years ago this was what most people thought about him, and the notion was supported by horrible little plaster busts which made him look the perfect eighteenth-century dummy. I bought one of these busts when I was at school, but when I first heard the G minor Quintet I realised that it couldn't have been written by the smooth, white character on my mantelpiece and threw the bust into the wastepaper basket. I afterwards discovered the Lange portrait [169] which, although no masterpiece, does convey the single-mindedness of genius. Of course a lot of Mozart's music is in the current eighteenth-century style. He was so much at home in this golden age of music, and so completely the master of its forms, that he didn't feel it necessary to destroy them. Indeed he loved the clarity and the precision that had been brought to perfection in the music of his time. I like the story of Mozart sitting at table absentmindedly folding and refolding his napkin into more and more elaborate patterns, as fresh musical ideas passed through his mind. But this formal perfection was used to express two characteristics which were very far from the Rococo style. One of them was that peculiar kind of melancholy, a melancholy amounting almost to panic, which so often haunts the isolation of genius. Mozart felt it quite young. The other characteristic was almost the opposite: a passionate interest in human beings, and in the drama of human relationships. How often in Mozart's orchestral pieces – concertos or quartets – we find ourselves participating in a drama or dialogue; and of course this feeling reaches its natural conclusion in opera.

Opera, next to Gothic architecture, is one of the strangest inventions of western man. It could not have been foreseen by any logical process. Dr Johnson's much quoted definition, which as far as I can make out he never wrote, 'an extravagant and irrational entertainment', is perfectly correct;

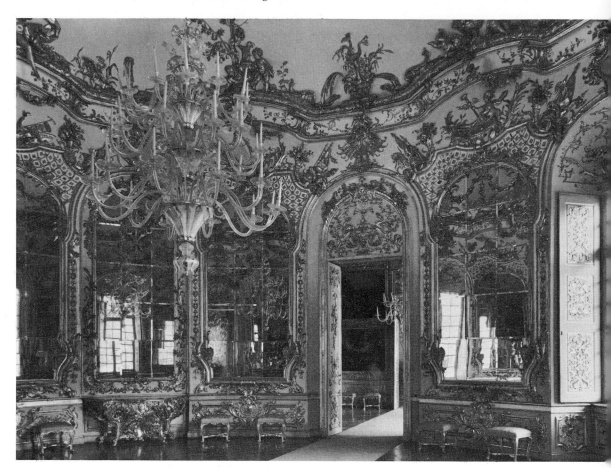

and at first it seems surprising that it should have been brought to perfection in the age of reason. But just as the greatest art of the early eighteenth century was religious art, so the greatest artistic creation of the Rococo is completely irrational. Opera, of course, had been invented in the seventeenth century and made into a form of art by the prophetic genius of Monteverdi; it came to the north from Catholic Italy and flourished in Catholic capitals – Vienna, Munich and Prague. Indignant Protestants used to say that Rococo churches were like opera houses – quite true, only it was the other way on. The opera house in the Residenz at Munich, by Cuvilliés, is exactly like a Rococo church. Opera houses came in when churches went out and they expressed so completely the views of this new profane religion that for one hundred years they continued to be built in Rococo style, long after that style had gone out of fashion. In Catholic countries, not only in Europe but in South America, the opera house is often the best and largest building in the town.

What on earth has given opera its prestige in western civilisation – a prestige that has outlasted so many different fashions and ways of thought? Why are people prepared to sit silently for three hours listening to a performance of which they do not understand a word and of which they very seldom know the plot? Why do quite small towns all over Germany and Italy still devote a large portion of their budgets to this irrational entertainment? Partly, of course, because it is a display of skill, like a football match. But chiefly, I think, because it *is* irrational. 'What is too silly to be said may be sung' – well, yes; but what is too subtle to be said, or too deeply felt, or too revealing or too mysterious – these things can also be sung and only be sung. When, at the beginning of Mozart's *Don Giovanni*, the Don kills the Commendatore, and in one burst of glorious music the murderer, his mistress, his servant and the dying man all express their feelings, opera provides a real extension of the human faculties. No wonder that the music is rather complicated, because even today our feelings about *Don Giovanni* are far from simple. He is the most ambiguous of hero-villains. The pursuit of happiness and the pursuit of love, which had once seemed so simple and life-giving, have become complex and destructive, and his refusal to repent, which makes him heroic, belongs to another phase of civilisation.

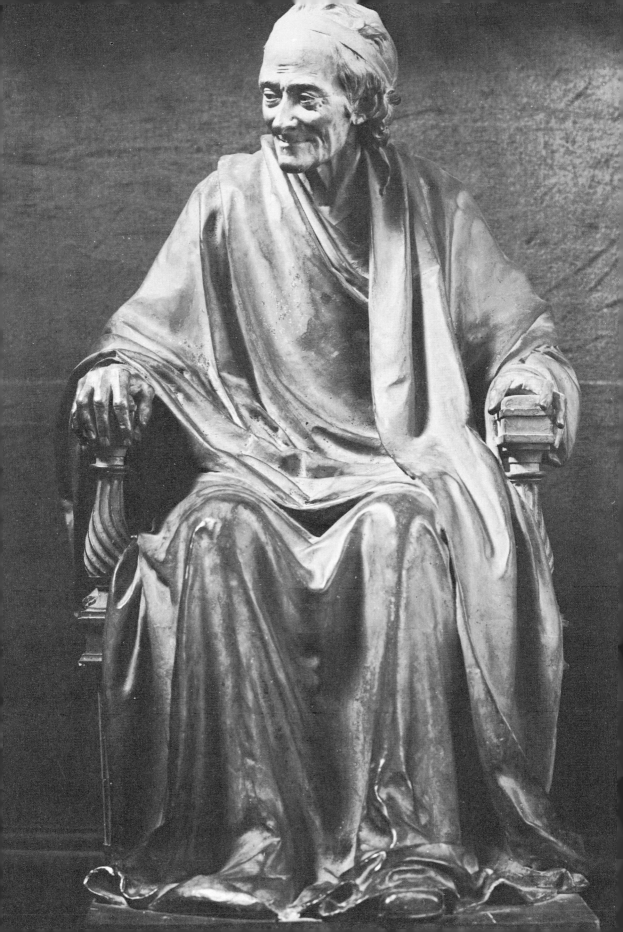

10 The Smile of Reason

The busts of the successful dramatists of eighteenth-century Paris stand in the foyer of the Comédie Française, the national theatre of France, which, strange as it may seem to us today, did a great deal, for a hundred years, to promote good sense and humanity. What witty, intelligent faces! And here is the wittiest and most intelligent of them all; in fact, at a certain level, one of the most intelligent men that has ever lived, Voltaire [171]. He is smiling – the smile of reason. Perhaps this state of mind originated with the French philosopher Fontenelle who, by living to be nearly a hundred, bridged the seventeenth and eighteenth centuries – the world of Newton and the world of Voltaire. He held a position known as 'perpetual secretary' of the Academy of Science. He told someone that he had never run and never lost his temper. A friend asked him if he had ever laughed. He said: 'No, I have never made ha ha.' But he smiled, and so do all the other distinguished writers, philosophers, dramatists and hostesses of the French eighteenth century: Crébillon, Diderot, Marivaux, D'Alembert.

It seems to us shallow – we've got into deep water in the last fifty years. We feel that people ought to be more passionate, more convinced – or, as the current jargon has it, more committed. Indeed, the civilised smile of eighteenth-century France may be one of the things that have brought the whole concept of civilisation into disrepute. This is because we forgot that in the seventeenth century, with all its outpourings of genius in art and science, there were still senseless persecutions and brutal wars waged with unparalleled cruelty. By 1700 people had begun to feel that a little calm and detachment wouldn't come amiss. The smile of reason may seem to betray a certain incomprehension of the deeper human emotions; but it didn't preclude some strongly held beliefs – belief in natural law, belief in justice, belief in toleration. Not bad. The philosophers of the Enlightenment pushed European civilisation some steps up the hill, and in theory, at any rate, this gain was consolidated throughout the nineteenth century. Up to the 1930s people were supposed not to burn witches and other members of minority groups, or extract confessions by torture or pervert the course of justice or go to prison for speaking the truth. Except, of course, during wars. This we owe to the movement known as the Enlightenment, and above all to Voltaire.

Although the victory of reason and tolerance was won in France, it was

171 Houdon, *Voltaire*

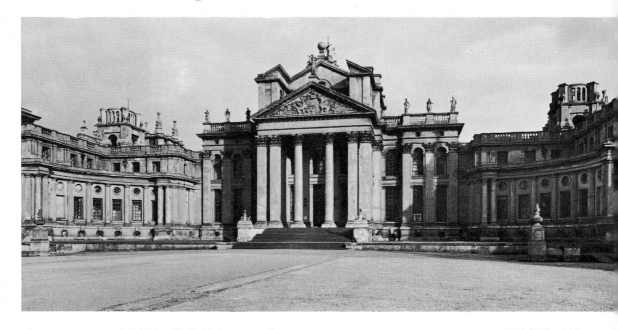

initiated in England and the French philosophers never concealed their debt
to the country that, in a score of years, had produced Newton, Locke and
the Bloodless Revolution. In fact they tended to overrate the extent of
political freedom in England and to exaggerate the influence of English men
of letters. All the same, when Montesquieu and Voltaire visited England in
the 1720s, it had enjoyed half a century of very vigorous intellectual
life; and although Swift, Pope, Steele and Addison might give and receive
some hard knocks in print, they weren't physically beaten up by the
hired gangs of offended noblemen, or sent to prison (except Defoe) for
satirical references to the Establishment. Both these things happened to
Voltaire, and as a result he took refuge in England in 1726.

It was the age of great country houses. In 1722 the most splendid of all
had just been completed for Marlborough, the general who had been victorious over Voltaire's country: not the sort of idea that would have worried
Voltaire in the least, as he thought of all war as a ridiculous waste of human
life and effort. When Voltaire saw Blenheim Palace [172] he said, 'What a
great heap of stone, without charm or taste,' and I can see what he means. To
anyone brought up on Mansart and Perrault, Blenheim must have seemed
painfully lacking in order and propriety. It contains some vigorous inventions, but they are not always happily combined. Perhaps this is because
the architect, Sir John Vanbrugh, although a man of genius, was really an
amateur. Moreover, he was a natural romantic, a castle-builder, who didn't
care a fig for good taste and decorum.

Eighteenth-century England was the paradise of the amateur; by which I mean, of men rich enough and grand enough to do whatever they liked, who nevertheless did things that require a good deal of expertise. One of the things they chose to do was architecture. Wren began as a brilliant amateur and, although he made himself into a professional, he retained the amateur's freedom of approach to every problem. And two of his chief successors were amateurs by any definition. Sir John Vanbrugh wrote plays, and Lord Burlington was a connoisseur, collector and arbiter of taste – the sort of character nowadays much despised. But he built, among other things, a small masterpiece of domestic architecture, Chiswick House [173]; and looking at the ingenious way in which the outside staircase is related to the portico, one may wonder whether many professional architects today could handle these problems of design as expertly as Lord Burlington has done. Of course, it's only a miniature. Behind the portico is a building about the size of an old parsonage, which was not intended for day-to-day existence, but for social occasions, conversation, intrigue, political gossip and a little music.

In a way these eighteenth-century amateurs were the inheritors of the Renaissance ideal of universal man. Leon Battista Alberti, the typical universal man of the Renaissance, had also been an architect, and if we may still consider architecture to be a social art – an art by which men may be enabled to lead a fuller life – then perhaps the architect should touch life at many points and not be too narrowly specialised.

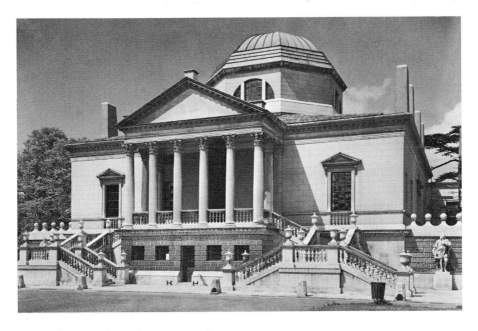

173 Burlington, Chiswick House, London

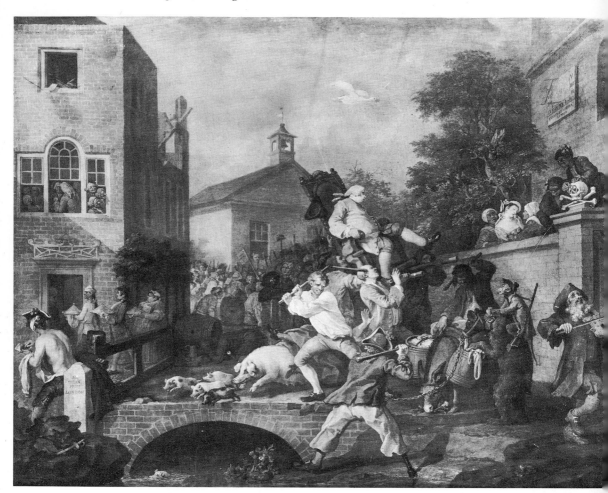

Eighteenth-century amateurism ran through everything: chemistry, philosophy, botany and natural history. It produced men like the indefatigable Sir Joseph Banks (who refused to go on Captain Cook's second voyage unless he was allowed to have *two* horn players to make music for him during dinner). There was a freshness and freedom of mind in these men that is sometimes lost in the rigidly controlled classifications of the professional. And they were independent, with all the advantages and disadvantages to society which result from that condition. They wouldn't have fitted into our modern utopia. I recently heard a professor of sociology say on television: 'What's not prohibited must be made compulsory.' Not a suggestion that would have attracted those eminent visitors, Voltaire and Rousseau, who drew inspiration from our philosophy, our institutions and our tolerance.

But as usual there was another side to this shining medal; and of this we have an exceptionally vivid record in the work of Hogarth. I am not myself an admirer of Hogarth, because his pictures are always such a muddle. He seemed entirely without the sense of space which one finds even in mediocre Dutch painters of the seventeenth century. But one can't deny that he had a gift of narrative invention, and in later life he did a series of pictures of an election that are better designed than the *Rake's Progress*, and a very convincing comment on our much cracked-up political system. He shows us the polling booth with imbeciles and moribunds being persuaded to make their marks. We see the successful candidate [174], like a fat, powdered capon, borne in triumph by his bruisers, who are still carrying on their private feuds; and I must confess that Hogarth conquers my prejudice by the figure of a blind fiddler, a real stroke of imagination outside the usual range of his moralising journalism.

The truth is, I think, that eighteenth-century England, in the aftermath of its middle-class revolution, had created two societies, very remote from one

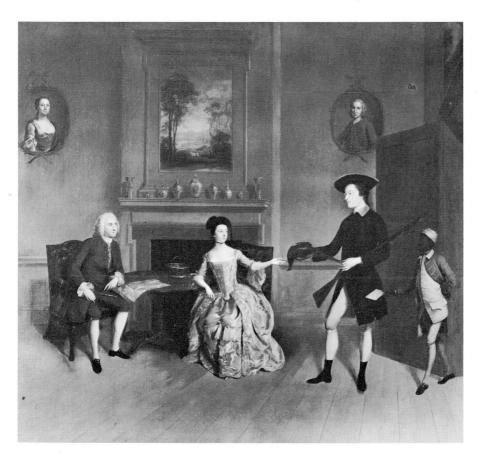

175 Devis, *Portrait group*

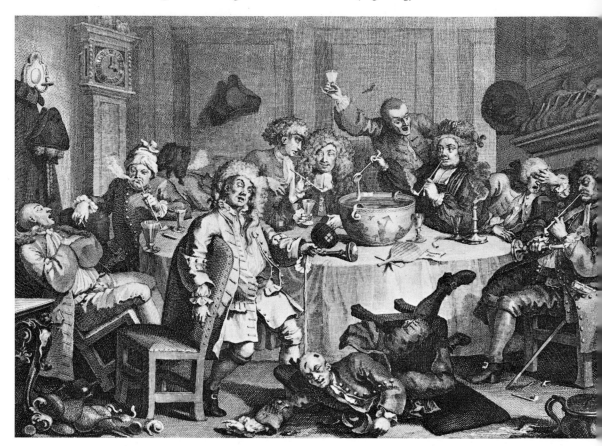

another. One was the society of modest country gentlemen, of which we
have a perfect record in the work of a painter called Devis – comically stiff
and expressionless in their cold, empty rooms [175]. The other was the urban
society, of which Hogarth has left us many records, confirmed by the plays
of his friend Fielding. Plenty of animal spirits, but not what we could, by
any stretch, call civilisation. I hope you will not think it too facile if I compare a print by Hogarth called *A Midnight Modern Conversation* [176] with a
picture painted in the same decade called *A Reading from Molière* [34, facing
p. 253] by the French artist de Troy. In this series I have tried to go beyond
the narrower meaning of the word civilised. But all the same it has its
value: one can't deny that the de Troy is a picture of civilised life. Even the
furniture contrives to be both beautiful and comfortable at the same time.
And one reason is that whereas all the characters in Hogarth's *Midnight
Conversation* are male, five out of the seven figures in the de Troy are women.

In talking about the twelfth and thirteenth centuries I said how great an
advance in civilisation was then achieved by a sudden consciousness of

feminine qualities; and the same was true of eighteenth-century France. I think it absolutely essential to civilisation that the male and female principles be kept in balance. In eighteenth-century France the influence of women was, on the whole, benevolent; and they were the creators of that curious institution of the eighteenth century, the salon. Those small social gatherings of intelligent men and women, drawn from all over Europe, who met in the rooms of gifted hostesses like Madame du Deffand and Madame Geoffrin, were for forty years the centres of European civilisation. They were less poetical than the court of Urbino, but intellectually a good deal more alert.

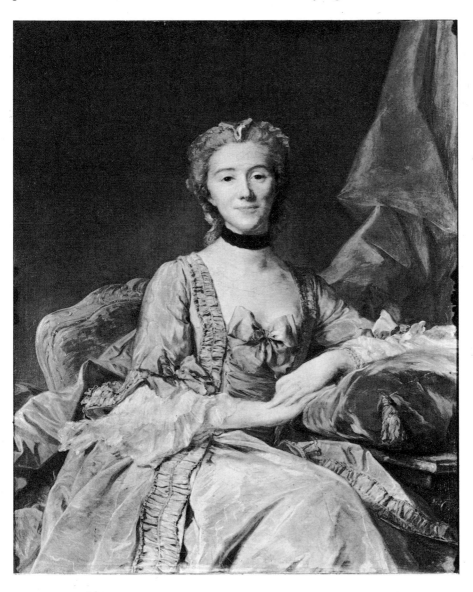

177 Perronneau, *Madame de Sorquainville*

178 Gabriel, Petit Trianon, Versailles

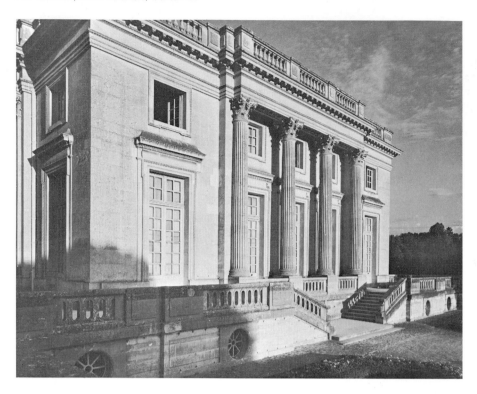

The ladies who presided over them were neither very young nor very rich: we know exactly what they looked like because French artists like Perronneau [177] and Maurice-Quentin De La Tour portrayed them without flattery, but with a penetrating eye for their subtlety of mind. Only in a highly civilised society could ladies have preferred this kind of likeness to the glossy fakes of fashionable portraiture.

How did these ladies do it? By human sympathy, by making people feel at ease, by tact. Solitude no doubt is necessary to the poet and the philosopher, but certain life-giving thoughts are born of conversation, and conversation can flourish only in a small company where no one is stuck-up. That is a condition which cannot exist in a court, and the success of the Parisian salons depended very largely on the fact that the court and government of France were not situated in Paris, but in Versailles. It was a separate world; indeed the courtiers of Versailles always referred to it as *ce pays-ci* – this country of ours. To this day I enter the huge, unfriendly forecourt of Versailles with a mixture of panic and fatigue – as if it were my first day at school. I must add in fairness that even in the eighteenth century, when its intellectual glory had passed, the enclosed society of Versailles produced some admirable works of architecture and design. The Petit Trianon [178],

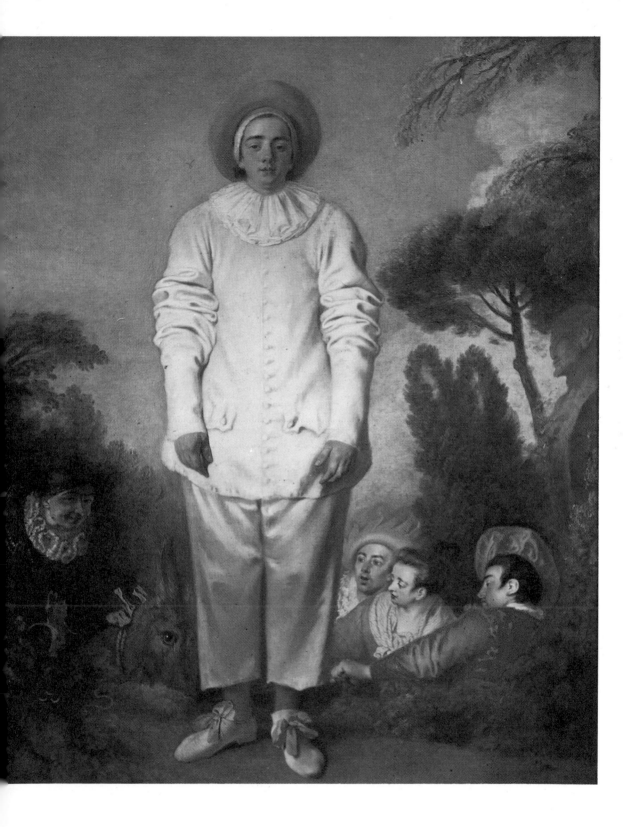

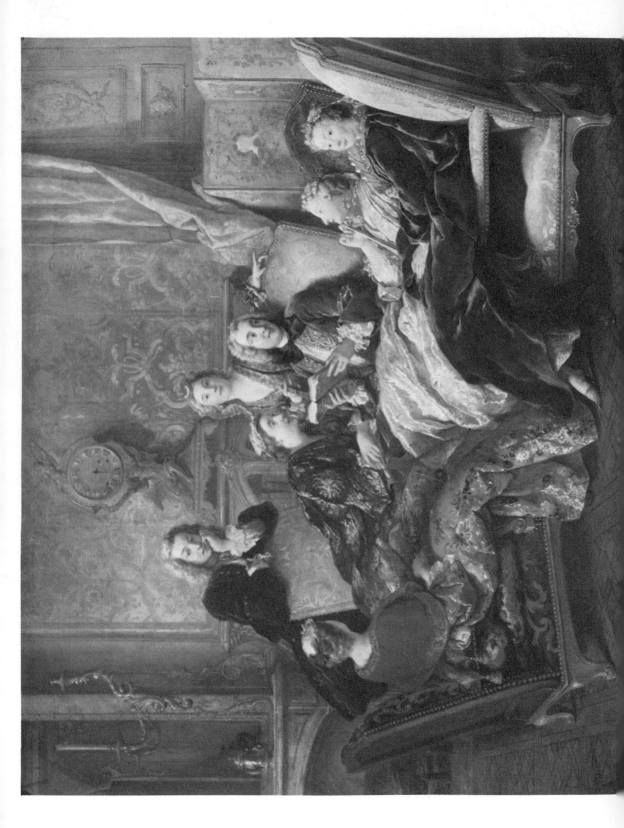

built by the great architect Jacques-Ange Gabriel for Louis XV, is as near to perfection as may be. Of course, the very word perfection implies a limited aim, but it also implies striving for an ideal. The tact and self-control and delicate precision of every statement in that beautiful façade was never achieved in its innumerable derivatives; by varying them a hairsbreadth they become banal, and by the smallest overemphasis they become vulgar.

However, if one turns from the arts of design to the play of intellect, then life at Versailles in the eighteenth century had little to offer, and Parisian society was fortunate to be free from the stultifying rituals of court procedure and the trivial day-to-day preoccupations of politics. Another thing that helped to keep the eighteenth-century salons free from too much toadying and pomposity is that the French upper classes were not oppressively rich. They had lost a lot of money in a financial crash brought about by a financial wizard, a Scot named John Law. A margin of wealth is helpful to civilisation, but for some mysterious reason great wealth is destructive. I suppose that, in the end, splendour is dehumanising, and a certain sense of limitation seems to be a condition of what we call good taste.

An example is Chardin, the greatest painter of mid-eighteenth-century France. No one has ever had surer taste in colour and design. Every area, every interval, every tone, gives one the feeling of perfect rightness. Well, Chardin did not depict the upper classes, still less the court. He sometimes found his subjects in the gentle bourgoisie, dressing or addressing their children [35, facing p. 260]; sometimes among the working class, where I think he was happiest because, in addition to the people, he loved the pots and barrels [179]. They have the basic nobility of design of something that has had to serve a human need unchanged for many centuries. Chardin's pictures show that the qualities immortalised in verse by La Fontaine and Molière – good sense, a good heart, an approach to human relationships both simple and delicate – survived into the mid-eighteenth century, and survive to this day in French country districts and in what the French call the *artisanat*.

The salons where the brightest intellects of France were assembled were more luxurious, but still not overwhelming. The rooms were of a normal size, and the ornament (for in those days people couldn't live without ornament) was not so elaborate as to impose a formal behaviour. People could feel that they had natural human relationships with one another. We have a complete record of how people lived in mid-eighteenth-century France, because although there were no great painters, except Chardin, there were innumerable minor artists, like Moreau le Jeune, who were content to record the contemporary scene, and so are still of interest to us after two hun-

34 de Troy, *La Lecture de Molière*

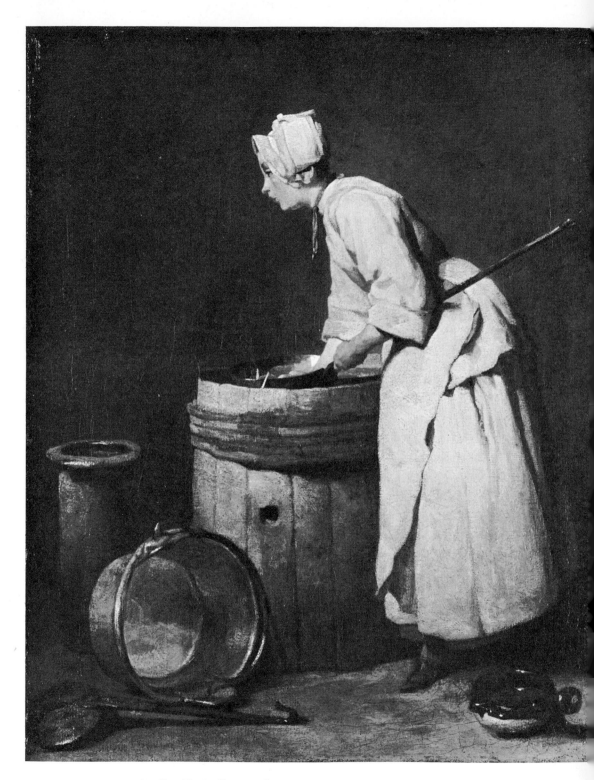

179 Chardin, *The Scullery Maid*

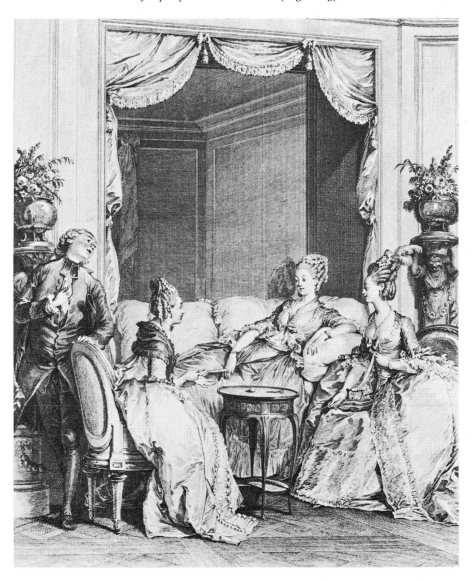

dred years – which artists who want to 'express themselves' will not be. They show us every hour in a young lady's life: how she pulled on her stockings before the fire paid a call on a friend who was about to have a baby (*'n' ayez pas peur, ma bonne amie'*) [180], gave the children a *canard* – a lump of sugar soaked in coffee [36, facing p. 261], chattered too much at a musical tea-party (*'un peu de silence s'il vous plait'*), received a billet doux from a young admirer, appeared superbly dressed at the opera, and at last went sleepily to bed. Well, nobody but a sourpuss or a hypocrite would deny that this was an agreeable way of life. Why so do many of us instinc-

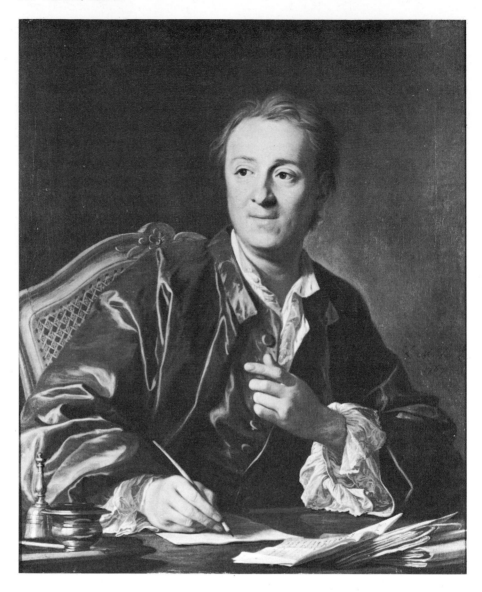

tively react against it? Because we think it is based on exploitation? Do we really think that far? If so, it is like being sorry for animals and not being vegetarians. Our whole society is based on different sorts of exploitation. Or is it because we believe that this kind of life was shallow and trivial? Well, that simply isn't true. The men who enjoyed it were no fools. Talleyrand said that only those who experienced the social life of eighteenth-century France had known the *douceur de vivre* – the sweetness of living – and Talleyrand was certainly one of the most intelligent men who has ever taken up politics. The people who frequented the salons of eighteenth-century

France were not merely a group of fashionable good-timers: they were the outstanding philosophers and scientists of the time. They wanted to publish their very revolutionary views on religion. They wanted to curtail the power of a lazy king and an irresponsible government. They wanted to change society. In the end they got rather more of a change than they had bargained for, but that is often the fate of successful reformers.

The men who met each other in the salons of Madame du Deffand and Madame Geoffrin were engaged on a great work – an encyclopedia or *Dictionnaire Raisonné des Sciences, des Arts et des Métiers*. It was intended to advance mankind by conquering ignorance. Once more the idea was imitated from England, where Chambers's *Encyclopedia* had been published in 1751. It was a gigantic enterprise – eventually there were twenty-four folio volumes – and of course it involved a great many contributors; but the dynamo of the whole undertaking was Diderot. We can see him, smiling the smile of reason, in a picture by van Loo [181] which enraged him: he said he had been made to look like an old cocotte who was still trying to be agreeable. He was a many-sided man of high intelligence, a novelist, a philosopher, even an art critic, the great supporter of Chardin – and in the Encyclopedia he wrote articles on everything from Aristotle to artificial flowers. One of his charms is that you never know what he is going to say or do next. Any generalisation about the eighteenth century could be confounded from the writings of Diderot.

The aims of the Encyclopedia seem harmless enough to us. But authoritarian governments don't like dictionaries. They live by lies and bamboozling abstractions, and can't afford to have words accurately defined. The Encyclopedia was twice suppressed; and by its ultimate triumph the polite reunions in these elegant salons became precursors of revolutionary politics. They were also precursors of science. The illustrated supplement of the Encyclopedia is full of pictures of technical processes, most of which, I must admit, had changed very little since the Renaissance. In the last quarter of the eighteenth century science was fashionable and romantic, as one can see from the work of Wright of Derby. His picture of an experiment with an air pump [182] brings us to the new age of scientific invention. It is an admirable example of narrative painting: the natural philosopher, with his long hair and dedicated stare, the little girls who can't bear to witness the death of their pet cockatoo, the sensible middle-aged man who tells them that such sacrifices must be made in the interest of science, and the thoughtful man on the right who is wondering if this kind of experiment is really going to do mankind much good. They are all taking it quite seriously; but nonetheless science was to some extent an after-dinner occupation, like

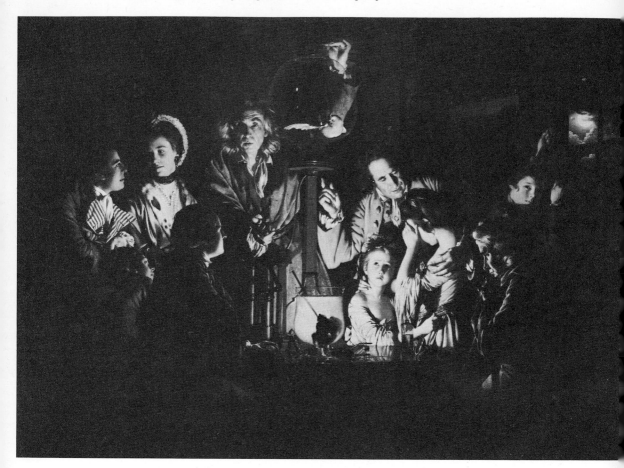

playing the piano in the next century. Even Voltaire, who spent a vast amount of time on weighing molten metal and cutting up worms, was only a dilettante. He lacked the patient, pedestrian realism of the experimenter, and perhaps such tenacity exists only in a milieu where quick-wittedness is less highly valued.

In the eighteenth century it emerged in a country where civilisation still had the energy of newness – Scotland. The Scottish character (and I am myself a Scot) shows an extraordinary combination of realism and reckless sentiment. The sentiment has passed into popular legend. The Scots seem to be proud of it, and no wonder. Where, but in Edinburgh, does a romantic landscape come right into the centre of the town? But it's the realism that counts and that made eighteenth-century Scotland – a poor, remote and semi-barbarous country – a force in European civilisation. Let me name some eighteenth-century Scots in the world of ideas and science: Adam Smith, David Hume, Joseph Black and James Watt. It is a matter of historical fact that these were the men who, soon after the year 1760, changed the whole current of European thought and life. Joseph Black and James Watt discovered that heat and, in particular, steam could be a source of power – I needn't describe how that has changed the world. In *The Wealth of Nations* Adam Smith invented the study of political economy, and created a social science that lasted up to the time of Karl Marx, and beyond. Hume, in his *Treatise of Human Nature*, succeeded in proving that experience and reason have no necessary connection with one another. There is no such thing as a rational belief. Hume, as he himself said, was of an open, social and cheerful humour, and was much beloved by the ladies in the Paris salons. I suppose they had never read that small book which has made all philosophers feel uneasy till the present day.

All these great Scotsmen lived in the grim, narrow tenements of the Old Town of Edinburgh, piled on the hill behind the castle. But in their lifetime two Scottish architects, the brothers Adam, had produced one of the finest pieces of town planning in Europe – the new town of Edinburgh [183].

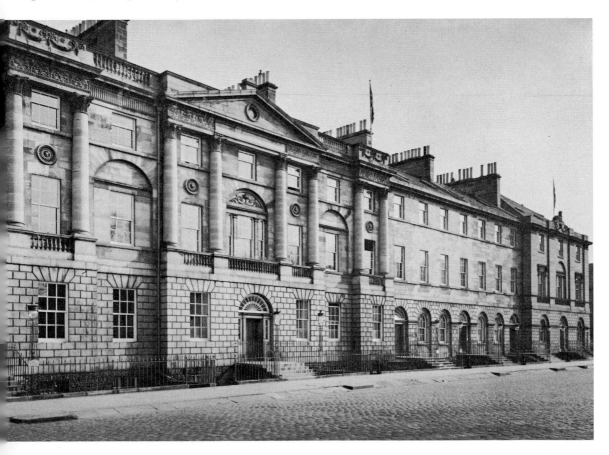

183 Robert Adam, Charlotte Square, New town, Edinburgh

In addition they exploited, and I think one may almost say invented, the strict, pure classicism that was to influence architecture all over Europe – even in Russia, where another Scot named Cameron practised it in a spectacular manner. And then, a Scot having popularised neo-classicism, Sir Walter Scott popularised the Gothic Middle Ages and furnished the imagination of the romantically-minded for a century. Add to these James Boswell, who wrote one of the most permanently entertaining books in the English language; Robert Burns, the first great popular lyricist; and Raeburn who painted the members of his remarkable society with an inspired directness – and one must admit that a survey of civilisation cannot omit Scotland. Through the practical genius of the Scots and English those technical diagrams in the Encyclopedia were superseded, and before the political revolutions of America and France had taken effect, a far deeper and more catastrophic transformation was already under way: what we call the Industrial Revolution.

If, on the practical side, the scene must change to Scotland, on the moral side we must return to France – not to Paris, but to the borders of Switzerland. For it was there, a mile or two from the frontier, that Voltaire had made his home. After several bad experiences, he had become suspicious of authority and liked to live in a place where he could slip out of reach. He did not suffer from his exile. He had made a lot of money by speculation, and his last commodious bolt-hole, the Château de Ferney, is a large agreeable country house. He planted a splendid avenue of chestnuts and a green tunnel of cut beeches, where he could take his constitutional on a hot day. It is said that when he was visited by the self-important ladies of Geneva he would receive them seated on a bench at the far end. It amused him to see how they struggled to prevent their mountains of fashionable hair from becoming entangled in the branches. I suppose the chestnuts have grown a good deal taller and the beech tunnel could not disturb the most towering *chevelure*; but most of Ferney has remained as Voltaire left it. In this agreeable setting he thought of the devastating witticisms with which he would destroy his enemies [184].

Voltaire is one of those writers whose virtue is inseparable from his style; and true style is untranslatable. He himself said: 'One word in the wrong place will ruin the most beautiful thought.' To quote from his writings in translation would ruin the wit and irony which was his peculiar gift. They still make one smile – the smile of reason; and to the end of his life Voltaire could not resist a joke. But on one subject he was completely serious – justice. Many people in his lifetime, and since, have compared him to a monkey. But when it came to fighting injustice he was a bull-dog. He never

35 Chardin, *La Toilette de Matin*

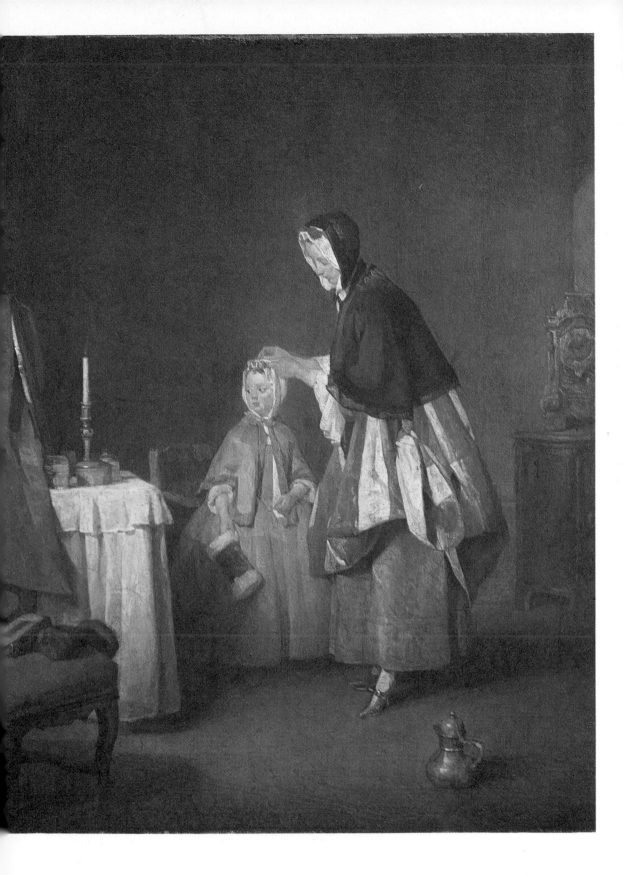

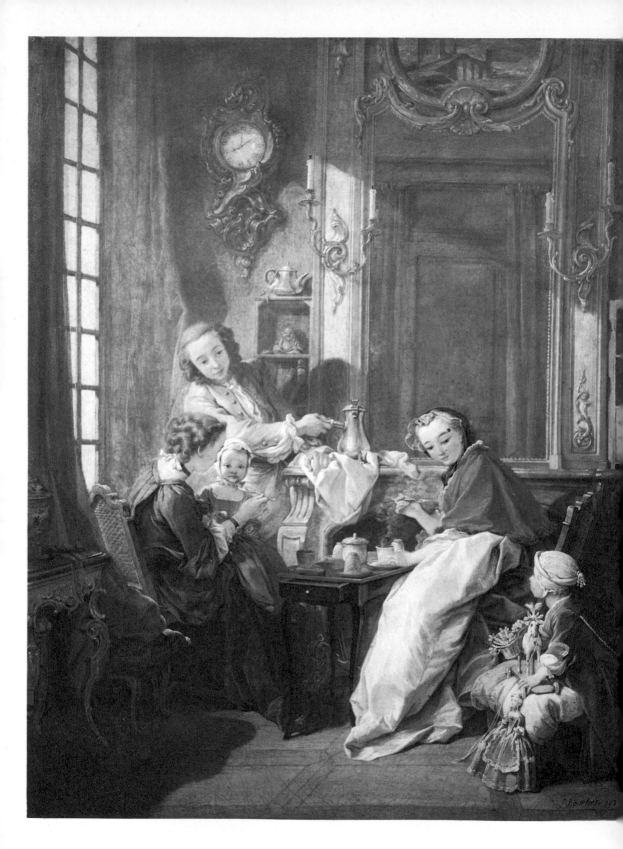

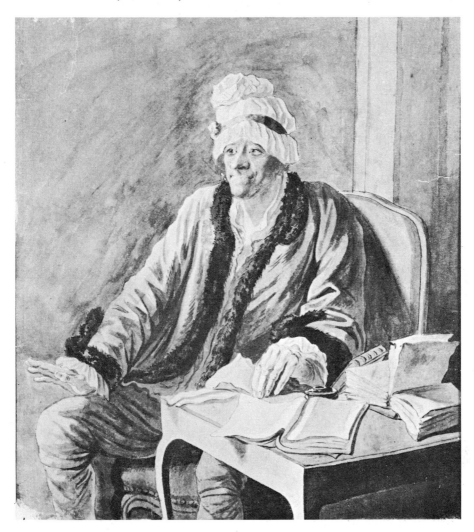

let go. He pestered all his friends, he wrote an unending stream of pamphlets and finally he had some of the victims living at his expense at Ferney. Gradually the world ceased to think of him as an impudent libertine but as a patriarch and sage; and by 1778 he at last felt it safe to return to Paris. He was eighty-four. No victorious general, no lone flyer, has ever been given such a reception. He was hailed as the universal man and the friend of mankind. People of all classes crowded round his house, drew his carriage and mobbed him wherever he went. Finally, his bust was crowned on the stage of the Comédie Française. Naturally, it killed him, but he died triumphant.

The remarkable thing about the frivolous eighteenth century was its seriousness. It was, in many ways, the heir to Renaissance humanism, but there was a vital difference. The Renaissance had taken place within the framework of the Christian Church. A few humanists had shown signs of scepticism, but no one had expressed any doubts about the Christian religion as a whole. People had the comfortable moral freedom that goes with an unquestioned faith. But by the middle of the eighteenth century serious-minded men could see that the Church had become a tied house – tied to property and status and defending its interests by repression and injustice. No one felt this more strongly than Voltaire. *'Ecrasez l'infâme'* – untranslatable! 'Crush the vermin', perhaps. It dominated his later life and he bequeathed it to his followers. I remember H. G. Wells, who was a kind of twentieth-century Voltaire, saying that he daren't drive a car in France, because the temptation to run over a priest would be too strong for him. All the same, Voltaire remained a kind of believer, whereas several of the contributors to the Encyclopedia were total materialists who thought that moral and intellectual qualities were due to an accidental conjunction of nerves and tissues. It was a courageous belief to hold in 1770, but it was not (and never will be) an easy one on which to found or maintain a civilisation. So the eighteenth century was faced with the troublesome task of constructing a new morality, without revelation or Christian sanctions.

This morality was built on two foundations: one of them was the doctrine of natural law; the other was the stoic morality of ancient republican Rome. The concept of nature, and its great exponent, Jean-Jacques Rousseau, belongs in my next chapter, but one can't understand the new morality of the Enlightenment without reckoning with the belief that the simple goodness of natural man was superior to the artificial goodness of sophisticated man. The complement to this agreeable delusion was an ideal of virtue drawn, for the most part, from Plutarch. His *Parallel Lives* was almost as widely read in the eighteenth century as the *Roman de la Rose* had been in the fifteenth and had, through example, an equal influence on conduct. Those grim, puritanical heroes of the Roman republic, who sacrificed themselves and their families in the interests of the state, were taken as models for a new political order; and they were made more memorable by the pictorial imagination of the painter Jacques Louis David.

David was an exceptionally gifted painter. He could have made a fortune depicting the beautiful women and highly polished men of his time; but he chose to be a moralist. He said to his young pupil, Baron Gros: 'You love art too well to occupy yourself with frivolous subjects. Quick, quick, my friend, turn the pages of your Plutarch.' His first great programmatic picture was the *Oath of the Horatii* [**37**, facing p. 268], painted in 1785. It created an effect which those of us who remember the first appearance of Picasso's *Guernica* may be able faintly to imagine. The *Oath of the Horatii* is the supreme picture of revolutionary action, not only in its subject, but in its treatment. Gone are all the melting outlines and pools of sensuous shadow of Fragonard, and in their place are firmly outlined expressions of will. The unified, totalitarian gesture of the brothers, like the kinetic image of a rotating wheel, has an almost hypnotic quality. Even the architecture is a conscious revolt against the refined, ornamental style of the time. The Tuscan columns, only recently rediscovered in the temple of Paestum, assert the superior virtue of the plain man. Two years later David painted an even more grimly Plutarchian picture, the lictors bringing back to the house of Brutus the bodies of his two sons whom he had condemned to death for treachery: one of those incidents in Roman history that do not appeal to us but which were completely in harmony with French feeling on the eve of the Revolution, and help us to understand many incidents in the next five years. The *douceur de vivre* had lost its hold on European man some years before 1789. In fact the new morality had already inspired a revolution outside Europe.

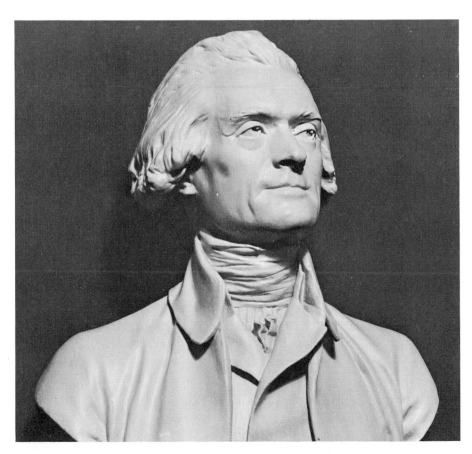

185 Houdon, *Thomas Jefferson*

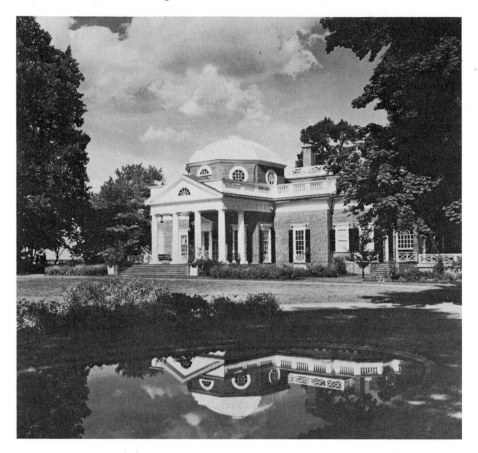

Once more we must leave the ancient focus of civilisation, and look at a young, underpopulated country where civilised life still had the freshness of a new and precarious creation: America. Here on the border territory of the Indian, a young Virginian lawyer elected in the 1760s to build his home. His name was Thomas Jefferson [185] and he called his house Monticello, the little mountain [186]. It must have been an extraordinary apparition in that wild landscape. Jefferson made it up out of the book of the great Renaissance architect Palladio, of which he is said to have owned the only copy in America. But of course he had to invent a great deal of it himself, and he was highly inventive. Doors that open as one approaches them, a clock that tells the days of the week, a bed so placed that one gets out of it into either of two rooms, all this suggests the quirky ingenuity of a creative man working alone outside any accepted body of tradition.

But Jefferson wasn't a crank. He was the typical universal man of the eighteenth century, linguist, scientist, agriculturist, educator, town-planner and architect: almost a reincarnation of Leon Battista Alberti, even down to a love of music, the management of horses, and what, in a lesser man, one might have called a touch of self-righteousness. Jefferson wasn't as good an architect as Alberti, but then he was also President of the United States; and as an architect he was by no means bad. Monticello was the beginning of that simple, almost rustic, classicism that stretches right up the eastern seaboard of America, and lasted for one hundred years, producing a body of civilised, domestic architecture equal to any in the world.

Jefferson is buried in the grounds of Monticello. He left instructions for his tomb. On it were to be inscribed the following sentences, 'and not a word more': 'Here was buried Thomas Jefferson, author of the Declaration of American Independence, of the Statute of Virginia for Religious Freedom, and Father of the University of Virginia.' Nothing about being President; nothing about the Louisiana Purchase – the Jeffersonian pride and independence that has annoyed a large section of American opinion ever since. Well, the establishment of religious freedom that earned him so much hatred and abuse in his own day we now take for granted. But the University of Virginia [187] is still a surprise. It was all designed by Jefferson, and is full of his character. He called it an academical village. There are ten

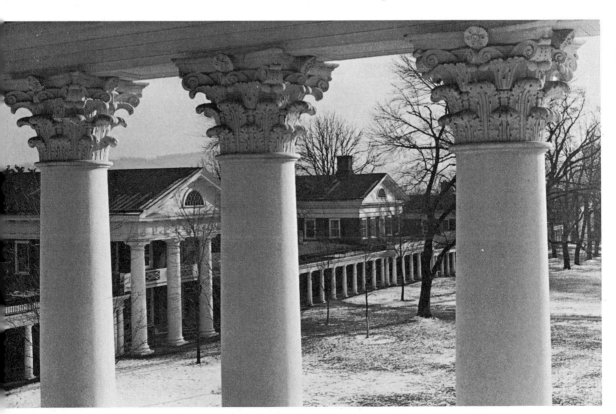

187 Jefferson, The University of Virginia, Charlottesville

pavilions for ten professors, and between them, behind a colonnade, the rooms of the students, all within reach, and yet all individual: the ideal of corporate humanism. Then outside the courtyard are small gardens that show his love of privacy. They are enclosed by serpentine walls which were Jefferson's speciality. The serpentine form was an economy. It meant that the wall could be only one brick thick, without buttresses; but it also conformed to Hogarth's 'line of beauty'. The low, open lines of the academical village, the use of covered ways between the buildings, and the great trees in each small garden give this classic enclosure something of the character of a Japanese temple. Jefferson's romanticism is shown by the way in which he left the fourth side of his courtyard open, so that young scholars could look across to the mountains still inhabited by the Indians who had been his father's friends.

How confidently in their semi-wild domain the Founding Fathers of America assumed the mantle of republican virtue, and put into practice the notions of the French Enlightenment. They even called on the great sculptor of the Enlightenment, Houdon, to commemorate their victorious general. The resulting statue of Washington [188] stands in the Capitol at Richmond, Virginia, designed by Thomas Jefferson on the model of the Maison Carrée at Nîmes. This chapter began with Houdon's statue of Voltaire, smiling the smile of reason; it could end with Houdon's statue of Washington. No more smiles. Houdon saw his subject as that favourite Roman republican hero, the decent country gentleman, called away from his farm to defend his neighbours' liberties; and, in moments of optimism, one may feel that, through all the vulgarity and corruption of American politics, some vestige of this first ideal has survived.

The capital city named after the first President is also the child, the overgrown and somewhat inarticulate child, of the French Enlightenment. It was laid out by a French engineer named l'Enfant, under the direction of Jefferson and is certainly the most grandiose piece of town planning since Sixtus V's Rome. The huge grassy spaces, the long straight avenues with their public buildings floating at the intersections like classical icebergs, unrelated, as it would seem, to the shops and houses that surround them, may seem to lack the essential vitality of America. But for the immigrants from the old world, with their countless differing traditions and ideas, a new myth had to be created. And this gives to the vast white monuments to Washington, Lincoln and Jefferson a moving quality that such pieces of masonry usually lack. Inside the Jefferson Memorial (the last to be built) are quotations from his writings. First the noble, indestructible words of the Declaration of Independence: 'We hold these truths to be self-evident: that

188 Houdon, *George Washington*

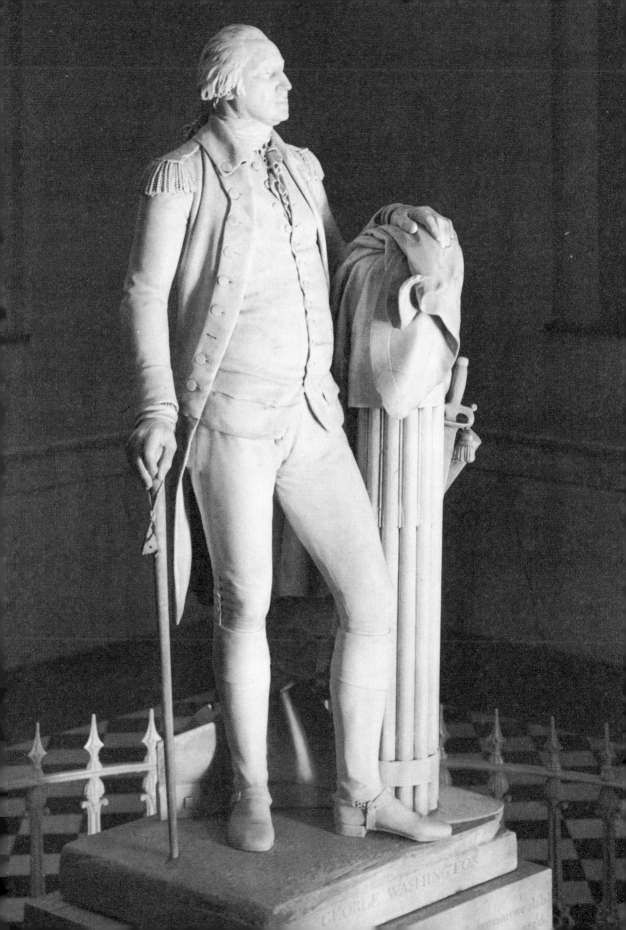

all men are created equal, that they are endowed by their creator with certain inalienable rights, among these are life, liberty and the pursuit of happiness, that to secure these rights governments are instituted among men.' 'Self-evident truths' . . . that's the voice of eighteenth-century enlightenment. But on the opposite wall are less familiar words by Jefferson, that still give us pause today : 'I tremble for my country when I reflect that God is just, that his justice cannot sleep forever. Commerce between master and slave is despotism. Nothing is more certainly written in the book of fate than that these people are to be free.' A peaceful-looking scene, a great ideal made visible. But beyond it what problems – almost insoluble, or at least not soluble by the smile of reason.

37 David, *Oath of the Horatii*

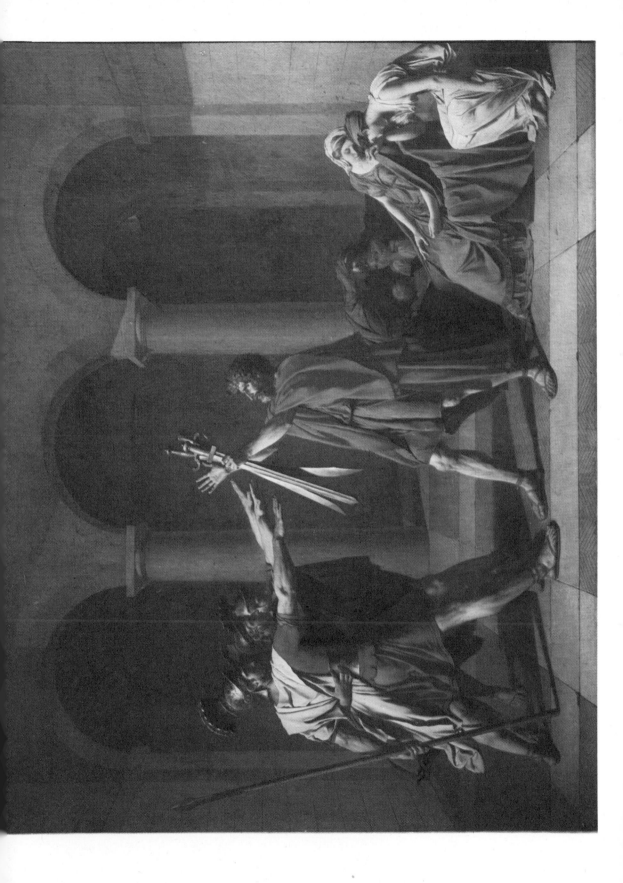

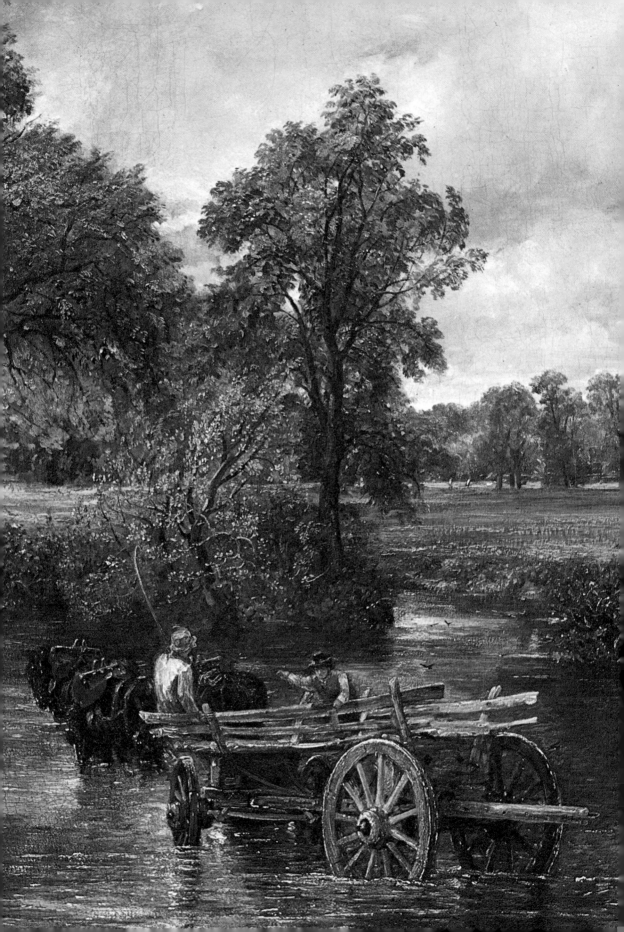

11 The Worship of Nature

For almost a thousand years the chief creative force in western civilisation was Christianity. Then, in about the year 1725, it suddenly declined and in intellectual society practically disappeared. Of course it left a vacuum. People couldn't get on without a belief in something outside themselves, and during the next hundred years they concocted a new belief which, however irrational it may seem to us, has added a good deal to our civilisation: a belief in the divinity of nature. It's said that one can attach fifty-two different meanings to the word 'nature'. In the early eighteenth century it had come to mean little more than common sense, as when in conversation we say: 'but naturally'. But the evidences of divine power which took the place of Christianity were manifestations of what we still mean by nature, those parts of the visible world which were not created by man and can be perceived through the senses. The first stage in this new direction of the human mind was very largely achieved in England – and perhaps it was no accident that England was the first country in which the Christian faith had collapsed. In about 1730 the French philosopher Montesquieu noted: 'There is no religion in England. If anyone mentions religion people begin to laugh.'

Montesquieu saw only the ruins of religion and although he was a very intelligent man he couldn't have foreseen that ruins, in the literal sense of the word, were part of the very subtle way in which faith in divine power was to trickle back into the Western European mind. The ruins of the Age of Faith had become part of nature – or rather they had become a sort of lead into nature through sentiment and memory. They helped to evoke that curious frame of mind which, in the early eighteenth century, was the usual prelude to the enjoyment of natural beauty, a gentle melancholy. Beautiful poetry was inspired by this mood – Gray's 'Elegy' and William Collins's 'Ode to Evening':

> Then lead, calm vot'ress, where some sheety Lake
> Cheers the lone Heath, or some time-hallow'd Pile,
>   Or up-land Fallows grey
>   Reflect its last cool Gleam.

> But when chill blust'ring Winds, or driving Rain,
> Forbid my willing Feet, be mine the Hut,
>   That from the Mountain's Side,
>   Views Wilds, and swelling Floods,

And Hamlets brown, and dim-discover'd Spires,
And hears their simple Bell, and marks o'er all
  Thy Dewy Fingers draw
  The gradual dusky Veil.

Very beautiful, but not very like nature, any more than were the pictures by Gainsborough and Wilson which were painted in the same decade [189].

William Collins is not a familiar name outside England. The same is true of all the eighteenth-century English nature poets, even James Thomson, who was, in his day, the most famous poet in Europe. Most of the great extensions of our faculties go back to an individual of genius. But not the emotional response to nature. It first appears in minor poets and provincial painters, and even in fashions; for example, the fashion that took the

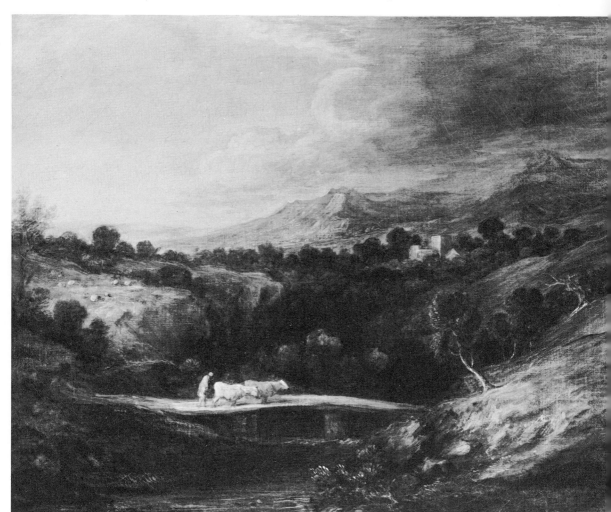

189 Gainsborough, *Landscape with Bridge*

straight avenues of formal gardens and changed them into twisting paths with pseudo-natural prospects: what were known all over the world for a hundred years as English gardens, and were the most pervasive influence that England has ever had on the look of things in Europe, except, perhaps, for men's fashions in the early nineteenth century. Trivial? Well, I suppose that all fashions seem trivial, but are serious. When Pope described 'this scene of man' as 'a mighty maze of walks without a plan' he was expressing a profound change in the European mind.

So much for nature in the first half of the eighteenth century. Then in about the year 1760 this English prelude of melancholy minor poets and picturesque gardens touched the mind of a man of genius, Jean-Jacques Rousseau. Although to some extent he derived his love of nature from England, it was among the lakes and Alpine valleys of Switzerland that his absorption in nature first became a sort of mystical experience. For over two thousand years mountains had been considered simply a nuisance: unproductive, obstacles to communication, the refuge of bandits and heretics. It is true that in about 1340 Petrarch had climbed one and enjoyed the view at the top (and then been put to shame by a passage from St Augustine); and early in the sixteenth century Leonardo da Vinci had wandered about in the Alps, ostensibly to study botany and geology, but his landscape backgrounds suggest that he was moved by what he saw. No other mountain climbs are recorded; and to Erasmus, Montaigne, Descartes, Newton, practically any of the great civilisers I have mentioned in this series, the thought of climbing a mountain for pleasure would have seemed ridiculous. I should add that this is not altogether true of painters. For example, Pieter Breughel, on his way from Antwerp to Rome in 1552, made drawings of the Alps which show something more than a topographical interest, and were later used with moving effect in his paintings.

However, the fact remains that when an ordinary traveller of the sixteenth and seventeenth centuries crossed the Alps it never occurred to him to admire the scenery – until the year 1739, when the poet Thomas Gray, visiting the Grande Chartreuse, wrote in a letter: 'Not a precipice, not a torrent, not a cliff, but is pregnant with religion and poetry.' Amazing! Might have been Ruskin. In fact I don't think that the full force of alpine poetry was expressed till the time of Byron and Turner. But in the middle of the eighteenth century a good many people seem to have recognised the charm of the Swiss lakes and enjoyed them in a comfortable, dilletantish sort of way. There even arose a Swiss tourist industry that supplied travellers in search of the picturesque with mementoes and produced one remarkable, almost forgotten artist, Caspar Wolf, who anticipated Turner by

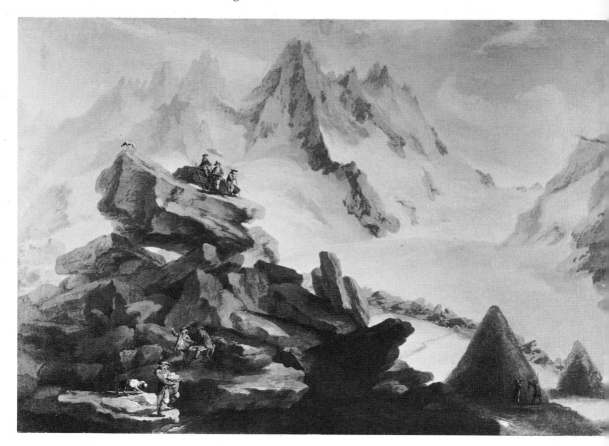

almost thirty years [190]. But like the eighteenth-century English nature
poets, this is a provincial overture, which might never have become a part
of contemporary thought without the genius of Rousseau [191].

Whatever his defects as a human being, and they were clearly apparent to
all those who tried to befriend him, Rousseau *was* a genius: one of the most
original minds of any age and a writer of incomparable prose. His solitary
and suspicious character had this advantage: it made him an outsider – he
didn't care what he said. As a result he was cruelly persecuted. For half his
life he was hounded out of one country after another. In 1765 he seemed
safely established in the small principality of Môtiers, but the local parson
stirred up the people against him, and they stoned him – broke his windows.
He took refuge on an island in the Lake of Bienne and there he had an experience so intense that one can almost say it caused a revolution in human
feeling. In listening to the flux and reflux of the waves, he tells us, he
became completely at one with nature, lost all consciousness of an independent self, all painful memories of the past or anxieties about the future,

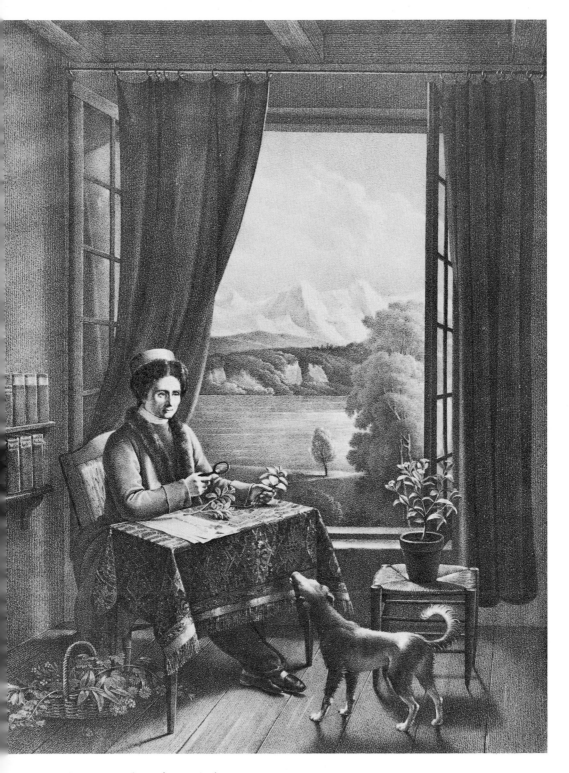

191 Rousseau at Bienne (engraving)

everything except the sense of being. 'I realised', he said, 'that our existence is nothing but a succession of moments perceived through the senses.'

I feel therefore I am. A curious discovery to have been made in the middle of the Age of Reason. But a few years earlier the Scottish philosopher, Hume, had reached the same conclusion by logical means. It was an intellectual time-bomb, which after sizzling away for almost two hundred years has only just gone off, whether to the advantage of civilisation seems rather doubtful. It had a certain effect in the eighteenth century, and became part of the new cult of sensibility. But no one seems to have realised how far abandonment to sensation might take us, or what a questionable divinity nature might prove to be: no one except the Marquis de Sade who saw through the new god – or goddess – from the start! 'Nature averse to crime,' he said in 1792, 'I tell you that nature lives and breathes by it, hungers at all her pores for bloodshed, yearns with all her heart for the furtherance of cruelty.'

Well, the Marquis was what used to be called a rank outsider and his unfavourable view of nature is hardly mentioned in the eighteenth century. On the contrary, Rousseau's belief in the beauty and innocence of nature was extended from plants and trees to man. He believed that natural man was virtuous. It was partly a survival of the old myth of The Golden Age, and partly a feeling of shame at the corruption of European Society – a feeling first expressed by Montaigne in the last admirable pages of his essay *On Cannibals*. But Rousseau expanded it into a philosophy in his *Discourse on the Origin of Inequality*. He sent a copy to Voltaire, who replied in a letter which is a famous example of Voltairian wit: 'No one has ever used so much intelligence to persuade us to be stupid. After reading your book one feels that one ought to walk on all fours. Unfortunately during the last sixty years I have lost the habit.' It was a dialectical triumph, but no more, because belief in the superiority of natural man became one of the motive powers of the next half-century; and less than twenty years after Rousseau had propounded his theory, it seemed to have been confirmed by fact. In 1767 the French explorer Bougainville arrived in Tahiti, and in 1769 Captain Cook stayed there for four months in order to observe the transit of Venus. Bougainville was a student of Rousseau. It isn't surprising that he should have found in the Tahitians all the qualities of the noble savage. But Captain Cook was a hard-headed Yorkshireman, and even he couldn't help comparing the happy and harmonious life that he had discovered in Tahiti [192] with the squalor and brutality of Europe. Soon the brightest wits of Paris and London were beginning to ask whether the word civilisation was not more appropriate to the uncorrupted islanders of the South Seas than to

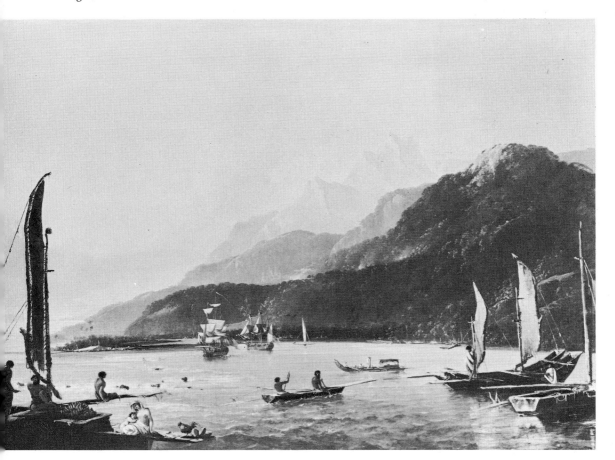

the exceptionally corrupt society of eighteenth-century Europe.

Some such idea was put to Dr Johnson in 1773 by 'a gentleman who ex-patiated to him on the happiness of savage life'. 'Do not allow yourself,' he replied, 'to be imposed on by such gross absurdity. It is sad stuff. If a bull could speak he might as well exclaim: "Here am I with this cow and this grass; what being can enjoy greater felicity!"' Without going as far Dr Johnson, who, in his hatred of cant, had momentarily forgotten the Christian doctrine of the soul, the student of European civilisation may observe that Polynesia produced no Dante, Michelangelo, Shakespeare, Newton or Goethe; and although we may all agree that the impact of European civilisation on places like Tahiti was disastrous, we must also allow that the very fragility of those Arcadian societies – the speed and completeness with which they collapsed on the peaceful appearance of a few British sailors followed by a handful of missionaries – shows that they were not civilisations in the sense of that word which I have been using.

Although the worship of nature had its dangers, the prophets of the new religion were earnest and even pious men whose whole aim was to prove that their goddess was respectable, and even moral. They achieved this curious intellectual feat by approximating nature and truth. Far the greatest man to apply his mind to this exercise was Goethe. The word 'nature' appears throughout his work – on almost every page of his theoretical and critical writings – and is claimed as the ultimate sanction for all his judgements. It is true that Goethe's Nature is slightly different from Rousseau's Nature. He meant by it not how things seem, but how things work if they are not interfered with. He saw all living things – and he was a distinguished botanist who made his own drawings of the plants that he observed [193] – as striving for fuller development through an infinitely long process of adaptation. I might almost say that he believed in the gradual civilisation of plants and animals. It was the point of view that was later to lead to Darwin and the theory of evolution. But this analytic and philosophic approach to nature had less immediate effect on people's minds than the purely inspirational approach of the English Romantic poets, Coleridge and Wordsworth.

Coleridge looked at nature in the high mystical manner. This is how he addressed the Swiss mountains in his 'Hymn Before Sun-rise, in the Vale of Chamouni':

> O dread and silent mount! I gazed upon thee,
> Till thou, still present to the bodily sense,
> Didst vanish from my thought: entranced in prayer
> I worshipped the Invisible alone.

Very Germanic, and best illustrated [**39**, on facing page] by a German landscape painter, Caspar David Friedrich. I have often wondered if this great artist was known to Coleridge, their outlooks are so similar.

Wordsworth's approach to nature was religious in the moral Anglican manner. 'Accuse me not,' he said, 'of arrogance'

> If having walk'd with Nature
> And offered, as far as frailty would allow,
> My heart a daily sacrifice to truth
> I now affirm of Nature and of Truth
>   That their Divinity
> Revolts offended at the ways of men.

That nature should be shocked by human behaviour does seem to me rather nonsense. But one mustn't lightly accuse Wordsworth of arrogance or silliness. By the time he wrote those lines he had lived through a great deal. As a young man he went to France, lived with a spirited French girl and had

39 Caspar David Friedrich, *Man looking at mountains, with rainbow*

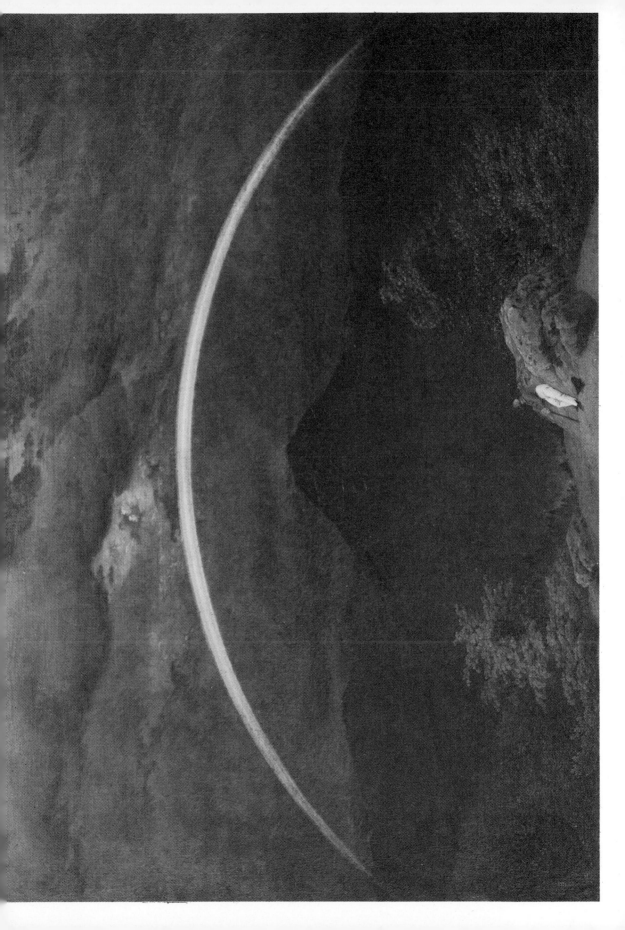

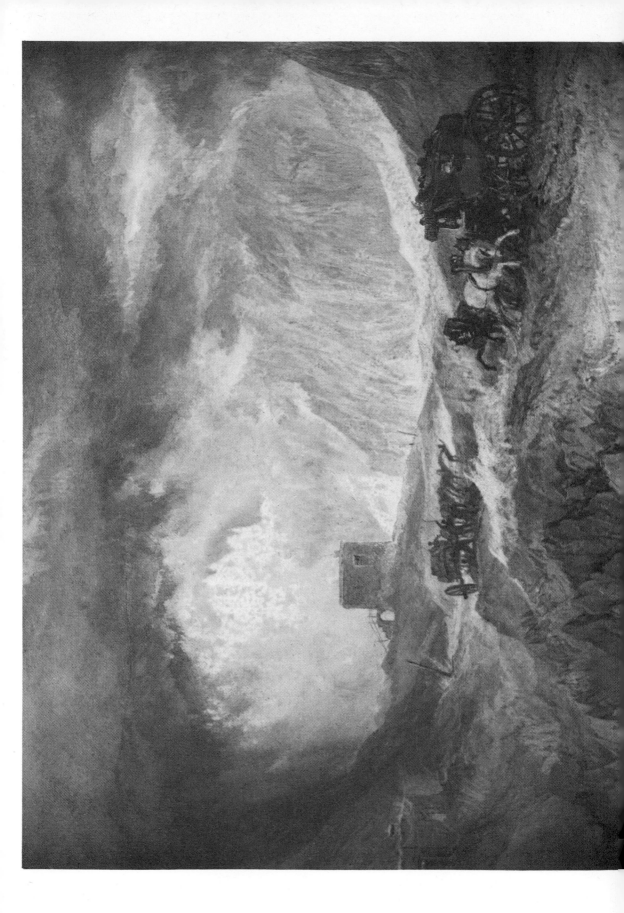

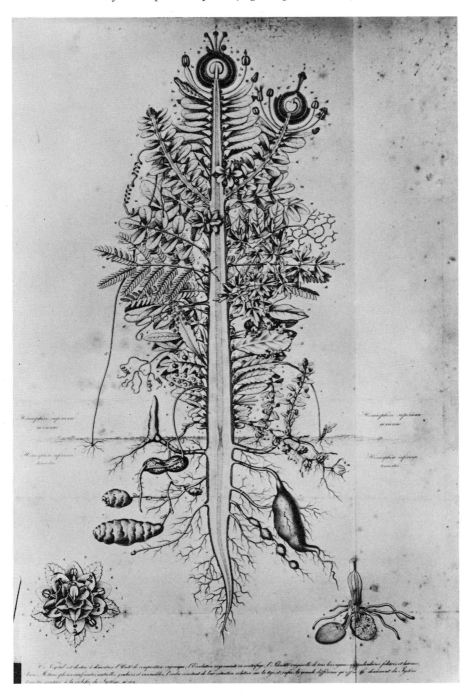

a daughter; he became involved in the French Revolution – an ardent Girondiste – and but for a chance might easily have had his head chopped off in the September Massacres.

He returned to England disgusted with the political aspect of the Revolution, but not the less attached to its ideals; and he set out to describe in verse the truth about the hardships of poor people as they had never been described before. He wrote poems without a glimmer of comfort or hope. He walked for miles alone, on Salisbury Plain and in Wales, talking only to tramps and beggars and discharged prisoners. He was utterly crushed by man's inhumanity to man. And finally he came to Tintern. Of course he had always been observant of natural beauty – his earliest poems show us that. But in August 1793, like Rousseau on the island of St Pierre, he recognised that only total absorption in nature could heal and restore his spirit. He returned to Tintern five years later and recaptured some of those first feelings:

> Though changed, no doubt, from what I was when first
> I came among these hills; when like a roe
> I bounded o'er the mountains, by the sides
> Of the deep rivers and the lonely streams,
> Wherever nature led: more like a man
> Flying from something that he dreads than one
> Who sought the thing he loved. For nature then
> To me was all in all. – I cannot paint
> What then I was. The sounding cataract
> Haunted me like a passion: the tall rock,
> The mountain, and the deep and gloomy wood,
> Their colours and their forms, were then to me
> An appetite; a feeling and a love,
> That had no need of a remoter charm,
> By thought supplied, nor any interest
> Unborrowed from the eye.

Unlike many of his successors in the nineteenth century, Wordsworth had earned the right to lose himself in nature. And so, after all, had Rousseau, because the author of the *Reveries of a Solitary Walker* was also the author of *The Social Contract*, the gospel of revolution. I stress this because a sympathy with the voiceless and the oppressed, be they human or animal, does seem to be a necessary accompaniment to the worship of nature – and has been ever since St Francis. Robert Burns, at the first dawn of Romantic poetry, would not have written 'A man's a man for a' that', if he hadn't also felt deeply distressed at disturbing a field mouse's nest. The new religion was anti-hierarchical: it proposed a new set of values; and this was implied in Wordsworth's belief that it was based on right instincts rather than learning. This was an extension of Rousseau's discovery of immediate feeling but with the addition of the word 'moral': because Wordsworth

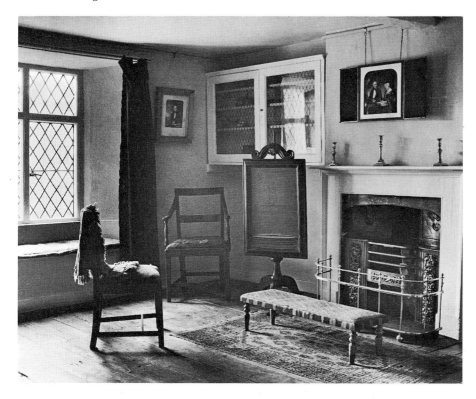

recognised that simple people and animals often show more courage and loyalty and unselfishness than sophisticated people, and also a greater sense of the wholeness of life:

> One impulse from a vernal wood
> May teach you more of man,
> Of moral evil and of good,
> Than all the sages can.
>
> Sweet is the lore which Nature brings;
> Our meddling intellect
> Mis-shapes the beauteous forms of things:–
> We murder to dissect.

What was it that made Wordsworth turn from man to nature? It was the reappearance in his life of his sister Dorothy. They first set up house together in Somerset. Then, driven by a strong instinct, they returned to their native country and settled in a cottage at Grasmere. It was in the steep-sloping garden and the tiny sitting-room [194] that Wordsworth wrote his most inspired poems. The journal which Dorothy kept in these years shows how often his poems originated in one of her vivid experiences; and Wordsworth knew it.

> She gave me eyes, she gave me ears;
> And humble cares, and delicate fears.

In the new religion of nature this shy, unassuming woman was the saint and prophetess.

Unfortunately the feelings for each other of brother and sister were too strong for the usages of this world:

> thou my dearest Friend,
> My dear, dear Friend; and in thy voice I catch
> The language of my former heart, and read
> My former pleasures in the shooting lights
> Of thy wild eyes. Oh! yet a little while
> May I behold in thee what I was once,
> My dear, dear Sister! and this prayer I make,
> Knowing that Nature never did betray
> The heart that loved her.

The burning heat of romantic egotism! Both Byron and Wordsworth fell deeply in love with their sisters. The inevitable prohibition was a disaster for both of them. Wordsworth suffered most, because although Byron became restless and cynical, he did write 'Don Juan'; whereas Wordsworth, after the heartbreaking renunciation of Dorothy, gradually lost inspiration, and although quite happily married to an old school friend, wrote less and less poetry that one can read without an effort. And Dorothy became simple-minded.

In the same years that English poetry took its revolutionary course English painting also produced two men of genius, Turner and Constable. A few months before Wordsworth had settled in the Lake District, Turner had painted a picture of Buttermere [195] which is one of his earliest masterpieces. However, Wordsworth's real kinship was not with Turner but with Constable. They both were countrymen, with strong appetites rigidly controlled. They both grasped nature with the same physical passion. 'I have seen him,' said Leslie, Constable's biographer, 'admire a fine tree with an ecstasy like that with which he could catch up a beautiful child in his arms.' Constable never had the least doubt that nature meant the visible world of tree, flower, river, field and sky, exactly as they presented themselves to the senses; and he seems to have arrived instinctively at Wordsworth's conviction that by dwelling with absolute truth on natural objects he would reveal something of the moral grandeur of the universe [38, facing p. 269]. Only by concentrating on the shining, variable surface of appearance would he discover

> That motion and the spirit that impels
> All thinking things, all objects of all thoughts
> And rolls through all things.

Then, both Wordsworth and Constable loved their own places, and never tired of the things which had entered their imaginations as children. Constable said: 'The sound of water escaping from mill-dams, old rotten banks, shiny posts and brickwork – these scenes made me a painter – and I am grateful.' We have got so used to this approach to painting that it is difficult for us to see how strange it was to love shiny posts and rotten banks more than heroes in armour, at a time when all serious artists aspired to go to Rome and paint vast pictures of subjects from Homer and Plutarch.

Constable hated grandeur and pomposity and like Wordsworth his cult of simplicity sometimes seems to me to verge on the commonplace. A picture like his *Willows by a Stream* [196] is the forerunner of a quantity of

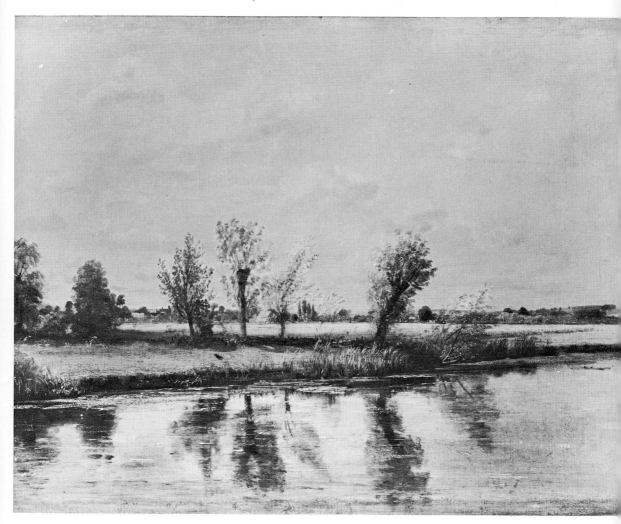

mediocre painting, just as Wordsworth's poems to small celandines and daisies anticipated a quantity of bad poetry. It was rejected from the Academy when it was painted. 'Take away that nasty green thing,' they said. For a hundred years it would have been the one of his works most likely to be accepted. But when Constable really trusted his emotions, his rustic subjects [197] do achieve that quality by which, as Wordsworth said. 'the passions of men are incorporated with the beautiful and permanent forms of nature'.

The simple life: it was a necessary part of the new religion of nature, and one in strong contrast to earlier aspirations. Civilisation, which for so long had been dependent on great monasteries and palaces, or well-furnished salons, could now emanate from a cottage. Even Goethe at the court of

Weimar preferred to live in a small and simple garden house; and Dove Cottage was extremely humble. No carriages rolled up to this door – which reminds me how closely the worship of nature was connected with walking. In the eighteenth century a solitary walker was viewed with almost as much suspicion as he is in Los Angeles today. But the Wordsworths walked continually – De Quincey calculated that by middle age the poet had walked 180,000 miles. Even the unathletic Coleridge walked. They thought nothing of walking sixteen miles after dinner to post a letter. And so, for over a hundred years, going for a country walk was the spiritual as well as the physical exercise of all intellectuals, poets, and philosophers. I am told that in universities the afternoon walk is no longer part of intellectual life. But for a quantity of people walking is still one of the chief escapes from the pressures of the material world, and the countryside where Wordsworth walked, in solitude, is now almost as crowded with pilgrims as Lourdes or Benares.

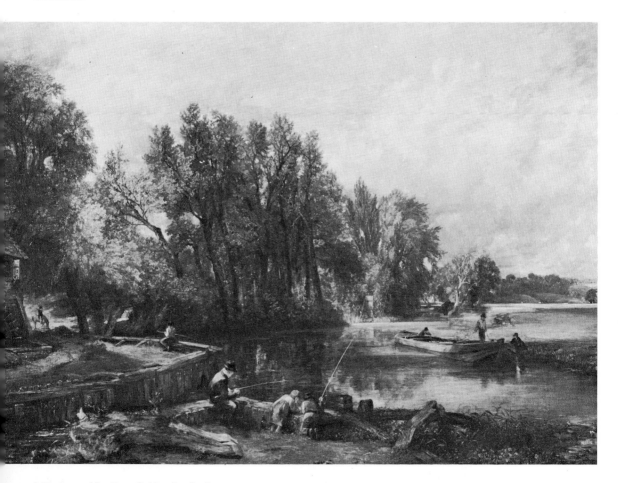

197 Constable, *Boys fishing by the Stour*

The resemblances between Wordsworth and Constable, which seem so obvious to us, did not occur to their contemporaries: partly, I suppose, because Constable was hardly known till 1825, by which time Wordsworth had long since lost inspiration; and partly because Constable painted flat country whereas Wordsworth, and indeed the whole cult of nature, was associated with mountains. This, combined with Constable's lack of finish, was what led Ruskin to underrate him, while devoting a good part of his life to the praise of Turner. Turner was the supreme exponent of that response to nature felt by Gray in the Grande Chartreuse – what one might call the picturesque sublime; and sometimes his storms and avalanches seem preposterous, just as Byron's rhetoric is preposterous. But I suppose that the new religion required assertions of power and sublimity more obvious than those provided by daisies and celandines [40, facing p. 277].

Don't think that I am trying to belittle Turner. He was a genius of the first order – far the greatest painter that England has ever produced; and although he was prepared to work in the fashionable style, he never lost his intuitive understanding of nature. No one has ever known more about natural appearances, and he was able to fit into his encyclopedic knowledge memories of the most fleeting effects of light – sunrises, passing storms, dissolving mists, none of which had ever been set on canvas before.

For thirty years these brilliant gifts were exploited in a series of pictures which dazzled his contemporaries, but are too artificial for modern taste. But all the time Turner was perfecting, for his own private satisfaction, an entirely new approach to painting which was only recognised in our own day. Briefly, it consisted of transforming everything into pure colour, light rendered as colour, feelings about life rendered as colour. It's quite difficult for us to realise what a revolutionary procedure this was. One must remember that for centuries objects were thought to be real because they were solid. You proved their reality by touching or tapping them – people still do. And all respectable art aimed at defining this solidity, either by modelling or by a firm outline. 'What is it,' said Blake, 'that distinguishes honesty from knavery, but the hard and wiry line of rectitude?'

Colour was considered immoral – perhaps rightly, because it is an immediate sensation and makes its effect independently of those ordered memories which are the basis of morality. However, Turner's colour was not at all arbitrary – what we call decorative colour. It always started as the record of an actual experience. Turner, like Rousseau, used his optical sensations to discover the truth. 'I feel therefore I am.' It's a fact which you can verify by looking at Turner's pictures in the Tate Gallery: the less defined, the more purely colouristic they are, the more vividly do they

41 Turner, *Waves breaking on a lee shore*

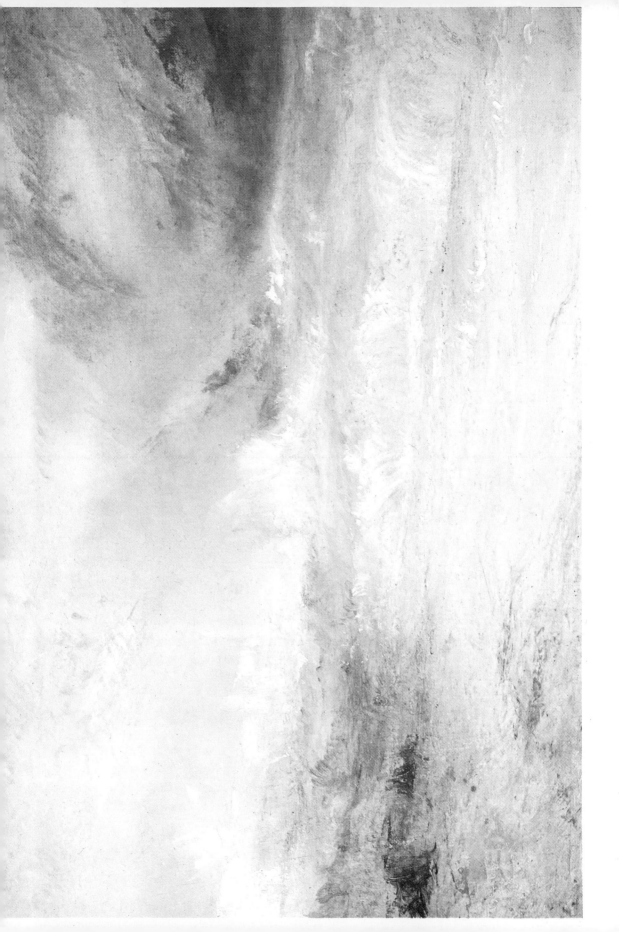

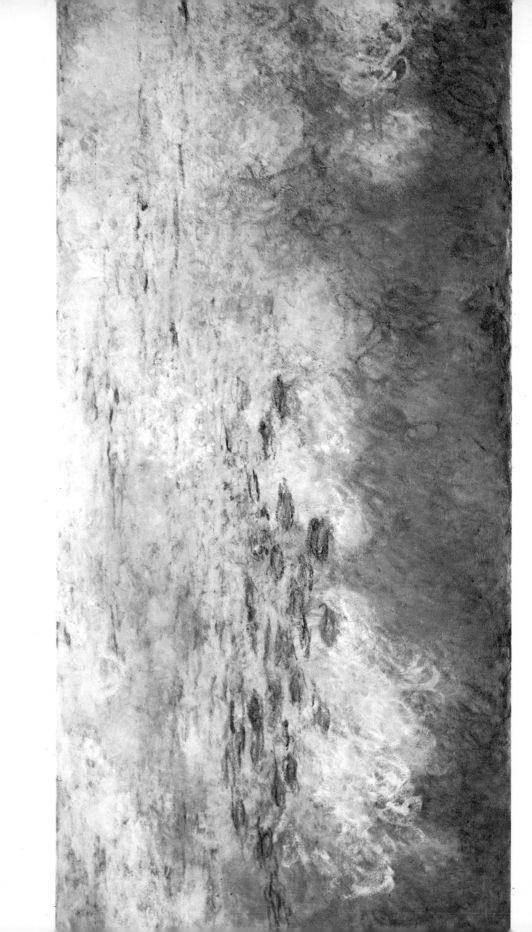

convey a total sense of truth to nature [41, facing p. 284]. Turner declared the independence of colour and thereby added a new faculty to the human mind.

I don't suppose that Turner was conscious of his relationship with Rousseau. But the other great prophet of nature, Goethe, meant a lot to him. Although he had practically no education, he painfully read Goethe's works, in particular his *Theory of Colour,* and he sympathised with Goethe's feeling for nature as an organism, as something that works according to certain laws. This, of course, was one of the things about Turner that delighted Ruskin, so that his enormous defence of the artist, which he called by the wholly misleading title of *Modern Painters,* became an encyclopedia of natural observation. Just as the Middle Ages produced encyclopedias in which inaccurate observations were used to prove the truth of the Christian religion, so Ruskin accumulated very accurate observations of plants, rocks, clouds, mountains, in order to prove that nature worked according to law [198]. Well, perhaps it does. But not the kind of law that human beings have concocted for themselves. Nobody today would take seriously Ruskin's belief that nature is subject to, or illustrates, Moral Law. All the same, when he says, 'The power which causes the several portions of a plant to help each other we call life. Intensity of life is also intensity of helpfulness. The ceasing of this help is what we call corruption,' he does seem to me to have drawn from his observations a moral at least as convincing as most of those that can be drawn from Holy Writ. And it helps to explain why, for fifty years after the publication of *Modern Painters,* Ruskin was considered one of the chief prophets of his time.

All these aspects of the new religion of nature meet and mingle where the old religions had also focused their aspirations: the sky. Only instead of the influential movements of the planets or a vision of a celestial city, the nature-worshippers concentrated on the clouds. In 1802 a Quaker named Luke Howard read a paper on the 'Modification of Clouds', which tried to do for the sky what Linnaeus had done for plants. The result so much delighted Goethe that he wrote a poem to Howard. Luke Howard also influenced the painters. Constable read his work and was confirmed in his belief that clouds must be collected and classified: he did hundreds of cloud studies [199], noting on the back the month, the time of day and the direction of the wind. Ruskin said of himself that 'he bottled clouds as carefully as his father [who was a wine merchant] had bottled sherries'.

But clouds are proverbially lawless. Even Ruskin gave up the attempt in despair. So for the time being, the sky appealed less to the analytically-minded than to those worshippers of nature who abandoned themselves to

42 Monet, *Water-lilies*

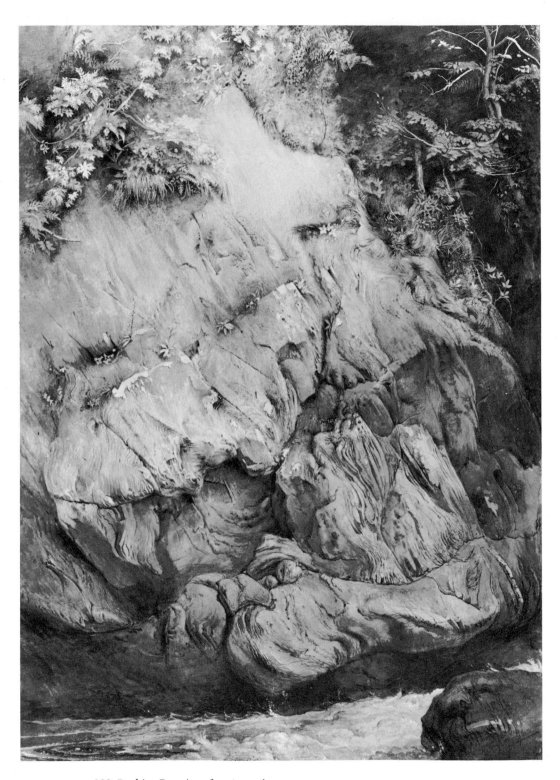

198 Ruskin, *Drawing of gneiss rock*

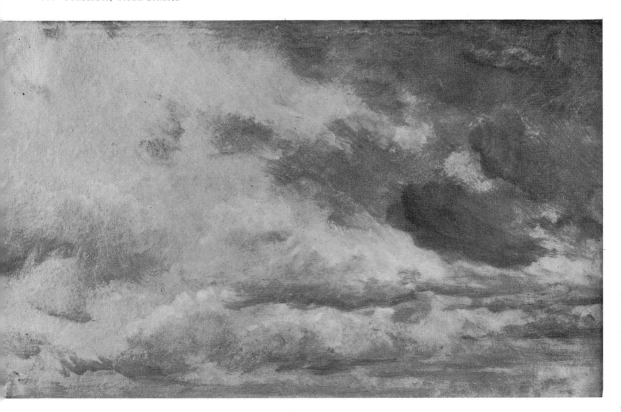

Rousseau's sensuous reverie. 'The whole mind,' said an early writer on Romanticism, 'may become at length something like a hemisphere of cloud scenery, filled with an ever moving train of changing, melting forms.'

Constable said that in landscape-painting clouds are the chief organ of sentiment. And for Turner they had a symbolic meaning. In his work clouds the colour of blood became symbols of destruction. He identified skies of peace and skies of discord. His chief aim in life was to see the sun rise above water: he owned a number of houses from which he could see this happening. And he was particularly fascinated by the line where the sky and the sea join each other, that mingling of the elements which seems, by its harmony of tone, to lead to a general reconciliation of opposites. In order to observe these effects, he lived by the seaside in East Kent – believed by the neighbours to be an eccentric sea-captain called Puggy Booth, who even in retirement could not stop looking out to sea.

'A dialogue between the sea and the sky': the title that Debussy gave to part of his *La Mer*. It was written sixty years later, but there is no feeling of shock in associating it with a much earlier work of art, because Turner painted in a style absolutely outside his own time – perhaps the first great

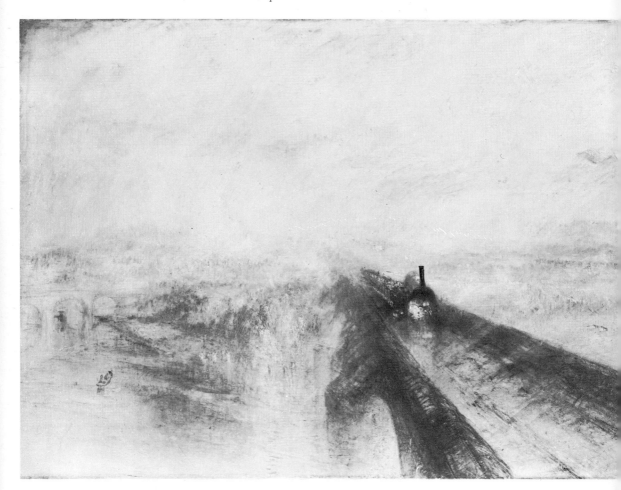

artist to do so. Even exhibited pictures like *Rain, Steam, Speed* [200] have no relation to anything that was being done in Europe, or was to be done for almost a century. In 1840 they must have looked absolutely crazy, and indeed were usually referred to as 'another of Mr Turner's little jokes'.

Turner was brought up in the tradition of the picturesque, by which only certain outstanding combinations in nature are suitable material for art. But the picturesque never took root in France. French painters preferred Constable, and echoed his saying, 'I never saw an ugly thing in my life'. It was a kind of egalitarianism, and Courbet, who was a communist by conviction, painted some of the most literal transcripts of nature ever offered as art. They come very close to that truly democratic form of art, the coloured postcard. This straightforward, naturalistic landscape-painting continued to be the popular style of painting for almost a hundred years – and would be still, I believe, if any modern painter could do it with conviction. But at a critical moment its place was taken by photography, and the three great lovers of nature of the late nineteenth century, Monet, Cézanne and Van Gogh, had to make a more radical transformation.

The enraptured vision that first induced Rousseau to live in the world of sensation had one more triumph in the nineteenth century. Curiously enough, it also came from looking at ripples – the sun sparkling on water and the quavering reflection of masts. It took place in 1869, when Monet and Renoir used to meet at a riverside café called La Grenouillière. Before that meeting they had both followed the ordinary naturalist style. But when they came to those ripples and reflections, patient naturalism was defeated [201].

All one could do was to give an impression – an impression of what? Of light, because that is all that we see. It was a long time since the philosopher

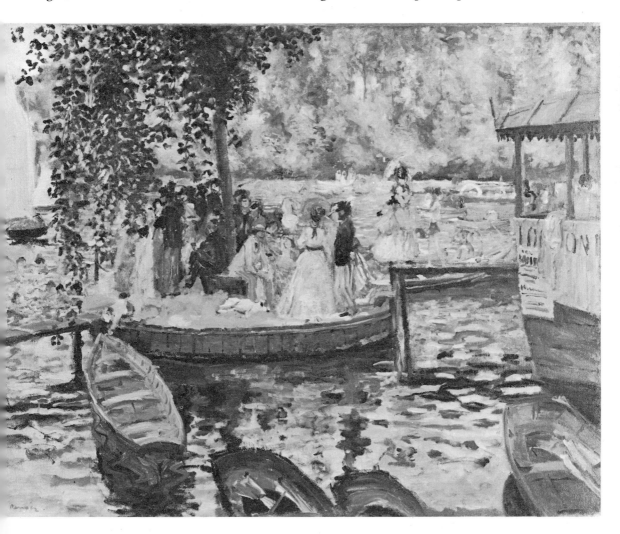

201 Renoir, *La Grenouillière*

Hume had come to the same conclusion, and the Impressionists had no idea that they were following up a philosophical theory. But Monet's words, 'light is the principle person in the picture', gave a kind of philosophic unity to their work, so that the great years of Impressionism have added something to our human faculties as well as delighting our eyes. Our awareness of light has become part of that general awareness, that heightening of sensibility so marvellously described in the novels of Proust, which seemed, when we first read them, almost to give us new senses.

When one thinks how many beautiful Impressionist pictures there are in the world, and of what a difference they have made to our way of seeing, it is surprising how short a time the movement, as a movement, lasted. The periods in which men can work together happily inspired by a single aim last only a short time – it's one of the tragedies of civilisation. After twenty years the Impressionist movement had split up. One party thought that light should be rendered scientifically, in touches of primary colour, as if it had passed through a spectrum. This theory inspired an impeccable painter, Seurat. But it was too remote from the first spontaneous delight in nature, upon which, in the end, all landscape-painting must depend.

On the other hand Monet, the original unswerving Impressionist, when he found that straightforward naturalism was exhausted, attempted a kind of colour symbolism to express changing effects of light: for example, he painted a series of cathedral façades in different lights – pink, blue and yellow – which seem to me too far from experience. Then he turned to the water-lily garden which he had made in his grounds, and the enraptured contemplation of the clouds reflected on its surface was the subject of his last great masterpieces [**42**, facing p. 285].

In the two rooms of the Nympheas in Paris he expands his sensations into one continuous form, like a symphonic poem. This poem takes its point of departure from experience, but the stream of sensation becomes a stream of consciousness. And how does the consciousness become paint? That is the miracle. By a knowledge of each effect so complete that it becomes instinctive, and every movement of the brush is not only a record but also a self-revealing gesture. All the same, the strength of will needed to carry through this transformation must have been enormous and perhaps Monet would never have achieved it without the support of his friend Georges Clemenceau. That great old warrior had will to spare from saving his country for keeping Monet at work. Time and again Monet, who was going blind, wrote that he could do no more. Whereupon M. Clemenceau would leave the Cabinet room and drive down to Monet's studio and beg him to take up his brush. Once more Monet would immerse himself in his pool of memories and sensations. Total immersion: this is the ultimate reason why the love of nature has been for so long accepted as a religion. It is a means by which we can lose our identity in the whole and gain thereby a more intense consciousness of being.

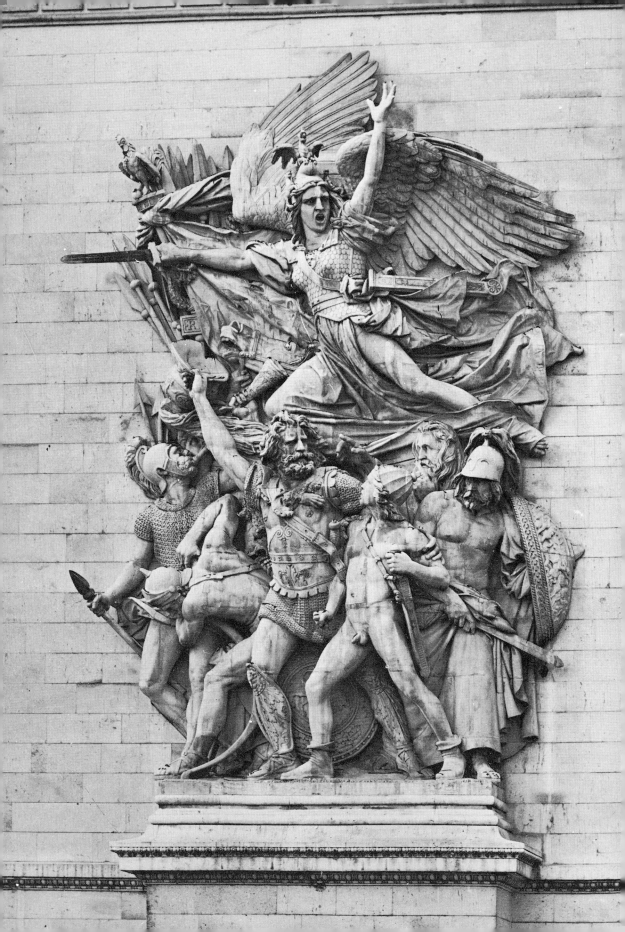

12 The Fallacies of Hope

The reasonable world of an eighteenth-century library is symmetrical, consistent and enclosed. Symmetry is a human concept, because with all our irregularities we are more or less symmetrical and the balance of a mantelpiece by Adam or a phrase by Mozart reflects our satisfaction with our two eyes, two arms and two legs. And consistency: again and again in this series I have used that word as a term of praise. But enclosed! That's the trouble: an enclosed world becomes a prison of the spirit. One longs to get out, one longs to move. One realises that symmetry and consistency, whatever their merits, are enemies of movement. And what is that I hear – that note of urgency, of indignation, of spiritual hunger. Beethoven. The sound of European man once more reaching for something beyond his grasp. We must leave the trim, finite interiors of eighteenth-century classicism and go to confront the infinite. We have a long, rough voyage ahead of us, and I cannot say where it will end, because it is not over yet. We are still the offspring of the Romantic movement, and still victims of the Fallacies of Hope.

I have used the metaphor of the sea because all the great Romantics, from Byron onwards, have been obsessed by this image of movement and escape.

> Once more upon the waters! yet once more!
> And the waves bound beneath me as a steed
> That knows his rider. Welcome to their roar!
> Swift be their guidance, wheresoe'er it lead!

In Romantic art it usually led to disaster. The escape from symmetry was also an escape from reason. The eighteenth-century philosophers had attempted to tidy up human society by the use of reason. But rational arguments were not strong enough to upset the huge mass of torpid tradition that had grown up in the last hundred and fifty years. In America it might be possible for a new political constitution to be achieved: but it took something more explosive to blast the heavy foundations of Europe, just as it had in the Reformation.

Once more the process began with Rousseau. He gave the appeal to the heart, rather than the head, universal currency, extending it from love and education to politics. 'Man was born free and is everywhere in chains.' What an opening sentence, like the first scene of *Hamlet*. Towards the end of the eighteenth century, as rational argument declines, vivid assertions take its place, and no one coined them with a sharper stamp of inspiration than William Blake. His *Marriage of Heaven and Hell*, written in about 1789, is a handbook of anti-rational wisdom comparable to Nietzsche's *Zarathustra*. 'The road of excess leads to the palace of wisdom.' 'The tigers of wrath are wiser than the horses of instruction.' 'Energy is the only life and is from the body; and Reason is the bound and outward circumference of Energy.'

At almost the same date in Scotland a more earthily human voice was raised in protest against hierarchy, the voice of Robert Burns. Poets had lived in poverty before his time, but they had mostly been poor scholars who preferred the hand-to-mouth, knock-about life of the town to a comfortable parsonage. Burns was the first great poet to be born in a cottage with only one room and an earth floor, to have spent more than half his life as a farm labourer, and to have used this experience as material for poetry. He was admittedly more at home as a writer of heart-warming songs than as a political thinker; but in one of his lyrics he produced a line that has echoed down the centuries like Rousseau's opening – 'A man's a man for a' that,' or, more explicitly, in the last lines:

> It's coming yet, for a' that,
> That man to man the warld o'er
> Shall brothers be for a' that.

Complementary to this appeal of justice and natural law was the feeling that custom, prudence, reasonable foresight, had become a drag on the human spirit.

> Sound, sound the clarion, fill the fife,
> Throughout the sensual world proclaim,
> One crowded hour of glorious life
> Is worth an age without a name.

Those lines, written by an obscure English poet named Mordaunt before the year 1790, outlasted revolutionary virtue, and are still the basis of romantic movies. These were the impulses that showed themselves like flames shooting up through cracks in the earth's crust during the 1780s. Then, as we all know, came the eruption; and because these fires had for so long been burning under the surface of the eighteenth century, the French Revolution evolved from the protest of a few discontented lawyers, through the honourable grunts and groans of bourgeois constitutionalism, to the raw cry of a popular movement. None of the intervening solutions would do.

In June 1789 the first phase, the liberal bourgeois phase, of the revolution came to a climax. The members of the National Assembly had found themselves locked out of their usual meeting place and went off full of virtuous

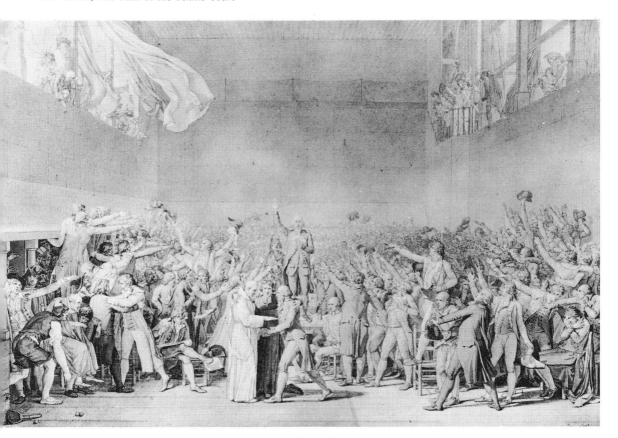

indignation to a covered tennis court, where they swore an oath to establish
a constitution. David, the painter of republican virtue, was commissioned
to record the scene. His unfinished picture was cut up, but in the drawing
for it [203] we see the repeated gestures of the *Oath of the Horatii* transposed
into modern dress. In the centre is a group symbolising the union of the
Church and the better aristocrats (actually the monk was not present: like
all propaganda pictures it is not strictly accurate); on either side are figures
in an ecstasy of enthusiasm for constitutional government; and on the
right (this is historically correct) is the one delegate who wouldn't swear to
support it. To our eyes, disenchanted by one hundred and fifty years of
democratic eloquence and fifty years of propaganda painting (none of it
as good as David), the whole thing may seem slightly absurd. And in fact
the early phases of the Revolution were pedantic and confused. It seemed
as if the forces of obstruction could be met only on their own terms. The
constitutional, one might almost say the American, phase of the French
Revolution belonged to the Age of Reason. Three years later we hear the
sound of the new world, when certain honest citizens of Marseilles grow

impatient at 'an executive that does not act', and undertake the amazing feat of marching, in a sweltering July, all the way from Marseilles to Paris, tugging three pieces of cannon and singing a new song – the Marseillaise.

Breathes there a man with soul so dead, who can listen to that marching song without emotion, even today. No wonder that the finest spirits of the time were enraptured, that Blake began a poem on the French Revolution which nobody reads, and Wordsworth wrote the lines that everybody quotes, and I must quote again:

> For mighty were the auxiliars which then stood
> Upon our side, we who were strong to love!
> Bliss was it in that dawn to be alive,
> But to be young was very heaven!

And Wordsworth goes on to say how the revolution seemed to bring Rousseau's dreams of natural man and travellers' tales of his enchanted existence into reality. It was no longer confined to

> some secreted island, Heaven knows where!
> But in the very world, which is the world
> Of all of us.

At this point the revolution was the Romantic movement in action. And perhaps its greatest legacy to posterity has been its message to the young that those who are strong in love may yet find a way of escaping from the rotten parchment bonds that tie us down.

The moving fact about the early revolution is that men's belief in a new world was so concrete and sharp that they could decide to change the calendar – making the year 1792 Year One, and renaming the months. The change of years was a nuisance, but the new names of the months – Ventose, Thermidor, Brumaire and so forth, the windy one, the hot one, the misty one – are poetical, and I wish they had survived. They express the love of nature which had become so closely entwined with the revolution. The same desire to return to nature affected women's fashions. All the artificial framework of the eighteenth century is thrown away, and the dresses follow the lines of the body with graceful simplicity [204]. No more high, pow-dered wigs, but flowing locks, with a simple bandeau. Madame Récamier, the most famous and inaccessible beauty of the time, posed for David with naked feet.

A more formidable undertaking was to replace Christianity by a religion of nature. It sometimes went rather too far: for example, it was proposed to pull down Chartres Cathedral and build in its place a temple of wisdom. There was a good deal of profanation and blasphemy, and a vast amount of destruction: Cluny, St Denis, many of the sacred places of civilisation were

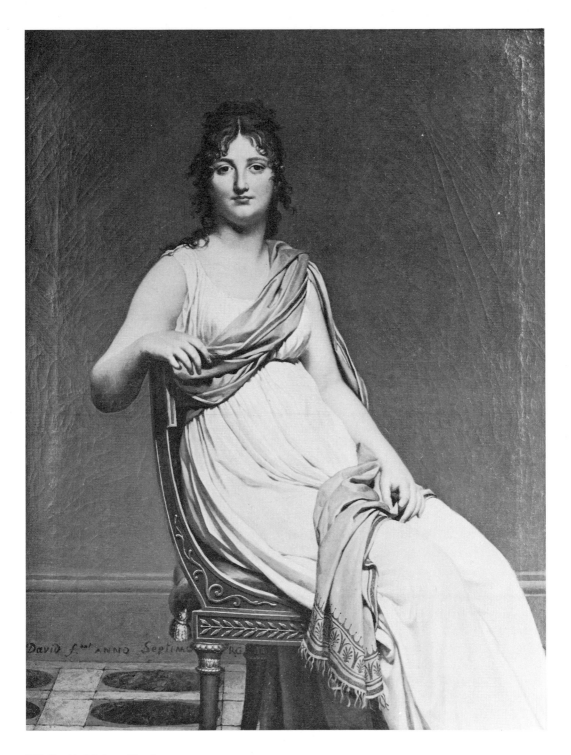

204 David, *Madame Verninac*

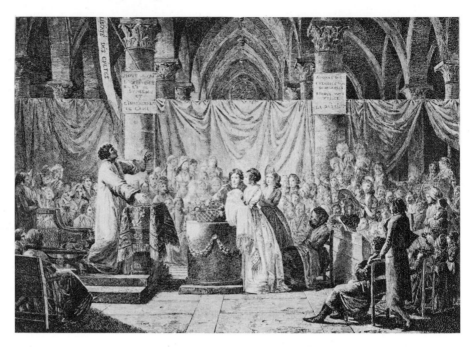

partially destroyed and their contents looted. On the other hand, there is something rather touching about the religion of nature as we see it in a print [205] of baptism according to the new rite, taking place in a de-Christianised church. People who hold forth about the modern world often say that what we need is a new religion. It may be true, but it isn't easy to establish. Even Robespierre, who was an enthusiast for a new religion and had powerful means of persuasion at his command, couldn't bring it off.

And on the name Robespierre one remembers how horribly all this idealism came to grief. Most of the great episodes in the history of civilisation have had some unpleasant consequences. But none have kicked back sooner and harder than the revolutionary fervour of 1792; because in September there took place the first of those massacres by which, alas, the revolution is chiefly remembered. No one has ever explained, in historical terms, the September Massacres, and perhaps in the end the old-fashioned explanation is correct, that it was a kind of communal sadism. It was a pogrom – a phenomenon with which we have since become familiar. And it was given fresh impetus by another well-known emotion – mass panic. In July 1792 the Committee of Public Safety had officially proclaimed *La patrie en danger* – 'the country in peril'; which was followed by the usual corollary: *Ils nous ont trahis* – 'there are traitors among us'. We know what that means. How many innocent German governesses and art-historians suffered in our last

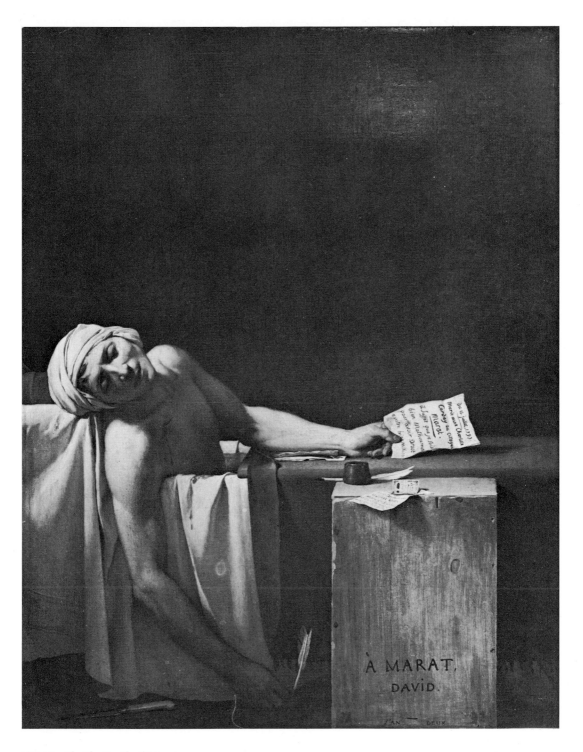

206 David, *The Death of Marat*

two wars, if not by execution, then by extradition and drowning on the way to Canada. In 1792 France *was* in danger and there really were traitors, starting with the King and Queen, who had encouraged the intervention of outside powers. France was fighting for her life against the forces of ancient corruption; and for a few years her leaders suffered from the most terrible of all delusions. They believed themselves to be virtuous. Robespierre's friend St Just said: 'In a republic which can only be based on virtue, any pity shown towards crime is a flagrant proof of treason.'

But reluctantly one must admit that a great many of the subsequent horrors were simply due to anarchy. It's a most attractive political doctrine, but I'm afraid it's too optimistic. The men of 1793 tried desperately to control anarchy by violence, and in the end were destroyed by the evil means they had brought into existence. With what mixed feelings one looks at David's picture [206] of Marat murdered in his bath. David painted it with deep emotion. The picture was intended to immortalise the memory of a great patriot, worthy of the tradition of Brutus. Few propaganda pictures make such an impact as a work of art. Yet Marat cannot escape responsibility for the September Massacres, and thus for the first cloud to overcast Wordsworth's dawn and darken the optimism of the early Romantics into a pessimism that has lasted to our own day.

One of the things that makes the French Revolution so confusing to read about is the great number of names that appear on every page, and disappear without a trace. Worse than a Russian novel. And the reason for this is that for almost ten years it produced no great men, except perhaps Robespierre. The revolutionary spirit lived on after his death, but it had no leaders. French politics was the same *mêlée* of self-seeking that it was to become so often in the next one hundred and fifty years. Then, in 1798, the French got a leader with a vengeance.

With the appearance of General Bonaparte the liberated energies of the revolution take a new direction – the insatiable urge to conquer and explore. But what has this to do with civilisation? War and imperialism, so long the most admired of human activities, have fallen into disrepute (except, I suppose, in Russia), and I am enough a child of my time to hate them both. But I recognise that, together with much that is destructive, they are symptoms of a life-giving impulse.

> See here, my boys: see what a world of ground
> Lies westward from the midst of Cancer's line,
> Unto the rising of this earthly globe;
> Whereas the sun, declining with our sight,
> Begins the day with our Antipodes . . .

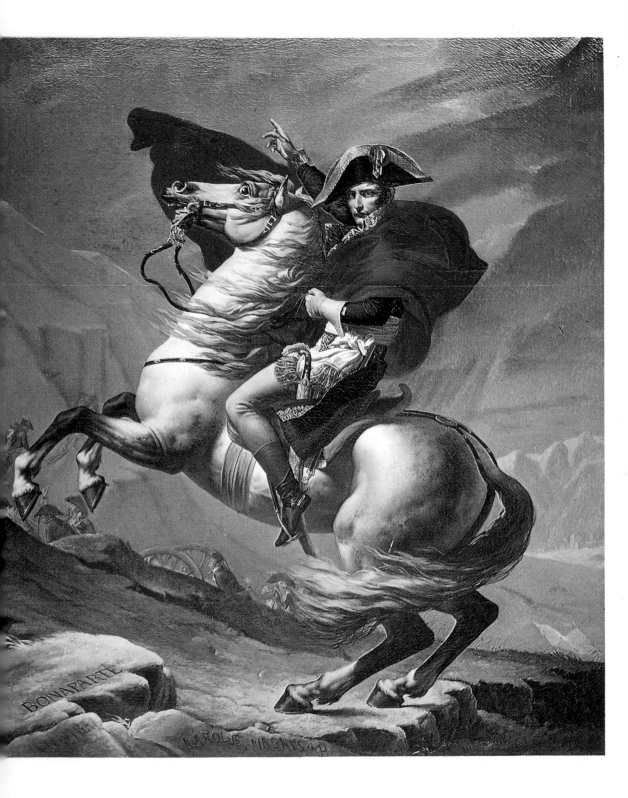

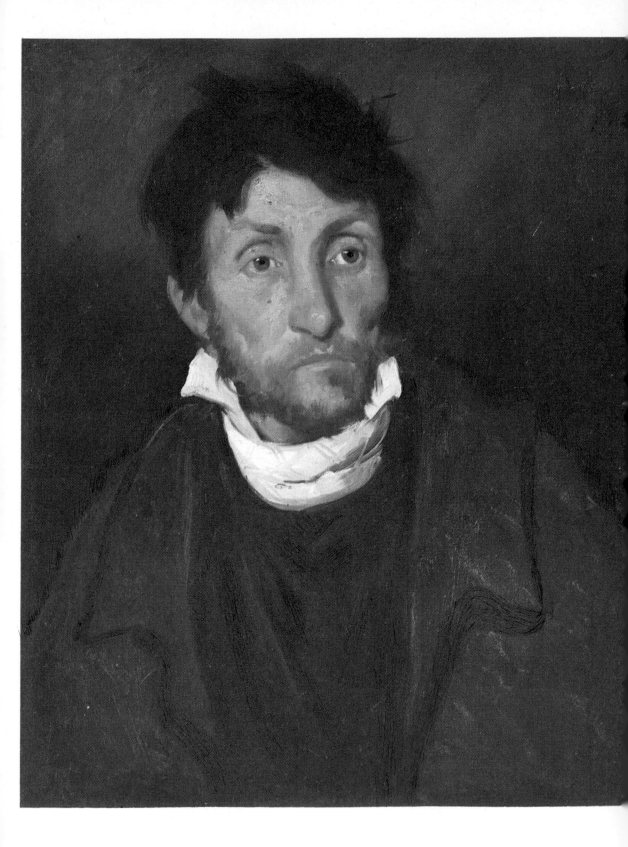

And from th' Antarctic Pole eastward behold . . .
As much more land, which never was descried,
Wherein are rocks of pearl that shine as bright
As all the lamps that beautify the sky!
And shall I die, and this unconquered.

How many great poets, artists and scientists could have spoken these words, that Marlowe put into the mouth of the dying Tamburlaine. In the field of political action they have become odious to us. But I have an uneasy feeling that we cannot have one thing without another. Ruskin's unwelcome sentence, 'No great art ever yet rose on earth but among a nation of soldiers,' seems to me historically irrefutable – so far.

The need to conquer was only one part of Napoleon's paradoxical character. There was also the political realist, the great administrator, the author, or at least the editor, of that classic corpus of law, the Code Napoleon. In his portraits we can watch the young revolutionary soldier dissolve into the First Consul (with vestiges of revolutionary intensity in his face); and in two years he becomes the successor of Charlemagne. An extraordinary portrait [208] by Ingres in the Musée de l'Armée in Paris makes conscious reference to both late Roman ivories and tenth-century miniatures of the Emperor Otto the Third. And those little gold insects on the velvet robe are there because they had been discovered on the robe of Childeric, first King of the Franks in the fifth century, whose coffin had been recently exhumed.

So in one mood Napoleon believed that he was reviving the great tradition of unity and stability by which the ideals of Greece and Rome were transmitted to the Middle Ages. To the end he maintained that Europe would have been better off if it had been united under his rule. It may be true. But it could never happen because the realistic ruler was dominated by the romantic conqueror; and the static, hieratic Emperor painted by Ingres is forgotten when we look at David's Bonaparte [43, facing p. 300] crossing the Great St Bernard. There he is truly the man of his time.

Of course, this dream of limitless conquest goes back to Alexander the Great, whose perfectly senseless expeditions to India may be seen as the original protest against classical enclosure. One of Napoleon's favourite pictures was the work of a sixteenth-century German painter, Altdorfer, representing the victory of Alexander over the Persian King. Napoleon looted it from Munich and hung it in his bedroom, where he could contemplate every day this glowing symbol of the great adventure. This was the period when the limits of history were extended beyond the known world of Livy and Thucydides to the remote ages of the East and the primitive West.

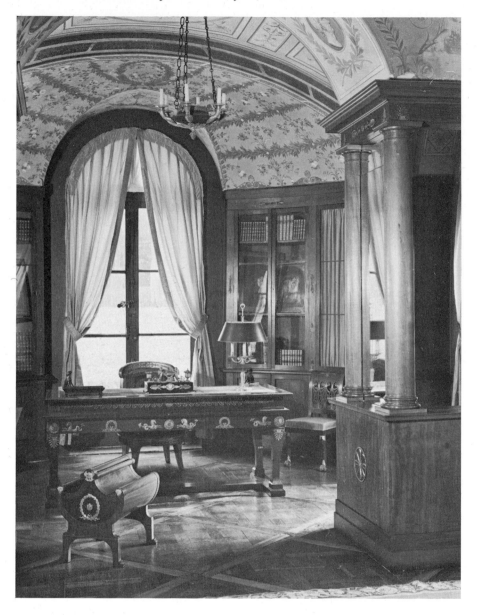

For fifty years the great minds of Europe were enchanted by a poem called 'Fingal', said to have been written by a Gaelic bard called Ossian. Actually it was a kind of fake, put together out of scraps of evidence by an enterprising Scot named Macpherson. But this did not prevent Goethe from admiring it; or Ingres, the high priest of Classicism, from painting an enormous picture of Ossian's dream. 'Fingal' was Napoleon's favourite poem. Ossian is the first hero we see on the painted ceiling of Napoleon's

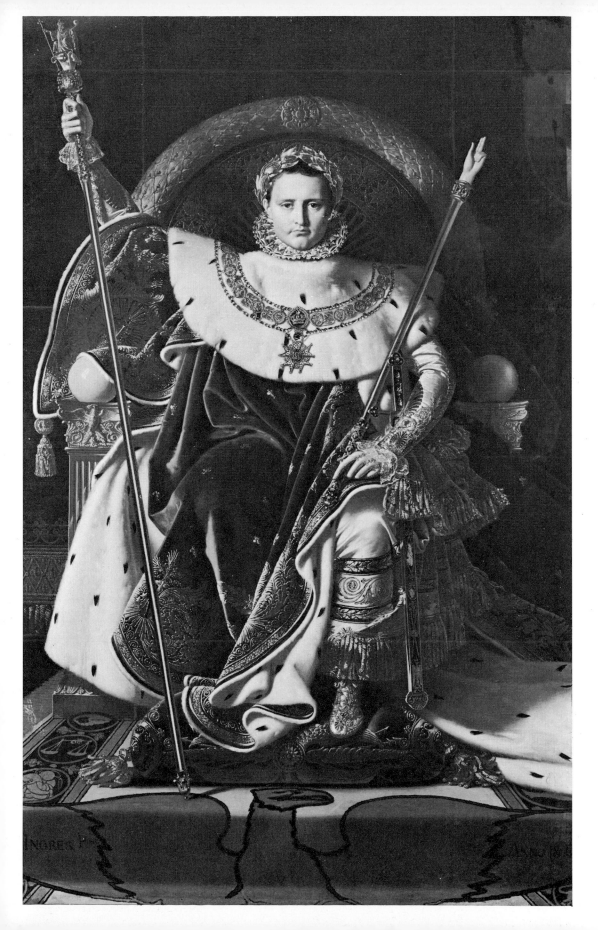

304

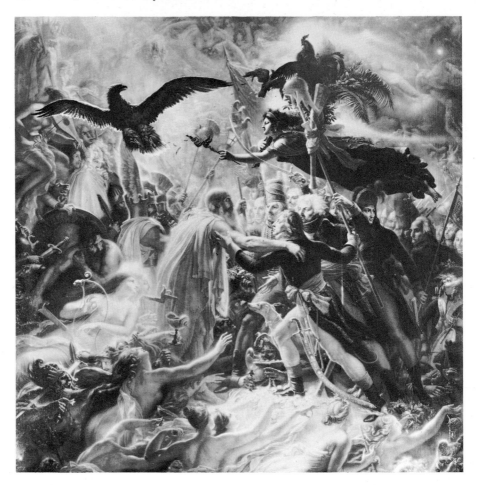

library [207] at Malmaison, and he took an illustrated copy of 'Fingal' on all his campaigns. Its heaven was not tarnished by the approval of the old regime. He ordered the glossiest of his painters, Girodet, to depict the souls of his own warriors – his marshals – being received by Ossian in Valhalla [209]. Painfully reminiscent of Hitler and Wagner. And yet one can't quite resist the exhilaration of Napoleon's glory. Communal enthusiasm may be a dangerous intoxicant; but if human beings were to lose altogether the sense of glory, I think we should be the poorer, and when religion is in decline it is an alternative to naked materialism.

And what, in all this glory, had happened to the great heroes that spoke for humanity in the revolutionary years? Most of them were silenced by fear – fear of disorder, fear of bloodshed, fear that, after all, human beings were not yet capable of liberty. Few episodes in history are more depressing than the withdrawal of the great Romantics – Wordsworth saying that he would give his life for the Church of England; or Goethe that it was better to support a lie than admit political confusion in the state. But two of them did not retreat, and so have become the archetypal Romantic heroes: Beethoven and Byron. Different as they were (and it is hard to think of two more different men) they both maintained an attitude of defiance to social convention, and they both believed unshakably in freedom. It is a curious paradox that Byron, with his legendary good looks, wit and knowledge of the world, was expelled from society, while Beethoven, small, hairy and uncouth, Beethoven, who quarrelled with a friend every month and insulted a patron every week, was treated with patience, sympathy and even affection by the Viennese aristocracy. This may be because genius was valued more highly in Vienna than in London. But I think the chief reason was that Beethoven's bad manners were the index of a noble simplicity, and they made him a more satisfactory symbol of the new world than Byron. The aristocratic society of Vienna, although it had settled for a century of conservative politics, could not resist the new character of the European spirit, especially when it took the form they understood best – music.

Beethoven was not a political man, but he responded to the generous sentiments in the Revolution. He admired Napoleon because he seemed to be the apostle of revolutionary ideals. Also, it must be confessed, because he liked supremacy. He said that if he knew as much about strategy as he did about counterpoint he would give Napoleon a run for his money. He dedicated to General Bonaparte one of his greatest works, the Third Symphony. But just before it was performed he heard that Napoleon had been proclaimed Emperor. He tore off the dedication page and was with difficulty prevented from destroying the score. The two revolutionary concepts that were dearest to him were freedom and virtue. As a young man in Vienna he had seen Mozart's *Don Giovanni* and had been shocked by its cynicism. He determined to write an opera in which virtuous and unwavering love should be associated with freedom. The subject rumbled about in his mind for years, providing first of all the *Leonora Overture*, and finally *Fidelio*, where, in addition to the themes of justice and virtuous love, he gives us the greatest of all hymns to liberty, as the victims of injustice struggle up from their dungeons towards the light. 'O happiness to see the light,' they say, 'to feel the air and be once more alive. Our prison was a tomb. O freedom, freedom come to us again.' This cry, this hope echoed through all the revolutionary movements of the nineteenth century. We tend to forget how many there were – in France, Spain, Italy, Austria, Greece, Hungary, Poland, and always the same pattern: the same idealists, the same professional agitators, the same barricades, the same soldiers with

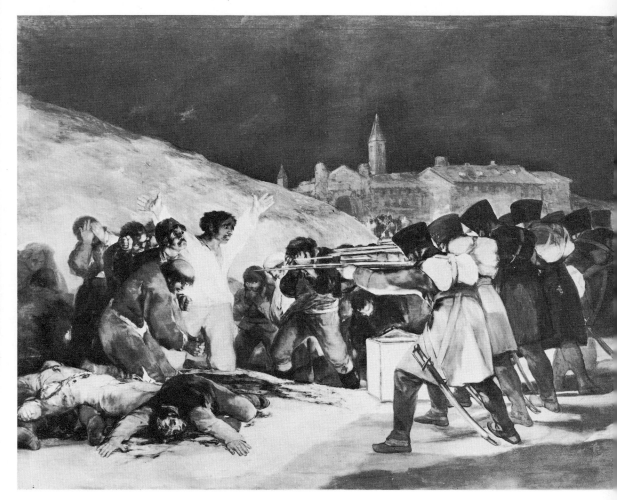

drawn swords, the same terrified civilians, the same savage reprisals. In the end one can't say that we are much further forward. When the Bastille fell in 1792 it was found to contain only seven old men who were annoyed at being disturbed. But to have opened the doors of a political prison in Germany in 1940 or Hungary in 1956 – then one would have known the meaning of that scene in *Fidelio*.

Beethoven, in spite of his tragic deafness, was an optimist. He believed that man had within himself a spark of the divine fire revealed in his love of nature and his need for friendship. He believed that man was worthy of freedom. The despair that poisoned the Romantic movement had not yet entered his veins. Where did this poison come from? Already in the eighteenth century there had been a taste for horror, and even Jane Austen's heroines had liked to frighten themselves by reading Gothic novels. But it seemed to be a mere fashion that would pass. Then in the 1790s the horrors became real, and by about 1810 all the optimistic hopes of the eighteenth century had been proved false: the Rights of Man, the discoveries of science, the benefits of industry, all a delusion. The freedoms won by revolution had been immediately lost either by counter-revolution or by the revolutionary government falling into the hands of military dictators. In Goya's picture of a firing squad [210], called *3 May 1808*, the repeated gesture of those who had raised their arms in heroic affirmation becomes the repeated line of the soldiers' rifles as they liquidate a small group of inconvenient citizens. Well, we are used to all this now. We are almost numbed by repeated disappointments. But in 1810 it was a new discovery, and all the poets, philosophers and artists of the Romantic movement were shattered by it.

The spokesman of this pessimism was Byron. He would probably have been a pessimist anyway – it was part of his egotism. But appearing when he did, the tide of disillusion carried him along, so that he became, after Napoleon, the most famous name in Europe. From great poets like Goethe and Pushkin, or great men of action like Bismarck, down to the most brainless schoolgirl his works were read with an almost hysterical enthusiasm which, as we struggle through the rhetorical nonsense of *Lara* or *The Giaour*, we can hardly credit; because it was Byron's bad poetry not *Don Juan* that made him famous. Byron, who was very much a man of his time, wrote a poem about the opening of a prison – the dungeon of the Castle of Chillon. He begins with a sonnet in the old revolutionary vein – 'Eternal Spirit of the chainless Mind! Brightest in dungeons, Liberty!' But when, after many horrors, the prisoner of Chillon is released, a new note is heard.

> At last men came to set me free;
>   I ask'd not why, and reck'd not where;
> It was at length the same to me,
> Fetter'd or fetterless to be,
>   I learn'd to love despair.

Since that line was written how many intellectuals down to Beckett and Sartre have echoed its sentiment. This negative conclusion was not the whole of Byron. The prisoner of Chillon had looked from his castle wall onto the mountains and the lake, and felt himself to be a part of them. This was the positive side of Byron's genius, a self-identification with the great forces of nature: not Wordsworth's daisies and daffodils, but crags, cataracts and colossal storms: in short, with the sublime.

Consciousness of the sublime was a faculty that the Romantic movement added to the European imagination. It was an English discovery, related to

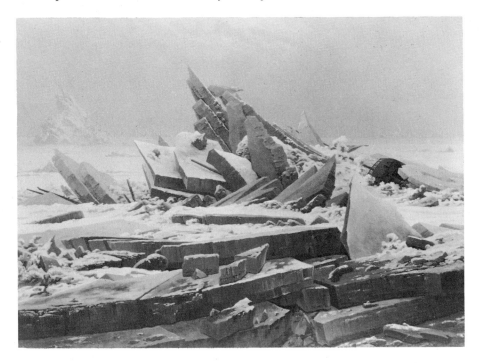

the discovery of nature: not the truth-giving nature of Goethe, nor the moralising nature of Wordsworth, but the savage incomprehensible power outside ourselves, that makes us aware of the futility of human arrangements. As so often Blake gave it the most memorable expression: 'The roaring of lions, the howling of wolves, the raging of the stormy sea and the destructive sword are portions of eternity too great for the eye of man!' Too great for the eye of man? As the Revolution turned into the Napoleonic adventure, the sublime became visible and within reach; and this was a feeling that was given popular expression by Byron. He was irresistible because he had identified himself with these fearful forces. 'Let me be', he says to the stormy darkness, 'a sharer in thy fierce and far delight, a portion of the tempest and of thee.' He forced Blake's 'portions of eternity' to admit him; and his friend Shelley's famous lines about him in 'Adonais' are correct – 'The Pilgrim of Eternity, whose fame over his living head like Heaven is bent.'

But participation in the sublime was almost as much of a strain as the pursuit of freedom. Nature is indifferent or, as we say, cruel. No great artist has ever observed these violent, hostile moods of nature as closely as Turner; and he was without hope – those are not my words, but the final judgement of Ruskin, who knew him and worshipped him. Turner was a great admirer of Byron and used quotations from Byron's poems in the titles of his pictures. But *Childe Harold* was not pessimistic enough for him, so he wrote a fragmentary poem to provide himself with titles. He called it 'The Fallacies of Hope'. Bad poetry, good pictures. One of the most famous of them represents an actual episode in the slave trade, another of the contemporary horrors that troubled the Romantic imagination: Turner called it *Slavers throwing overboard the dead and dying – typhoon coming on.* For the last fifty years we have not been in the least interested in the horrible story, but only in the delicate aubergine of the negro's leg and the pink fish surrounding it. But Turner meant us to take it seriously. 'Hope, hope, fallacious hope,' he wrote, 'where is thy market now?'

About twenty years earlier the German Romantic landscape-painter, Caspar David Friedrich, had made his name with a picture of a ship in the ice, *The Wreck of the 'Hope'* [211]. This, too, was an actual episode, of which he had read an account in the newspapers. And at almost the same date Géricault, the most Byronic of all painters, had also made his name with a picture of disaster at sea [212]. The frigate *Medusa* foundered on her way to Senegal – a hundred and forty-nine of the passengers were put onto a raft, which was to be towed by sailors in the pinnaces. After a time the crew grew tired of this fatigue and cut the ropes, leaving the raft to drift out to sea and condemning the passengers to almost certain death. Miraculously there were a few survivors, from whom Géricault learnt the full horrors of the episode; he even found the ship's carpenter who had made the raft, and had him make a model of it in his studio. He took a workroom near a hospital, so that he could study dying men. He gave up his life of pleasure, shaved his head and locked himself in with corpses from the morgue. He was determined to paint a masterpiece, and I think he succeeded; but the odd thing is that, in spite of being so carefully documented, the whole work looks like a piece of grandiose picture-making. For his formal language Géricault has looked to an earlier heroic age – the High Renaissance – to Michelangelo's *Deluge* and his Athletes in the Sistine, and even, in this painting, to Raphael's *Transfiguration*. Not the least Byronic thing about Géricault was his reliance on the tradition of rhetoric. However, the *Raft* was intended, and originally accepted, as a piece of what we call social realism, and Géricault planned to follow it up with two even larger pictures with more revolutionary themes: one the opening of a prison of the Inquisition (I should doubt if he had heard of *Fidelio*, which was then considered a failure) and another of the slave trade, for which he made some drawings. Neither of them was painted; he had worn himself out, and confided to his friends that he longed for death.

In order to restore his spirits he visited London, partly because he admired English painting, partly because he had a passion for horses – one

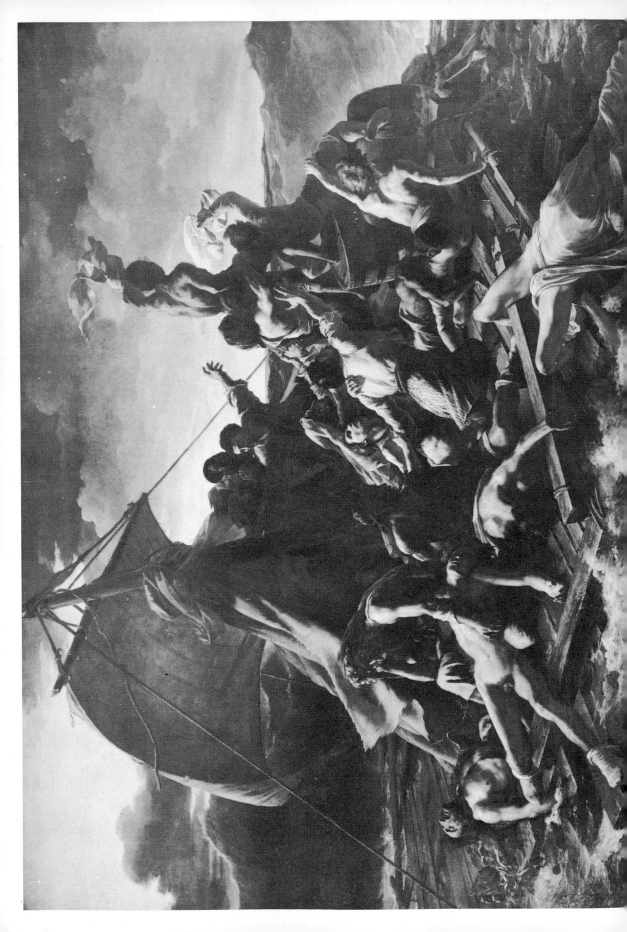

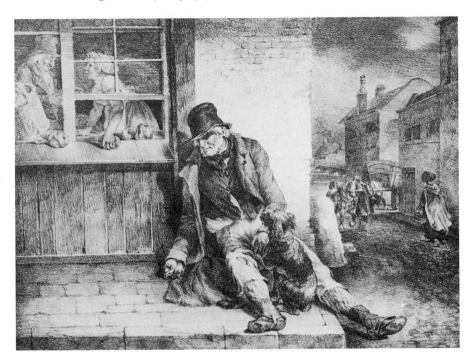

might say that in Romantic imagery the horse is the complement to the ship-wreck – and England was then the country of the horse. He did a picture of the Derby, and in a series of drawings and lithographs he did justice to the animal weight and brutality of the English scene [213]. On his return to Paris he painted a series of portraits of lunatics [**44**, facing p. 301] which I think are among the great pictures of the nineteenth century. They carry into painting the Romantic impulse to explore beyond the bounds of reason. By this time Géricault was dying of some internal injury, which he aggravated by riding the most unruly horses he could find. No strong man has ever sought death more resolutely. He died at the age of thirty-three, a little younger than Byron, considerably older than Shelley and Keats.

Fortunately, he left a spiritual heir whose pessimism was supported by a more powerful intellect – Delacroix. When Delacroix's first large picture, *Dante and Virgil crossing the Styx*, was exhibited, people asked Géricault if he had not painted it, to which he replied: 'I wish I had.' Two years later in 1824 Delacroix painted a picture in which he is entirely himself – *The Massacre of Scios* [214]. As with almost all the masterpieces of Romantic painting, it represents an actual event, and it reflects the generous senti-ments of those liberals like Shelley and Byron who dreamed that Greece might yet be free. There is protest and compassion in this picture, more perhaps than Delacroix was ever to show again.

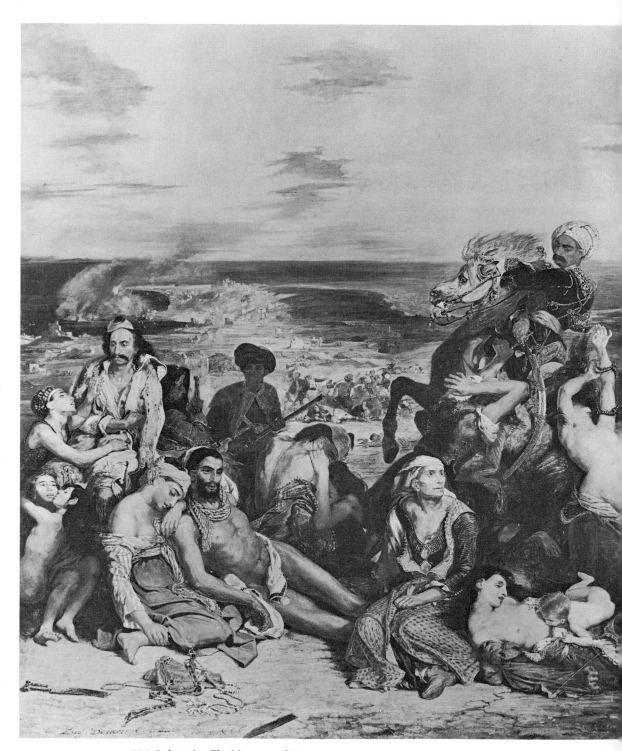

214 Delacroix, *The Massacre of Scios*

Revolutionary sentiments, which had gone underground under the restored Bourbon monarchy, could still show themselves in sympathy with other victims of oppression. In 1830, after some of the stupidest episodes in the whole of European history, Charles X and his Prime Minister managed to provoke a revolution. It was short and limited – a poor affair compared to the revolutions that preceded and followed it – but it showed that the fires had never died out, and that the young romantics of the 1820s still felt the glow of 1792. Indeed, the Republican Army was commanded by one of the leaders of the original revolution, Lafayette. Delacroix joined the National Guard (he said he did so because he liked the uniform) and painted a picture of Liberty guiding the people. It is one of the few programmatic pictures of revolution that has any claim to be a work of art, but it is far from being one of his best works and he never again allowed his art to be influenced by contemporary politics. On the contrary, he had the utmost contempt for the age in which he lived, for its crass materialism and complacent belief in progress; and his art is almost entirely an attempt to escape from it. He escaped into the subjects of romantic poetry, in particular that of Shakespeare, Byron and Walter Scott. Some of his greatest pictures were inspired by Byron, and he had a Byronic power of self-identification with the forces of the sublime – in particular 'the roaring of lions and the destructive sword'. Baudelaire said that when an idea shot through his mind his muscles quivered with impatience and his eyes shone like a tiger stalking its prey. At feeding-time in the Paris Zoo he was overwhelmed with happiness. His great pictures of lion-hunts [215] are the most personal of all his works.

Delacroix also made a physical escape from the prosperous bourgeois society of his time. In 1834 he went to Morocco. It had occupied his imagination for some time, but when he got there the reality was rather different from what he had expected. Instead of the sensual ferocity of his Byronic dreams, he found an ancient way of life that, he maintained, was far more Classical than the waxwork Classicism of the academics. He said that the gestures of the Arabs were like those of Cato the Elder.

Delacroix had a small circle of friends, poets and writers, including Chopin, the only man he loved and admired without reservation. Baudelaire said that Chopin's music was like 'a bird of brilliant plumage, fluttering over the horrors of the abyss'. He could well have extended the metaphor to Delacroix's painting (of which he was a passionate admirer), adding however that the abyss did not horrify Delacroix in the least: on the contrary, he gloried in it. As luck would have it one of Delacroix's friends, Thiers, became Prime Minister, and gave him many public commissions, including the library of the French parliament house. It was typical of Delacroix that

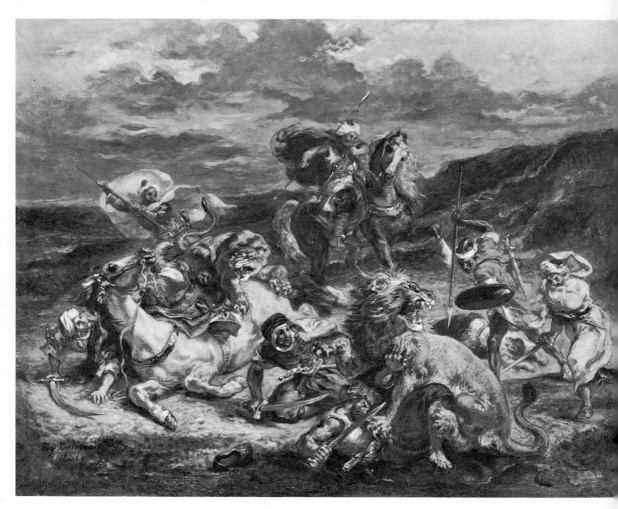

the most impressive of these decorations represents Attila the Hun, trampling on the remains of antique civilisation [45, facing p. 320]. No one realised better than Delacroix that we had got through by the skin of our teeth; and in certain moods he would have added: 'was it worth it?' But in the end, somewhat reluctantly, he would have answered yes. He was consciously the heir of the finest spirits of Western Europe – Dante, Michelangelo, Tasso, Shakespeare, Rubens, Poussin – their names appear constantly in his writings and their works inspired his paintings. Perhaps his last word on the subject is in a large mural painting in the church of St Sulpice (and Delacroix, although not a Christian, was the only great religious painter of the nineteenth century) representing Jacob wrestling with the angel [216]. In the shadow of great oaks, symbols of his primitive nature, man·has struggled all night to resist that gift of spiritual perception that will so greatly sadden and complicate his existence; he charges like a bull against the impassive angel; but in the end he must succumb to his destiny.

Delacroix valued civilisation all the more because he knew that it was fragile and he would never have been so naive as to look for an alternative in Tahiti. By all accounts Gauguin was far from naive, and it is surprising that he didn't take more trouble to inform himself about Tahiti which, when he went there, had already been corrupted by Europeans for almost a century. His Byronic hatred of the society of his time had made him determined to escape from European civilisation, whatever the cost. Like Delacroix he did not find what he expected, but he managed to mould what he found into a reflection of his dream; and what he discovered in Tahiti was, after all, very much what Delacroix had discovered in Morocco — nobility, dignity, timelessness. The courage with which he clung to his dream through every disaster was really heroic, and makes us forget the

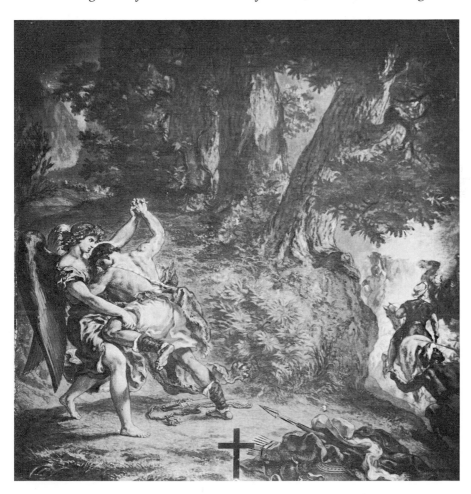

216 Delacroix, *Jacob wrestling with the Angel*

many sordid and grotesque incidents of his life there. His *Women of Tahiti* is a masterpiece equal to Delacroix's *Women of Algiers*. But one is left wondering what had gone wrong with the European spirit that so long a journey and so great a renunciation were necessary.

The early nineteenth century created a chasm in the European mind as great as that which had split up Christendom in the sixteenth century, and even more dangerous. On one side of the chasm was the new middle class nourished by the Industrial Revolution. It was hopeful and energetic, but without a scale of values. Sandwiched between a corrupt aristocracy and a brutalised poor, it had produced a defensive morality, conventional, complacent, hypocritical. The brilliant cartoonists of the day, Daumier, Gavarni and Gustave Doré have left us a convincing record of these stout gentlemen [217], tightly buttoned into their long coats, but still looking rather nervous and carrying their umbrellas as if to ward off aggression. On the other side of the chasm were the finer spirits – poets, painters, novelists, who were still heirs of the Romantic movement, still haunted by disaster, still Jacob wrestling with the angel. They felt themselves – and not without reason – to be entirely cut off from the prosperous majority. They mocked at the respectable middle class and its bourgeois king, Louis Philippe, called them philistines and barbarians. But what could they put

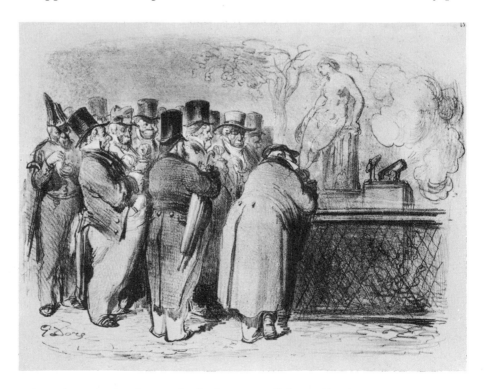

217 Doré, *Men setting their watches by the noon gun* (lithograph)

218 Rodin, *Eve*

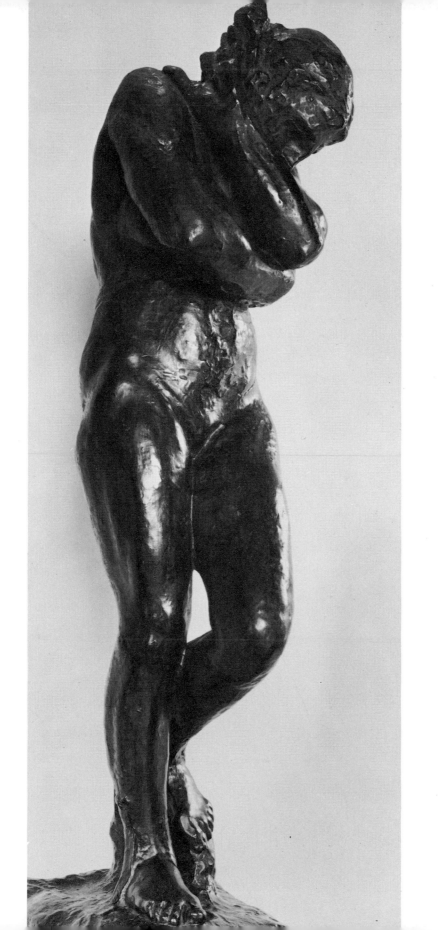

317

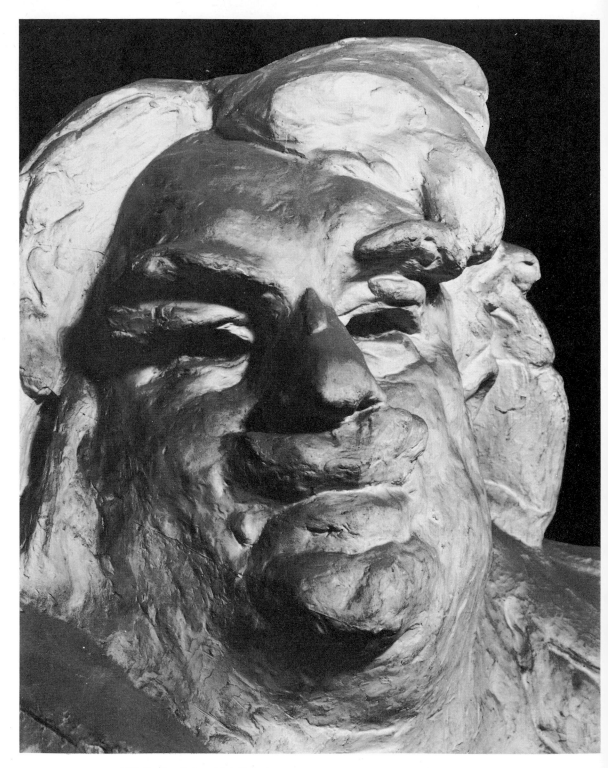

219 Rodin, *Balzac* (detail)

in place of middle-class morality? They themselves were still in search of a soul.

The search went on throughout the nineteenth century: in Kierkegaard, in Schopenhauer, in Baudelaire, in Nietzsche; and in the visual arts, in the sculptor Rodin. He was the last great Romantic artist, the direct heir of Géricault, Delacroix and Byron. His greatest disappointment was that he didn't win the competition to do the Byron memorial in Hyde Park. Like them his abundant animal spirits did not allay – but rather enhanced – his view of mankind's tragic destiny; and like them there is sometimes, in his expressions of despair, a trace of rhetorical exaggeration. But what an artist he was! Only twenty years ago he was still under the cloud of critical disapproval: 'the judgment of posterity'. He was an inventor of symbolic poses that stay in the mind, and sometimes like all oversimplified statements of diffused feelings they are rather too obvious. The famous *Thinker*, seen in isolation, is a tiresome generalisation, but in its original position its meaning is clear. It is in the centre of the composition known as *Gate of Hell*, which Rodin used as a repository for all his small figures. Originally it was quite small. All Rodin's figures were made within the stretch of his fingers and thumb, and took their life from his hands [218]. They lost some of their vitality when they were enlarged by assistants, and more still when they were copied in marble. The title of *Gate of Hell* was suggested to Rodin by Dante's lines: 'Abandon hope, all ye who enter here'. I don't suppose he had read very far in the *Divine Comedy*, and he didn't make his figures with Dante in mind, but in response to strong sensual impulses. I find that the total effect of the gates, the continuous swirling and floating in Art Nouveau rhythms, makes me feel slightly sea-sick; but the individual figures are saved by the force and freedom of their modelling, every form (as Rodin said) thrusting outwards at its point of maximum tension. And the hundreds of plaster models made for these figures give an impression of creative power equal to that of the seventeenth century.

Rodin always professed his admiration for Greek and Gothic sculpture, but his own work is a mixture of Baroque and Romantic traditions, not only in content but in style. However, he did one piece which is dateless – very ancient or very modern, depending on which way you look at it. This is his monument to Balzac [219]. Balzac had been dead for many years when Rodin received the commission, and the commemorative figure had to be an ideal likeness – a serious obstacle to him, as he always worked direct from nature. All he had to go on was the knowledge that Balzac was short and fat and worked in his dressing-gown. Yet he had also to make Balzac look immense – the dominating imagination of his age, and yet transcending his age. He set about the problem in a peculiar way: he made five or six figures of a fat naked man to satisfy his sense of Balzac's physical reality; and after contemplating them for several months, he chose one of them, which he covered with a cast of drapery indicative of the famous dressing-gown. In this way he contrived to give the figure both monumentality and movement. The result is to my mind the greatest piece of sculpture of the nineteenth century – indeed the greatest since Michelangelo. But this is not the way in which it struck Rodin's contemporaries when it was exhibited at the Salon of 1898. They were horrified. Rodin was a hoax, a swindler. They even raised the cry of *la patrie en danger*, which shows how seriously the French take art. The crowds surging round it, insulting it and threatening it with their fists, were unanimous on one point of criticism: that the attitude was impossible and that no body could exist under such draperies. Rodin, sitting nearby, knew that he had only to strike the figure with a hammer, and the draperies would fall off, leaving the body visible. Hostile critics said that it was like a snowman, a dolmen, an owl and a heathen god – all quite true, but we no longer regard them as terms of abuse. Balzac's body has the timelessness of a druidical stone, and his head has the voracity of an owl. The real reason why he made people so angry is the feeling that he could gobble them up, and doesn't care a damn for their opinions. Balzac, with his prodigious understanding of human motives, scorns conventional values, defies fashionable opinion, as Beethoven did, and should inspire us to defy all those forces that threaten to impair our humanity: lies, tanks, tear-gas, ideologies, opinion polls, mechanisation, planners, computers – the whole lot.

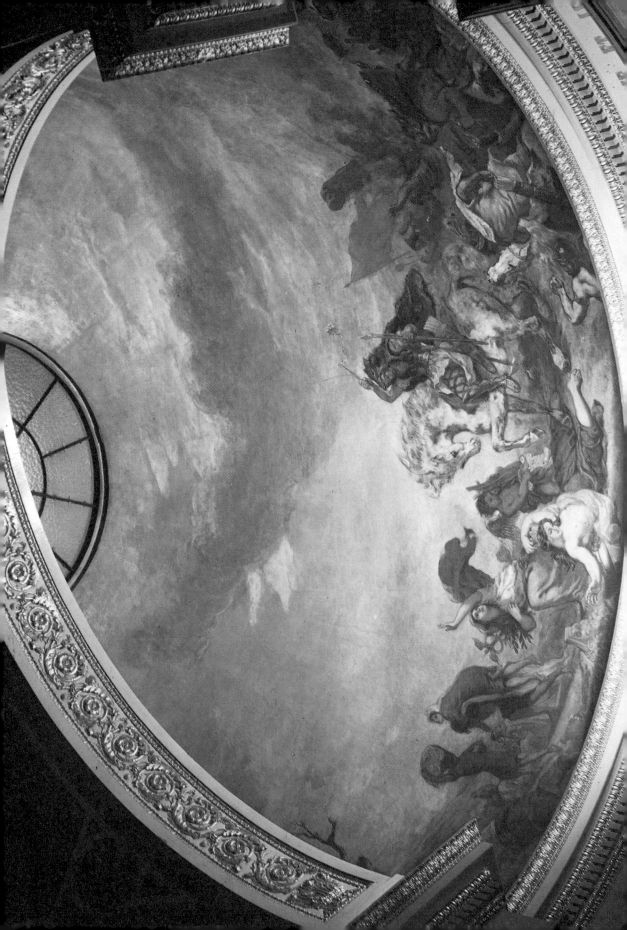

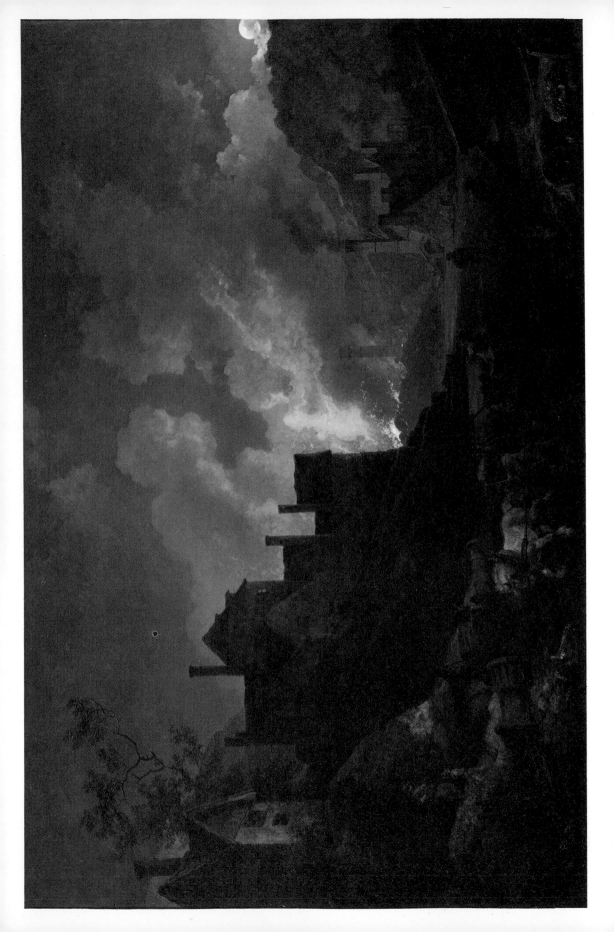

13 Heroic Materialism

Imagine an immensely speeded up movie of Manhattan Island during the last hundred years. It would look less like a work of man than like some tremendous natural upheaval. It's godless, it's brutal, it's violent – but one can't laugh it off, because in the energy, strength of will and mental grasp that have gone to make New York, materialism has transcended itself. Dorothy Wordsworth said about the view of London from Westminster Bridge that 'it was like one of Nature's own grand spectacles'. Well, nature is violent and brutal, and there's nothing we can do about it. But New York, after all, was made by men. It took almost the same time to reach its present condition as it did to complete the Gothic cathedrals. At which point a very obvious reflection crosses one's mind: that the cathedrals were built to the glory of God, New York was built to the glory of mammon – money, gain, the new god of the nineteenth century. So many of the same human in-gredients have gone into its construction that at a distance it does look rather like a celestial city. At a distance. Come closer and it's not so good. Lots of squalor, and, in the luxury, something parasitical. One sees why heroic materialism is still linked with an uneasy conscience. It has been from the start. I mean that historically the first discovery and exploitation of those technical means which made New York possible coincided exactly with the first organised attempt to improve the human lot.

The first large iron foundries like the Carron Works or Coalbrookdale [46, on facing page], date from round about 1780: Howard's book on penal reform was published in 1777 and Clarkson's essay on slavery in 1785. This may have been no more than a coincidence, because at that time most people thought of the application of mechanical power to industry as something to be proud of. The early pictures of heavy industry are optimistic. Even the workers didn't object to it because it was hellish but because they were afraid that machinery would put them out of work. The only people who saw through industrialism in those early days were the poets. Blake, as everybody knows, thought that mills were the work of Satan. 'Oh Satan, my youngest born . . . thy work is Eternal Death with Mills and Ovens and Cauldrons.' And Burns, passing the Carron Iron Works in 1787, scratched these lines on a window-pane:

> We cam na here to view your warks,
>   In hopes to be mair wise,
> But only, lest we gang to Hell,
>   It may be nae surprise.

46 De Loutherbourg, *Coalbrookdale by Night*

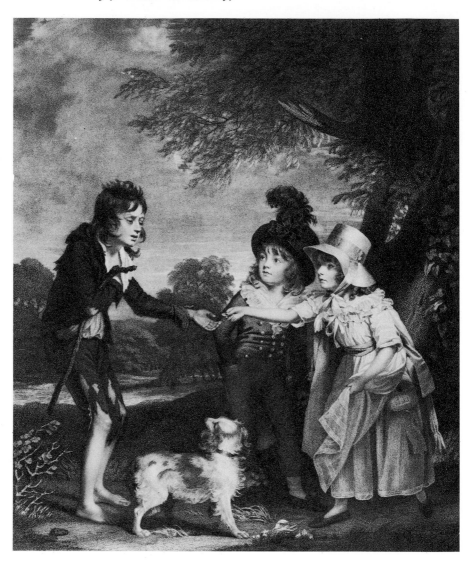

It took a longish time – over twenty years – before ordinary men began to
see what a monster had been created.

Meanwhile the spirit of benevolence was growing. Prisons were reformed, Sir Frederick Eden published the first sociological survey called
the *State of the Poor*, and overshadowing everything else was the movement to abolish the slave trade. I have often heard it said by people who
want to seem clever that civilisation can exist only on a basis of slavery, and
in support of their thesis they point to the example of fifth-century Greece.
If one defines civilisation in terms of leisure and superfluity, there is a grain
of truth in this repulsive doctrine. I have tried throughout this series to

define civilisation in terms of creative power and the enlargement of human faculties; and from that point of view slavery is abominable. So, for that matter, is abject poverty. Throughout the great ages of human achievement which I have been discussing, the mass of voiceless people have had a hard time. Poverty, hunger, plagues, disease: they were the background of history right up to the end of the nineteenth century, and most people regarded them as inevitable – like bad weather. Nobody thought they could be cured: St Francis wanted to sanctify poverty, not to abolish it. The old Poor Laws were not designed to abolish poverty but to prevent the poor from becoming a nuisance. All that was required was an occasional act of charity. I remember an English mezzotint after Beechey, entitled *Rustic Charity* [220], representing a pretty little girl diffidently holding out her hand to a shivering, ragged boy. Under it are written the lines: 'Here, poor boy without a hat, take this halfpenny.' Not an indication of very serious concern. But slaves and the trade in slaves, that was something different: for one thing it was contrary to Christian teaching; for another it was esoteric – it wasn't something that surrounded one like the air, as home-made poverty did. And the horrors it involved were far more horrible: even the unsqueamish stomachs of the eighteenth century were turned by accounts of the middle passage [221]. It has been estimated that over nine million slaves died from heat and suffocation on their way from Africa to America: a remarkable figure, even by modern standards.

So the anti-slavery movement became the first communal expression of the awakened conscience. It took a long time to succeed. There were huge

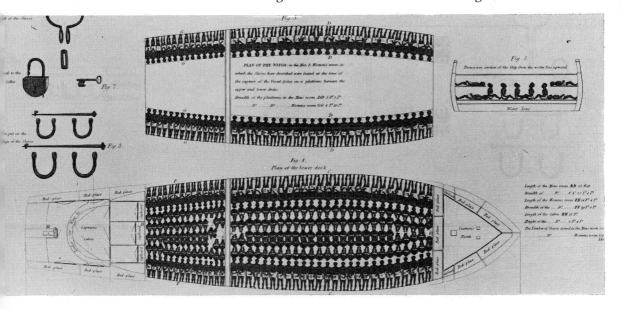

221 Plan of Slave Ship

323

vested interests involved. Slaves were *property* and even the most ardent revolutionaries, even Robespierre himself, never doubted the sacred rights of property. The most respectable people in England supported slavery: Mr Gladstone's first speech in Parliament was in its favour. But Clarkson had produced unanswerable statistics, and Wilberforce stuck to his aims with legendary charm and devotion. The trade was prohibited in 1807, and as Wilberforce lay dying in 1835, slavery itself was abolished.

One must regard this as a step forward for the human race, and be proud, I think, that it happened in England. But not too proud. The Victorians were very smug about it, and chose to avert their eyes from something almost equally horrible that was happening to their own countrymen. England had entered the war with France in the first triumphant consciousness of her new industrial powers. After twenty years England was victorious, but by failing to control her industrial development she had suffered a defeat, in terms of human life, far more costly than any military disaster.

In its early stages the Industrial Revolution was also a part of the Romantic movement. And here I may digress to say that painters had for long used iron foundries to heighten the imaginative impact of their work with what we call a romantic effect; and they had introduced them into pictures as symbolising the mouth of hell. The first to do so (as far as I know) was Hieronymus Bosch in about 1485. He came from a region of the Low Countries which was one of the first parts of Europe to be industrialised, and as a child the blast of iron foundries must have added a real image to the imaginary horrors that filled his mind. Bosch was much admired in Venice, and in the work of Giorgione and his followers – the first self-conscious Romantics – the iron foundry appears as the mouth of the pagan underworld. The same furnaces spouting fire reappear in the Romantic landscape-painters of the early nineteenth century, in Cotman and occasionally in Turner (too rarely – he ought to have been to the Industrial Revolution what Raphael was to Humanism). The most curious instance is the minor painter known, quite wrongly, as Mad Martin, who assimilated the dramatic effects and even the architecture of industrialism, and used them as the basis of his illustrations to Milton and the Bible. His panoramas of Satan's Kingdom, vaster and more sinister than the film sets of D. W. Griffiths, were a genuine development of the contemporary style, and he was the first to see the importance to the early nineteenth-century imagination of the tunnel.

However, the influence of the Industrial Revolution on Romantic painting is a side issue, almost an impertinence, when compared to its influence on human life. I needn't remind you of how cruelly it degraded and exploited a mass of people for sixty or seventy years. It was not so much the

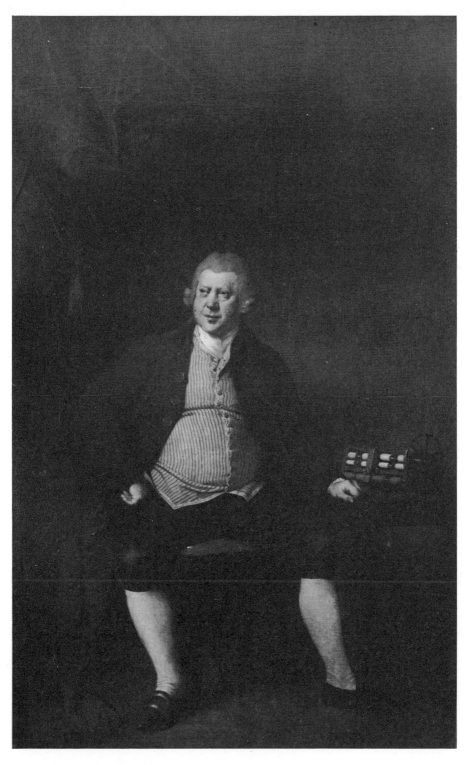

222 Wright of Derby, *Arkwright*

nature of the work as its organisation. Early iron foundries had been small affairs – almost family businesses – and in its early stages the industrial movement had positively helped small men to escape from the more hopeless poverty of rural life. What was destructive was *size*. After about 1790 to 1800 there appeared the large foundries and mills which dehumanised life. Arkwright's spinning frame, invented about 1770, is always quoted as the beginning of mass production, on the whole rightly; and the man we see faithfully recorded for us by Wright of Derby [222] is typical of the new potentates who were to dominate industry until the present day. He and his like gave England a flying start in the economy of the nineteenth century, but they also produced that dehumanisation which obsessed almost every great imaginative writer of the time. Long before Carlyle and Karl Marx – in fact in about 1810 – Wordsworth had described the arrival of a night shift:

> Disgorged are now the ministers of day;
> And, as they issue from the illumined pile,
> A fresh band meets them, at the crowded door –
> And in the courts – and where the rumbling stream
> That turns the multitude of dizzy wheels,
> Glares, like a troubled spirit, in its bed
> Among the rocks below. Men, maidens, youths,
> Mothers and little children, boys and girls,
> Enter, and each the wonted task resumes
> Within this temple, where is offered up
> To Gain, the master idol of the realm,
> Perpetual sacrifice.

This new religion of gain had behind it a body of doctrine without which it could never have maintained its authority over the serious-minded Victorians. The first of its sacred books – printed in 1789 – was the *Essay on the Principle of Population* by a clergyman named Malthus, which demonstrated that population will always increase faster than means of subsistence. In consequence, misery and want were bound to be the lot of the majority of mankind. This depressing theory, which cannot be altogether brushed aside, even today, had been put forward in a scientific spirit. Unfortunately Malthus's text contained such phrases as 'man has no claim of right to the smallest portion of food'. And these were used to justify the inhuman exploitation of labour. The other sacred books were the economic theories of Ricardo, also a most earnest man writing in a scientific spirit – but inexorable. Free enterprise and the survival of the fittest: one can see how they looked like laws of nature – and in fact were both to become involved with Darwin's theories of natural selection.

When I call them sacred books I am not joking. Malthus and Ricardo were taken as gospels by the most serious and even pious men, who used them to justify actions they would never have thought of defending on human grounds. Hypocrisy? Well, hypocrisy has always existed – where would the great comic writers have been without it, from Molière downwards. But the nineteenth century, with its insecure middle class dependent on an inhuman economic system, produced hypocrisy on an unprecedented scale. For the last forty years or so, the word hypocrisy has been a sort of label attached to the nineteenth century, just as frivolity was attached to the eighteenth century – and with about as much reason. The reaction against it continues; and although it is a good thing to have cleared the air, I think that this reaction has done harm by bringing into discredit all professions of virtue. The very words 'pious', 'respectable', 'worthy', have become joke words, used only ironically.

Mass-hypocrisy is often referred to as Victorian. But in fact it dates from the very beginning of the century. Here is Blake in 1804: 'Compell the poor to live upon a crust of bread by soft mild arts. When a man looks pale with labour and abstinence, say he looks healthy and happy; and when his children sicken, let them die; there are enough born, even too many, and our Earth will be overrun without these arts.' Well, much as one hates the inhuman way in which the doctrines of Malthus were accepted, the terrible truth is that the rise in population did nearly ruin us. It struck a blow at civilisation such as it hadn't received since the barbarian invasions. First it produced the horrors of urban poverty and then the dismal counter-measures of bureaucracy and regimentation. It must have seemed – may still seem – insoluble; yet this doesn't excuse the callousness with which prosperous people ignored the conditions of life among the poor on which to a large extent their prosperity depended, and this in spite of the many detailed and eloquent descriptions that were available to them. I need mention only two – Engels's *Conditions of the Working Classes in England*, written in 1844, and the novels written by Dickens between 1840 and 1855, between *Nicholas Nickleby* and *Hard Times*.

Engels's book is presented as documentation, but is in fact the passionate cry of a young social worker, and as such it provided, and has continued to provide, the emotional dynamo of Marxism. Marx read Engels – I don't know who else did: that was enough. Everybody read Dickens. No living author has ever been more hysterically beloved by a larger cross-section of the community. His novels produced reform in the law, in magistrates' courts, in the prevention of public hanging – in a dozen directions. But his terrible descriptions of poverty had very little practical effect: partly be-

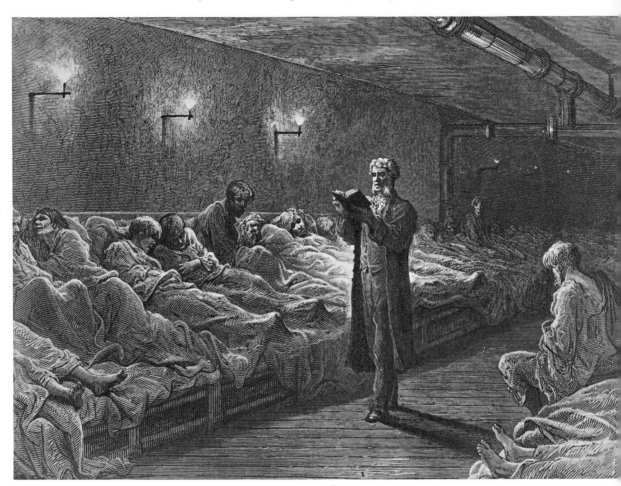

cause the problem was too big; partly because politicians were held in the intellectual prison of classical economics; and partly, one must admit, because Dickens himself, for all his generosity of spirit, took a kind of sadistic pleasure in the horrors he described. Dickens's early illustrators were too comical and pictorially incompetent to convey his feelings about society. The images that fit Dickens are by the French illustrator Gustave Doré. He was originally a humorist; but the sight of London sobered him. His drawings [223] were done in the 1870s, after Dickens's death. But one can see that things hadn't changed much. Perhaps it took an outsider to see London as it really was, and it needed someone of Doré's marvellous graphic skill to make this great slice of human misery credible.

I suppose that Dickens did more than anyone to diffuse an awakened conscience, but one mustn't forget the practical reformers who preceded him: at the beginning of the period, the Quaker, Elizabeth Fry [224], who in an earlier age would certainly have been canonised, because her spiritual influence on the prisoners at Newgate was really a miracle. And in the middle of the century Lord Shaftesbury, whose long struggle to prevent the exploitation of children in factories puts him next to Wilberforce in the history of humanitarianism.

The early reformers' struggle with industrialised society illustrates what I believe to be the greatest civilising achievement of the nineteenth century, humanitarianism. We are so much accustomed to the humanitarian outlook that we forget how little it counted in earlier ages of civilisation. Ask any decent person in England or America what he thinks matters most in human conduct: five to one his answer will be 'kindness'. It's not a word that would have crossed the lips of any of the earlier heroes of this series. If you had asked St Francis what mattered in life, he would, we know, have answered 'chastity, obedience and poverty'; if you had asked Dante or Michelangelo they might have answered 'disdain of baseness and injustice'; if you had asked Goethe, he would have said 'to live in the whole and the beautiful'. But kindness, never. Our ancestors didn't use the word, and they did not greatly value the quality – except perhaps in so far as they valued compassion. Nowadays, I think we under-estimate the humanitarian achievement of the nineteenth century. We forget the horrors that were taken for granted in early Victorian England: the hundreds of lashes inflicted daily

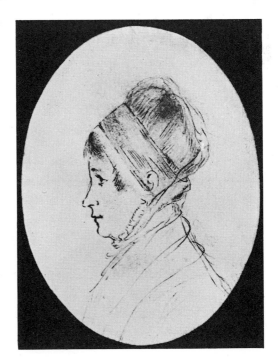

224 Elizabeth Fry

on perfectly harmless men in the army and navy; the women chained together in threes, rumbling through the streets in open carts on their way to transportation. These and other even more unspeakable cruelties were carried out by agents of the Establishment, usually in defence of property.

Certain philosophers, going back to Hegel, tell us that humanitarianism is a weak, sloppy, self-indulgent condition, spiritually much inferior to cruelty and violence, and this point of view has been eagerly accepted by novelists, dramatists and theatrical producers. It is of course true that kindness is to some extent the offspring of materialism, and this has made anti-materialists look at it with contempt, as a product of what Nietzsche called a slave morality. He would certainly have preferred the other aspect of my subject, the heroic self-confidence of men for whom nothing was impossible, the men who forced the first railways over England.

The application of steam to manufacture had only intensified what had existed before. Wordsworth's factory was powered by water. But the railway engine created a situation that was really new: a new basis of unity, a new concept of space – a situation that is still developing. The twenty years after Stephenson's Rocket had made its momentous journey along the Manchester-Liverpool Railway were like a great military campaign: the will, the courage, the ruthlessness, the unexpected defeats, the unforeseen victories. The Irish navvies who built the railways were like a *grande armée*, ruffians who yet had a kind of pride in their achievement. Their marshals were the engineers.

At the very beginning of this series I said that I thought one could tell more about a civilisation from its architecture than from anything else it leaves behind. Painting and literature depend largely on unpredictable individuals. But architecture is to some extent a communal art – at least it depends upon a relationship between the user and the maker much closer than in the other arts. Judged by its architecture in a narrow sense of the word, the nineteenth century does not come off too well. There were many reasons for this. One of them was the enlarged historical perspective which allowed architects to employ a quantity of different styles. This wasn't such a disaster as people used to suppose. For example, I think that the Houses of Parliament look much better in their pseudo-Gothic dress than they would have done in a classical style, which itself, after all, would have been an imitation of antiquity. Barry's design is beautifully related to the bend of the river, and Pugin's Gothic pinnacles melt into the misty London air. However, I must admit that the public buildings of the nineteenth century are often lacking in style and conviction; and I believe this is because the strongest creative impulse of the time didn't go into town halls or country

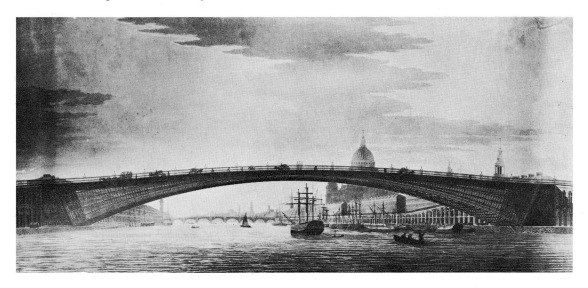

houses, but into what was then thought of as engineering; and at this date it was only in engineering that men could make full use of the new material that was going to transform the art of building – iron. The first Iron Age had been a turning point in civilisation; and one can say the same for the second. In 1801 Telford did a design of London Bridge [225], a single span of iron. It is superb and dateless. It was never carried out, and perhaps was beyond the technical skills of the time. But in about 1820 Telford did bring off the Menai Bridge [226], the first great suspension bridge, an idea that combines beauty and function so perfectly that it has hardly been varied, only expanded, down to the present day.

In sixteenth-century Florence Vasari wrote the *Lives of the Painters*. In nineteenth-century England Samuel Smiles, that reliable barometer of his time, wrote the *Lives of the Engineers*. Smiles believed above all in good sense and moderation, and perhaps for that reason he scarcely mentioned the most extraordinary product of this movement, a man who deserves to rank with the earlier heroes in this series, Isambard Kingdom Brunel. Brunel was a born romantic. Although the son of a distinguished engineer, brought up in a business that depended on sound calculations, he remained all his life in love with the impossible. In fact as a boy he fell heir to a project which he himself believed to be impossible: his father's plan for the construction of a tunnel under the Thames. At twenty his father put him in charge of the work, and thus began the sequence of triumphs and disasters that were to mark his whole career. We have records of both: a painting [227] of the grand dinner held in the tunnel when it was half way across, with father Brunel congratulating his son, and behind them a table full of notables. It is typical

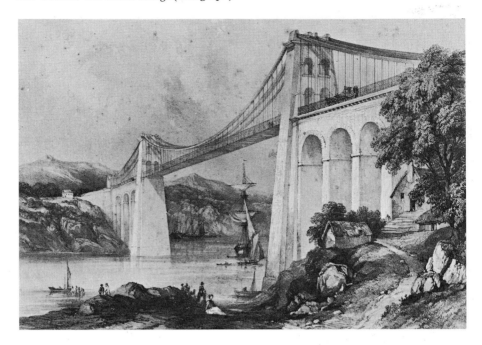

of Brunel that in the next bay of the tunnel there was an equally good dinner for a hundred and fifty of his miners. Two months later the shield collapsed and the water poured in for the third time, and we have drawings of the corpses being fished out of the water. In the end the tunnel was completed. That was the way with Brunel's designs: they were so bold that shareholders were frightened and withdrew – sometimes, I am bound to say, with reason. Even his bridge at Clifton [228], for long the most beautiful suspension bridge in the world, was finished thirty years after it was designed. But one thing he did push through and complete, the Great Western Railway. Every bridge and every tunnel was a drama, demanding incredible feats of imagination, energy and persuasion, and producing works of great splendour. The greatest drama of all was the Box Tunnel [229], two miles long, on a gradient, and half of it through rock, which Brunel, against all advice, left unprotected. How on earth did they do it? By men with pickaxes working by torchlight and horses to pull away the debris. There were floods, collapses: it cost the lives of over a hundred men. But in 1841 a train steamed through, and from that day forward, for over a century, every small boy dreamed of becoming an engine-driver. Brunel's last work was the bridge over the Dart at Saltash; it was completed just in time for him to cross it on the first train, lying on his death-bed.

The Saltash Bridge [232] is less picturesque than the Clifton Suspension Bridge, but in fact it was a far more original piece of engineering, and involved all the principles of construction, both in the sinking of the central pier and in the cantilever, that were to be followed by engineers for a century. Brunel is the ancestor of New York; and I must say he looks it. We have his photograph [230], complete with cigar, standing in front of the chains used in launching – or rather, failing to launch – his vast steamship, the *Great Eastern*. This was his most grandiose dream. The first steamship to cross the Atlantic, in 1838, had been only seven hundred tons. Brunel's *Great Eastern* was to be twenty-four thousand tons – a floating palace. The amazing thing is that he got it built at all. But no doubt he had taken too big a leap forward, and although the *Great Eastern* ultimately floated and crossed

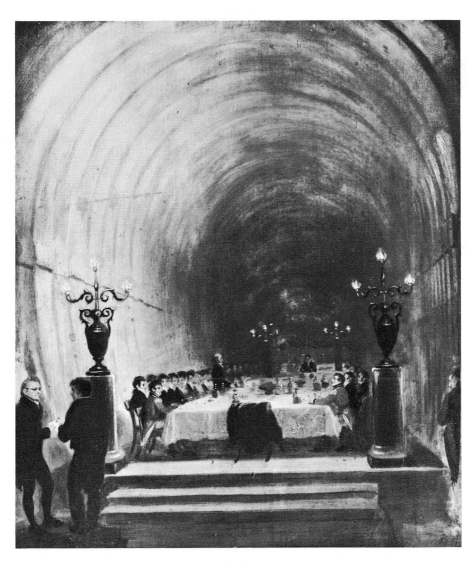

227 Dinner held in Brunel's half-completed Thames tunnel

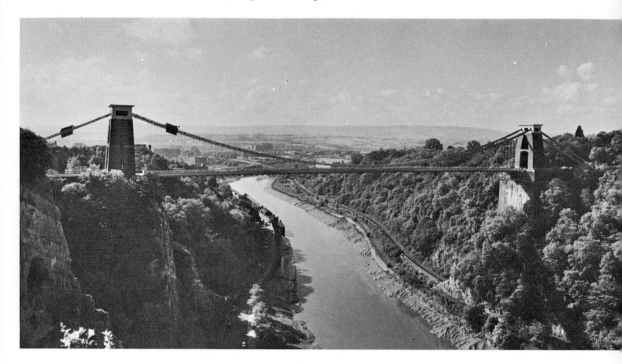

the Atlantic, the delays and disasters it had involved killed its designer. But the transatlantic liner was one more way in which the nineteenth century created its new world of shape, its own architecture.

'The shapes arise!' said Walt Whitman, writing in the 1860s.

> Shapes of factories, arsenals, foundries, markets,
> Shapes of the two-threaded tracks of railroads,
> Shapes of the sleepers of bridges, vast frameworks, girders, arches.

I fancy that Walt Whitman was thinking of Brooklyn Bridge [231], designed by a great engineer called Doebling in 1867. Its towers were for long the tallest buildings in New York – in fact, all modern New York, heroic New York, started with Brooklyn Bridge. 'Vast frameworks, girders, arches.' Whitman would have been equally delighted with the Forth Bridge, and so am I, although it is an anachronism, a sort of prehistoric monster – a brontosaurus of technology. Because by the time it was built, 1892, the new shapes had gone in the other direction, the way of lightness and economy, the characteristics of the suspension bridge.

The new Forth Bridge is our own style, which expresses our own age as the Baroque expressed the seventeenth century, and it is the result of a hundred years of engineering. It is a new creation, but it is related to the past by one of the chief continuous traditions of the western mind: the tradition of mathematics. For this reason the builders of the Gothic cathedrals, the great architects and painters of the Renaissance – Piero della Francesca and Leonardo da Vinci, and the great philosophers of the seventeenth century – Descartes, Pascal, Newton and Wren, would all have looked at it with respect.

It may seem rather odd to consider nineteenth-century art in terms of tunnels, bridges and other feats of engineering. Certainly this point of view would have horrified the more sensitive spirits of the time. Ruskin's rage against railways produced masterpieces of invective, although, characteristically, he also wrote a rhapsodic description of a railway engine. An answer to these aesthetes would have been a visit to the Great Exhibition of 1851. The building, the so-called Crystal Palace [233], was a piece of pure engineering on Brunel's principles (and in fact greatly admired by him). It

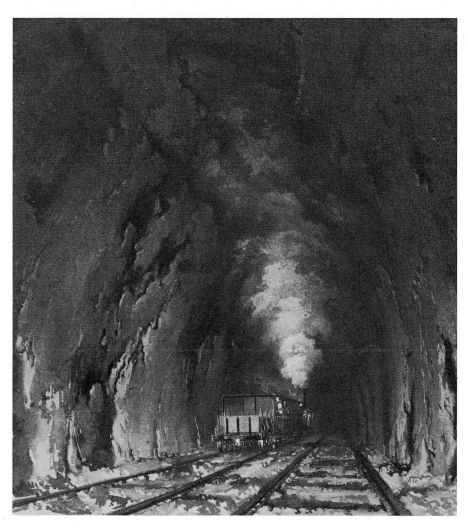

229 Box Tunnel (wash drawing)

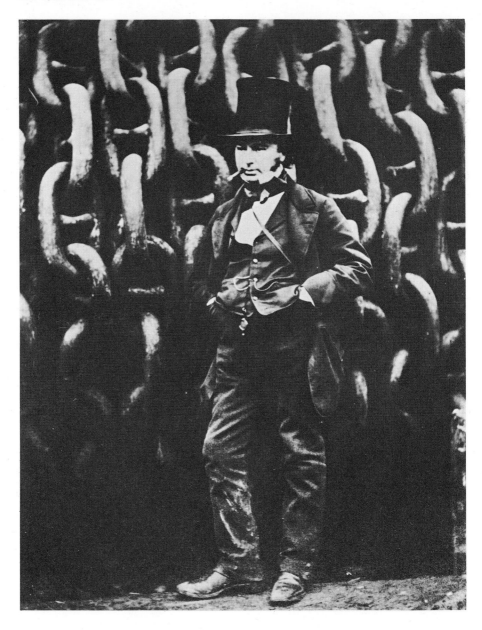

was impressive, in a somewhat joyless style, and was praised by the 'functionalist' architects of the 1930s. But inside this piece of engineering was *art*. Well, funny things happen in the history of taste. But I doubt if many of the works of art so trustingly admired in the Great Exhibition will come back into favour: the reason being that they do not express any real conviction and so are not controlled by any stylistic impulse. The new shapes of the time were based on straight lines – the straight lines of iron girders, the

47 Seurat, *La Baignade*

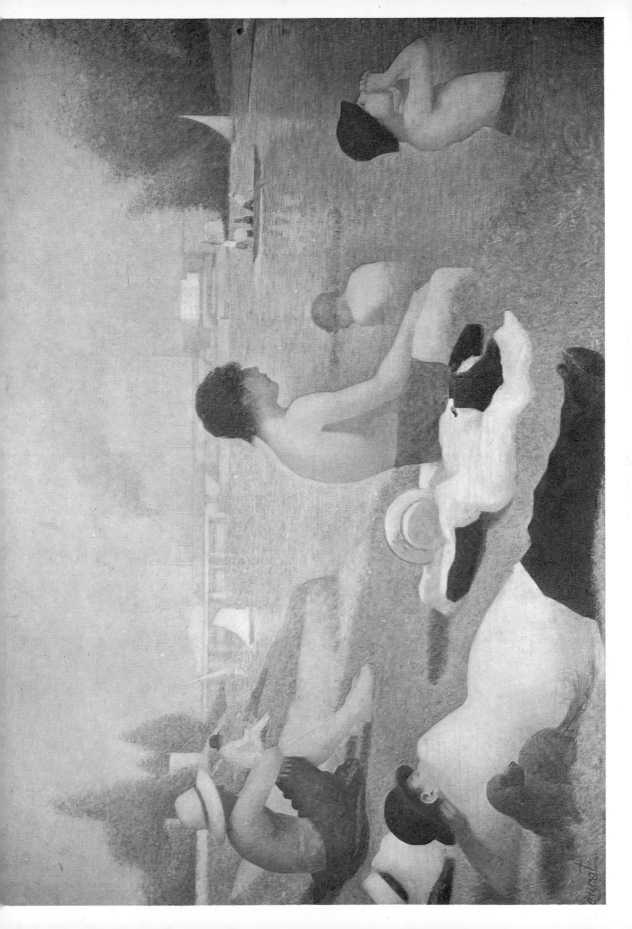

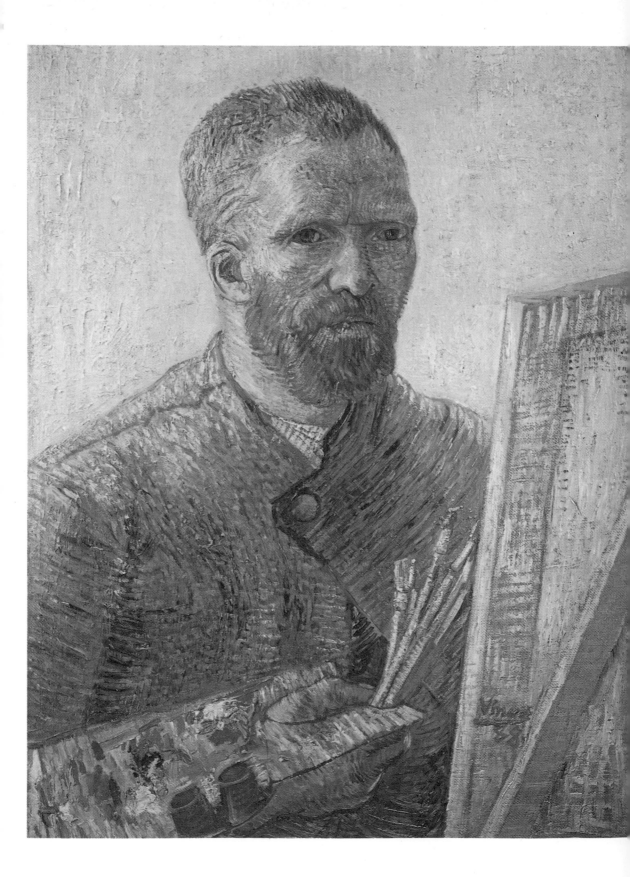

straight streets of industrial towns: the shortest way between two points. The ornamental art exhibited in the Crystal Palace was based on curves – unctuous, elaborate and purposeless curves, which caricature the luxury art of the preceding century.

Of course, works of art in the conventional sense, pictures and sculpture, were being produced at the time of the Great Exhibition – but for the most part not very good ones. It was one of those slack periods in the history of art which occur in almost every century. The great artists – Ingres and Delacroix – had grown old; and their work (other than portraiture) was concerned entirely with legend and mythology. The younger artists tried to cope with the present and showed what is called a social consciousness. In England the most famous attempt was made by Ford Madox Brown in a picture called

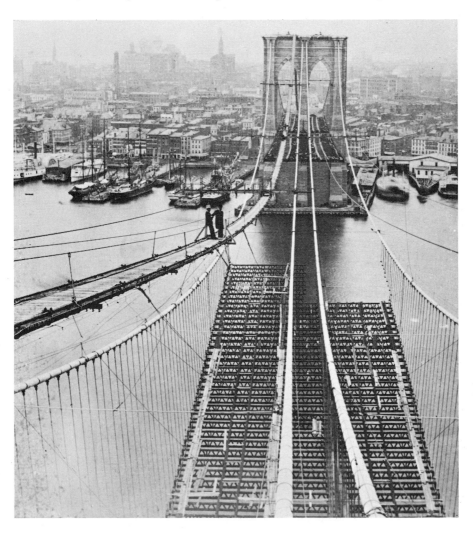

231 The construction of Brooklyn Bridge

48 Van Gogh, *Self-portrait with Palette*

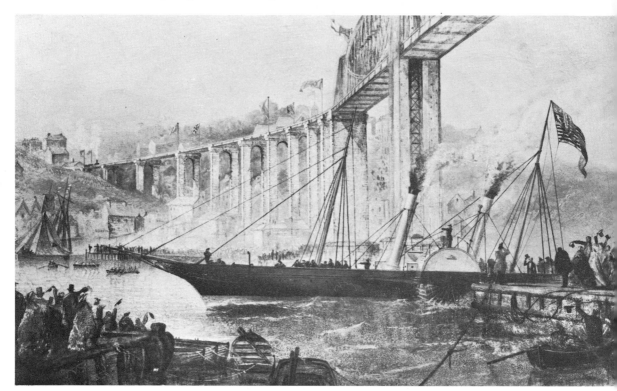

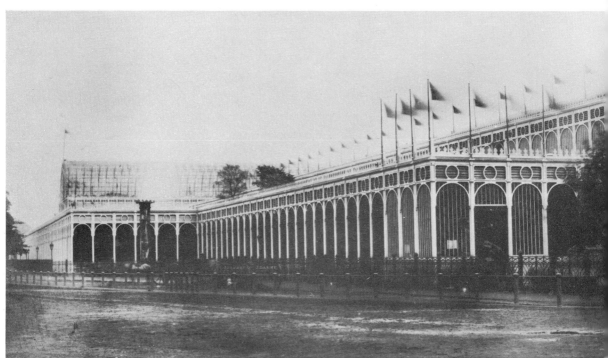

233 Paxton, The Crystal Palace, 1851

Work [236], begun in 1852. It projects the philosophy of Carlyle, who stands
on the right grinning sardonically (with his friend Frederick Denison
Maurice, the Christian Socialist). At the centre of his composition are the
navvies, on whose labour all nineteenth-century prosperity depended,
heroically strong, although, as always with Madox Brown, slightly grotesque. They are the men who made the Box Tunnel, and why they should
be digging such an enormous hole in this quiet street in Hampstead I can't
imagine. Round them are the idlers, elegant and fashionable, furtive and
destitute, or merely naughty. Madox Brown looked at people, especially at
cruel people, with an intense gaze which saves his work from the usual
banality of social realism. All the same, this is descriptive painting, and as
such, slightly provincial. But in France, at exactly the same time, there
emerged two painters whose social realism was in the centre of the European
tradition – Gustave Courbet and Jean François Millet. They were both
revolutionaries; in 1848 Millet was probably a communist, although when
his work became fashionable the evidence for this was hushed up; Courbet
remained a rebel and was put in prison for his part in the Commune – very
nearly executed. In 1849 he painted a picture of a stonebreaker – alas,
destroyed in Dresden during the war. He intended it as a straightforward
record of an old neighbour, but it was seen by his friend Max Buchon who
told him that it was the first great monument to the workers etc., etc.
Courbet was delighted by this idea, and said that the people of his native
town of Ornans wanted to hang it over the altar in the local church. This, if
it were true, which I very much doubt, would have been the beginning of
its status as an *objet de culte*, which it has retained till the present day. It is
indispensable to all Marxist art-theorists. The following year Courbet
painted an even more impressive example of his sympathy with ordinary
people in his enormous picture of a funeral at Ornans [235]. By abandoning
all pictorial artifice, which must inevitably involve a certain amount of
hierarchy and subordination, and standing his figures in a row, Courbet
achieves a feeling of equality in the presence of death.

Millet's work is less well thought of today, because at the end of his life
he did a number of sentimental pictures that became popular. But his
drawings of men and women working in the fields [234] are more unflinching
than those of Courbet, and based on closer experience. No wonder they
became a determining influence on Van Gogh. They remind one of a passage
by the seventeenth-century essayist, La Bruyère, in which for the first time
the peasant was forced into the consciousness of polite society: 'Scattered
about the countryside are certain wild animals, both males and females.
They are black, livid, burnt by the sun and attached to the soil that they dig

with invincible obstinacy. But they seem to make articulate sounds and when they stand upright they show a human face : and in fact they are men.

Throughout this series I have used works of art to illustrate various phases of civilisation. But the relationship between art and society is not at all simple and predictable. A pseudo-Marxist approach works fairly well for the decorative arts and for mediocrities like Wright of Derby, but artists of real talent always seem to slip through the net and swim away in the opposite direction. Take a picture like Seurat's *Baignade* [47, facing p. 336), unquestionably one of the greatest pictures of the nineteenth

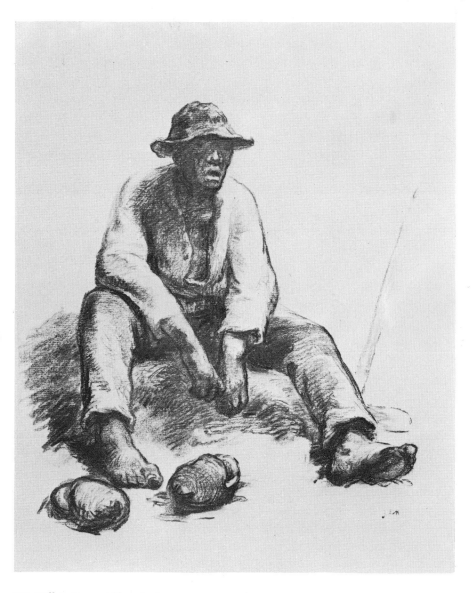

234 Millet, *Peasant* (drawing)

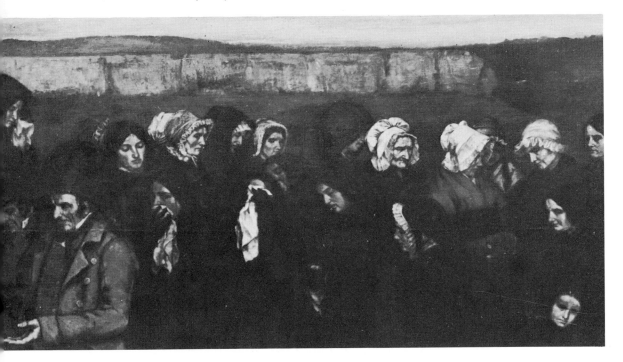

century. There are factory chimneys in the background and, in the foreground, a bowler hat, boot-tabs and other proletarian emblems; but to classify the *Baignade* as a piece of social realism would be absurd. The point of the picture is not its subject, but the way in which it unites the monumental stillness of a Renaissance fresco with the vibrating light of the Impressionists. It's the creation of an artist independent of social pressures.

Never before in history have artists been so isolated from society and from official sources of patronage as were the so-called Impressionists. Their sensuous approach to landscape through the medium of colour seems to have no connection with the intellectual currents of the time. In their best years – from 1865 to 1885 – they were treated as madmen or completely ignored. And yet there can be no reasonable doubt that they were the painters by whom those years will be remembered. The greatest of them, Cézanne, retired to Aix-en-Provence, where provincial incomprehension allowed him freedom to work out his difficult aims. Others were to cultivate their sensations in country districts of the Isle de France. But one of them, Renoir, continued for a time to live in Paris, and to represent the life around him. He was poor, and the people he painted were neither grand nor rich. But they were happy. Before one makes gloomy generalisations about the late nineteenth century – the miseries of the poor, the oppressive luxury of the rich, and so forth – it's as well to remember that two of the most beautiful pictures of the period are Renoir's *Boating*

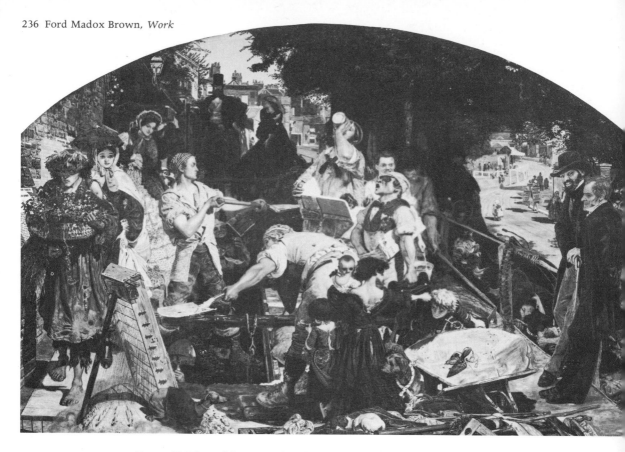

Party [237] and his *Moulin de la Galette*. No awakened conscience, and no heroic materialism. No Nietzsche, no Marx, no Freud. Just a group of ordinary human beings enjoying themselves.

The Impressionists did not set out to be popular. On the contrary, they became resigned to public ridicule; but in the end they achieved a modest measure of success. The only great painter of the nineteenth century who longed for popularity in the widest possible sense was, ironically enough, the only one who achieved absolutely no success in his lifetime, Vincent Van Gogh [48, facing p. 337]. In its earlier phase the awakened conscience had taken a practical, material form. Even Elizabeth Fry, with her powerful religious gifts, had lots of common sense. But in the later part of the nineteenth century feelings of shame at the state of society became more intense. Instead of benevolent action there arose a need for atonement. No one expressed this more completely than Van Gogh in his pictures, his drawings, his letters and his life. His letters (and they are among the most moving records of a human spirit that have come down to us) show that he was a profoundly religious man. For the first part of his working life he was torn between two vocations, painter and preacher; and for some years the preacher was in the ascendant. Preaching wasn't enough. Like St Francis, he had to share the poverty of the poorest and most miserable of his fellow men – and conditions in industrial Belgium were probably more degraded than in thirteenth-century Umbria. It wasn't the hardships that made him give up this way of life: it was his unconquerable need to paint. At first he hoped to unite his conflicting impulses by doing drawings and pictures of very poor people to show with what courage and dignity they supported their condition – in fact he wished to continue the work of Millet. Millet was his god: he describes doing seven copies of the *Sower*, one after another, in a week. He continued to reproduce and re-create Millet's images all his life, even when the bright sun of the south had changed his colour from dark green and brown to orange and yellow, even when the intensity of his feelings had driven him mad.

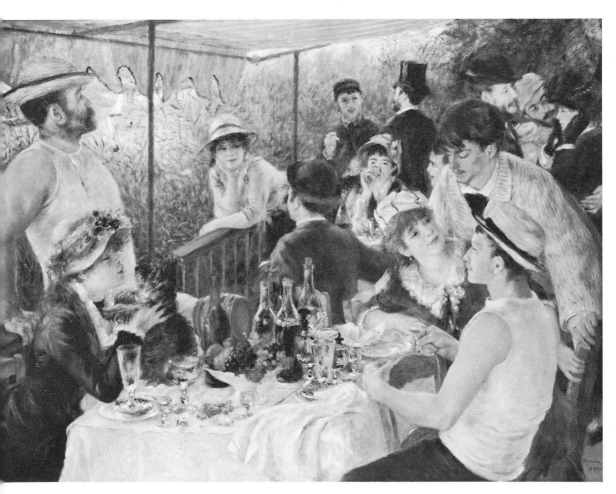

237 Renoir, *Boating Party*

Van Gogh's hero – the hero of almost all generous-minded men in the late nineteenth century – was Tolstoy. With his desire to reach the people, Tolstoy welcomed the appearance of the cinema, and wanted to write a film script. It was too late; but at least he himself could be filmed, and so we can see the last great man of this series as he lived and moved. We can see him sawing wood, expressing the feeling that one must share the life of working people, partly as a sort of atonement for years of oppression, partly because that life was nearer to the realities of human existence. We can see him talking to peasants, mounting his horse – even walking unhappily with the Countess. Tolstoy towered above his age as Dante and Michelangelo and Beethoven had done. His novels are marvels of sustained imagination; but his life was full of inconsistencies. He wanted to be one with the peasants, yet he continued to live like an aristocrat. He preached universal love, but he quarrelled so painfully with his poor demented wife that at the age of eighty-two he ran away from her. After a nightmare journey he collapsed at a country railway station. He was laid out on a bed in the station-master's house, and there, with all the horrors of modern publicity stewing outside the station, he died. Almost his last words were: 'How do peasants die?' After his death, when the peasants were singing a lament, soldiers were sent in with drawn swords to stop them mourning him. However, there was no way of preventing the funeral, and of this too we have a piece of film which shows the long procession winding up the valley, the weeping peasants, the busybodies and the broken-hearted disciples. A new kind of historical document, and one of the most moving.

That scene took place in 1910. Within two years Rutherford and Einstein had made their first discoveries: so a new era had begun even before the 1914 War. It is the era in which we are still living. Of course science had achieved great triumphs in the nineteenth century, but nearly all of them had been related to practical or technological advance. For example, Edison, whose inventions did as much as any to add to our material convenience, wasn't what we would call a scientist at all, but a supreme 'do-it-yourself' man – the successor of Benjamin Franklin. But from the time of Einstein, Niels Bohr and the Cavendish Laboratory, science no longer existed to serve human needs, but in its own right. When scientists could use a mathematical idea to transform matter they had achieved the same quasi-magical relationship with the material world as artists. Look at Karsh's photograph of Einstein [238]. Where have we seen that face before? The aged Rembrandt.

In this series I have followed the ups and downs of civilisation historically, trying to discover results as well as causes; well, obviously I can't do that any longer. We have no idea where we are going, and sweeping, confident

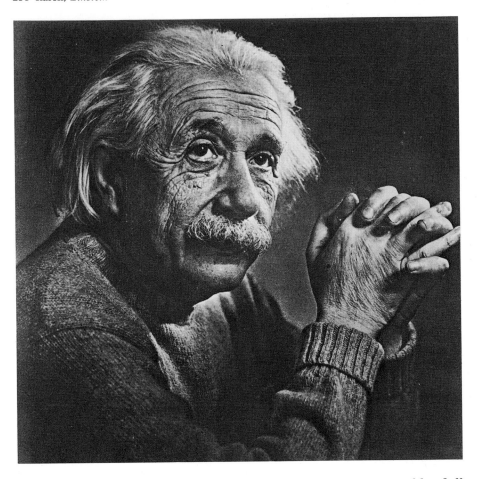

articles on the future seem to me, intellectually, the most disreputable of all forms of public utterance. The scientists who are best qualified to talk have kept their mouths shut. J. B. S. Haldane summed up the situation when he said: 'My own suspicion is that the universe is not only queerer than we suppose, but queerer than we can suppose.' 'I saw a new heaven and a new earth, for the old heaven and the old earth had passed away.' Which reminds us that the universe so vividly described in the Book of Revelation is queer enough; but with the help of symbols not beyond description. Whereas our universe cannot even be stated symbolically. And this touches us all more directly than one might suppose. For example, artists, who have been very little influenced by social systems, have always responded instinctively to latent assumptions about the shape of the universe. The incomprehensibility of our new cosmos seems to me, ultimately, to be the reason for the chaos of modern art. I know next to nothing about science, but I've spent my life in trying to learn about art, and I am completely baffled by what is taking place today. I sometimes like what I see, but when I read modern critics I realise that my preferences are merely accidental.

However, in the world of action a few things are obvious – so obvious that I hesitate to repeat them. One of them is our increasing reliance on machines. They have ceased to be tools and have begun to give us directions. And unfortunately machines, from the Maxim gun to the computer, are for the most part means by which a minority can keep free men in subjection.

Our other speciality is our urge to destruction. With the help of machines we did our best to destroy ourselves in two wars, and in doing so we released a flood of evil, which intelligent people have tried to justify with praise of violence, 'theatres of cruelty' and so forth. Add to this the memory of that shadowy companion who is always with us, like an inverted guardian angel, silent, invisible, almost incredible – and yet unquestionably there and ready to assert itself at the touch of a button; and one must concede that the future of civilisation does not look very bright.

And yet when I look at the world about me in the light of this series, I don't at all feel that we are entering a new period of barbarism. The things that made the Dark Ages so dark – the isolation, the lack of mobility, the lack of curiosity, the hopelessness – don't obtain at all. When I have the good fortune to visit one of our new universities, it seems to me that the inheritors of all our catastrophes look cheerful enough – very different from the melancholy late Romans or pathetic Gauls whose likenesses have come down to us. In fact, I should doubt if so many people have ever been as well-fed, as well-read, as bright-minded, as curious and as critical as the young are today.

Of course there has been a little flattening at the top. But one musn't overrate the culture of what used to be called 'top people' before the wars. They had charming manners, but they were as ignorant as swans. They did know something about literature, and a few had been to the opera. But they knew nothing about painting and less than nothing about philosophy (except for Balfour and Haldane). The members of a music group or an art group at a provincial university would be five times better informed and more alert. Naturally, these bright-minded young people think poorly of existing institutions and want to abolish them. Well, one doesn't need to be young to dislike institutions. But the dreary fact remains that, even in the darkest ages, it was institutions that made society work, and if civilisation is to survive society must somehow be made to work.

At this point I reveal myself in my true colours, as a stick-in-the-mud. I hold a number of beliefs that have been repudiated by the liveliest intellects of our time. I believe that order is better than chaos, creation better than destruction. I prefer gentleness to violence, forgiveness to vendetta. On the whole I think that knowledge is preferable to ignorance, and I am sure that human sympathy is more valuable than ideology. I believe that in spite of the recent triumphs of science, men haven't changed much in the last two thousand years; and in consequence we must still try to learn from history. History is ourselves. I also hold one or two beliefs that are more difficult to put shortly. For example, I believe in courtesy, the ritual by which we avoid hurting other people's feelings by satisfying our own egos. And I think we should remember that we are part of a great whole, which for convenience we call nature. All living things are our brothers and sisters. Above all, I believe in the God-given genius of certain individuals, and I value a society that makes their existence possible.

This series has been filled with great works of genius, in architecture, sculpture and painting, in philosophy, poetry and music, in science and engineering. There they are; you can't dismiss them. And they are only a fraction of what western man has achieved in the last thousand years, often after setbacks and deviations at least as destructive as those of our own time. Western civilisation has been a series of rebirths. Surely this should give us confidence in ourselves.

I said at the beginning that it is lack of confidence, more than anything else, that kills a civilisation. We can destroy ourselves by cynicism and disillusion, just as effectively as by bombs. Fifty years ago W. B. Yeats, who was more like a man of genius than anyone I have ever known, wrote a famous prophetic poem.

> Things fall apart; the centre cannot hold;
> Mere anarchy is loosed upon the world,
> The blood-dimmed tide is loosed, and everywhere
> The ceremony of innocence is drowned;
> The best lack all conviction, while the worst
> Are full of passionate intensity.

Well, that was certainly true between the wars, and it damn nearly destroyed us. Is it true today? Not quite, because good people have convictions, rather too many of them. The trouble is that there is still no centre. The moral and intellectual failure of Marxism has left us with no alternative to heroic materialism, and that isn't enough. One may be optimistic, but one can't exactly be joyful at the prospect before us.

Index

CIVILISATION
By KENNETH CLARK

When Kenneth Clark introduced his magnificent BBC television series *Civilisation* he emphasised that it was *not* a history of the arts, but a history of life-giving beliefs and ideas made visible and audible through the medium of art. The continuous praise and enthusiasm with which the series was received proves how successful he has been in making this 'personal' view an exciting and stimulating search into the sources and development of Western Civilisation.

For this book the author has revised the scripts of the thirteen television programmes. As he takes us from the fall of the Roman Empire to the present day, he does not attempt to give a complete record but concentrates on crucial civilising episodes – from Iona in the ninth century to France in the twelfth, from Florence to Urbino, from Germany to Rome, England, Holland and America. Against these historical backgrounds he shows us both the men who gave new energy to civilisation and expanded our understanding of the world and ourselves, and the works of genius, in architecture, sculpture and painting, in philosophy, poetry and music, in science and in engineering, which they produced and with which the series has been filled. In relating works of art to the history of civilisation Kenneth Clark's perception of their quality and the spirit they embody enables him to let us see a painting, a building or a piece of sculpture, whether it is something we know, like Raphael's *School of Athens*, or something we might not have thought of considering a work of art, like a Brunel bridge, with the excitement of new discovery.

The enormous television audience that has been delighted by Kenneth Clark's clarity and lucidity in covering and interpreting so wide a span of time, so versatile a range of ideas and their manifestations, will be in no doubt at all about the value and importance of this book.

On the front of the jacket is a detail from Raphael's fresco in the Vatican, known as the *School of Athens*. It shows Euclid (in fact a portrait of the architect Bramante) proving a geometrical theorem to a group of graceful young men, who are enraptured at the logic and clarity of his demonstration. On the back of the jacket is a later result of drawing diagrams – the old Forth Bridge.

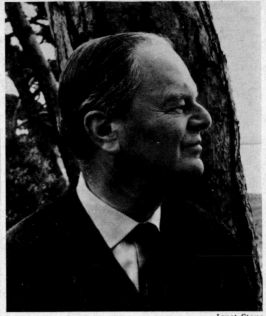

Janet Stone

Kenneth Clark was educated at Winchester and Trinity College, Oxford (Hon. Fellow, 1968). Worked for two years with Mr Bernard Berenson, Florence: Keeper of Department of Fine Art, Ashmolean Museum, Oxford, 1931-3: Director of National Gallery 1934–45: Surveyor of the King's Pictures 1933–44: Director of Film Division, later Controller, Home Publicity, Ministry of Information, 1939–41: Slade Professor of Fine Art, Oxford, 1946–50, and October 1961–2: Chairman Arts Council of Great Britain 1953–60: Chairman of the I.T.A. 1954–7: Chancellor, University of York, 1969: Trustee British Museum: Member of the Advisory Council Victoria and Albert Museum, The National Art Collections Fund, Conseil Artistique des Musées Nationaux: President, London Library. He was created a Peer in the Birthday Honours of 1969.

Books by Kenneth Clark
published by John Murray